# Final Report
## of the
## Minnesota Tax Study Commission

# Final Report
## of the
# Minnesota Tax Study Commission

Volume 1
Findings and Recommendations

Butterworths
St. Paul

**The Butterworth Group**

*United States*
Butterworth Legal Publishers, Austin
Butterworth Legal Publishers, Boston
Butterworth Legal Publishers, St. Paul
Butterworth Legal Publishers, Seattle
Butterworth Legal Publishers, Florida

*Canada*
Butterworth & Co. (Canada) Ltd., Toronto and Vancouver

*United Kingdom*
Butterworth & Co. (Publishers) Ltd., London

*Australia*
Butterworths Pty. Ltd., Sydney

*New Zealand*
Butterworths of New Zealand, Ltd, Wellington

*South Africa*
Butterworth Publishers (Pty.) Ltd., Durban

*Singapore*
Butterworth & Co. (Asia) Pte. Ltd.

Special thanks are given to the *St. Paul Pioneer Press and Dispatch* and cartoonist Jerry Fearing for permission to reproduce the cartoons on pages 17, 164, 263, and 304.

ISBN 0-86678-474-8 (set)
ISBN 0-86678-472-1 (volume 1)

Printed in the United States of America by Bolger Publications, Inc., 3301 Como Ave. S.E., Minneapolis, MN 55414

# Contents

## VOLUME 1
## FINDINGS AND RECOMMENDATIONS

### PART I
### THE INSTITUTIONAL AND ECONOMIC FRAMEWORK

### PART II
### ANALYSIS OF REVENUES

# ACKNOWLEDGMENTS

The production of a study of this magnitude can only succeed with the cooperation of many people who are not directly involved with the work on a day-to-day basis. And in Minnesota, the element of cooperation was enormous. In fact, there is no doubt that without their help, the quality of the report would have suffered greatly. In making this observation, it is important to note that the Minnesota government's reputation of having one of the nation's best set of fiscal analysts is well deserved.

It is difficult to place any ranking in making these acknowledgments. At or near the top of any list, however, would be Revenue Commissioner Arthur Roemer and Finance Commissioner Gordon Donhowe, Deputy Finance Commissioner Jay Kiedrowski, House Research Director Carole Pagones, State Planning Director Thomas Triplett and their staffs. At Finance, John Haynes deserves special thanks. At Revenue special mention must be made of the first-rate work of Research Director Daniel Salomone and Assistant Commissioner Dennis Erno, Corporate Tax Director Gerome Caulfield, and their colleagues Carole Wald, Tom Albrecht, and Lynn Reed (income tax), Nancy Edwardson (sales), Mark Misukanis and Carolyn Allmon (gross earnings), Jerry Garski (gross receipts and property), Tom Schmucker and Don Walsh (minerals), Rod Hoheisel (corporate and insurance), John Malach (income), Jerome Sicora (corporate), Jerry Silkey and Wallace Dahl (local government aid). And, Gordon Folkman's advice (Office of the Legislative Auditor) was often sought and always valuable.

Karen Baker and Steve Hinze at the Research Office of the House of Representatives worked many hours, often on short notice, in order to provide needed information on the impacts of alternative property tax packages, as did Thomas Stinson at the University of Minnesota. House staffers James Cleary and Mahomed Eldeeb assisted with the computer work. Other assistance with data collection and critical review was provided by John Post, Joel Michael, Keith Carlson, Dana Frey, John Peloquin, Pat Meagher, Steve Phenenger, Nancy Rooney, Dan Gjelten, and Peter Sausen, Edward Fuller, and Tom Melcher.

Persons from the private sector were also most helpful in providing technical advice and information. These include Steve Alnes, William Blazar, Donald Paterick, Patricia Westhoff, Lee Munnich, John Stone, Brian Osberg, Paul Gilge, Alfred France, William Toal, James Stuebner, Bill Kelly, Dan Vandermark, James Pratt, L. R. Bartley, Dick Brust, L. J. Schoenwetter, and Michael Stutzer. Members of several professional associations also gave hours of advice. The Insurance Federation of

Minnesota (Ralph Marlatt, Director) provided otherwise inaccessible data through a survey of their membership; and the Tax Section of the Minnesota Bar Association (through Jack Carlson) and the Society of CPAs (Bill Fraser) both held seminars for the Commission.

Finally, special acknowledgment must go to Attorney Maureen Warren of Chairperson Latimer's staff who gave much valuable advice and assistance on nearly every aspect of our work, and at Finance to Peg Kenny, Director of Administrative Management, and her associates, Karen Hinkemeyer and Deborah Patrin who helped establish and then monitor the Commission's budget for the state.

Funding for the publication of this report was provided by the Dayton Hudson Foundation, the Minnesota Bankers Association, and Minnesota Wellspring.

# EXECUTIVE ORDER NO. 83-33
## Providing for Creation of a
## Minnesota Tax Study Commission

I, RUDY PERPICH, GOVERNOR OF THE STATE OF MINNESOTA, by virtue of the authority vested in me by the Constitution and applicable statutes, do hereby issue this Executive Order:

WHEREAS, the tax system of Minnesota is complex, many-layered, often controversial and sometimes inequitable; and

WHEREAS, there has been no thorough review of the tax system, including both state and local taxes, for more than twenty-five years; and

WHEREAS, tax changes have been made piecemeal, without regard to the system as a whole and sometimes without knowledge of long-term effects; and

WHEREAS, confidence in the Minnesota tax system has suffered; and

WHEREAS, the citizens of Minnesota deserve a systematic and learned review of tax and economic policies in order to provide goals and directions for Minnesota into the twenty-first century;

NOW, THEREFORE, I order:

1. There is hereby created a Minnesota Tax Study Commission, its chairperson and members to be appointed by the Governor.

2. It shall be the duty of this Commission to obtain funds from private and public sources in order to hire a staff and perform the research necessary for an extensive study of state and local taxes and economic goals.

3. Funds received by the Commission shall, upon their acceptance by the State Treasurer and Commissioner of Finance pursuant to Minnesota Statutes Chapter 7, become the property of the State of Minnesota. Such Funds shall be subject to all standard state accounting methods and procedures and shall further be subject to all appropriate auditing requirements and mechanisms.

4. The Commission is charged with providing the citizens and policymakers of Minnesota a descriptive and analytical survey of the Minnesota economy and of the tax structure as it now exists. The Commission is expected to synthesize research already completed, but perform new research when required.

5. The Commission's goal will be, after extensive research and discussions with citizens throughout the state, to recommend tax policies which will remove inequities, promote economic growth, stabilize revenues for state and local governments, meet the needs of Minnesota's people, and provide Minnesota with a competitive position among the states.

6. The Commission's study shall include, but shall not be limited to the interrelationships of state and local governments through taxes and state aid payments, the relationship between taxes and business expansion, the need for and usage of property tax relief programs, the state sales tax and its base, simplification of the income tax system, optional local taxes, the effect of tax policy on development of jobs, the use of tax policy to foster growth industries, tax policy relating to agricultural land, the problems of border areas because of interstate tax differences, the relationship of state spending levels to tax revenues, the appropriate mix of taxes, and the effect of taxes on Minnesota's position among state rankings.

7. The Commission may issue reports as it deems fit, but shall make a full report and recommendation to the Governor and Legislature by December 15, 1984.

8. The Commission may adopt its own rules for the conduct of meetings, hearings, and deliberations, but the goal will be to invite wide public participation and enhancement of the public's knowledge about the Minnesota tax system.

Pursuant to Minnesota Statutes 1982, Section 4.035, this Order shall be effective 15 days after publication in the State Register and filing with the Secretary of State and shall remain in effect until it is rescinded by proper authority or it expires in accordance with Section 4.035, Subdivision 3.

IN TESTIMONY WHEREOF, I hereunto set my hand this 8th day of August, 1983.

# Commission Members and Staff

## MEMBERS OF THE COMMISSION

Chairperson
George Latimer, Mayor
City of Saint Paul

Vice Chairperson
Geri Joseph
Director of International Programs
Hubert Humphrey Institute of Public Affairs
University of Minnesota
Former Ambassador to the Netherlands

Norbert Berg, Deputy Chairman
Control Data Corporation

Earl Craig
Owner and Principal
The Earl Craig Company

Kenneth Dayton
Oakleaf Associates

Jan Dietrich, President
Local 17/Hotel &
Restaurant Union

Marvin Hanson
Farmer

Michael Kahleck
Farmer

Jean Keffeler
Northwestern Bell

Robert Killeen, Director
United Auto Workers,
Subregion 10

Elliott Perovich, Director
Regional Transit Board

Sidney Rand
President Emeritus
St. Olaf College
Former Ambassador to Norway

Leonard Schaeffer, President
Group Health Plan

Gary Tankenoff
Hillcrest Development

Charles Weaver
Holmes and Graven

Mark Willes
Executive Vice President
General Mills Corporation

## COMMISSION STAFF

Executive Director
Robert D. Ebel

Research

John R. Bartle
Michael E. Bell
John H. Bowman
Julia M. Friedman
Therese J. McGuire
Lisa A. Roden

Administration

Renae A. Rogers
Loriann Sarafolean

*xi*

MINNESOTA TAX STUDY COMMISSION
400 NORTH ROBERT STREET
SUITE 920
ST. PAUL, MINNESOTA 55101
612-297-1133

December 15, 1984

The Honorable Rudy Perpich
Governor
State of Minnesota
130 State Capitol
Saint Paul, Minnesota 55155

Dear Governor Perpich:
　On behalf of the Minnesota Tax Study Commission, we take pleasure in transmitting this Report that fulfills your Executive Order No. 83-33 providing for a systematic and evenhanded analysis of the Minnesota state and local tax system. During the past fifteen months, the Commission examined the economic, demographic and fiscal impacts of nearly every type of state and local tax and its alternatives. The results of this work are presented in this two-volume report.
　Volume I presents the findings and recommendations of the Commission, followed by a detailed set of information that provides the factual, institutional, and analytical background against which the Commission considered the various tax issues and reached its conclusions. In the process of writing this Report, the Commission engaged the services of several technical experts to prepare research papers on a wide range of concerns pertaining to Minnesota's tax and revenue system. The quality of these papers is such that they are of value beyond our purpose here. Accordingly, they are presented as Volume II of this report.
　The tax policy goals and recommendations set forth herein represent a coordinated program of tax reform for Minnesota's future. They provide for an equitable, simple, efficient and competitive state/local tax system, a system that the people of Minnesota can understand and control, and that will meet their needs into the twenty-first century. As such, the Report merits earnest consideration by all citizens and their elected representatives.
　The report is the product of many hours of private study and public debate by a group of Minnesotans who represent a broad cross section of

this state and who gave many, many hours of their time to this effort. The Commission addressed the important fiscal issues and questions that all Minnesotans must face in the years ahead. The Commission served without remuneration and with a commitment to lay out directions for tax policy that will continue Minnesota's long tradition of structuring public policy in a manner that is to the benefit of all of Minnesota's citizens.

Respectfully Submitted,


Members of the Commission

# Part I

# The Institutional and Economic

# Framework

# 1

# Summary of Findings and Recommendations

## INTRODUCTION

Historically, Minnesotans have demonstrated a commitment to excellence and equity in the responsibilities they assign to their government.

They sought excellence in education, in health and welfare, in the quality of community life, and in individual opportunity and creativity. They accepted taxes higher than the national average as the price they were willing to pay.

They pursued equity not only in the services they asked of their government but also in the method of paying for them. Minnesota became known for fiscal innovations undertaken to spread the tax burden with fairness.

Intricately constructed systems need periodic examination because, over the years, small actions taken in response to specific needs become an unwieldy collection of rules. Policies adopted to address concerns within the state have produced harmful comparisons to other states. A major concern arising in recent years has been whether Minnesota's tax structure inhibits economic growth and is achieving the equity goals once promised for it.

The Minnesota Tax Study Commission was created by the executive order of Governor Rudy Perpich to conduct a systematic and evenhanded examination of the Minnesota system. The charge was to recommend tax policies that will remove inequities, promote economic growth, provide Minnesota with a competitive position among the states and meet the needs of Minnesota's people as they move into the twenty-first century.

The commission began with a thorough review of the demographic and economic trends in the state. It then examined nearly every recognized tax device and the alternatives available to the state. It carefully considered the historical reasons for our tax system, the views of the public regarding Minnesota's present taxes, and the present intergovernmental relationships. The result is this report to the people of Minnesota. It is a set of guiding principles, goals, and recommendations that will provide a simple, rational, and fair state/local tax system, a system that the people of Minnesota can understand and control.

## CRITERIA FOR JUDGING A STATE/LOCAL TAX SYSTEM

### GUIDING PRINCIPLES FOR TAX REFORM

The commission first established a set of principles that make explicit the philosophical framework as well as the practical limits for the recommendations that follow. These principles are:

- *Public values embodied in the tax law should be explicit and visible.* The Minnesota tax system is an expression of community relationships among individuals and between the people and their government. Giving tax relief to classes of taxpayers is not inherently wrong; however, preferential treatment should be clearly shown and satisfy an agreed-upon set of policy goals. Policy should be written in a manner that does not obscure which class of individuals or institutions actually bears the tax burden when another class receives relief.
- *Use of the state/local tax system to achieve social and economic goals should be minimized.* Our recommendation is practical, not philosophical. A state operates in an "open economy" characterized by a free flow of goods, services, and factors of production across its borders. Openness requires a fiscal system competitive with those in other states, and it restricts a state's ability to secure major changes in the distribution of income or in the levels of output and prices through budget policy.
- *Within limits dictated by economic reality, Minnesota's tax burden should be distributed according to ability to pay.* Minnesota state and local taxes paid as a percentage of income should increase with higher income. But the overall or net effect of the tax system is more important than the effect of a specific tax such as that on income.
- *The standard for government's fiscal accountability should be high.* With respect to different levels of government, this principle requires open and clear communication between the level that mandates services and the unit that levies the taxes to pay for those services. The principle also requires that tax policy be enacted visibly and explicitly rather than through thoughtless expediency or neglect.
- *Although reform of the tax system inevitably creates winners and losers, that is no reason for inaction.* Devices to "hold harmless" or "grandfather" existing arrangements will imbed inequities within the system and thwart reform. If some transition mechanisms are required, they should be of short duration.

### GOALS FOR MINNESOTA'S TAX SYSTEM

The commission adopted six goals for Minnesota's tax system and recommends their continuing use in examination of the system. They are:

- *Equity.* Tax burdens should be distributed according to the principles of benefits received and ability to pay; they should also be consistent with the overall distributional objectives of the state. For those activities to which the benefits principle does not apply, ability to pay requires that individuals with equal economic capacities pay the same amount of tax ("horizontal equity") and persons with a greater capacity bear larger tax burdens ("vertical equity").

- *Certainty/Predictability.* Taxes should be designed to give fiscal certainty to the taxpayer and government and lessen the need for ad hoc legislative changes.
- *Simplicity.* Tax law should be easily understood by taxpayers in order to minimize administrative and compliance costs.
- *Neutrality.* Taxes should be designed to avoid unintended interference with private (consumer, worker, producer) economic decisions.
- *Competitiveness.* Minnesota's tax rates and tax burden distribution should be compared to those of other states, and then evaluated for their effects on the growth of the state's economy and employment, and on the migration of residents as the state competes for economic activity.
- *Political Accountability.* Changes in tax burden or distribution of the tax burden should be the result of explicit and/or fully disclosed legislative actions rather than the effect of hidden or complex economic and institutional (e.g., intergovernmental) arrangements.

These goals do not stand in isolation from each other. Tradeoffs are essential in making tax policy because no perfect tax or tax mix exists. The challenge to policymakers is to design a tax structure that achieves these goals while, at the same time, it remains consistent with the guiding principles stated above.

## HIGHLIGHTS OF FINDINGS

A detailed discussion of the commission's findings, conclusions, and recommendations is provided in subsequent chapters. Here are the essential elements:

- *Powerful economic, demographic, and technological changes are occurring in Minnesota, the nation, and the world.* Although these changes are largely beyond control or manipulation by Minnesota (or by any state government), they cannot be ignored in the design of the state's tax structure. Indeed, quite the opposite is true: in designing a tax structure that will enable Minnesota to compete for jobs in the coming years, and thereby provide an environment that enhances the quality of life for all its citizens, the state must have a fiscal structure that flows with and captures the fiscal benefits of these powerful changes. Attempts to use a state/local tax system to reverse these economic, demographic, and technological trends will only result in a failed and costly policy.

- *The clear evidence is that Minnesota's economy has been and continues to be among the strongest and healthiest of the fifty states.* Minnesota's relative strength stems in part from the productivity and creativity of its people. Unfortunately, it is also clear that Minnesota's overall tax burden has become so high relative to other states that its economic and employment growth, and the social benefits that accompany growth, are being slowed as a result. It follows that tax reform in Minnesota requires overall tax reduction. In turn, tax reduction requires that the growth in public spending be slowed.

- *Consistent with other tax policy goals and institutional (e.g., legal) constraints, taxes should be broadly based.* Broad-based taxation not only enhances accountability by spreading the burden of paying for government among all its beneficiaries, it also decreases the possibility of the combination of a narrow base and a high statutory rate—a situation that makes intolerable the structural deficiencies inherent in all taxes.

- *Minnesota's state and local tax system is unnecessarily complex and cumbersome.* This is particularly noticeable in its system of property taxation and intergovernmental aid. The complexity results from tax changes that have been made without regard to the system as a whole and sometimes without knowledge of their likely long-term effects. Because Minnesotans have a decreased understanding of their tax system, they have less confidence in it. Diminished confidence poses a serious concern in a democracy, and particularly in this state, which has historically had a tradition of openness between the people and their government.

- *The likelihood of sweeping changes in the federal tax code strengthens the case for reform of the state and local tax system.* It will be easier to determine the likely fiscal impacts of proposed or actual federal changes, if Minnesota policymakers and taxpayers are able to work from a clear and explicit state/local tax system. Without such a system, the debate on the implications of federal change will be chaotic and the policy response uncertain.

## THE ECONOMIC AND INSTITUTIONAL FRAMEWORK

To make informed judgments regarding specific tax proposals, it is important for policymakers to understand the basic institutional and economic forces that influence the fiscal system. Accordingly, before looking at the Minnesota state and local system on a tax-by-tax basis, the commission made an in-depth examination of the following five topics:

- The relationship of the Minnesota revenue system to the Minnesota economy;
- The state's recent fiscal history, which provides the current setting for policy decisions;

- An examination of how Minnesota's fiscal system compares to those of the other states;
- The role that taxes play in the decision to create private sector employment;
- The fiscal relationship between the State of Minnesota and its local units of government.

### MINNESOTA'S ECONOMY

An understanding of the fundamental forces that characterize Minnesota's economy at present—and which are likely to do so in the future—is essential to formulate tax policies that will adjust to changing economic circumstances. State and local tax systems do affect people's behavior and their welfare. To accomplish the objectives laid out in the commission's statement of goals, state and local tax systems must take into account the policy boundaries imposed by economic trends and forces beyond any state's control. In terms of the economy, these forces are both structural and cyclical.

*Structural forces.*    With the exception of agriculture, which in terms of overall employment and earnings is twice as important in Minnesota as it is for the nation's economy, Minnesota's economic profile (the distribution of state employment and earnings by major industry group) is similar to that of the nation's. And, like the nation, Minnesota is shifting from a "goods" producing economy of agriculture, mining, construction, and manufacturing, toward the "service" producing activities of wholesale and retail trade, services, finance, transportation, communications, utilities, and government. This is true even though manufacturing is the largest state industry in terms of real earnings.

In long-term growth (1969-79), Minnesota has demonstrated an above-average capacity to employ its people and generate new jobs. This record was due to two factors: (a) national growth trends, and (b) the ability of most local industries to outperform their national counterparts. The common perception that Minnesota's above-average growth was primarily due to a specialization in fast growing industries was not supported by the commission's analysis.

*Cyclical forces.*    The Minnesota nonfarm economy tends to move with the nation in recession and recovery. Prior to the 1980-82 recession, it was frequently advanced that the diversified nature of the Minnesota economy insulated the state from the disruptive effects of the national business cycle. Actually, Minnesota's economy has long exhibited a significant degree of sensitivity to changing national economic conditions. During the 1974-75 recession, Minnesota was quite sensitive to the national downturn, but it was less affected in employment losses because of its disproportionately large agricultural sector. In contrast, in 1980-82, Minnesota found itself in a deeper and longer lasting recession than did the nation as a whole (5.8% decline in employment versus 2.2% nationally). The severity of the last recession can be attributed to the simultaneous downturn of Minnesota's farm and nonfarm economies.

Economic recovery, especially in the Twin Cities metropolitan area, has restored Minnesota's above-average rate of growth. However, the state's future growth may be restrained by lingering weakness in two of its long-time basic industries, mining and agriculture. Mining is entering a period of structural decline primarily due to the decline in the U.S. steel industry. Growth in agriculture is being slowed by both structural and cyclical factors; however, the long-term outlook for agriculture is much more favorable than that for mining.

Tax reform is needed to capture the fiscal benefits of the broad economic and demographic trends. When Minnesota's changing economy is examined for the long-run revenue generating potential of its various industry sectors, it can be concluded that it will be necessary to: (a) rely on all major tax sources (no one source can capture economic growth in all industries); and (b) within the bounds of other tax policy objectives, to use taxes that are broadly based.

## A RECORD OF FISCAL UNCERTAINTY

At present, the State of Minnesota is experiencing a large and permanent or "structural" surplus (FY 1986) in its general fund: quite a different story from the years of 1981 and 1982. Then the state faced a general fund deficit situation that led to six special sessions of the legislature. In view of this record, the commission recognized that in addition to designing tax policies that would promote fiscal stability, the tax system had to be reconciled with state spending policies. Although an examination of the expenditure structure was clearly beyond the purpose and scope of the commission, the issue of overall budget policy and tax level was a critical part of its concern. For this reason, the commission examined three overall budget issues: the level of the present surplus, the process by which spending decisions were made, and the budget reserve account.

Regarding the surplus, the commission analyzed the budget numbers and determined that as a result of a series of significant tax increases made in response to the 1981-82 fiscal crisis, the Minnesota government would be permanently "overtaxing" its citizens by about 5% in 1986. This finding, when combined with further evidence that the level of the personal income tax was discouraging employment growth in certain key industries, led to the recommendation that tax reform requires overall tax reduction. As described below, the change in the structure of the general sales tax plus the recommendation to return the "structural surplus" made possible a large reduction in personal income taxes.

To help the state get a handle on its more fundamental and longer-term problems of erratic spending and tax changes made piecemeal, the commission made the following recommendations: after the governor's budget message in odd-numbered years, the legislature should pass a budget resolution setting formal biennial fiscal policy goals. These policy goals should serve as "fiscal boundaries" for the legislature's debate on individual budget items.

MEASURING TAX BURDEN AND TAX EFFORT

Among the first questions raised in Minnesota tax discussions is whether tax burdens or efforts are higher in this state than in others. And, indeed, throughout the year, Minnesotans receive a series of reports from a variety of governmental and public interest groups that show Minnesota's rank among the states

Most often these comparisons are made by dividing tax and spending aggregates by state population or personal income ("fiscal burden") or by dividing a state's capacity to tax (a hypothetical measure that assumes all states have the same average tax base available to them) by actual collections ("tax effort").

The popular use of these comparisons of tax and spending aggregates for the fifty states derives from their ability to provide a quick and easily calculated comparison. They are also simplistic and often misleading, and thus, they must be interpreted with caution. These ratios, which rely on standardized U.S. census definitions of "taxes" and "expenditures," make no allowance for differences in the quality and scope of public services, the ability to "export" taxes to nonresidents, the incidence of the tax burden, the fundamental economic explanations why one state spends or taxes more (or less) than another, and, of course, how the tax system is achieving or failing the policy goals set out for it.

These warnings notwithstanding, Minnesota is consistently shown to be a high-tax and high-expenditure state. Three measures used to compare the state-plus-local-tax burden are total taxes per capita, total taxes as a percentage of state personal income, and the tax effort index. As illustrated below by the most recent figures available from the United States Bureau of the Census, Minnesota's tax load is well above the U.S. average.

| | 1983 Tax Collections Per Capita | 1983 Taxes as a Percentage of State Personal Income | 1982 Tax Effort Index |
|---|---|---|---|
| Minnesota | $1,473 | 13.22% | 111 |
| U.S. Average | 1,216 | 11.06 | 100 |
| Minnesota Rank | 5 | 5 | 9 |

Since the commission recognized the many weaknesses as well as the strengths of these numbers, it did not make any recommendations based solely upon them.

## JOBS AND TAXES

Two facts—that long-term employment growth in Minnesota has generally been better than most of its neighboring states or the U.S. as a whole, and that Minnesota is a high-tax state relative to most other states—leave unanswered the question whether there is a relationship between taxes and changes in the level of employment in Minnesota.

One way to answer this question is to record actual employment growth rates for Minnesota and other states and then statistically relate them to taxes and other business climate factors in the states. Accordingly, the commission tested the extent to which a set of factors could be shown to explain (correlate in a statistically significant way) employment growth in manufacturing; transportation and public utilities; wholesale trade; retail trade; finance, insurance, and real estate (FIRE); and services. Total employment growth for these six industries was also analyzed.

The set of business climate factors tested as determinants of employment growth in this study was more extensive than any examined in other studies of this type. In addition to standard measures of the market (e.g., personal income), labor force (e.g., wages, work stoppages, education), climate, and energy prices, many fiscal variables were also examined. These included tax burden, tax trend, and progressivity for total taxes as well as for specific levies.

These results, which should be interpreted as a test of Minnesota's competitiveness relative to other states, not as a test of factors that explain Minnesota employment over time, are summarized in Table 1. Factors with an asterisk (*) indicate a positive relationship between the factor and the percentage change in employment (1973-80) for the industry group shown. Factors without an asterisk are inversely related to employment change. Look at the lists for each group or industry sector in Table 1. In four of the seven groups, tax burden trend is shown to be negatively associated with the rate of job growth. One can conclude with a high degree of confidence (as measured by statistical tests of significance) that if the total state/local tax burden tends to rise (fall) faster in Minnesota than in other states, a lower (higher) rate of job growth will be associated with that phenomenon, and that this relationship will be particularly evident in three key industries: manufacturing, services, and retail trade. Just why this relationship occurs is not revealed here. Several hypotheses are plausible, including the most basic: rising taxes leave less and less income for spending in the private sector; this results in fewer private sector jobs being created than it would if Minnesota's taxes were more in line with other states.

### TABLE 1
### The Factors that Mattered for Each of the Industries Examined

| Total Employment | Manufacturing | Transportation | Services |
|---|---|---|---|
| Wages | Tax Burden Trend | Work Stoppage | Wages |
| Tax Burden Trend | *Temperature | Electricity Costs | Electricity Costs |
| Electricity Costs | Percentage Manufacturing | *Temperature | Tax Burden Trend |
| *Education Expenditure | | Percent Manufacturing | *Temperature |
| *Temperature | | | *Per Capita Income |
| Percentage Manufacturing | | | |
| *Per Capita Income | | | |

| Wholesale Trade | Retail Trade | Finance, Insurance and Real Estate |
|---|---|---|
| Electricity Costs | Wages | Wages |
| Individual Income Tax | Electricity Costs | Labor Force Availability |
| Sales Tax | *Educational Expenditure | Electricity Costs |
| *Temperature | Tax Burden Trend | *Education Expenditure |
| Percentage Manufacturing | Individual Income Tax | Individual Income Tax |
| | Density of State | Density of State |
| | *Per Capita Income | *Per Capita Income |

Which specific taxes appear to matter the most? Of the taxes examined, the level of the individual income tax appears to present the greatest danger to job growth, particularly in Wholesale and Retail Trade and Finance, Insurance and Real Estate. In these the case emerges for a reduction in individual income taxes as part of any program of Minnesota tax reform. This case is buttressed by the evidence presented below—that the individual tax effort index in Minnesota is nearly twice that of the average U.S. state.

A few final comments are in order with respect to the relationship between certain business climate factors and the rate of growth of Minnesota private sector jobs. Several factors that were tested did not turn out to be significantly related to the rate of change of employment. This suggests that at present these nonsignificant factors are not causes for concern. The fiscal variables in this list included the retail sales tax and public welfare expenditures. Due to data limitations, no measure of the relationship between the property tax and job change could be estimated.

## THE INTERGOVERNMENTAL SYSTEM

For most states, an examination of the state/local tax structure can proceed with only a brief reference to the interplay between state and local finances. In Minnesota, however, finances of the state and its localities are intertwined. The result is a complex maze of explicit as well as implicit financial relationships. An idea of the magnitude of this interplay is evidenced by the fact that in 1982 local governments accounted for more than 70% of state-plus-local spending but collected only 26% of all state/ local taxes. This relationship is primarily the result of a series of property tax credit and local government aid programs enacted (and then expanded) since 1967.

A major purpose for setting up this system of credits and grants was to minimize the reliance on the property tax as a source of state/local revenues and instead rely more heavily on the more economically responsive ("elastic") state taxes. Between 1967 and 1975, in a series of actions that has been labeled the *Minnesota Miracle,** greater reliance was placed on the income tax, corporate net profits levy, and the general sales tax (adopted in 1967).

---

* The *Minnesota Miracle* refers to a set of innovative actions in the early 1970s in which the governor and the legislature joined to restructure state-local fiscal relations. While the legislature took over a more direct responsibility for levying taxes of all kinds from the state's political subdivisions, including school districts, it committed the state to return more revenues than ever before to local governments. In its *1972 Annual Report on Federalism of the U.S. Advisory Commission on Intergovernmental Relations,* John Shannon coined the term *Minnesota Miracle* and observed that Minnesota "[rewrote] the book on state fiscal policy toward local government."

The Minnesota Miracle was a bold set of actions, and it will remain basically intact even if all of this commission's recommendations are enacted in the next few years. However, the manner in which recent legislatures have attempted to make that philosophy operational has frustrated the very goals of tax relief and explicitness that were originally envisioned. To summarize:

- There are now nine tax credits and three refund programs intended to provide property tax relief. The resulting complexity, however, frustrates taxpayers and tax policymakers alike. At public hearings, several taxpayers complained that the system had become so complex they were reluctant to participate in their local city council hearings on tax matters. The result is a system controlled by technicians, not taxpayers. For the policymakers, the state-local linkages frustrate attempts to manage total public spending, since outlays for many state programs directly or indirectly affect outlays for local services;
- Property owners of like-valued and types of property may pay widely different property tax bills; and
- What is intended as property tax relief in the short run actually results in higher net property tax burdens over time. Why? Because the effect of the state financed property tax relief devices (on homesteads, prairie land, wetlands, and taconite areas) is to stimulate local spending (and, therefore, mill rates) to levels significantly higher than would otherwise occur. This is an important finding, not only from the perspective of political accountability but also from that of tax equity.

## THE "BIG THREE" TAXES: INCOME, SALES, AND PROPERTY

An examination of the long-run revenue producing potential of the state's changing economic structure in combination with its current institutional and intergovernmental arrangements forces the conclusions that in order to finance state and local government in the future, Minnesota must (a) rely on all major tax sources because no one tax can equitably or efficiently capture economic growth in all sectors, and (b) within the bounds of other tax policy objectives, use taxes that are broadly based.

Faced with these conclusions, the commission examined nearly all of the revenue sources currently available to Minnesota and then evaluated these devices vis-a-vis its set of guiding principles and normative tax policy goals. The topics examined ranged from the "Big Three" (general sales, personal income, and property taxes), which together account for 77% of Minnesota's total state-plus-local revenues, to alternatives to the corporate net income tax and the method for valuing farmland for property tax purposes. Because of their combined quantitative importance, the findings and recommendations regarding the personal income, sales, and property taxes are summarized first.

## THE PERSONAL INCOME TAX

Three facts stand out about the Minnesota state personal income tax. It is among the nation's most progressive (tax burden rises as income rises); it is so high that it is discouraging job growth in several of Minnesota's growing economic sectors; and it is overly complex from both the taxpayer's and tax administrators' view.

Of the several goals in designing a revenue system, the most basic for a state personal income tax relates to the last of these characteristics—viz, the need for tax simplicity.

The reality is that the structure of the state's income tax is intertwined with the federal individual income tax. Furthermore, because the federal income tax is so large relative to Minnesota's (or any state's) income tax, it is the federal law that largely dictates people's decisions regarding their tax behavior. An apt analogy is that of a small boat (the state tax) following a large ship (the federal code). The smooth path is set by the ship; and the boat is at peril if it gets too far out of line.

This is certainly not to say that the various economic incentives and disincentives of the federal tax code are those that each state would wish to emulate if it could design its own law in isolation from the federal. Rather, as a practical matter, it is the federal structure, not the state, that affects people's tax behavior regarding consumption and investment decisions, and there is very little (if any) action that a state can take to undo these federal incentives.

However, once a state recognizes the power of the federal tax code, it can then design its own tax structure within those constraints. Specifically, it can determine the degree to which it can conform its tax base to federal code (several alternatives are available) in order to ease the burdens of taxpayer compliance and administration. What is desirable, therefore, is that a state adopt some degree of federal tax conformity—whether it be at a gross level (e.g., adopting the U.S. definition of adjusted gross income as the tax base), or along narrower lines (e.g., federal taxable income). Adopting a mish-mash of some tax base items and not others as Minnesota has done has little payoff, and it causes taxpayer confusion and increased problems of tax auditing.

Does this mean that a conforming state cannot control the distribution of its income tax burden? No. Once it conforms to some tax base, the distribution (e.g., the degree of progressivity) can be achieved in a straightforward manner by the setting of its own tax rate schedule. Tax base conformity achieves the simplicity. The distribution of the state income tax burden is another issue.

Finally, a state can control the use of its personal income tax by the relative quantitative importance it assigns to it in the total tax structure. Here the evidence is that in recent years Minnesota has gone too far. In an attempt to achieve a great degree of progressivity in its overall tax system, the legislature has pushed the income tax to a height that many believe—and empirical evidence supports their thought—is inhibiting job growth. The personal income tax is too high in Minnesota, and steps need to be taken to correct this tax imbalance.

## THE GENERAL SALES TAX

Minnesota was one of the last of forty-six states (including the District of Columbia) to enact a general retail sales tax. The Minnesota tax is levied at a rate of 6% to a narrow subset of consumer purchases and at a 2% rate to a broad set of capital purchases. Although sales taxes alone account for about 17% of state and local tax collections ($1.388 billion in FY 1985), Minnesota is less reliant on this source than are all but eight of the other sales tax states. The 6% rate on retail sales, one of the highest in the nation, is a misleading indicator of actual tax effort due to the narrowness of the consumer portion of the base. Indeed, the representative tax system (tax effort) index places Minnesota at 75% of the U.S. average. Thus, the sales tax, a major revenue source, is utilized less extensively by Minnesota than it is by the average (representative) U.S. state.

The purpose of utilizing so narrow a tax base (sales, income, and property) is, ostensibly, to lessen the regressive distribution (tax burden falls as income rises) of the sales tax burden. Thus, when faced with the choice between generating added state tax revenues from sales vs. the income tax, the general Minnesota policy has been to go with the income tax. There is merit to this choice. After all, if one has to raise a dollar from a progressive (e.g., income) vs. a regressive (e.g., sales) tax, the ability-to-pay criterion dictates the former.

But the meritorious nature of the argument is limited. This is so because Minnesota accomplishes the anti-regressivity goal in an obtuse way. By enacting specific "over-the-counter" exemptions for various items such as clothing and services sold to persons (ranging from hairstyling to auto repair), several problems arise. These are summarized below:

- *Ineffectiveness.* As a policy, the over-the-counter approach actually accomplishes little in terms of enhancing ability to pay taxation. As discussed in the full commission report, the effect of adding to the sales tax base some now tax-exempt items will have little effect on the "gressivity" of the tax. Indeed, if Minnesota adds the purchase of new clothing to the sales tax base, the effect is to lessen slightly the regressivity. Taxing services to persons slightly increases the regressivity. By adding these two tax base items together, one can pick up about 13% in added revenues (or alternatively, lower the sales tax rate from 6% to 5.3%), while leaving the distribution of the tax burden across income groups largely unaffected.

- *Inefficiency.* The over-the-counter approach is an inefficient way to accomplish the goal of reduced regressivity because the benefits of tax exemption accrue to high-income and low-income taxpayers alike. Consider food purchased for home consumption. At present it is exempt from the tax base. If it were taxed, the tax would be regressive—the lower one's income, the greater the percentage of the food tax. But the food exemption also costs the state a large amount of money—$259 million in FY1985. By taxing food, one gets a 19% larger tax base (or a lower equal yield tax rate of 5%). One solution is to take part of the revenue from taxing food and return it to lower-income persons who are most burdened by the additional regressivity of the tax. This can be achieved by packaging it with lower personal income taxes for low- and middle-income families. This is, in fact, why the commission recommended extending the sales tax base to new clothing and services to persons (see Table 2).* The result: a broader tax base, without the regressivity sting.

- *Inequity.*   There is more to the tax equity argument than the avoidance of regressivity (vertical equity). Equity also requires that taxpayers in similar economic circumstances (e.g., equal incomes) be treated similarly. The "equal treatment of equals" (horizontal equity) goal is violated if some families can avoid the sales tax by opting to buy tax exempt rather than taxable items. Because the Minnesota tax base is so narrow, examples of this equity problem abound. This is particularly evident in the fact that Minnesota taxes many consumer purchases of goods (e.g., hairstyling products) but then exempts the service side of the activity (hairstyling salon services).

- *Uncertainty and uncompetitiveness.*   By relying on a narrowly-based retail sales tax, Minnesotans bear two other costs. First, for a given state revenue yield, state tax collections are less stable than they otherwise would be. Because retail consumption (capital purchase) activity tends to be less (more) volatile over the business cycle, utilizing a broad retail base adds to the certainty of the entire revenue system. A more certain revenue flow reduces the need for constant ad hoc legislative tinkering of the revenue system. Second, when the revenue flow to the state is more certain, it is also more predictable for taxpayers. This certainty/predictability element adds to the competitiveness of the Minnesota economy. When a business firm makes a decision to locate or expand in a

---

*An alternative to targeting sales tax relief through an income-based personal income tax credit was rejected.

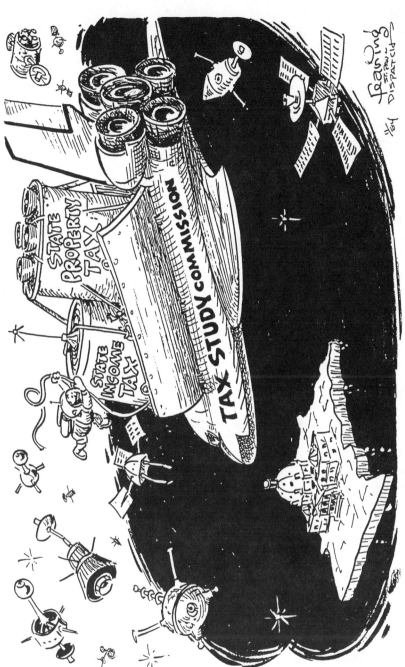

In November 1984 the space shuttle was sent on a mission to retrieve and repair a satellite that had become inoperative. Saint Paul cartoonist Jerry Fearing saw in that mission a message for Minnesotans.

given jurisdiction, it is making a commitment to the future. If a state gets a reputation for frequent ad hoc tax changes and/or having to resolve periodic fiscal crises with special legislative sessions (as Minnesota has), this becomes a negative factor in the decision by a business to locate or expand its operations here.

## THE REAL PROPERTY TAX

In Minnesota, as in other states, the real property tax is the mainstay of local revenue sources. Although the tax is second to the individual income tax as a source of state-plus-local own-source revenues in the Minnesota system ($2.7 billion in 1985), its importance in Minnesota is declining relative to other Minnesota revenue sources. Between 1965 and 1980 the relative importance of the property tax has decreased significantly—from 43% to 21% of own-source state/local revenues.

Again, however, aggregate statistics only tell part of the story. The declining share of the real property tax has been accomplished not only at a great cost in terms of the sacrifice of achieving (nearly all) the normative goals of good tax policy, but in fact, in a manner that so thwarts criteria of fiscal accountability that it actually leads to higher spending by local governments (and, therefore, higher mill rates) than would otherwise occur.

The commission put an enormous amount of time and other resources into analyzing and discussing the Minnesota property tax system, and the findings of fact are numerous. Here are the highlights:

- *Minnesota has the most complex property tax system in the nation.*    This is best illustrated by noting that there is no agreement on the number of classification categories—estimates run from twenty to seventy different classes. There are at least nine credits that can be applied against a taxpayer's property tax bill and three refund programs. The results are increased administrative burdens on the assessor (which negatively affect assessment quality), reduced taxpayer understanding, and a lack of government accountability.
- *Minnesota provides direct property tax relief to taxpayers through three basic approaches.*
    *Classification* alters the tax base by assessing different types of property at different percentages of market value;
    *Credits* make the net property tax bills of certain property owners less than their gross property tax bills; and
    *A refund program* (a circuit breaker) returns a varying portion of net property taxes paid to taxpayers eligible to claim such a refund.
- *Although designed to reduce tax burdens, Minnesota's system of property tax relief is encouraging higher, not lower, mill rates.*  Over time, Minnesota's property tax credits (homestead, wetlands, native prairie, and

taconite credits) which offset part or sometimes all of the increase in a taxpayer's property tax bill, have a significant stimulative effect on local government expenditure. Credits tend to be more stimulative than the block grant local government aid (LGA) that is paid in a lump sum to cities. Commission research shows that dollar-for-dollar, Minnesota's system of property tax credits, which are ostensibly designed to give tax relief, stimulate local mill rates up to three times more than would occur if the same dollars were distributed through LGA.

- *Overall, there is a basic inconsistency in the assumptions underlying Minnesota's direct property tax relief system.* Some programs are designed as though taxes are passed on to renters and others as though the property tax burden is borne by the owner of the property. The circuit breaker and a few of the credits provide relief to both homeowners and renters, recognizing the former circumstance while the classification system and most of the credits give preferential treatment to homeowners (homesteads), acknowledging the latter circumstance.

- *Tax classification is a crude and inefficient property tax relief tool.* If such relief is desirable, there are far superior techniques. Moreover, classification creates additional administrative problems that make difficult the job of the assessor, which is to value property equitably. This administrative burden becomes particularly severe with respect to mixed-use property.

- *For many of the credits, the program designs may not be compatible with the stated goals of the programs.* This criticism is most apt concerning the wetlands, native prairie, and the state school agricultural credits. One overriding design problem is that, although credits would be justified if they provided relief for those with low or no ability to pay taxes, proxies for "need" such as age or disability are used rather than measures such as income and the value of real estate wealth held.

- *The classification system and the credit programs combine so that the burden of the net property tax is the smallest for residential homesteads and agricultural property.* For example, the effective net property tax rate in 1984 was 1.2% for residential homesteads and 0.7% for agricultural homesteads. By contrast, the effective rate for apartments was 3.5% and for commercial-industrial property, 4.4%.

- *The effective rate on agricultural property has declined significantly in recent years.* Between 1973 and 1984 the equalized market value of farm property rose three times as fast as farm property taxes. Minnesota's effective rate on agriculture is below the rates of neighboring states and the national average.

- *The present circuit breaker is designed to coincide with the existing system of tax credits, and as such it is complex and poorly understood.* The circuit breaker provides a greater percentage of relief (up to a maximum) to a low-income/high-property-value taxpayer than to a taxpayer with both low income and low property value. And at every included income level, there is an abrupt cap on the amount of circuit breaker relief available. As taxes rise and taxpayers reach the cap, the share of extra tax borne by the lowest-income taxpayer rises from 5% to 100% of new tax levies. For moderate-income taxpayers, the extra tax share jumps from 50% to 100%. With credits removed, some taxpayers with very-low-valued homes receive no relief from the state and pay all new taxes themselves as taxes rise. Other taxpayers with both incomes and homes of moderate value get 100% relief from additional taxes. This second group of taxpayers has a strong incentive to vote for all property tax increases knowing that the state will pay their share of the cost of new public services.

- *A desirable alternative to the circuit breaker is a taxpayer relief program based on income and property wealth that treats renters and homeowners the same.* The amount of tax relief for any taxpayer would be a percentage of the total tax bill. For some taxpayers the percentage would be zero; they receive no assistance. No taxpayer would receive 100% property tax relief. For households with the same property wealth, the percentage of state-paid relief would fall smoothly as income rose— higher-income households get a smaller percentage of property tax relief. The percentage becomes zero above some income level. For households with the same income, the percentage of state-paid relief would fall smoothly as the home value (real estate wealth) rises—wealthier households would get a smaller percentage of relief. The relief percent becomes zero above some property value.

## A BALANCED PACKAGE

Early in its deliberations, the commission recognized it could not carry out its mission without addressing the interplay among taxes on individual income, sales, and property.

These taxes are inextricably linked in their overall effects. For example, a state's progressive individual income tax is the most effective tool available for offsetting the inherently regressive effect of property and general consumption (sales) taxes. The degree to which each of the taxes is used— the tax mix—has important implications for fiscal stability, competitiveness, equity, and accountability.

After debating several potential tax packages, the commission agreed upon a set of policy directions and a plan of implementation for each of the three taxes. *Although this is not the only package that could correct the distortions noted above, it does illustrate a combination of changes explicitly addressing the tradeoffs in the commission's stated tax policy goals and principles.* Thus, it shows that in an overall budget context, the recommendations can be made operational. A summary is provided in Table 2. More detailed recommendations on each of the areas of study are presented at the end of each section of the full report.

TABLE 2

### Personal Income Tax

| Future Policy Directions | Implementation* (\$ CY 85) |
|---|---|
| • Reduce use of taxes shown to have negative effects on employment growth.<br>• Make Minnesota's tax system more competitive by reducing taxes that exhibit tax efforts well above the other states.<br>• Use the progressive personal income tax as a tool for offsetting tax regressivity inherent in other parts of the Minnesota fiscal system.<br>• Simplify the tax in order to facilitate taxpayer compliance and government administration.<br>• Add to the certainty and predictability of revenues.<br>• Promote accountability. | • Reduce the level of the income tax and lower effective tax rates on all income classes (20% or \$477 million); and target the income tax for further reductions in the future.<br>• Concentrate tax cuts in low- and middle-income groups; fund a property tax credit targeted to low-middle income homeowners, farmers, and renters designed to offset the additional tax burden for those least able to pay.<br>• Conform to federal taxable income while maintaining a separate Minnesota tax rate schedule.<br>• Eliminate the "federal deductibility" provisions and reduce effective tax rates accordingly.<br>• Adopt complete tax indexing whereby the legislature must explicitly vote to approve higher personal income taxes that occur as the result of the interplay of inflation and a progressive income tax structure. |

### General Sales and Use Tax

| Future Policy Directions | Implementation (\$ CY 85) |
|---|---|
| • Increase horizontal tax equity (equal treatment of equals).<br>• Add to the overall stability of the Minnesota fiscal system.<br>• Change the Minnesota tax mix by relying more heavily on sources for which there is an "excess capacity to tax" relative to the other states. | • Broaden the sales tax (now among the nation's most narrowly based) to personal services and new clothing.<br>• Maintain the present 6% tax rate (\$177 million in new revenues). |

*The numbers are used solely to illustrate this reform package can be made operational.

The Property Tax

| Future Policy Directions | Implementation ($ FY 85) |
|---|---|
| • Simplify and make explicit the tax structure and its impact. | • Reduce the number of classifications (estimates range from 20 to 70) to three [residential, homestead and agriculture; residential nonhomestead and apartments; and all other property with assessed to market value ratios of 1/3, 2/3, and 3/3, respectively.]. |
| • Give preferential treatment to homeowners and farmers. | |
| • Eliminate the "expenditure stimulation" effect of a tax credit system that automatically encourages higher property tax levels. | • Eliminate the nine existing property tax credits and three refund programs, thereby creating a windfall to the state general fund of approximately 30% of gross property tax collections ($803 million). |
| • Improve the accountability of the intergovernmental system. | |
| • Add to property tax equity by designing a tax that more closely approximates a tax on wealth as measured by real estate value. | • Relieve this fiscal windfall in the form of tax relief through a combination of reduced mill rates and grants to equalize fiscal disparities among localities ($624 million) and an income/wealth property tax credit ($180 million) targeted to low-income homeowners and small farm homesteads (520 acres and below). |
| • Directly and explicitly address the need to reduce the property tax burden on low- and middle-income households and small farm homesteads. | |
| • Free local assessors from administrative encumbrances that prevent them from carrying out the task of fairly and accurately assessing property. | • Classification reform plus retention of the comparable sales approach to agricultural land. |

# BRINGING IT ALL TOGETHER:
## A SUMMARY OF OTHER MAJOR RECOMMENDATIONS

As noted, the commission examined the Big Three taxes used by Minnesota as well as nearly every other state/local revenue source and their alternatives. The findings and rationale for each of the commission's recommendations are laid out in detail in the full commission report. They are summarized below:

• Maintain the top corporate net income tax rate of 12% and the use of the alternative apportionment formula for multistate income.

• Apply the same corporate income tax to both financial and nonfinancial corporations.

• Retain domestic unitary combination in the apportionment of multistate income and continue to reject the worldwide unitary combination.

• Maintain the current general business tax structure but do not preclude further consideration of a value-added tax.

• Maintain the current status of health premium taxes on insurers and continue the exemption of fraternal, domestic, and township mutuals from the tax premium base.

- Maintain the corporate income tax on insurance companies as well as the provision permitting taxable firms to deduct their premium tax payments in computing their tax liability.
- Maintain the gross receipts tax on telephone and telegraph companies for one or two years to permit planning for replacement of the tax with a property tax that treats telecommunication business as other commercial/industrial activities are treated.
- Eliminate the labor credit on the taconite occupation and royalty taxes, and lower the current statutory rate of 15% to the current effective rate of 6.75%.
- Allow the taconite amendment to the Constitution to expire in 1989 and thereafter base the occupation tax on statute, adjusting it so its burden is similar to that imposed on net income from other business sources.
- Rewrite, simplify, and clarify the tax levy limitation laws for municipalities.
- Retain the comparable sales approach for valuation of farmland rather than applying the concept of agricultural use-value.
- Classify all forested lands under the same rules as agricultural land.
- Retain the present unit-value method of valuing railroad operating property but examine whether greater use of an ad valorem approach can be used.
- Continue the prohibition against new local general sales and local income taxes.
- Avoid the practice of earmarking revenues for specific expenditures except in clear user charge cases.
- Continue the phased-in transfer of motor vehicle excise tax revenues to the highway and transit funds.
- Implement a system of variable tax rates under which motor vehicle fuel and licenses taxes would be increased automatically when highway costs increase, as measured by the federal operation and maintenance cost index.
- Replace the per-unit taxes on alcoholic beverages and cigarettes with ad valorem taxes so the taxes rise as the price of the product rises.

# 2

# The Minnesota Economy

In order to make informed tax policy decisions for the next decade, it is imperative that policymakers understand the nature and direction of change in the Minnesota economy. Accordingly, the purpose of this chapter is to lay out the demographic and economic forces that have been and are shaping the tax policy environment in Minnesota. Making these forces known to the policymakers will help them design a tax (revenue) system that flows with and "captures" the fiscal benefits of economic change.

This chapter begins with a brief overview of the demographic and structural change of the Minnesota economy over the past twenty years. Then, by shift-share analysis, it identifies the long-term employment growth trends in Minnesota's economy vis-a-vis the national economy. Next, it examines how the state economy has performed during the cyclical ups and and downs of the 1970s and early 1980s. Finally, it considers the revenue implications of the long-term trends in the state economy.

## OVERVIEW[1]

DEMOGRAPHICS

*Population.* At 4.1 million inhabitants in 1980, Minnesota ranks twenty-first among the states in terms of population. Although it grew more slowly than the nation during the 1970s (7.1% compared to 11.5% nationally), it was the fastest growing state in the twelve-state north central region.[2] This trend is expected to continue in the 1980s, with Minnesota's population reaching 4.3 million by the end of the decade.

Minnesota's population is heavily concentrated within the Minneapolis-St. Paul metropolitan area. In 1980, about one-half of all Minnesotans lived within the seven-county metropolitan area. A less apparent feature of the state's settlement pattern is that about one-third of its population resides in rural areas, and that is significantly higher than the national average (26%).

During the 1970s, slightly more people moved into Minnesota than moved out, thus reversing a thirty-year trend of net outmigration. About half of the state's immigrants and outmigrants came from and went to other north central states. However, most mobile Minnesotans who changed residence between 1975 and 1980 moved within the state. This propensity to move locally is higher than the national figure (75%). However, it is not a state that relatively large numbers of people leave. In 1980 three of every four residents were born in the state, a number which is also above the national average (64%).

*Labor Force.* During the 1970s, Minnesota's labor force increased by 30%, a rate of growth that was fueled by the entrance of the baby-boom generation into the labor force and the increased participation of women in the labor force. Although the state's labor force expanded as fast as the nation's, its labor force participation rates stood well above the national averages for both males and females, and its unemployment rate was lower than the national average. Together, these characteristics indicate that Minnesota demonstrated an above-average capacity to employ its people.

The rate of labor force growth is expected to lessen in the late 1980s and early 1990s as fewer new, young workers enter the labor force. The increasing experience of those already in the labor force should permit gains in productivity that were not possible during the 1970s when the state and national economies were absorbing large numbers of inexperienced workers.

## EMPLOYMENT AND EARNINGS: STRUCTURE AND GROWTH

*Structure.* The Minnesota economy is generally characterized by its industrial diversity and structural similarity to the national economy. In 1982, the distribution of state employment by major industry groups varied from the national pattern by less than 2% in nine of eleven total sectors. However, the state is not a scaled-down replica of the national economy. Agriculture is twice as important to Minnesota, even though it is declining as a share of both state employment and earned income. Professional services and certain durable manufacturing industries, such as nonelectrical machinery, fabricated metals, and scientific instruments, are also of greater importance to the state economy than to the national economy.

*Growth.* Minnesota has generated jobs faster than most other north central states and the nation as a whole. Between 1969 and 1982, employment increased by 26% in Minnesota compared to 22% nationally. The state also outpaced the national economy in terms of real earned income growth, with state earnings (adjusted for inflation) rising by 16.2% compared to 14.8% nationally over the thirteen-year period.

*Shift to services.* Like the nation, Minnesota is shifting to a service-based economy. During the 1969-82 period, state growth in employment and earnings was dominated by the service-producing industries, i.e., wholesale and retail trade; services; finance, insurance, and real estate (FIRE); transportation, communications, and public utilities (TCPU); and government. By 1982, nearly three-fourths (72%) of the state's work force was employed in these industries compared to 65% in 1969. Conversely, the state's goods-producing industries—agriculture, mining, construction, and manufacturing—have declined as a percentage of total employment. However, unlike the service-producing industries, the goods-producing industries' share of total state earnings is greater than their employment share.

*Relative strength in manufacturing.*    When examined apart from other goods-producing industries, manufacturing has been a strong performer in Minnesota. It was the state's largest industry in terms of real earnings in 1982, despite a long-term decline in its proportional share of state employment. It was also the only goods-producing industry that experienced gains in employment and real earnings throughout the 1969-82 period. Although such gains were modest, they stand in sharp contrast to the experience of the national manufacturing industry, which suffered declines in both employment and earnings over the period.

## SOURCES OF ECONOMIC CHANGE: SHIFT-SHARE ANALYSIS

At first glance, the Minnesota economy resembles the national economy in terms of the relative size and diversification of its major industry sectors. Yet, the state's employment growth in the 1970s far surpassed that of the nation.

The incongruity between economic structure and growth raises two questions: (1) On an industry-by-industry basis, how did Minnesota's employment growth adhere to or vary from that of the nation's? and (2) Why did some industries expand more (less) rapidly in Minnesota than nationally? This chapter addresses the first question by using a descriptive device—shift-share analysis—to examine systematically Minnesota's employment growth in relation to the nation's. Shift-share identifies which state industry groups followed or departed from the national pattern of employment growth. The second question, which examines the whys of economic growth, is addressed in chapter 4.

Before discussing the results of the Minnesota analysis, a brief explanation of the shift-share technique may be helpful. The technique begins by breaking Minnesota's employment growth into three components—national growth, industry mix, and local performance. National growth recognizes that the course of economic events in the nation is a major influence on state employment growth. A state's industries are linked in many ways with industries across the country; therefore, a state economy changes as a function of national economic change.

But state growth seldom reflects national changes precisely. One reason is industry mix, i.e., a state specialization in certain types of industries. If a state specializes in rapidly (slowly) expanding industries, its economy should grow more rapidly (slowly) than does the nation's. Another reason is local performance, i.e., the competitive advantage or disadvantage of state industry groups with respect to their counterparts nationally. If most state industry groups gain an advantage over similar industries in other states due, for example, to favorable access to inputs and markets, they are likely to grow faster than do their competitors in other states (and vice versa if they are at a competitive disadvantage).

To summarize, national growth sets the standard for state employment growth (i.e., employment growth in each state industry group equivalent to national employment growth in the aggregate), and industry mix and local performance account for growth in excess or less than that standard. Together, the sum of these three factors equals the absolute change in state employment, by sector and in total, for a given period.

THE MINNESOTA EXPERIENCE

The Minnesota analysis was performed for the period 1969 – 79 using employment as the measure of economic growth. It revealed that:

- *National Growth.* About three-fourths of the jobs generated in Minnesota from 1969-79 were attributable to national growth trends (i.e., employment in most state industry groups increased at least as rapidly as the national rate of growth for all industries combined).
- *Industry Mix.* A state specialization in the rapidly expanding sectors of the national economy did not fully explain Minnesota's above-the-national-average rate of employment growth. In 1969, Minnesota's employment base was evenly split between the rapidly and slowly growing sectors of the national economy in the 1970s.
- *Local Performance.* The factor that did account for Minnesota's above-average employment growth was the ability of most of its industries to outperform their national counterparts. Nearly all of Minnesota's industry groups—regardless of their fast- or slow-growth qualities—grew faster in Minnesota than they did nationally. This allowed Minnesota to increase its share of the nation's total employment (from 1.86% in 1969 to 1.98% in 1979).

Shift-share analysis also demonstrated how interindustry differences in the state and national employment bases contributed to Minnesota's above-average employment growth. For example:

All subsectors of the service, trade, and FIRE industries, which were fast-growth industries nationally, grew even faster in Minnesota, with the exception of banking. This growth allowed the state to accumulate a larger share of the nation's service, trade, and financial activity.

Many subsectors of Minnesota's manufacturing industry did not exhibit the slow growth typical of that industry as a whole. Lumber and wood products, printing and publishing, scientific instruments, fabricated metals, and nonelectrical machinery (the latter three industries contain many of Minnesota's high technology industries) grew significantly faster in Minnesota than they did nationally. Overall, manufacturing was able to expand its employment base in Minnesota by gathering the fast-growth segments of the industry.

## CYCLICAL CHANGE IN THE MINNESOTA ECONOMY

*Recession.* Prior to the 1980-82 recession, it was frequently advanced that the diversified nature of the Minnesota economy insulated the state from the disruptive effects of peaks and troughs in the national business cycle. Actually, Minnesota's economy has long exhibited a significant degree of sensitivity to changing national economic conditions. Minnesota (especially its nonfarm economy) tends to move with the nation in recession and recovery.

During the 1974-75 recession, Minnesota was quite sensitive to the national downturn, even though it was not hit as hard in terms of employment losses. The stronger performance of the state economy then was largely attributable to the moderating effect of its disproportionately large agricultural sector. Farm exports were growing, thus bringing new income to Minnesota which bolstered the growth of its nonfarm economy.

In contrast, Minnesota recently found itself in a deeper and longer lasting recession than that occurring nationally. Between 1980 and 1982, the state lost more than 100,000 jobs for a decline of 5.8% compared to 2.2% nationally. Most economists attributed the greater severity of the recession in Minnesota to the simultaneous downturn of its farm and nonfarm economies, which had not been affected concurrently in previous recessions.

*Recovery.* During the first half of 1983, Minnesota's economic recovery slightly lagged behind the nation's, but it has since gained additional strength. By April 1984 the state reached its prerecession nonfarm employment peak of 1.79 million and has since expanded. The most recent employment data indicate that Minnesota is among the fastest growing states in the nation.

*Outlook.* Minnesota is expected to outperform the national economy in the 1980s, assuming continued national economic recovery and expansion. Moderate gains in consumer spending and a strong comeback in capital spending is expected to generate above-average growth in several of Minnesota's key industries, such as services, trade, and durable manufacturing. In total, nonagricultural employment is expected to reach a new high of 1.95 million by the end of 1986.

The state's future growth, however, may be restrained by weakness in two of its long-time basic industries—mining (chapter 14) and agriculture (chapter 19).

Minnesota's taconite mining industry is suffering from the decline of the U.S. steel industry, which is currently plagued by obsolete equipment, excess capacity, and increasingly stiff foreign competition. In order to regain its edge in domestic and world markets, industry analysts expect steel companies to become smaller and more efficient, and increasingly to use cheaper, imported sources of iron ore for domestic steel production. These changes imply a reduced demand for Minnesota taconite, and thus, fewer mining jobs. The taconite industry is unlikely to return to pre-1980 levels of production and employment.

Despite a slight improvement in 1983, farm income is expected to decline through 1987. The combination of rising production costs, large crop supplies, and weak demand for farm exports is expected to depress commodity prices and, thus, farm incomes. As has been true since 1980, the farm sector is caught in a significant cost/price squeeze.

Overall, Minnesota's economic growth is likely to be most affected by the course of national economic events. At present, the external forces creating the greatest uncertainty for Minnesota are the mounting federal deficit, high real interest rates, and, especially for the farm, a strong dollar and low/ declining commodity prices.

## THE LONG-RUN REVENUE POTENTIAL OF THE MINNESOTA ECONOMY

Given what is known about Minnesota's changing economy, what can be said about the long-run revenue potential of its state/local tax system? This relationship can be explored in general terms by analyzing the potential of each sector of the state economy to generate directly and indirectly the four major types of tax base: individual income, business income and receipts, consumption, and property.[3] Revenue-generating potential depends on several industry characteristics, such as each sector's share of total state employment and earnings; its rate of employment and earnings growth; its property, labor or capital intensity; wage scale; and overall profitability. From these indicators, general conclusions can be drawn regarding each sector's share of total state employment and earnings; its rate of employment and earnings growth; its property, labor or capital intensity; wage scale; and overall profitability. From these indicators, general conclusions can be drawn regarding each sector's ability to contribute to the four types of tax bases. For example, a large, growing, high-wage industry group is likely to have high individual income tax revenue potential, and a growing industry group with a wide profit margin is likely to be a key contributor to business income revenue productivity.

The findings of this discussion are summarized in Figure 1. Again, it is important to emphasize that these findings relate to the long-run revenue

FIGURE 1
Summary of Tax Revenue Potential—Economic Structure Relationships

| Industry | Revenue Potential | | | |
|---|---|---|---|---|
| | Personal Income | Business Income/ Receipts | Consumption | Property |
| Agriculture | Low | Low | Moderate | Moderate to High |
| Mining | Low | Low | Low to Moderate | Low to Moderate |
| Construction | Low to Moderate | Low to Moderate | Low to Moderate | Low to Moderate |
| Nondurable Manufacturing | Low | Moderate to High | Low | Moderate to High |
| Durable Manufacturing | High | Moderate to High | High | Low to Moderate |
| Transportation | Low to Moderate | Low | Low to Moderate | Moderate |
| Communications | Low to Moderate | Low to Moderate | Low to Moderate | Low to Moderate |
| Public Utilities | Moderate | Moderate to High | Moderate | High |
| Wholesale Trade | Moderate | High | Moderate to High | Low to Moderate |
| Retail Trade | Low | Low | High | Moderate to High |
| Finance & Insurance | Moderate to High | Moderate to High | Moderate to High | High |
| Services | Low | Low | Moderate to High | Moderate to High |
| Government | Moderate to High | — | Moderate | — |

Goods-Producing ↕

Service-Producing ↕

*Source:* Lisa Roden, "Long-Term and Cyclical Change in the Minnesota Economy," Staff Papers, volume 2 of this final report.

potential of the Minnesota economy. They should not be interpreted as revenue projections or tax policy options. This analysis indicates, however, that in order to finance Minnesota's public sector in the years ahead, it will be necessary to rely on all major tax sources (no one tax can capture the economic growth in all industries), and, within the bounds of other tax policy objectives, to use taxes that are broadly based. However, balancing these other objectives with the dictates of long-term changes in the state economy will require state policymakers to make some difficult choices. As is discussed in subsequent chapters of this report, this is particularly true with respect to the need to change Minnesota's tax mix towards more consumption taxes and away from the personal income tax.

## ENDNOTES

1. This chapter is based on a detailed study by Lisa A. Roden, "Long-Term and Cyclical Change in the Minnesota Economy," in *Staff Papers,* vol. 2 of the *Final Report of the Minnesota Tax Study Commission,* ed. Robert D. Ebel and Therese J. McGuire (St. Paul: Butterworth Legal Publishers, 1985), 000-00.

2. The Bureau of Economic Analysis of the U.S. Department of Commerce includes twelve states in the north central region: Illinois, Indiana, Michigan, Ohio, Wisconsin, Iowa, Kansas, Missouri, Nebraska, North Dakota, South Dakota, and Minnesota.

3. Each of these tax bases represents the potential or comprehensive tax base that Minnesota starts with before any narrowing through exclusions, exemptions, deductions, preferential assessments, or credits, *viz:* "personal income" refers to the total income of individuals, of which earnings comprises the largest share; "business income receipts" includes not only net income or profit, but also rent, wages, and interest; "consumption" refers to that part of personal income not saved—a much broader concept than "sales" taxes although both conventional general sales and selected sales taxes are included here; and, "property" includes both real and personal property at its full market value.

# 3

# Minnesota's Budget and Budget Process

Tax policy is not made in isolation. Several factors set the framework for discussion of tax structure and tax levels, which are only parts of the total budget equation. This chapter examines three aspects of the state budget. The first section reviews the recent history of the state's fiscal policies and makes projections into the near future. The second section examines the state's budget reserve, its purpose and structure. A third section explains and evaluates the current process by which the budget is made. The chapter then concludes with a recommendation for spending goals and full disclosure of the overall level of the state budget in order to rationalize tax policy more fully.

Clearly, the particular budgetary considerations facing Minnesota will change in the future. However, the historical and institutional settings examined here provide an important framework for making tax policy in the years ahead.

## REVIEW OF MINNESOTA'S FISCAL POLICIES: 1957-87

State spending policies have a crucial influence on tax levels. In recent years, there has been an important interplay between spending and tax levels in Minnesota. This relationship can be seen by comparing state fiscal policy during the period spanning 1975 to 1979 with the period between 1980 and 1987 (estimated).

The earlier period represented a time of relatively good "fiscal health." The tax base and rates established in 1975 changed little during the period. Between 1975 and 1979 tax revenue increased, largely as a result of economic factors, at approximately the same rate as spending.

Between 1980 and 1982, however, the state experienced major fiscal problems with the general fund, expending over $900 million more than it collected between FY 1980 and FY 1982. The result was a fund deficit of $624 million as of June 30, 1982.

The magnitude of that fiscal crisis required a complex, comprehensive array of tax increases, revenue/expenditure shifts, and expenditure reductions to bring the state's budget back into balance by the end of FY 1983. Although it appears on the surface that these fiscal policies were evenly divided between those affecting revenues and those affecting expenditures, the evidence is that Minnesota taxes in order to spend and not vice versa.

## MINNESOTA'S STATE AND LOCAL FISCAL SYSTEM, ONE OF FISCAL INTERDEPENDENCY

Since 1957, Minnesota state and local finances have undergone significant changes. The most profound change is that today the state is the primary collector of tax revenue, while local governments continue to be the primary spenders. In 1957, 49% of total state/local taxes in Minnesota were collected by the state and 51% by local governments. Local governments, on the other hand, accounted for 73% of total state/local spending. By 1982 the local share of taxes had declined to 26% while still accounting for over 70% of total government spending.

This trend can be attributed to four distinct policy developments during the period:

- *The 1967 Tax Reform and Relief Act,* which enacted a state general sales tax to finance a local government aid program, and two property tax relief programs, the homestead credit and the circuit breaker refund.
- *The Omnibus Tax Bill of 1971 (Minnesota Miracle),* which enacted a school foundation aid program, reformed local government assistance, established levy limitation on local governments, and enacted the agricultural credit program. To finance these programs several tax measures were also adopted that increased revenue from statewide nonproperty sources.
- *State assumption of a greater share of spending for public welfare programs (the mid-1970s),* which have shielded the county-collected proportion of the property tax from financing the surge in public welfare benefit costs.
- *Expansion of direct property tax relief payments* in the form of credits and refunds to individuals throughout the 1970s.

The institutionalization of these programs has not only had a profound impact on the state/local fiscal system, it has also altered the purpose of state government, and, as a consequence, the accountability of Minnesota's local governments.

In 1957, state operating expenditures accounted for one-half of all state spending, while intergovernmental transfer payments accounted for only 38%. By 1975, 50% of state outlays were distributed back to local units of government and only 28% of the outlays were spent directly for state operating purposes. If direct property tax relief payments—state-paid property tax credits and refunds—are also considered as a type of aid to local governments, then nearly 60% of total state outlays provided direct or indirect fiscal assistance to local governments in 1975.

Since 1975, however, the relative growth in state intergovernmental transfer payments declined slightly, and by 1982 transfer payments accounted for only 44% of total state outlays. This decline was offset partly by state payments for property tax relief, which increased from 9% of total state outlays to over 12% during the period.

It is also reasonable to interpret the increase in state welfare benefit expenditures as yet another form of indirect aid to local governments (counties). Accordingly, in 1982 nearly 60% of total state outlays was devoted to direct or indirect fiscal assistance to local governments. This analysis is based upon expenditures made from all state funds as opposed to the general fund only. If only expenditures from the general fund were examined, then nearly 70% of state spending is for the purpose of either directly or indirectly assisting local governments.

As a result of these policies, state tax effort increased significantly from 5.7% of total state personal income in 1967 to 9% in 1979, while local tax effort declined from 5.3% to 3.6% during the same period. By 1982, the state's tax effort was 8.4% and local taxes represented only 3% of the state's personal income. Correspondingly, total state and local tax effort increased only slightly during the entire period, from 11% in 1967 to 11.4% in 1979.

The implication of these state/local fiscal policies for evaluating tax reform in Minnesota is straightforward. If state tax cuts are recommended, any corresponding reductions made in state spending may merely shift the financial responsibility to local governments. Depending on which state programs are reduced, the net reduction on state and local taxes can be something far less than what was originally reduced at the state level.

GROWTH IN STATE TAX REVENUE: 1975-87 (ESTIMATED)

Table 1 shows the estimated revenue impact of major tax laws for FY 1982 through FY 1987. Much of the new tax revenue has been generated from the general sales tax, where the state increased its rate from 4% to 6% and expanded its base to include such items as the sale of candy and soft drinks. As a result of this legislation, the state in FY 1983 collected an estimated $322 million in new tax revenue and may collect as much as $597 million in FY 1987.

Laws affecting the state's personal income tax were also responsible for generating new tax dollars for the state. The most important legislation was the 7% and 10% surtax rates, which affected FY 1982 - FY 1984. Of the new personal income tax dollars, it is estimated that the surtax provisions generated $63 million in FY 1982, $170 million in FY 1983, and approximately $100 million in FY 1984.

TABLE 1
Summary of Estimated-Revenue Impact of Major Tax Law Changes:
FY 1982 - FY 1987 (estimated)
($ Millions)

| Major Tax Source | Fiscal Years | | | | | |
| --- | --- | --- | --- | --- | --- | --- |
| | 1982 | 1983 | 1984 | 1985 | 1986 | 1987 |
| Personal Income | $139 | $268 | $188 | $ 87 | $ 86 | $ 99 |
| General Sales | 159 | 322 | 473 | 515 | 552 | 597 |
| Motor Vehicle | 16 | 25 | 63 | 55 | 59 | 63 |
| Corporate Income | 0 | (27) | (11) | (15) | (17) | (17) |
| Total State Laws | $314 | $588 | $713 | $641 | $ 679 | $ 742 |
| Federal Tax Law Changes | $ 59 | $149 | $216 | $271 | $ 338 | $ 411 |
| TOTAL IMPACT | $373 | $737 | $929 | $912 | $1,017 | $1,153 |

*Source:* Office of Legislative Auditor staff computations and estimates provided by the Departments of Revenue and Finance, April 1984.

In addition to state tax law changes, federal tax policies have also had a significant impact on state tax revenues. As shown in table 1, the department of revenue estimated that in FY 1983, the state revenues may have increased as much as $149 million in additional revenue as a result of changes in federal tax law. By FY 1987, the state may benefit by as much as $411 million. Much of this revenue gain from federal tax policies was a result of reductions in federal personal income tax rates. Since the State of Minnesota allows taxpayers to deduct federal tax liability, any reduction in federal taxes results in an increase in Minnesota taxable income. However, under the current tax law, the reverse is also true—if federal taxes go up, Minnesotans will pay less in state personal income taxes.

GROWTH IN STATE SPENDING: 1975-87 (ESTIMATED)

Between 1975 and 1982, state general fund expenditures increased from $1.9 billion to over $4.1 billion, a rate of growth approximating 12% per year. The Minnesota Department of Finance estimates that general fund expenditures will increase at a 6.3% average annual rate to nearly $5.8 billion by the end of FY 1987. If this rate of increase is realized for this latter period, then it will represent a growth rate approximately two-thirds of that experienced between 1979 and 1982 when state general fund expenditures grew at 9% per year.

Approximately 80% of state general fund expenditures can be associated with seven major program categories.[1] Among these categories in 1975, aid to school districts accounted for 34% of total state general fund expenditures. The school district and relative proportion of general fund expenditures declined to 29% in FY 1982 and is estimated at only 22% in FY 1987.

Between 1975 and 1982, combined state expenditures for property tax relief, medical assistance and general assistance medical care (MA/GAMC), and general support to local governments increased at an average annual rate exceeding 15%. Total expenditures for these three programs amounted to $512 million in 1975, 27% of state general fund expenditures. By FY 1982, expenditures for these programs increased to nearly $1.4 billion and represented over 34% of general fund expenditures.

As indicated earlier, the department of finance estimates that general fund expenditures are anticipated to increase at a relatively slower rate of 6.3% per year between FY 1984 and FY 1987. This is largely a product of anticipated slower growth in general support aids to local governments and expenditures for direct property tax relief. This is significantly slower than the rate of growth experienced in the late 1970s when these expenditures increased by more than 24% per year.

State-paid direct property tax relief payments are also anticipated to slow significantly. Projections for the 1986-87 biennium show expenditures for these programs increasing by only 4% per year. This can be compared to a 16% annual rate realized between FY 1975 and FY 1982.

On the other hand, of the seven major program areas, the most significant growth, by far, is expected to occur in MA/GAMC, increasing by a projected 17% per year during this period. If these estimates are realized, MA/GAMC expenditures will amount to over $850 million by the end of FY 1987 representing, alone, nearly 15% of total state general fund expenditures.

## GROWTH IN TAXES AND SPENDING: A PERIOD OF FISCAL STABILITY VS. A PERIOD OF FISCAL WOES

The period between 1975 and 1979 represented a time of relatively good fiscal health. During this period, there were few major tax law changes and what actions were taken resulted in tax savings to Minnesotans. Tax revenue from major sources increased at a rate of 13.6% per year; tax revenue would have increased slightly faster if no law changes were enacted. A strong argument could be made that, between 1975 and 1979, the tax system, which benefited greatly from the high rate of inflation during that period, generated revenues at such a fast rate that it actually stimulated state spending. The system produced the revenues, so, the dollars were spent.

Between 1979 and 1982 the fiscal pattern changed. During this period, tax revenue from major sources increased 7.1% per year, while general fund expenditures increased at 9% per year. Much of the growth in tax revenue realized during this period occurred in FY 1982 when state legislative action increased taxes by $314 million. If that legislation had not occurred, revenues from major tax sources would have increased by only 3.1% for the period. This gap between the growth in state taxes and spending began with tax and spending policies adopted during the 1979 legislative session. Actions were taken to slow the growth in tax revenue while at the same time increasing spending for major programs.

## THE 1979 LEGISLATIVE SESSION: TAX AND SPENDING POLICIES PROVIDED THE IMPETUS FOR FISCAL DIVERGENCY

In 1979, lawmakers decided that the revenue-generating capacity of the tax system may have exceeded spending demands and was overburdening the taxpayer. As a result, several policies were adopted that either cut tax revenue or were designed to diminish the system's revenue—elasticity during periods of rapid inflation. Major legislation included:

- Personal credits increased to $55 in 1979 and to $60 in 1980, and indexed thereafter;
- Standard deduction increased to 10%, up to a maximum of $2,000, indexed as of 1981;
- Low-income credit increased and indexed as of 1981;
- Income tax brackets indexed by 85% of percentage change in the (Minneapolis/St. Paul) consumer price index;
- Top income tax rate reduced from 17% to 16%;
- Pension exclusions increased, nonresident pensions not taxed.

Also, in 1979 the legislature took action that either allowed or provided for major spending increases to occur over the 1981 biennium. As a result of legislation that occurred in 1979, state tax revenue from major sources increased by only 7% during the 1981 biennium, while spending for major programs increased by over 23%. Clearly, this policy mix was not very conducive for fiscal stability.

The fiscal impact of this divergency in tax and spending policy can be best illustrated by examining two policy decisions—the indexation of the personal income tax and increased homestead credit benefits. The state began the 1980-81 biennium with a $281 million fund balance. Indexation of tax brackets, credits, and deductions reduced state tax revenue by $302 million for the biennium, while legislative increases to the homestead credit increased the state's liability for property tax relief by $124 million.* The combined fiscal impact of these two policies totaled nearly $426 million, exceeding the fund balance by $145 million. By the end of FY 1982, these two policies had a fiscal impact of $723 million, representing over 115% of the total general fund deficit of $624 million realized on June 30, 1982.

---

*As discussed in chapter 7, indexation cannot be said to be a true tax cut measure. Rather it is a device that promotes honesty and legislative accountability by preventing higher generated revenues as a result of the interplay between a progressive income tax and inflation. Indexation merely requires that income tax increases be explicit.

ANALYSIS OF THE GENERAL FUND BUDGET BALANCING
ACTIONS IN THE 1982-83 BIENNIUM

After enjoying several years of relatively stable finances, the general fund began exhibiting fiscal problems in August 1980. The sources of these difficulties are complex, but most agree that a national recession coupled with certain modifications to the tax system—primarily indexing the individual income tax—had stalled the general fund's revenue growth. In addition, while various factors contributed to slowing the rate of growth in tax revenue, the state continued to pursue a relatively fast rate of growth in spending. The combination of divergent tax and spending policies, compounded by an economic recession, quickly resulted in fiscal instability.

The problems experienced during the 1980-81 biennium were certainly painful, but they were solved, primarily through restructuring the cash flow of a few major revenue and expenditure programs. Individual income tax collections were accelerated and an additional $60 million was received during the biennium. School aid payments totaling $241 million were deferred into the 1982-83 biennium. In all, $300 million of adjustments were required, but relatively few programs were affected.

By contrast, revenue shortfalls plagued the general fund throughout the 1982-83 biennium. Six special legislative sessions were called so that the finances could be adjusted and nearly $2 billion of financial modifications became necessary during the biennium. The time lag required to institute many of the financial changes resulted in the $624 million general fund deficit on June 30, 1982, the mid-point of the biennium. Accordingly, facing up to fiscal recovery was necessary during FY 1983 so that the biennium would end without a fund deficit.

Table 2 illustrates the fiscal impact of the series of budget balancing acts that were implemented during the 1982-83 biennium. On the surface, it appears the actions were evenly divided between those affecting revenues and those affecting expenditures. However, a closer examination reveals that of the total $1.8 billion fiscal adjustment, 37% was generated with new and now permanent taxes. The 19% expenditure reduction, which will be discussed later, was basically a temporary decline, and offset somewhat by local tax increases.

Nearly $900 million of state budget savings were achieved during the 1982-83 biennium through actions decreasing expenditures. However, only a small amount of these expenditure reductions were ultimately translated into service cuts trimming back programs. The largest share, $548 million, represents a restructuring of payment schedules or shifts from one biennium to the next. These actions resulted in a temporary remedy that afforded a one-time budget savings.

Of the $331 million cut from expenditures during FY 1983, $262 million may have increased local tax efforts because of the extensive

TABLE 2
State General Fund
Fiscal Impact of Budget-Balancing Actions
1982-83 Biennium
($ Millions)

|  | Biennium | | 1982-83 Biennium | Percent of Total |
|  | 1982 | 1983 | Totals | Adjustment |
| --- | --- | --- | --- | --- |
| Revenue Enhancements: | | | | |
| Temporary Taxes (income surtax) | $ 63 | $ 170 | $ 233 | 13.0% |
| New Taxes | 251 | 418 | 669 | 37.2 |
| Subtotal: Revenues | $314 | $ 588 | $ 902 | 50.2% |
| Expenditure Actions: | | | | |
| Cuts[a] | $ 17 | $ 331 | $ 348 | 19.4% |
| Shifts | 68 | 480 | 548 | 30.5 |
| Subtotal Expenditures[a] | $ 85 | $ 811 | $ 896 | 49.8% |
| TOTAL FISCAL IMPACT | $399 | $1,399 | $1,798 | 100% |

Source: Office of the Legislative Auditor, staff computations.
[a]Expenditure cuts do not include amounts eliminated from state department appropriations for salary, supplies, and equipment.

intergovernmental fiscal relationships between the state and its local government units. The remaining $69 million of expenditure reductions could not have resulted in increased local taxes. They were either temporary declines in state financing and/or shifts in financial obligations to a nontax revenue source.

In sum, the impact of the 1982-83 cuts were either translated into increased local property taxes, future increases in state spending, or at best, a temporary reprieve in tax burdens. This demonstrates the difficulties of implementing long-term declines in state expenditure commitments and, consequently, the level of taxation.

GENERAL FUND FINANCES: 1984-87 (ESTIMATED)

Through FY 1987, revenues are expected to exceed spending, keeping the state budget well in the black. However, as Exhibit 1 illustrates, the state's projected level of spending through 1987 is only affordable if some of the new and temporary state taxes enacted since 1980 remain in place (the only exception being the personal income surtax which, under this projection, was repealed January 1, 1984). The graph clearly shows that had these new tax laws not been enacted, the level of revenues (line C) would not have been able to sustain the level of general fund expenditures as currently projected.

EXHIBIT 1

General Fund Revenues and Expenditures
Actual and Projected
Showing Impact of State Tax Laws Since FY 1981
Trendlong: 1978-1987 Est.

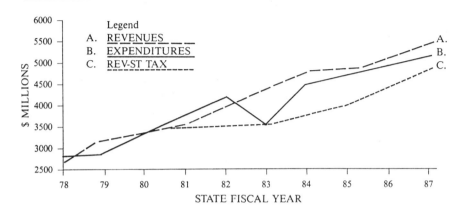

*Source:* Office of the Legislative Auditor staff computations (FY 1978 – FY 1983). Projections based on data provided by the Department of Finance, April 17, 1984.

Finally, it is important to emphasize that these projections of revenues and expenditures assume moderate economic growth for the state through FY 1987. If another recession occurs in 1985-86, the state will be faced with another deficit situation by the end of FY 1987. This is likely to occur despite the fiscal actions taken since 1980, a current, relatively large fund balance, and a projected rate of growth in state general fund expenditures slower than that experienced over the last ten years.

## CONCLUSION: TAX REFORM—TAX REDUCTION

Based on the evidence, a strong argument could be made that since 1980 the state's tax policy has responded to spending demands rather than expenditure policy responding to revenue constraints. The legislative response to the recent budget crises has been to increase taxes, borrow, and alter its cash flow in order to bring revenues back in line with spending. Although it could be argued that such policies are necessary because it is difficult to adjust expenditures in the short run, the state has chosen to maintain all the new and "temporary" taxes enacted since 1980 other than the income tax surcharge, which was repealed retroactively to January 1984.[2]

This puts Minnesota in a fiscal situation quite different from the 1980-82 period. There is now a structural surplus in the general fund of approximately $250 million to $300 million. That is, when all state revenues (not just taxes) are taken into account, Minnesota has an annual, built-in divergence (surplus) of revenues over expenditures in the $250 million - $300 million range.[3] This indicates that the Minnesota Legislature is in a position in 1985 to enact a significant and permanent tax cut of an amount equal to at least 5% of its general fund resources in FY 1986.[4] In short, although tax reform can be accomplished on a total "equal yield" or "revenue neutral" basis, Minnesota has the opportunity to combine tax reform with tax reduction. This combination of actions will not only eliminate the permanent overtaxing of Minnesotans by their state government, but it will also minimize fiscal losses that inevitably accrue to some taxpayers as a result of a major restructuring of a tax system.

## MINNESOTA'S BUDGET RESERVE ACCOUNT

### BUDGET RESERVE FUNDS IN OTHER STATES

In recent years several states have established budget reserves to be used when general fund projections fall short because of unexpected recessions. The reserve funds are not large enough nor are they intended to enable a state to weather severe recessions without increasing taxes and/or cutting spending. Rather, the purpose is to provide a contingency fund for general fund deficits and to ease cash flow problems resulting from revenue projection errors. These funds enable policymakers to cover unexpected revenue shortfalls without having to change tax rates or expenditure levels on short notice. Thus, these contingency funds lend stability to the tax structure, and ad hoc tinkering with rates to solve a short-term problem can be avoided.

Nineteen states currently have some form of budget reserve. These reserves differ in how they are funded and also in the conditions for withdrawal. For determining flows into the funds, three methods are used: appropriation, surpluses up to a certain percentage of general fund revenue, and formulas based on real personal income. Withdrawals from the funds are either specified by appropriation, automatically withdrawn for revenue shortfalls, set by special legislative session, specified by per capita income formulas, or determined as part of the budget plan.

### THE BUDGET RESERVE ISSUE IN MINNESOTA, CONCERNS DURING THE 1970S: PROBLEMS OF BUDGET SURPLUSES

The issue of a budget reserve first materialized in the mid-1970s. The primary concern, however, was not from fear of revenue shortfalls but rather from substantial revenue surpluses. From this initial concern, no legislative action was enacted nor proposed for at least two reasons: first, many officials thought Minnesota's economy was "recession proof," due to the mild impact of the 1974-75 recession in Minnesota; and second, the large surpluses that were experienced during that period created more of a political concern than a budget management problem.

Between 1975 and 1979, Minnesota's fiscal condition was characterized by a tax system that generated revenues faster than the growth in personal income.[5] This period was also characterized by relatively accurate revenue projections that slightly underestimated tax receipts. Total tax receipts were underestimated by 0.7% in 1975, 2.4% in 1977, and by 1.6% in 1979. The dollar impact of these errors resulted in unexpected gains of $14.1 million in 1975, $59.2 million in 1977, and $51.9 million in 1979.

Correspondingly, this underforecasting of revenues contributed to the substantial surpluses realized in the general fund during this period. The unrestricted balance in the state's general fund exceeded $200 million in all but one of the five years between 1975 and 1979, and exceeded $300 million in 1975 and 1976. At the end of FY 1979, the unrestricted general fund balance exceeded $234 million and represented 7.2% of total state spending.

The continued experience of having relatively large general fund balances prompted the governor and the 1979 legislature to pursue its policy of tax cuts that, for the time being, resolved the budget reserve issue.

## THE ESTABLISHMENT OF A BUDGET RESERVE ACCOUNT

Because of the severe fiscal problems experienced during the 1982-83 biennium, the budget reserve issue was resurrected. This time, however, the issue was not overtaxation and government accountability, but rather a concern for budget stability and sound fiscal management.

Governor Rudy Perpich, in his 1983 budget message, recommended to the legislature that the state be prepared to manage up to a 5% variance in revenue forecasts. In order to do this, he proposed that the legislature either establish a $500 million budget reserve fund or a $250 million reserve along with a "shared risk" provision that would reduce local government aids, up to an additional $250 million. A compromise was reached between the governor and the legislature and a $250 million account was established. In addition, the legislature also adopted a provision to suspend income tax indexing if a deficit larger than the amount in the budget reserve is forecasted.

In 1984, the governor proposed and the legislature approved increasing the budget reserve from $250 million to $375 million. Currently, the governor is proposing to increase the budget reserve to $500 million for the 1986-87 biennium.

The budget reserve is administered as follows. In implementing the budgetary reserve requirement on July 1, 1983, the department of finance did not specifically segregate $250 million in cash or other assets in a separate account in the state treasury. To do so would have been virtually impossible as all cash on hand on July 1, 1983, was needed for expenditures during the first few months of FY 1984. The department interpreted Minnesota Statute Section 16A.15, Subdivision 6 as requiring a budgetary reserve rather than an actual cash reserve account. The department implemented the statute by establishing a $250 million reserve of fund balance in the accounting records for the general fund. The intent of such a reserve is to make this portion of the fund balance unavailable for appropriation or expenditure. Fund balance is the difference between total assets and total liabilities. On a budgetary basis the projected fund balance at the end of a biennium represents the difference between estimated revenues and expenditures during the two-year period added to the balance at the beginning of the biennium. By implementing the budgetary reserve, the department is saying that by the end of the biennium, revenues (plus the beginning balance) will exceed expenditures by at least $375 million.

In addition to providing a cushion, the budgetary reserve provides a means of alleviating the cash flow problems of the general fund. In recent years, the fund has encountered cash flow difficulties because of the uneven timing of revenues and expenditures. Despite recent changes in the state's payment schedules for several major programs, these cash flow problems will persist into the future bienniums. In effect, short-term borrowing has been necessary during the first part of the fiscal year when expenditures exceeded revenues.

Based on recent experience, fiscal year revenue projections have been in error by approximately plus/minus 8% to 10%. Table 3 shows the impact of a plus/minus 9% error to FY 1987 revenues as forecasted by the department of finance in July 1984. As can be seen, the effect on the general fund balance is very significant. Under the "control" forecast, revenues totaling 9% above projections would result in an unrestricted balance of $1 billion. However, if revenues are 9% less than projected, $60.2 million would have to be transferred from the budget reserve account to balance the budget at the end of FY 1987. The impact under the pessimistic forecast is equally as great. A plus/minus 9% error could result in an unrestricted fund balance as high as $620 million or require $422 million to be transferred from the budget reserve, reducing the reserved amount to $78 million at the end of fiscal year.

## IMPLICATIONS FOR TAX REFORM

A budget reserve provides a fiscal cushion that can help stabilize budgetary problems resulting from either unexpected downturns in the

TABLE 3
Estimated Impact of a Plus/Minus Projection Error*
on Current Forecasted Fiscal Year 1987 General Fund Balance

| | Control Forecast | | | Pessimistic Forecast | | |
|---|---|---|---|---|---|---|
| | As Forecasted | +9% Error | -9% Error | As Forecasted | +9% Error | -9% Error |
| Total Revenue | $6,021,042 | $6,562,936 | $5,479,148 | $5,789,293 | $6,310,329 | $5,268,257 |
| Balance Forwarded | $664,173 | $664,173 | $664,173 | $584,628 | $584,628 | $584,628 |
| Total Resources | $6,685,215 | $7,227,109 | $6,143,321 | $6,373,921 | $6,894,957 | $5,852,885 |
| Total Expenditures | $5,697,797 | $5,697,797 | $5,697,797 | $5,769,095 | $5,769,095 | $5,769,095 |
| Total Balance | $987,418 | $1,529,312 | $445,524 | $604,826 | $1,125,862 | $83,790 |
| Restricted Balance | $505,703 | $505,703 | $505,703 | $505,703 | $505,703 | $505,703 |
| Total Unrestricted Balance | $481,715 | $1,023,609 | ($60,179) | $99,123 | $620,159 | ($421,913) |
| Net Amount Left In Budger Reserve | $500,000 | $500,000 | $439,821 | $500,000 | $500,000 | $78,067 |

*Source:* Office of legislative auditor staff computations based on department of finance projections as of July, 1984.
*This estimate of potential impact of projection error does not accumulate the assumed error rate through previous fiscal years. If the plus/minus 9 percent error rate was applied in fiscal years 1985-1987 this could significantly improve or worsen the outcome produced in this simple analysis of fiscal year 1987 alone.

economy or unanticipated impacts from tax reform itself. It is important to recognize that along with stability in the tax structure can come inflexibility, but if future recessions are truly temporary, it may not be appropriate to change the entire tax structure; rather it may be more prudent to use a budget reserve. Tax rates should be changed for purposes such as alleviating a perceived overburden or improving the distribution of the burden, but one could argue that they should not be changed for temporary fluctuations in the economy. A reserve fund can provide this stability.

However, basic tax reform can have a significant impact on both the size and design of a budget reserve fund. For example, any new mix of taxes or new tax structures will affect the system's degree of responsiveness to changes in the economy and in inflation, thereby making revenues more or less predictable. In addition, changes in state-paid property tax credits, school aids, or local government aid programs significantly affect the state's cash flow pattern. Thus, establishment of a budget reserve may only be part of a tax reform package; a well-crafted design is also important.

## MINNESOTA STATE BUDGET PROCESS

Mechanically, Minnesota's budget process works well. Every two years, it produces a balanced budget before the start of the biennium. Substantively, however, it has a critical shortcoming—a limited amount of debate is devoted to the overall level of the state budget and tax spending. The lack of early and ongoing attention to this matter tends to encourage state tax policy to respond to spending demands rather than expenditure policy responding to revenue constraints. Because the budget process can influence state spending and therefore state tax structure and levels, it is appropriate to examine it as part of this tax policy study. Accordingly, this section describes the process by which the governor and legislature arrive at the overall taxing and spending levels for the upcoming biennium. It focuses on the interaction between the executive and legislative branches as well as the internal workings of the legislature with respect to the state's biennial budget. The budgeting relationship of the governor and legislature with the state agencies is not considered here.

## OVERVIEW

During an eleven-month period that occurs every other year, the governor and legislature review thousands of individual revenue and expenditure items, culminating in the adoption of a two-year budget before the start of the new biennium. Because the Minnesota Constitution prohibits borrowing to finance operations across bienniums, the adopted budget must be balanced. In the event of revenue shortfalls (such as those experienced in 1981 and 1982), it may be necessary for the legislature to meet in special session so that mid-biennium adjustments can be made to bring the budget into balance.

The governor is Minnesota's chief budget officer. As such, he both starts and ends the budget process. The governor, with the assistance of the department of finance, submits a biennial budget to the legislature. Once acted upon by the legislature, the governor can veto individual items or entire appropriation bills, thus giving him final say on the budget.

The legislature follows the governor's lead because its time and resources for budget work are limited. From the time it convenes to adjournment five months later, the legislature must not only adopt a budget but also address many other policy issues. If it had to build a budget from scratch, it would be difficult for the legislature to complete its other responsibilities. Maintaining the budget planning, development, and administrative functions in the executive branch is also advantageous to sound fiscal management.

The state budget process can be divided into two stages: budget preparation and budget adoption. *Budget preparation* begins in the spring of each even-numbered year and ends in late January of each odd-numbered year with the governor's budget address to the legislature. The *budget adoption* stage starts in late January of each odd-numbered year and ends in mid- to late-May with the passage of the biennial budget by the legislature and its approval by the governor. During its session in even-numbered years, the legislature may adjust budget decisions made in the previous year.

During the course of the budget process, there are relatively few statutory requirements that the governor and legislature must abide by. Of these, the most important requirements are that:

- the governor present a biennial budget to the legislature in January of each odd-numbered year;
- a budget is adopted before the start of a new biennium; and,
- the state's budget is balanced at the time of adoption and at the close of each biennium.

Generally, the governor and legislature work with one hard-and-fast deadline: that all budget actions of one biennium are completed before the start of the next biennium.

## THE MAKING OF THE BUDGET: THE GOVERNOR'S ROLE

Through work with state agencies and the legislature, the governor sets the tone of the biennial budget discussion. For example, in May 1984, Governor Perpich directed state agencies to keep their budget increases for the next biennium at or below 14% and to include no increase in positions. Based on guidelines such as these (which may change as budget preparation advances), the governor puts together his proposed budget for submission to the legislature.

On the expenditure side, the executive budget is considerably more than just an extrapolation of previous spending practices. However, the governor's ability to make major changes in state spending policy is limited by past legislative decisions and by the fact that most state/local spending is at the local level. For example, the level of state aid to school districts for the 1986 school year was set by the 1984 legislature. Thus, 22% of the budget for the first year of the 1985-87 biennium was in place before the governor even announced his budget guidelines for that biennium. With respect to medical assistance and general assistance medical care, the legislature must change existing policies, service programs, and/or eligibility requirements in order to have a significant effect on spending in these areas. In addition, since most welfare programs are carried out by local units of government, it is difficult for the state to control these expenditures directly.

## THE LEGISLATOR'S ROLE

Legislators and their staffs do not become formally involved in the budget process until after the legislature convenes and the governor presents his proposed budget. Previous to that time, however, there are frequent, informal consultations between the house and senate leadership and the executive, particularly as the legislative session approaches.

Immediately following the governor's budget message in January, the proposed budget is divided into three parts and referred to three committees in both the house and senate. In the house the appropriations, tax, and education committees all produce major fiscal policy legislation. Similarly, in the senate, the finance, tax, and education committees, also write funding legislation. Basically, their responsibilities divide as follows:

- The appropriations and finance committees review the proposed budget for income maintenance and medical assistance, state agencies, and institutions. These include institutions such as the University of Minnesota and state hospitals.
- The house and senate tax committees review proposals for property tax relief and local government aids.
- The house and senate education committees review the aid proposals for K-12 education. Education aids are also reviewed by the house appropriations and senate finance committees.

In addition to these committees, policy committees (e.g., agriculture, economic development, and commerce) in both houses are regularly involved in the review process. State law requires that the governor's budget recommendation include funding for only "current law" programs. New programs must be kept separate and labeled "specific change items." The legislature's policy committees must act favorably on these programs before they can go through the budget review process. Because they can use their authority to bring legislative initiatives into the budget and to delay or stop the governor's initiatives, the policy committees are important participants in the budget process.

Once distributed to the committees, the various parts of the biennial budget are separately examined through a lengthy budget hearing process. These hearings provide legislators, interest groups, and the public with the opportunity to express their views on the separate budget items. The committees reviewing various segments of the governor's proposal begin their work without any formal instructions or directions from the legislature as a whole. As such, the governor's recommendation is their baseline. The committees and their subcommittees may reallocate funds within a particular category, rejecting the governor's recommendation for one of their own. Fiscal committees are not free to make significant changes in the total size of major budget items or to shift dollars among themselves. Both are closely controlled by the legislative leadership. If a fiscal committee or subcommittee seeks to exceed the governor's recommendation, it must justify its claim to the leadership and quite probably to the majority caucuses in both the house and senate as well as the governor, should he choose to join the debate. This review modification process is informal; there are no rules or statutes that guide or require it.

## RECONCILIATION OF EXECUTIVE AND LEGISLATIVE DIFFERENCES

The governor's proposals as modified by the legislature are enacted through a minimum of six conference committee reports—one from each division/subcommittee of the appropriations/finance committees and one each on taxes and school aids. These conference committee reports originate with at least twelve bills—six from the house and six from the senate. As a result, there is no floor debate by the legislature as a whole on the total budget and tax spending package. Prior to this time, some consideration has been given to the total package by the spending committees and through informal discussions among legislators. And recently, the initial meetings of both the house appropriations and senate finance committees have been used to overview the budget as proposed by the governor. Similar overview sessions are also held by both the tax and school aids committees. However, in no case do these committees take any action (binding or otherwise) regarding the overall size of the governor's proposed budget. Rather, debate and action is focused throughout the legislative session on the various items which make up the governor's proposal.

Final review and spending decisions are made as the session draws to a close. During the closing days, coordination of final subcommittee and committee work is vital. Their bills must sum to a balanced budget. For this work, legislative leaders depend on balance sheets and estimates prepared by the department of finance. In effect, they yield to the executive branch for the information necessary to reconcile revenues and expenditures. Typically, the budget and tax spending bills passed by the legislature exceed the governor's initial request (averaging 108% over the last seven bienniums).

The informal nature of Minnesota's budget process makes the state's budget deliberations both open and private. The process is open to virtually every member of the legislature. Eighty-four percent of the senate's members are on a tax or spending committee. In the house, almost 60% of the members are on one or more of these committees. At the same time, the state's budget process is not entirely public. Its informality leads to numerous private negotiations and coordinating sessions.

## EVALUATION OF MINNESOTA'S BUDGET PROCESS

There is one major shortcoming in Minnesota's budget process: the extremely limited amount of attention that is devoted to the overall level of the state budget and tax spending. This characteristic may be accentuated by the informal mechanisms that are used to coordinate legislative review of the governor's proposed budget. Such mechanisms are not without virtue. The informal approach to budget review has merit in that it opens the process to all members of the legislature and yet keeps the budget responsibilities of individual legislators manageable by using a relatively large number of committees. However, the result is a review process that is piecemeal and does little to encourage legislative debate and action on the total size of the state budget.

There are at least three ways the legislature could structure debate and action on overall tax and spending issues. For example, it could:

- debate and pass a "budget resolution." It would occur shortly after the governor makes his budget and tax spending recommendations. It would require no changes in legislative procedures prior to the governor's fiscal message.
- establish an "affordability committee" similar to that used by the Maryland legislature. This committee would be charged with the task of developing spending guidelines to be recommended to the governor. The process would probably result in two sets of fiscal guidelines for the pending legislative session: one proposed by the legislature's affordability committee and the other by the governor. However, it could conceivably result in a single budget resolution, such as that described above.
- restructure its budget review process around a central budget committee composed in whole or in part by members of the current appropriations, finance, and tax committees. Such structure would promote closer attention to the fiscal impacts of individual budget actions.

These proposals differ with respect to leadership roles in the budget process. The first proposal recognizes and maintains executive leadership in matters of fiscal policy. The other two proposals attempt to give more of that responsibility to the legislature, actions that could potentially weaken the budgeting power of the governor. Overall, however, the proposals have the same goal: to bring greater legislative and public attention to Minnesota fiscal policies.

## RECOMMENDATIONS

### NEED FOR SPENDING GOALS AND FULL DISCLOSURE OF THE LEVEL OF THE STATE BUDGET

In order to insure that all of Minnesota's fiscal policies (especially the overall level of public spending) is debated and the result of deliberate action by the governor and legislature, the commission recommends the following three-part process:

- In the late spring of every even-numbered year, the governor should announce spending goals for the next biennium. These goals should describe the governor's objectives with respect to the overall level of state and local government spending. In presenting the goals, the governor should disclose their likely consequences with respect to the quality or quantity of public services and the effective tax rates for both state and local governments.

• Following the governor's announcement, public hearings sponsored by the house and senate tax and/or appropriations/finance committees regarding the governor's spending goals should be held. The results of these hearings should be published and distributed to the legislature by August of that year.

• After the governor's January budget message, the legislature should pass a budget resolution setting formal fiscal policy goals for the next biennium. These goals should serve as fiscal boundaries for the legislature's debate and action on the governor's budget proposal.

The legislature should pass its budget resolution before consideration of any individual budget items. The legislature may pass subsequent budget resolutions in response to changes in fiscal conditions or budgetary preferences. However, no budget should be adopted which has spending levels above those prescribed in the most recent budget resolution.

THE BUDGET RESERVE

The commission recognizes that fiscal prudence requires the state to maintain a budgetary reserve account. Accordingly, the commission recommends that Minnesota include a reserve fund as a permanent part of its fiscal structure.

## ENDNOTES

1. The seven categories that will account for an estimated 81.7% of general fund financing in FY 1987 are aid to schools (22.1% of total general fund expenditures), postsecondary education (16.6%), direct property tax relief (15.3%), medical assistance and general assistance for medical care (14.8%), local government aid plus general support (6.5%), debt service (2.9%), and income maintenance (3.5%).

2. The only temporary tax to be repealed was the income tax surcharge, which was repealed retroactively to January 1, 1984, by the 1984 legislature. At the same time the state's budget reserve was increased from $250 million to $375 million for the biennium.

3. This estimate includes an increased budget reserve for the biennium of $500 million. Data based on October 1984 department of finance projections of a constant services budget and existing (1984) revenue system.

4. Some policymakers argue that the tax reduction might be as much as $500 million if the present structural surplus is combined with a budget process (e.g., budget resolution on overall expenditure levels) that will limit expenditure growth.

Remarks by William Schreiber, Chair, Tax Committee of the House of Representatives, Fiscal Chairman's Seminar, National Conference of State Legislatures, January 5, 1985 (Denver).

5. During this period, the state's total personal income increased at an average rate of 11.7% per year, while tax revenues from major sources increased at an average annual rate of 13.2%.

# 4

# Minnesota Fiscal Comparisons

Among the first and most frequently raised issues in state/local fiscal policy discussions are those pertaining to the extent of the fiscal or budget "pressure" (the government's viewpoint) or the "burden" of financing the government (taxpaying public's viewpoint). The question usually posed within this context is: "Are fiscal pressures or tax burdens higher in this state than in others?" Although this question is certainly not new to state fiscal discussions, it has taken on increased importance in Minnesota in recent years as the result of a growing concern regarding the state's ability to compete with other parts of the country in attracting new investments and jobs.

There are several measures that have been devised to address the comparison question, and it is the purpose of this chapter to present and evaluate the available data. As will become clear, the measures that are used both here as well as in other tax burden studies have advantages as well as shortcomings. Therefore, it is important that the attendant numbers be interpreted with care.

The chapter begins with a look at the level and functional distribution of Minnesota state and local spending, and then examines in detail the burden and performance of the tax system that has been designed to pay for these expenditures. In order to make interstate comparisons, it is necessary to focus on amounts spent and taxed by state plus local governments. Because one state may perform functions that in another state are left to localities, comparisons of state government finances (or of local government finances) could be quite misleading.

## EXPENDITURE LEVELS AND TRENDS

As discussed in chapter 1, the most useful approach to the analysis of the Minnesota tax system is to take each tax and, for a given required revenue yield, ask what is the "best" design of that tax or its alternatives. Then, a search for the best system is a search for the best mix of those taxes. Thus, a tax study such as this one can be accomplished, while at the same time, an in-depth examination of the expenditures financed by those taxes can be avoided.

This is not to say, however, that expenditures can be altogether ignored. There are several cases in which the tax and expenditure decisions are not even mechanically separable. This is particularly true in Minnesota with respect to the interrelationships among various tax relief devices and state aid outlays and the use of earmarked tax levies—all topics that will be carefully examined in later chapters.

Equally important to recognize is that even if there is no direct accounting relationship between taxes and spending, there are certain fundamental and practical relationships between expenditures and taxes that have special relevance. Two key relationships can be identified.

First, governments tax to spend. As will become clear below, when all the warnings are given regarding the weaknesses of various tax burden and performance indicators, the conclusion is that Minnesota is a high-tax state. And that, in turn, reflects the fact that the state is a high spender.

The special importance of this finding is that the task of providing Minnesotans with a set of recommendations that will achieve a balance among the fiscal goals laid out in chapter 1 becomes more difficult as spending pressures increase. This is true even if voters feel that the level of Minnesota public spending is about right. Why? Because every tax has inherent structural deficiencies and inequities. Thus, if a given tax or mix of taxes is too heavily relied upon, those deficiencies and inequities may become intolerable. And, if the political system does not adequately respond to this situation, the voters may institute absolute, inflexible solutions (such as writing specific tax law into the Constitution) without regard to agreed upon public needs. In the long run, such a solution may only worsen the fiscal problem it was designed to address. Accordingly, if policymakers find that even the "best" of tax systems is either now or in the future likely to be under too much stress, then it must come to grips with the expenditure level issue. Whether this excessive stress is indeed the case is something that should become evident as this study progresses.

Second, despite the tendency for policymakers and observers alike to separate tax from expenditure decisions (a process that many argue is at present institutionalized in the present Minnesota legislative structure that lacks budget planning committees), the tax structure is often a product of the nature of changes in spending. That is, if spending decisions become erratic, so may the design of the tax system. For example, if government expenditures are permitted to rise at a rate beyond the tax system's ability automatically to generate new revenues as the economy grows, the legislature may need to meet on short notice to solve fiscal crises. The result can be a revenue system which meets none of the goals of a "good" tax system since it is characterized by tinkering and patchworking. This sort of environment occurred in 1980-83 and might occur again in the 1985-87 period, if a recession combines with present projected spending trends and the existing revenue structure. Conversely, it is also possible (though less likely) that revenues could become so automatically responsive to economic growth as to lead to unusually large surpluses in growth years and deficits in economic downturns, with the possible result that the tax system would again be subject to adjustments expedient in the short run but which build in long-run, structural defects.

Minnesota may be particularly vulnerable to this problem of erratic budget determination due to the fact that many state spending programs are effected through a most complex and many-layered intergovernmental system. Indeed, that system is so complex that some participants at the commission's public hearings testified that only a handful of experts really understand how the total system works. Similarly, the executive order creating this commission specifically cited the problem of "tax changes (that) have been made piecemeal without regard to the system as a whole and sometimes without knowledge of long-term effects."

Accordingly, the purpose here is to recognize explicitly that "good" tax policy is in certain ways inextricably tied to expenditure policy. Thus, it is appropriate to begin the examination of the Minnesota state and local tax system by first taking a look at the level and composition of Minnesota expenditures.

Two conventional approaches to identifying state/local expenditure changes are presented below—viz, expenditure levels as a percent of state personal income and per capita spending by function. Each of these measures is a ratio of a spending amount in the numerator divided by a common denominator that is available for all states. By computing these ratios, one can make statements about a given state's spending behavior over time as well as the rank of a given state relative to others. Although these ratios give one a useful first glance at Minnesota's spending picture, these measures also have serious defects, which, if not clearly recognized, can lead to misleading policy conclusions. For example, the measures not only require one to assume that what is treated as a public expenditure in one state is also a public function in another (however, North Dakota does not have publicly provided kindergartens, Minnesota does), but also that the economies being compared have similar economic and demographic characteristics. These and similar defects are discussed below.

LEVEL OF SPENDING

In order to make fiscal comparisons between Minnesota and other states, it is necessary to use data compiled by the Bureau of the Census of the U.S. Department of Commerce. This is worth mentioning because the census definitions of what constitutes "direct expenditures," "intergovernmental spending and revenues," and even specific taxes or nontax revenues (e.g., user fees and charges) are often not quite the same as those used by a specific state or local government. Because states themselves lack agreement on these terms, the census uses its own definitions in order to have a consistent method for making interstate comparisons. The differences between how a state/local area defines an item or category and the U.S. census approach are not so significant, however, to make the census data unreliable for comparative purposes. Nevertheless, one should be aware that it is not an easy task to look at the census numbers presented in this chapter and then find the exact same number in Minnesota financial reports.[1]

Table 1 presents data relating Minnesota's state and local general expenditures (all expenditures, including capital outlay, but excluding utility expenditures, liquor stores expenditures, and insurance-trust expenditures) as a percent of state personal income for selected years over the period 1966-83. To facilitate comparisons, the numbers in parentheses show individual state/local spending to income ratios as a percentage of the U.S. average state/local spending to income ratio. The states shown in the table have been chosen to include Minnesota's four neighbors as well as to reflect a variety of economic and fiscal circumstances. Data for all fifty states plus the District of Columbia are available elsewhere.[2]

The data illustrate that Minnesota is a high-expenditure state relative to both its neighbors and to the U.S. average. This high standing has generally held true throughout the last decade and a half (and, in fact, all of the post-WWII period) relative to the rest of the nation; but it is only in recent years that it has become particularly noticeable when compared to its border states. In terms of national rankings, Minnesota has moved from 13% above the national average and a ranking of the fourteenth highest state in 1980 to 19% above the nation's average and a ranking of tenth in 1983.

## PER CAPITA AND FUNCTIONAL COMPARISONS

Per capita spending information is provided in the next two tables. In examining the data, three fiscal years (FY) were chosen in order to reflect periods of special interest to Minnesotans:

1967-68 Pre-Minnesota Miracle
1975-76 Mid-late Miracle
1981-83 Post-budget Crisis

The Table 2 data show that in terms of the current dollar and percentage distribution of state and local spending by function, with three exceptions, the functional shares have been about the same. But the exceptions are the big three of spending activities, and they account for nearly 60% total state/local expenditures in FY 1982—educational (all levels), highways, and public welfare. A review of the data shows that a smaller share of the public's budget is going to education and highways, and that an increasing share is being spent on public welfare. As for the remaining smaller spending categories, per capita expenditures are rising most rapidly for interest on general debt.

TABLE 1

Minnesota State and Local Direct General Expenditure
in Relation to State Personal Income Compared with Selected States
Selected Years, 1983-66

| State | 1983 % | 1983 * | 1980 % | 1980 * | 1976 % | 1976 * | 1966 % | 1966 * |
|---|---|---|---|---|---|---|---|---|
| United States | 18.07 | (100.0) | 19.03 | (100.0) | 20.32 | (100.0) | 15.75 | (100.0) |
| MINNESOTA | 21.57 | (119.4) | 21.46 | (112.8) | 23.70 | (116.6) | 17.93 | (115.2) |
| New York | 22.67 | (125.5) | 24.08 | (126.5) | 26.38 | (129.8) | 16.31 | (104.8) |
| Illinois | 15.73 | ( 87.1) | 16.47 | ( 86.5) | 17.45 | ( 85.9) | 11.72 | ( 75.3) |
| Michigan | 20.34 | (112.5) | 20.10 | (105.6) | 21.06 | (103.6) | 14.96 | ( 96.1) |
| Wisconsin | 19.93 | (110.3) | 21.14 | (111.1) | 21.82 | (107.4) | 17.24 | (110.7) |
| Iowa | 18.69 | (103.4) | 19.29 | (101.4) | 18.89 | ( 93.0) | 16.13 | (103.6) |
| North Dakota | 20.84 | (115.4) | 22.21 | (116.7) | 20.76 | (102.2) | 20.84 | (133.8) |
| South Dakota | 18.76 | (103.8) | 21.31 | (112.0) | 23.11 | (113.7) | 19.59 | (122.8) |
| Texas | 15.59 | ( 86.3) | 16.48 | ( 86.6) | 17.39 | ( 85.6) | 14.88 | ( 95.6) |
| Colorado | 16.97 | ( 93.9) | 18.03 | ( 94.7) | 21.53 | (106.0) | 19.24 | (123.6) |
| Wyoming | 29.55 | (163.6) | 26.64 | (129.5) | 27.56 | (135.6) | 27.18 | (174.6) |
| California | 17.97 | ( 99.4) | 19.04 | (100.1) | 22.06 | (108.6) | 18.41 | (118.2) |
| Alaska | 56.30 | (342.4) | 54.94 | (288.7) | 35.38 | (174.1) | 29.49 | (189.4) |
| Minnesota Rank | 10 | | 14 | | 13 | | 19 | |

*Source:* U.S. Advisory Commission on Intergovernmental Relations, *Significant Features of Fiscal Federalism*, Washington, D.C., 1982-1983 Edition (Washington, D.C., 1984) and U.S. Burea of The Census, *Government Finances in 1982-83* (Washington D.C., 1984).

*State percent related to U.S. average (U.S. = 100.0)

TABLE 2

Minnesota Per Capita State and Local, Direct General Expenditures
and Percent Distribution by Functional Category, Selected Years

| Function | 1967-1968 | | 1975-1976 | | 1982-1983 | |
|---|---|---|---|---|---|---|
| Education | $255 | (44.7%) | $549 | (40.3%) | $811 | (33.7%) |
| Highways | 97 | (17.0) | 154 | (11.3) | 241 | (10.0) |
| Public Welfare | 49 | ( 8.6) | 183 | (13.4) | 356 | (14.8) |
| Health & Hospitals | 39 | ( 6.8) | 93 | ( 6.8) | 207 | ( 8.6) |
| Police & Fire | 17 | ( 3.0) | 47 | ( 3.4) | 94 | ( 3.9) |
| Sewage & Sanitation | 19 | ( 3.2) | 49 | ( 3.6) | 60 | ( 2.5) |
| Local Parks & Recreation* | 7 | ( 1.2) | 29 | ( 2.1) | 90 | ( 3.7) |
| Financial Administration and General Control | 17 | ( 3.0) | 47 | ( 3.5) | 104 | ( 4.3) |
| Interest on General Debt | 17 | ( 3.0) | 49 | ( 3.6) | 154 | ( 6.4) |
| Other Expenditure | 55 | ( 9.6) | 162 | (11.0) | 287 | (11.9) |
| TOTAL | $572 | (100.0%) | $1362 | (100.0%) | $2404 | (100.0%) |

Source: U.S. Bureau of the Census, Governmental Finances, various years.

Note: Expenditures are in current dollars; percent details may not add to 100.0 due to rounding.

*For 1982-83, Local Parks and Recreation adds in spending for "natural resources."

These long-term, per capita changes in budget share suggest several possible areas for further inquiry:

- Are there technological changes and other innovations (ways of delivering the services) that explain why highway and education shares have fallen? If so, has productivity increased (e.g., improved road maintenance techniques) and/or the workload decreased (e.g., fewer students)?
- Can the source of the welfare expenditure increases be traced to larger numbers of poor people, changing federal priorities, increased generosity on the part of legislature, changes in the cost and standard of living that generate automatic dollar outlays for a given scope of services, or some combination of all these factors?
- Have there been alternative ways of delivering public services, such as redesigned public pricing techniques, voucher finance, privatization and contracting-out that are more cost effective than the standard pattern of social intervention, which is largely characterized by centralized regulatory bodies, governmental delivery of free services, and restricted grants to subordinate units of government? If so, to what extent have they or might they be employed in Minnesota?
- Is there reason for concern for the increasing shares in the more recent years going to some of the previously smaller, more stable categories such as interest on debt and spending on health and hospitals? That is, are we beginning to see new trends and growth pressures due to such factors as the condition of the nation's economy (e.g., permanently higher interest rates; a deterioration of the municipal bond market) and increasing costs of medical care and health care facilities?

The purpose of presenting the Table 2 data and then raising these questions regarding the trends in spending by functional categories is twofold. The first is to draw attention to the changes occurring on the expenditure side of the budget that may warrant further attention. The second is to remind that a decline or growth in a relative budget share may be as much a cause for jubiliation ("we are doing things better in terms of the delivery of public services") as of alarm ("potholes are getting worse and so are scholastic achievement test scores"). However, in order to answer these and similar questions, a systematic review of the determinants of state/local spending is needed, and that is as enormous an undertaking as is this tax study effort. It is also a separate task.

In this introduction to expenditures, we can, nevertheless, examine a few possible explanations for the observed expenditure changes. One can start by drawing some per capita income and spending comparisons between Minnesota and the U.S. average (Table 3) and four other states (Table 4).

Table 3 provides per capita expenditure functional data expressed as an index of the ratio of Minnesota spending to a U.S. average; the index is set equal to 100.0. Thus, in the column for FY 1982-83, the index number 115.8

TABLE 3
Per Capita State and Local Direct General Expenditure Indices
Minnesota and U.S. Average, State and Local Governments
Selected Fiscal Years
(State percent related to U.S. average, U.S. = 100.0)

| Function | 1967-68 | 1975-76 | 1982-83 |
|---|---|---|---|
| Education | 123.8 | 121.2 | 115.8 |
| Local Schools | 122.8 | 118.3 | 119.3 |
| Higher Education | 136.7 | 133.1 | 110.5 |
| Other | 60.6 | 104.3 | 93.3 |
| Highways | 134.0 | 138.6 | 144.1 |
| Public Welfare | 99.2 | 124.8 | 141.8 |
| Health and Hospitals | 103.2 | 96.4 | 109.9 |
| Police & Fire | 67.4 | 72.5 | 85.4 |
| Sewage & Sanitation | 136.8 | 128.5 | 124.6 |
| Local Parks & Recreation | 330.2 | 160.4 | 138.6 |
| Financial Administration and General Control | 92.9 | 104.7 | 116.6 |
| Interest on General Debt | 104.1 | 102.1 | 149.4 |
| Other Expenditure | 82.2 | 94.6 | 113.9 |
| TOTAL | 111.4 | 114.4 | 121.1 |

*Source:* U.S. Bureau of the Census, *Governmental Finances,* various years.
*Note:* U.S. data excludes Washington, D.C. in 1982-83.

indicates that Minnesota spent 15.8% more per state resident on education than did the average U.S. state and its local governments. Further category-by-category comparisons can be made for a given year by moving down the columns. Moving across the rows gives a perspective of how the Minnesota-to-U.S. relationships have changed over time.

The total expenditure row in Table 3 indicates that in 1967-68 the Minnesota state and local sector spent 11.4% more per capita than the average. By 1975-76 this difference had grown to 14.4%, and by 1982-83 Minnesota total state and local expenditures per capita were 21% higher than the U.S. average. Thus, the percentage by which Minnesota per capita expenditures exceed the U.S. has almost doubled since 1967.

One explanation for this relative increase might come from comparing Minnesota per capita income to the U.S. average. If Minnesota's income grew faster over the period than did that of the U.S. as a whole, then the relative increase in public expenditure may simply be a reflection of the preferences of a higher income population. Although, Minnesota per capita income did increase somewhat faster than the U.S. average over the period, the differences were minor for all three years examined (less than 1.6% in all three years). Thus, differences in per capita income cannot explain the differences in expenditure levels noted above.

To illustrate further how Minnesota compares to the U.S. in addition to comparing the level of total expenditures, a comparison of the functional distribution of the largest two spending categories—public welfare and education—is helpful. In the discussion of Table 2 above, one finding was that the Minnesota budget had shifted away from education and toward public welfare in terms of the budget allocated to each category. This change may simply reflect the national trend. In other words, it may be the case that the budget of the average state showed a similar trend over the period. As illustrated in Table 3 the shares of the U.S. average budget allocated to these categories changed in the same *direction* as these shares changed in Minnesota, but the Minnesota changes were much more dramatic. In 1967-68, Minnesota spent 23.8% more on education per capita than the U.S. average. If the share allocated to education in the U.S. budget fell at the same rate as that share in the Minnesota budget, then this difference would remain at 23.8%. But by 1975-76 this difference was only 21.2%, and by 1982-83 Minnesota spent 15.8% more on education per capita than the U.S. state and local governments taken as a whole. The data on expenditure components in Table 3 reveal that almost all of this relative decrease came in higher education. Thus, over the last decade and a half, Minnesota came closer to the average in terms of expenditure per capita on higher education but stayed at roughly 20% above the U.S. for expenditures for local schools.

What about welfare? In 1967-68 Minnesota spent almost the same amount per capita on public welfare as did the average state. By 1975-76 Minnesota spent 24.8% more per capita, and by 1982-83 that difference was 41.8%. Thus, even though the share of the U.S. state/local budget allocated to public welfare increased over the period as it did in Minnesota, the increase in Minnesota was again much more dramatic. That is, Minnesota showed a strong tendency to vary from the average in terms of the share of its budget allocated to public welfare. Whether this implies that Minnesota is spending "too much" on welfare relative to education is not clear, however, since 50% of that welfare spending is financed by federal aid, whereas only 8% of the Minnesota education budget is federally funded.[3] Finally, to keep a policy perspective here, it must be noted that the great bulk of welfare spending is for hospital and medical care. "Public welfare" does not translate to "public assistance."

Some further plausible reasons for these expenditure changes are suggested (not *shown* or *proven*) by comparing Minnesota not only to the U.S. average of expenditure on education and welfare, but also to four other states. The states selected were chosen in order to suggest some possible explanations as to why expenditures might differ among states and not to address whether Minnesota is doing "better" or "worse" than another state.

The answer to the better vs. worse question requires a much more thorough analysis than is provided here.

The data in Table 4 reveal some of the major facets of the Minnesota expenditure environment. For example, over the sixteen-year period Minnesota went from spending a greater share of its budget than Wisconsin on education and a smaller share than Wisconsin on public welfare to just the opposite arrangement. By 1982-83 Wisconsin spent 38% of its budget on education compared to 33.7% in Minnesota. On public welfare, Wisconsin spent 12.2% of its budget compared to 14.8% in Minnesota. This reversal occurred despite the fact that the two states had almost identical values of income and total expenditure per capita throughout the period. Thus, Minnesota did not "keep up with the Joneses" but instead offered a combination of public services to its residents that differed from that offered in a similar, neighboring state.

Comparisons also aid in drawing some conclusions about trends in overall expenditures. That the expenditures per capita in South Dakota have declined relative to Minnesota can be illustrated using figures displayed in Table 4. In all three years, South Dakota income per capita was about 85% of Minnesota income but total expenditure per capita in South Dakota fell from 98% of Minnesota expenditures per capita in 1967-68 to 83% in 1975-76 to 74% in 1982-83. Thus it follows that total spending as a percentage of total state income was greater in South Dakota than in Minnesota in 1967-68, about the same in the two states in 1975-76, and greater in Minnesota in 1982-83.

Michigan, whose per capita income was higher than Minnesota's until the most recent period, spent consistently less per capita than Minnesota. This illustrates that it is possible for a state to spend less and inflict a lower tax burden, but the question of where the cuts would be made is difficult to answer. In 1982-83 Michigan spent a greater percentage of its budget on both public welfare and education than Minnesota. For Minnesota to emulate Michigan in terms of its total tax burden, difficult decisions would have to be made about which programs to cut.

In all three years, New York had a higher per capita income than did Minnesota, and it spent more per capita. Also in all three years, New York spent a much smaller share of its budget on education than did Minnesota (although the gap narrowed) and New York spent a larger share on public welfare than Minnesota did. This higher-expenditure and higher-income state chose to allocate its budget differently from Minnesota, spending a smaller share on education and a greater share on welfare.

In summary, differences in per capita income levels and trends across the states cannot explain differences in per capita expenditure levels and trends across the states. Minnesota, in any one year and across the years, has chosen expenditure levels and functional distributions different from the average, and these differences are not solely the result of different per capita

TABLE 4
A Comparison of Minnesota State Per Capita Income and
State/Local Expenditures to the U.S. and Four States

| | United States | Minnesota | Wisconsin | South Dakota | New York | Michigan |
|---|---|---|---|---|---|---|
| **1967-1978** | | | | | | |
| Income Per Capita | $3159.0 | $3116.0 | $3156.0 | $2590.0 | $3759.0 | $3396.0 |
| Total Expenditures Per Capita | 512.4 | 570.8 | 570.7 | 560.7 | 703.9 | 538.0 |
| Percent Spent on Education | 40.2 | 44.7 | 41.6 | 46.2 | 33.8 | 47.1 |
| Percent Spent on Public Welfare | 9.6 | 8.6 | 10.0 | 6.2 | 13.6 | 8.7 |
| **1975-1976** | | | | | | |
| Income Per Capita | $5902.0 | $5807.0 | $5669.0 | $4924.0 | $6564.0 | $6173.0 |
| Total Expenditures Per Capita | 1190.5 | 1362.4 | 1236.1 | 1133.7 | 1735.4 | 1307.5 |
| Percent Spent on Education | 38.0 | 40.3 | 42.5 | 39.9 | 29.8 | 40.2 |
| Percent Spent on Public Welfare | 12.3 | 13.4 | 13.9 | 8.9 | 16.2 | 15.9 |
| **1982-1983** | | | | | | |
| Income Per Capita | $11107.0 | $11175.0 | $10774.0 | $9666.0 | $12314.0 | $10956.0 |
| Total Expenditures Per Capita | 1985.9 | 2404.4 | 2154.2 | 1788.8 | 2790.2 | 2237.9 |
| Percent Spent on Education | 35.3 | 33.7 | 38.0 | 35.6 | 29.6 | 35.5 |
| Percent Spent on Public Welfare | 12.6 | 14.8 | 12.2 | 9.6 | 15.9 | 17.6 |

*Source:* Staff Computations

income levels. Whether or not these findings imply that Minnesota is better than average or than a particular state depends in part on the relative value placed on the state's mix of expenditures. A relatively high level of spending, and therefore total tax burden, may be justified if the goods and services financed by that burden are desired by the individuals who must pay.

Finally, at the risk of becoming repetitive, it is important to reiterate the warning that because of the nature of the census data used in making interstate comparisons, there is danger in a too hasty conclusion regarding what the Minnesota expenditure structure ought to look like. The purpose of Tables 3 and 4 is to suggest the sort of questions one must ask when attempting to understand why spending by function changes over time. For example, the point of the Wisconsin-Minnesota comparison was to show that despite geographical proximity and similarity in income and overall spending characteristics, voters in the two states may differ in the combination of public services they want to provide. In the economist's jargon, the social preference function varies by jurisdiction. Nothing much more can be said at this point.

## COMPARING MINNESOTA TAXES

### TAX BURDENS

Several tax and tax-related measures are available as indicators of interstate (or interregional and international) variations of fiscal pressures. In general these aggregate indicators rely on four basic estimates: population, personal income, size of tax base, and tax collections. In this section, the focus is on how various arithmetic combinations of these four variables are conventionally used to make tax comparisons between Minnesota and selected other state/local jurisdictions. Each measure is designed to highlight different aspects of the Minnesota fiscal position. These measures include a straightforward presentation of collections by type of tax and a set of ratios that put collections in a numerator and population, income, and/or tax base in the (common) denominator. These ratios then permit interstate comparisons of "tax burden" or taxpayer capacity, a government's tax raising capacity, government "tax effort," and changes in fiscal pressure over time.

As with any aggregate fiscal measure of interstate variation, such as the expenditure data shown above, the tax indicators that are presented below have advantages and disadvantages; and, depending on the specific indicator being used, the significance of these merits and shortcomings varies. However, there are some points common to all.

The first is that the widespread use of these conventional measures is due largely to their ability to be quickly and consistently compared. The element of consistency here also explains why much greater reliance is made on tax and revenue rather than on expenditure indicators for interstate comparisons. In practice there is much more agreement (though it is certainly not complete) among state and local jurisdictions as to what constitutes a given tax or tax base than what is included in an expenditure category.

A second and equally important merit of aggregate indicators of interstate fiscal variation is their ease of calculation. This is particularly true of the simple ratios (which tend to be widely cited by various tax organizations) that relate tax collection information to personal income and population.

There are also five weaknesses common to these indicators. The first four are functions of their structure; the fifth is a matter of timing. To summarize:

- Implicit in their use is the assumption that state/local economies are "closed"—i.e., void of movement of goods and services, factors of production, and even consumers across their jurisdictional borders. Accordingly, the data fail to take into account that some states are better able than others to export taxes to nonresidents. There are two basic ways exporting occurs. The first is through the specific deductibility provisions of the U.S. Internal Revenue Code that allow real and personal property, general sales, and income taxes to be subtracted in computing federal taxable income. The second form of tax exporting results when nonresidents purchase goods and services that are both produced and taxed in Minnesota and then shipped out-of-state to a nonresident buyer or purchased within the state by a visitor. The out-of-state tourist to Ely who pays sales taxes on a restaurant meal or the out-of-state purchaser of a manufacturing or mining product that embodies some portion of the corporation franchise (income) tax are examples.

- Aggregate interstate comparisons give no evidence regarding the extent to which the states deliver a differing level or quality of public services to their citizens, yet, there are differences. Nevertheless the degree of effectiveness of a government in using tax dollars to benefit resident individuals and institutions is a matter not addressed in these comparisons.

- The numerators (e.g., tax collections) and common denominators (e.g., income, population) are assumed to be independent of one another. Thus the ratios ignore the possibility of the public budget-income creation interplay. It is plausible, however, that some of the income being taken in the form of taxes may have been created by the tax-expenditure process itself. For example, if tax rates become too high, they may reduce the state's tax base.

- Aggregate measures give no hint of the incidence of the tax collections— i.e., how the portion of taxes collected within a state are ultimately distributed among the citizens of the state; and

- For any one year the ratio for any given state may reflect historical accident. For example, a state's enactment of a temporary yet large income tax surcharge (e.g., Minnesota's surtax in 1981 and Wisconsin's 10% surtax in 1983, now both repealed) designed to meet an unexpected revenue shortfall could lead to an overstatement in the personal income tax ratio. Similarly, a major one-time tax reduction could bias the ration downward.

As noted, it is important to keep these warnings in mind when making interstate comparisons of the sort about to be presented. Such tax burden ratios do not tell the whole story about such concerns as taxpayer equity and business climate. However, because these weaknesses apply to the indicators of each of the states presented, it can be plausibly argued that, when viewed over time, the ratios give a useful picture of how a specific state compares with others.

TAX MIX

A first glance at how Minnesota's revenue system compares to other states is provided in Table 5, which shows the percentage distribution of state and local general revenue by type of revenue source. The numbers in the parentheses are index numbers, which are presented to facilitate quick comparisons of the relationship of Minnesota both to specific states and a U.S. state and local average.

As indicated, one cannot get much from these numbers beyond a first look at the sources of a state/local system's revenues. What can be usefully said about the data in Table 5 is that they show the wide range of diversity among state and local tax systems, which in turn reflects the differing nature of the economic base among the states. The clearest example of this diversity revealed in the table is the ability of the fossil fuel rich states such as Alaska, Wyoming, and North Dakota to derive the bulk of their revenues from severance tax levies (included in "other taxes") on the production and income of that oil. The data also highlight the fact that different states will make different decisions regarding the appropriate mix of taxes they wish to use in raising public funds. For example, Washington, Texas, and South Dakota are all non-income-tax states—as the zeros in the personal income tax column dramatize. But, take a look at the taxes on consumption and property in relation to Minnesota. There are tradeoffs.

In contrast, Minnesota's total sources of revenue are, like most other states, more evenly spread across the sources shown although Minnesota makes a relatively heavier reliance on the individual income tax and charges and miscellaneous taxes. The data also show that, as a percent of total state/local revenues, Minnesota derives less from levies on property, sales, and federal aid than the average state.

TABLE 5
Percentage Distribution of Minnesota State/Local General Revenue, By Source
Compared to the U.S. Average and Other States
1983

| | Federal Aid | Property Taxes | General Sales Tax | Individual Income Taxes | Corporate Income Taxes | Other Taxes | Interest Earnings | Charges and Miscellaneous |
|---|---|---|---|---|---|---|---|---|
| United States | 18.5% (100.0) | 18.3% (100.0) | 13.3% (100.0) | 11.3% (100.0) | 2.9% (100.0) | 12.5% (100.0) | 5.4% (100.0) | 17.7% (100.0) |
| MINNESOTA | 16.6 (89.7) | 16.1 (88.0) | 9.3 (69.9) | 18.5 (163.7) | 2.4 (82.8) | 10.9 (87.2) | 6.8 (125.9) | 19.4 (109.6) |
| New York | 18.0 (97.3) | 20.8 (113.7) | 12.4 (93.2) | 18.6 (164.6) | 4.6 (158.6) | 8.2 (65.6) | 4.5 (83.3) | 12.8 (72.3) |
| Illinois | 19.2 (103.8) | 23.8 (130.1) | 14.5 (109.0) | 9.5 (84.1) | 2.6 (89.7) | 12.1 (96.8) | 5.1 (94.4) | 13.2 (74.6) |
| Michigan | 19.1 (103.2) | 24.2 (132.2) | 9.2 (69.2) | 13.3 (117.7) | 4.7 (162.1) | 6.7 (53.6) | 3.8 (70.4) | 19.0 (107.3) |
| Wisconsin | 17.8 (96.2) | 23.2 (126.8) | 11.0 (82.7) | 15.8 (139.8) | 3.1 (106.9) | 8.5 (68.0) | 3.7 (68.5) | 17.0 (96.0) |
| Iowa | 16.7 (90.3) | 23.8 (130.1) | 10.0 (75.2) | 12.6 (111.5) | 2.4 (82.8) | 10.6 (84.8) | 2.8 (51.9) | 21.1 (119.2) |
| North Dakota | 19.7 (106.5) | 13.7 (74.9) | 9.3 (69.9) | 2.2 (19.5) | 1.9 (65.5) | 20.3 (162.4) | 6.7 (124.1) | 26.2 (148.0) |
| South Dakota | 24.7 (133.5) | 20.8 (113.7) | 15.3 (115.0) | 0.0 (0.0) | 0.2 (6.9) | 12.5 (100.0) | 10.7 (198.1) | 15.8 (89.3) |
| Texas | 14.7 (79.5) | 21.4 (116.9) | 14.5 (109.0) | 0.0 (0.0) | 0.0 (0.0) | 22.2 (177.6) | 6.3 (116.7) | 20.0 (117.5) |
| Colorado | 15.5 (83.8) | 19.7 (107.7) | 17.3 (130.1) | 10.1 (89.4) | 0.9 (31.0) | 8.3 (66.4) | 6.7 (124.1) | 21.6 (122.0) |
| Wyoming | 17.0 (91.9) | 21.8 (119.1) | 9.7 (72.9) | 0.0 (0.0) | 0.0 (0.0) | 21.4 (171.2) | 9.2 (170.4) | 21.0 (118.6) |
| California | 18.9 (102.2) | 15.3 (83.6) | 16.9 (127.1) | 13.4 (118.6) | 4.5 (155.2) | 8.9 (71.2) | 5.4 (100.0) | 16.6 (93.8) |
| Washington | 17.9 (96.8) | 16.9 (92.3) | 27.6 (207.5) | 0.0 (0.0) | 0.0 (0.0) | 13.6 (108.8) | 6.2 (114.8) | 17.8 (100.6) |
| Alaska | 8.0 (43.2) | 7.1 (38.8) | 0.7 (5.3) | 0.0 (0.0) | 4.7 (162.1) | 28.8 (230.4) | 22.4 (414.8) | 28.2 (159.3) |

*Source:* Staff computations based on U.S. Census data, *Government Finances In 1982-83*, Washington, D.C., 1985.
*Note:* Index numbers set for U.S. percent equal to 100.0

What is not shown here, and what the several measures that are presented in the following sections are designed to correct, is how Minnesota's fiscal system stacks up against the other states once some economic base and/or demographic variables are taken into account.

## TAXES PER CAPITA

The ratio of taxes per capita (tax collections divided by population) is one of the most widely used measures of interstate variation in "tax burdens." Although this ratio is a much better indicator of interstate differences than tax collection data presented in isolation (since it provides a common denominator among the states) it is nevertheless a weak measure of tax burden and thus is subject to abuse and misinterpretation. Not only do per capita measures count each resident equally, regardless of their condition, degree of dependence, and taxpaying capacity, but the measure is also vulnerable to the criticism that it does not account for the role nonresidents play in the payment of taxes.

The data on per capita tax collections are presented in Table 6. The collections number includes monies derived from what one usually considers taxes (income, sales, property and excises) and excludes federal aid and other nontax revenue (e.g., user charges and fees). As such the data tend to reflect the internal or own-source and compulsory aspect of state/local revenue raising. And, according to Table 6, Minnesota has been consistently above both the national per capita burden and that of its neighboring states since the mid-1960s (the Wisconsin 1965 comparison is the only exception).

## TAXES AS A PERCENT OF INCOME

State and local revenues as a percent of personal income is a somewhat better measure of interstate burden variations than is the per capita data, but it can nevertheless be nearly as superficial due to its failure to address practical concerns identified in the introduction to this section. Moreover, in addition to this list of general shortcomings presented above, the personal income measure is flawed since the income denominator significantly understates the tax-wealth of energy-rich as well as tourist-rich states and overstates the taxing power of states confronted with diminished economic bases of property and sales. Indeed, in some cases the tax collections to personal income ratio can lead to absurd results. For example, consider the data in Table 7 that show that in 1982 Alaska collected general revenues of 102 cents of each $1 of Alaska personal income.[4] Similarly, Wyoming was taking 36 cents of each $1. That makes high-spending states like Minnesota and New York quite a bargain.

But those Alaska and Wyoming numbers include taxes collected on oil, which, because oil is sold nationwide, are largely exported and thus

TABLE 6
Per Capita State/Local Tax Collections
Minnesota and Selected States
1965 - 1983

| | 1983 | | 1980 | | 1975 | | 1965 | | % change 1975-1982 |
|---|---|---|---|---|---|---|---|---|---|
| United States | $1,216 | (100.0) | $ 987 | (100.0) | $ 664 | (100.0) | $264 | (100.0) | 83.1% |
| MINNESOTA | 1,473 | (121.1) | 1,125 | (114.0) | 754 | (113.6) | 299 | (113.3) | 95.4 |
| New York | 1,889 | (155.3) | 1,495 | (151.5) | 1,025 | (154.4) | 372 | (140.9) | 84.3 |
| Illinois | 1,255 | (103.2) | 1,084 | (109.8) | 730 | (109.9) | 266 | (100.8) | 71.9 |
| Michigan | 1,370 | (112.7) | 1,075 | (108.9) | 682 | (102.7) | 290 | (109.8) | 100.9 |
| Wisconsin | 1,425 | (117.1) | 1,061 | (107.5) | 719 | (108.3) | 318 | (117.4) | 98.2 |
| Iowa | 1,171 | ( 96.3) | 967 | ( 97.8) | 637 | ( 95.9) | 276 | (104.5) | 83.8 |
| North Dakota | 1,100 | ( 90.5) | 847 | ( 85.8) | 613 | ( 92.3) | 248 | ( 93.9) | 79.4 |
| South Dakota | 914 | ( 75.1) | 789 | ( 79.9) | 543 | ( 81.8) | 241 | ( 91.3) | 68.3 |
| Texas | 1,033 | ( 84.9) | 806 | ( 81.7) | 515 | ( 77.6) | 207 | ( 78.4) | 100.6 |
| Colorado | 1,166 | ( 95.9) | 990 | (100.3) | 631 | ( 95.0) | 292 | (110.6) | 84.8 |
| Wyoming | 2,443 | (200.9) | 1,399 | (135.7) | 697 | (105.0) | 278 | (105.3) | 250.5 |
| California | 1,337 | (109.9) | 1,172 | (118.7) | 869 | (130.9) | 361 | (136.7) | 53.9 |
| Washington | 1,306 | (107.4) | 989 | (100.2) | 676 | (101.0) | 294 | (111.4) | 93.2 |
| Alaska | 4,908 | (403.5) | 4,189 | (424.4) | 842 | (126.8) | 250 | ( 94.7) | 482.9 |

*Source:* Derived from U.S. Department of Commerce Bureau of the Census, *Governmental Finances*, December 1984, and U.S. Advisory Commission on Intergovernmental Relations, *Significant Features of Fiscal Federalism*, Washington, D.C., 1982-83 Edition (Table 30), 1984.

*Notes:* U.S. average for 1983 excludes Washington, D.C.
    U.S. average equals 100.0

TABLE 7
State and Local General Revenue in Relation to
State Personal Income, Minnesota and Selected States
1966-82

| | 1982 | | 1980 | | 1976 | | 1966 | |
|---|---|---|---|---|---|---|---|---|
| | % | Index* | % | Index* | % | Index* | % | Index* |
| U.S. | 18.8 | (100.0) | 19.8 | (100.0) | 20.4 | (100.0) | 15.6 | (100.0) |
| MINNESOTA | 22.0 | (117.0) | 22.3 | (112.6) | 23.7 | (116.2) | 18.8 | (120.3) |
| New York | 23.9 | (127.1) | 25.4 | (135.1) | 26.3 | (128.9) | 16.3 | (104.2) |
| Illinois | 16.5 | ( 87.8) | 17.6 | ( 88.9) | 17.2 | ( 84.3) | 12.3 | ( 78.9) |
| Michigan | 20.7 | (110.1) | 20.2 | (102.0) | 20.5 | (100.5) | 14.9 | ( 95.4) |
| Wisconsin | 20.6 | (109.6) | 21.3 | (107.6) | 22.3 | (109.3) | 16.7 | (107.0) |
| Iowa | 17.6 | ( 93.6) | 18.6 | ( 93.9) | 19.0 | ( 93.1) | 16.8 | (107.8) |
| North Dakota | 21.5 | (114.4) | 23.1 | (116.7) | 22.8 | (111.8) | 20.8 | (133.7) |
| South Dakota | 19.9 | (105.9) | 21.5 | (108.6) | 22.7 | (111.3) | 19.7 | (126.4) |
| Texas | 16.2 | ( 86.2) | 17.2 | ( 86.9) | 18.0 | ( 88.2) | 15.1 | ( 96.5) |
| Colorado | 18.1 | ( 96.3) | 20.0 | (101.0) | 21.6 | (105.9) | 19.5 | (124.7) |
| Wyoming | 36.2 | (192.6) | 28.6 | (144.4) | 28.6 | (140.2) | 26.2 | (168.1) |
| California | 18.9 | (100.5) | 20.2 | (102.0) | 22.8 | (111.8) | 18.0 | (115.2) |
| Washington | 18.3 | ( 97.3) | 19.8 | (100.0) | 20.5 | (100.5) | 18.1 | (116.0) |
| Alaska | 102.3 | (544.1) | 78.3 | (395.5) | 38.5 | (188.7) | 26.9 | (172.2) |

Sources: ACIR, *Significant Features of Fiscal Federalism 1982-83 Edition.* pp. 139-190; U.S. Department of Commerce, Bureau of the Census *Governmental Finances in 1975-76,* Table 17, pp. 47-49 and Table 26, p. 70; Bureau of the Census, *Governmental Finances in 1965-66.* Table 24, p. 50.
*State percent related to U.S. Average (U.S. = 100)

ultimately paid by nonresidents. Though Alaska and Wyoming provide extreme examples, it is nevertheless true that this same sort of distortion applies, albeit in a less spectacular manner, to all such state ratios.

## TAX PERFORMANCE

### THE REPRESENTATIVE TAX SYSTEM

An additional kind of information that is used in establishing relative fiscal balance among the states are "tax capacity" indices, which are most commonly used for judging the distribution of intergovernmental grants. The most traditional of these capacity measures is personal income (personal income per capita is also used) by state, i.e., a number that reflects the view that since all taxes are ultimately paid out of one's income, total or aggregate state personal income then represents the citizenry's overall ability or capacity to pay taxes in order to finance a given set of public goods and services. When aggregate income is viewed in this capacity manner, the ratios of taxes collected to incomes then provide a relative measure of a degree of fiscal pressures within the state.

A more sophisticated yardstick of tax capacity among states is the representative tax system (RTS) approach, which was developed by the staff of the U.S. Advisory Commission on Intergovernmental Relations (ACIR) in 1962 and which has been subsequently refined (though the basic methodology has remained the same).[5]

The representative tax system answers the following question: How would each of the fifty states rank on a revenue productivity scale if every state applied identical tax rates to each of the twenty-six commonly used tax bases in the U.S. state/local system? Thus "tax capacity" is defined as the amount of revenue that each state would raise if it applied a nationally uniform set of tax rates to its hypothetical tax base. The rates used in the calculation are representative since they are national average rates for each base. Thus, differences in estimated tax yields among the states reflect only the difference in state/local tax bases.

It is important to understand that for the RTS to work, the set of representative tax rates are applied in every state regardless of whether or not in practice a given state actually levies a particular tax. If this across-the-board computation were not made for all fifty states, tax capacity would be understated in states that do not choose to employ a full spectrum of taxes. For example, although neighboring South Dakota does not have a broad-based income tax, it is included in South Dakota's tax capacity because that base is available to tax (with the intensity of "use" presumed to equal a national average) even though the choice at this time is not to utilize it. Thus the different mix of revenue devices actually used from one state to the next does not affect the RTS yardstick of capacity to raise taxes.

TRENDS IN RTS TAX CAPACITY

With the representative tax system method, a given state's "tax capacity index" is defined as its per capita tax capacity divided by the average for all states with the index for the average set at 100. The tax capacity indices provide the measure for comparing the relative taxing potentials of any one state and local system among the states. Thus, a state with an index larger than 1.00 has an ability to raise revenue greater than the average or representative state. For example, in Table 8, which presents tax capacity indices for the selected set of states for various years, the 1981 index for North Dakota was 123. That means that North Dakota state/local system has a 23% greater ability to raise taxes than the representative or statistically average U.S. state. The 1981 New York index, which is 89, shows an 11% below-average ability to generate revenues then the representative state.

Further examination of Table 8 shows:

• Minnesota has generally exhibited a near average capacity to raise revenues since the mid-1970s. At present the Minnesota tax capacity is well

TABLE 8
Representative Tax System Capacity Indices
Minnesota and Selected States
1967-82 (1979-82)

|  | 1982 | 1980 | 1975 | 1967 |
|---|---|---|---|---|
| United States | 100 | 100 | 100 | 100 |
| MINNESOTA | 99 | 102 | 97 | 95 |
| New York | 91 | 90 | 98 | 108 |
| Illinois | 99 | 108 | 112 | 114 |
| Michigan | 93 | 97 | 101 | 104 |
| Wisconsin | 87 | 95 | 98 | 94 |
| Iowa | 96 | 105 | 106 | 104 |
| North Dakota | 115 | 108 | 101 | 92 |
| South Dakota | 87 | 90 | 94 | 91 |
| Texas | 130 | 124 | 111 | 98 |
| Colorado | 121 | 113 | 106 | 104 |
| Wyoming | 201 | 196 | 154 | 141 |
| California | 116 | 117 | 110 | 124 |
| Washington | 102 | 103 | 98 | 112 |
| Alaska | 313 | 260 | 155 | 99 |

*Source:* U.S. Advisory Commission on Intergovernmental Relations, *1982 Tax Capacity of the Fifty States,* Washington, D.C., September 1983, and preliminary report for 1982 (March 1985).

above that of neighboring South Dakota and Wisconsin, but below North Dakota and slightly less than that of Iowa.

- The trend in tax capacity disparities among Minnesota and its neighbors suggests that in the near future, at least, Minnesota's position is improving vis-a-vis everyone but North Dakota; and
- It is nice to have oil and coal.

## TOTAL TAX EFFORT

A complementary measure to the RTS tax capacity index is "tax effort." Whereas tax capacity refers to the relative size of a state's potential tax base, tax effort indicates the degree to which the aggregate tax base is exploited. Arithmetically, tax effort is the ratio of percentage of a state's actual tax collections to its tax capacity. A tax effort index is created by dividing each state's tax effort by the average for all states, which is set at 100. Thus, by exhibiting an overall tax effort index of 109 for the year 1981 (Table 9), Minnesota is seen as choosing to exploit its total tax base at a rate of 9% greater than the national average. In contrast, a state such as Colorado, which has a tax effort index of 84 is making a less than average national effort to utilize its potential tax base. It should be noted that a high tax effort index does not necessarily translate into a high burden on residents. Recall that the tax effort numerator—total state plus local collections—does not adjust for such factors as the mix of taxes employed or the ability to export taxes. For example, the data in Table 8 showed that Texas had a high 1981 capacity tax (132), a fact that is largely explained by the ability to apply a severance tax to oil. Yet, Table 9 shows a low tax effort for Texas. The reason is, in part, that because taxes on oil and gas are exported (and, interestingly, at a below than U.S. average severance tax effort), Texas is able to make low efforts for all their other taxes. In addition, a reduced level of expenditures is also reflected in that decision and the numbers (Table 1).

Given all these warnings, Table 9 provides the same sort of evidence as did the per capita tax burden data—viz, that Minnesota is about 9% above the national average tax burden, and that relative to the rest of the United States, the burden has been falling slightly since the mid-1970s. In 1981, Minnesota was the eleventh leading total tax effort state. Alaska was first, a result largely explainable by its non-Texas like decision to tax oil heavily. Of the nine other states ranked above Minnesota, six were on the east coast and two (Michigan and Wisconsin) were midwestern. Hawaii is the other high-ranking state.

TAX EFFORT AND CAPACITY BY TYPE OF TAX

The next tables provide a look at the tax capacity and tax effort estimates by type of tax. The first (Table 10) focuses on Minnesota and the second (Table 11) compares Minnesota with neighboring states. The data in these

TABLE 9
Tax Effort Indices, Minnesota
and Selected States, 1967-82

|  | 1982 | 1980 | 1979 | 1975 | 1967 |
|---|---|---|---|---|---|
| United States | 100 | 100 | 100 | 100 | 100 |
| MINNESOTA | 111 | 111 | 115 | 117 | 119 |
| New York | 170 | 167 | 171 | 160 | 138 |
| Illinois | 107 | 102 | 99 | 99 | 84 |
| Michigan | 120 | 116 | 113 | 106 | 100 |
| Wisconsin | 128 | 116 | 118 | 115 | 124 |
| Iowa | 105 | 96 | 93 | 93 | 104 |
| North Dakota | 83 | 79 | 78 | 92 | 97 |
| South Dakota | 91 | 88 | 84 | 87 | 107 |
| Texas | 66 | 65 | 65 | 68 | 75 |
| Colorado | 81 | 90 | 96 | 90 | 106 |
| Wyoming | 105 | 74 | 83 | 70 | 79 |
| California | 99 | 102 | 95 | 119 | 108 |
| Washington | 93 | 94 | 96 | 101 | 106 |
| Alaska | 180 | 166 | 129 | 101 | 106 |

*Source:* U.S. Advisory Commission on Intergovernmental Relations, *1981 Tax Capacity of the Fifty States,* Washington, D.C., September 1983, Table 6 and preliminary report for 1982 (March 1985).

tables are particularly useful: they go beyond the aggregate or total indices discussed above and show on a tax component basis where the status has an above-(below) average capacity to tax, where it is making a higher (lower) than average effort to tax, and give some idea of the relative dollar magnitudes of what the divergence between capacity and effort means to the state. To summarize from Table 10:

- For 1982, the most recent year for which the tax capacity and effort is available for all state/local tax systems, Minnesota's tax effort exceeded the national average for taxes on selective sales, personal and corporate income, and nonmineral severance taxes. It made a less than (U.S.) average effort for general sales, property, and estate and gift taxes.[6]
- There was an unused tax capacity of $280 million in the general sales tax, an amount that is equal to about 30% of what was then raised. The comparable percent for unused 1982 property tax capacity is about 10% of revenues collected, or about $144 million.
- Although the state has a below-average estate and gift tax capacity, its effort is even further below the representative U.S. state.

Tax effort and capacity indices by type of tax with Minnesota compared to its four neighboring states are presented in Table 11. Even when the relative total capacity and effort indices are taken into account, generalizations regarding the region's performance indicators are difficult to draw. Again, the key seems to be diversity, particularly with respect to tax effort. What

TABLE 10
Minnesota Per Capita Tax Capacity (RTS) and Tax Effort Indices
by Type of Tax - 1982

| Type of Tax | Tax Capacity Index | Tax Effort Index | Tax Revenue Less Capacity* |
|---|---|---|---|
| General Sales | 107.9 | 75.9 | $-280,191 |
| Total Selective Sales | 94.9 | 112.8 | 65,169 |
| Total License Taxes | 124.3 | 97.5 | - 5,024 |
| Personal Income | 92.9 | 184.5 | 709,373 |
| Corporate Income | 98.4 | 128.5 | 72,124 |
| Total Property | 105.3 | 90.6 | -143,745 |
| Estate and Gift | 84.5 | 68.9 | - 60,202 |
| Non-fuel Mineral Severance | 303.0 | 818.7 | 133,096 |
| TOTAL TAXES | 99.1 | 111.2 | $ 510,742 |

Source: U.S. Advisory Commission on Intergovernmental Relations, *Tax Capacity of the Fifty States,* Washington, D.C., September 1983, and preliminary report for 1982 (March 1985).

Note: U.S. average equals 100.0

*Thousands of dollars

TABLE 11
Tax Effort and Capacity Comparisons (1982)

Tax Capacity - As a Percentage of the U.S. Average

| Tax Source | Minnesota | Wisconsin | Iowa | North Dakota | South Dakota | Minnesota's National Rank |
|---|---|---|---|---|---|---|
| TOTAL | 99.1 | 86.8 | 96.0 | 115.1 | 87.4 | 22 |
| General Sales | 107.9 | 88.2 | 99.8 | 109.6 | 104.0 | 13 |
| Selective Sales | 94.9 | 92.4 | 98.2 | 107.3 | 99.4 | 36 |
| License Tax | 124.3 | 105.4 | 120.8 | 154.0 | 142.9 | 12 |
| Personal Income | 92.9 | 88.1 | 88.2 | 88.3 | 65.9 | 28 |
| Corporate Income | 98.4 | 90.3 | 85.5 | 93.0 | 67.1 | 17 |
| Total Property | 105.3 | 90.4 | 105.8 | 102.0 | 89.6 | 16 |
| Estate and Gift | 84.5 | 58.2 | 110.9 | 79.6 | 64.1 | 19 |
| Severance (all types) | 9.4 | 0.8 | 2.9 | 459.3 | 18.2 | 27 |

Tax Effort - As a Percentage of the U.S. Average

| Tax Source | Minnesota* | Wiconsin | Iowa | North Dakota | South Dakota | Minnesota's National Rank |
|---|---|---|---|---|---|---|
| TOTAL | 111.2 | 127.8 | 105.3 | 82.6 | 90.7 | 9 |
| General Sales | 75.9 | 88.2 | 69.2 | 76.6 | 107.7 | 34 |
| Selective Sales | 112.8 | 104.9 | 89.9 | 71.8 | 103.7 | 11 |
| License Tax | 97.5 | 82.5 | 137.7 | 82.6 | 80.4 | 19 |
| Personal Income | 184.5 | 183.8 | 128.5 | 27.2 | 0.0 | 5 |
| Corporate Income | 128.5 | 121.0 | 95.0 | 96.9 | 3.6 | 8 |
| Total Property | 90.6 | 136.6 | 117.3 | 81.9 | 121.5 | 23 |
| Estate and Gift | 68.9 | 211.3 | 242.8 | 57.0 | 179.3 | 25 |
| Severance (all types) | 817.7 | 57.1 | 0.0 | 161.5 | 196.0 | 1 |

*Source:* ACIR, *1982 Tax Capacity of the Fifty States,* Washington, D.C., March 1985 (preliminary)
*Note:* Rank is from highest to lowest

emerges is a pattern that was suggested in the Table 3 and 4 data on expenditures—viz, that for a variety of reasons, including tradition, even neighboring states vary in terms of the mix of taxes and expenditures that they use to carry out the public sector role.

## POLICY IMPLICATIONS

It is important at this point to reiterate a major point from above: the burden, tax capacity, and effort ratios are provided only in order to give an introductory overview as to how Minnesota compares with other states. They are not replete with policy implications. It would be hasty to conclude, for example, that because Minnesota consistently is above (below) another state in terms of burden ratios or tax effort index, that Minnesota taxes are "too high" ("too low"). Thus, it is an unhappy fact that each year so much public attention is given to various reports on state tax and expenditure rankings.

Several other factors are yet to be explored, regarding the role that taxes play in creating a total climate in Minnesota that promotes fiscal fairness and efficiency and enhances development of the economic base. A systematic examination and discussion of these and related topics thus begins in the following chapter on the relationship between state/local taxes and changes in private sector employment growth.

## ENDNOTES

1. Census treats the Minnesota homestead, agricultural, taconite, and wetlands credits as property tax reduction devices. However, the property tax refund (circuit breaker) and targeted relief programs, both property tax relief devices which are granted in the form of credits against the personal income tax, are counted as income tax reductions.

2. U.S. Advisory Commission on Intergovernmental Relations (ACIR), *Significant Features of Fiscal Federalism* (1982-83 ed.), Washington, D.C., 1984.

3. Minnesota receives slightly less federal aid revenues for both education and welfare than the U.S. per capita average. The per capita percentage comparisons of state local expenditures from federal aid are (U.S./Minnesota) as follows: education (9.4%: 8.0%) and public welfare (56.5%: 50.0%). The percentage for federal aid as a percent of total state/local revenues are U.S. (20.1%) and Minnesota (18.2%). U.S. Bureau of the Census, *Government Finances in 1982*, U.S. Department of Commerce, 1984.

4. General revenue includes all government revenue (including intergovernmental) except utility revenues, liquor store revenues, and insurance trust revenue.

5. The RTS methodology is described by the ACIR in *1981 Tax Capacity of the Fifty States*, Report A-93, ACIR, Washington, D.C. September 1983. For a summary

of the controversy see Steven D. Gold, "Measuring Fiscal Effort and Fiscal Capacity: Sorting Out Some of the Controversies," a paper presented at the Tax Roundtable of the Lincoln Institute of Land Policy, Cambridge, Massachusetts, April 27, 1984. Stephen Barro of SMB Economic Research Inc., Washington, D.C., is preparing a detailed assessment of the capacity and fiscal disparities for the U.S. Department of Housing and Urban Development, Washington, D.C.

6. Advisory Commission on Intergovernmental Relations (ACIR), *1982 Tax Capacity of the Fifty States* (Preliminary, March 1985). Tax-effort estimates are not made for component categories of the property tax base (residential, farm, commercial-industrial, and utility).

# 5

# Jobs and Taxes: The Effect of
# the Business Climate
# on Minnesota Employment

## INTRODUCTION

Two facts appear to be clear. First, Minnesota is a high-tax state. Second, recent, long-term employment growth in Minnesota has generally been higher than employment growth in most of its neighboring states and higher than the U.S. average. The purpose of the present study is to determine the relationship (if any) between these two facts, between taxes and changes in the level of employment in Minnesota.

Obviously, the Minnesota economy and thus its employment growth is tied closely to the national economy. No state can realistically have employment grow at a rate that differs widely from national trends. But there are differences in employment growth rates across the states. Even as some sectors of the national economy are growing and others declining, more of the growth and less of the decline is occurring in some states rather than in others. This study attempts to determine which factors explain these differences in state employment growth rates.

Many discussions of the business climate or tax climate center on various rankings of the states. For example, the Alexander Grant report[1] recently ranked Minnesota forty-three out of forty-eight states in its measure of the business climate. This low ranking resulted in large part because of the heavy emphasis placed on taxes in that study. These rankings can help document the first fact about Minnesota, that it is a high-tax state. But they do not address questions rising from the second fact, whether taxes affect employment. No attempt is made to bring the two facts together, to determine whether a poor tax climate ranking is a matter for concern.

One approach to determining whether taxes affect employment growth is to ask those individuals responsible for changing employment, i.e., the business persons who decide to relocate, to form new branches, to start a new business, or to expand on site. Surveys of the individuals responsible for location decisions can provide a guide as to which factors may be important. But surveys must be carefully designed to elicit the actual determinants of location decisions as respondents may have an incentive to exaggerate the importance of those factors that they feel are amenable to policy changes.

A second approach, which overcomes these problems, is to observe actual employment growth rates for Minnesota and the other states and then to statistically relate these growth rates to taxes and other factors in the states. These are the factors that compose business climate measures and that surveys, rankings, economic theory, and common sense would lead one to believe are important in explaining changes in employment. The questions that are addressed include the following: have the "bad" business climate states been low employment growth states? do taxes help explain the differences in growth rates or are tax differentials not large relative to other cost differentials, and, thus, not significant determinants of employment growth? By comparing Minnesota to the other states on employment growth and many cost factors, not just taxes alone, we can ask, other things being equal, do taxes matter?

In interpreting the results of the study it is important to remember that the analysis uses aggregate figures on employment. Our list of the significant and important factors for determining employment growth rates may not be relevant for any specific business location decision. It may, in fact, be the case that for a particular business location decision, a factor that we determine to be insignificant in explaining employment changes is the deciding factor. But, if a factor is not important for many such decisions, a statistical relationship cannot be detected between aggregate employment growth rates and the factor. This study attempts to determine which factors are important in explaining differences observed in aggregate employment growth rates across states.

In the next section, the statistical approach is described. The study is designed to address the specific concerns often expressed about the Minnesota business climate, including which factors (the high personal and corporate income tax rates, the overall tax effort, the change in tax effort) appear to explain Minnesota's (and other states') employment growth.

A final section discussing the implications of the results for tax reform follows. Some of the factors that are identified as being significant determinants are amenable to policy changes, others are not. For those that are, the issue is what Minnesota should do about these factors (taxes and others) to improve its employment growth rate.

## WHAT ARE THE DETERMINANTS OF EMPLOYMENT GROWTH?

This study compares employment growth rates to taxes, labor costs, the weather, energy costs, and other potential determinants of employment growth for the forty-eight contiguous states. It draws from previous work but expands the scope of inquiry into business location decisions in three ways.[2] First, it focuses on a recent period (1973 to 1980), a time characterized by significant shifts in employment among the states. Second, it analyzes employment growth in nonmanufacturing industries as well as manufacturing industries. In particular, employment change during the 1970s in six major industrial categories is analyzed using a statistical framework that relates employment growth to a set of factors hypothesized to be important. The industries studied include: manufacturing; transportation and public utilities; wholesale trade; retail trade; finance, insurance, and real estate (referred to as *finance* in the report); and services. Employment growth in the aggregate of these six industries is also analyzed.

The third way in which this study expands upon others is that the potential set of factors to be tested as determinants of employment is a far more extensive set than has been examined before. In addition to standard measures of market accessibility, labor force characteristics, energy prices, and climate, many fiscal variables are included to capture burden, trend, progressivity, expenditure, and announcement effects. Also, the explanatory variables include a mixture of the levels of and the percentage changes in the levels of certain factors.

EMPLOYMENT TRENDS IN MINNESOTA COMPARED TO OTHER STATES

As the study is an attempt to explain differences in employment growth rates between Minnesota and other states for the period from 1973 to 1980, it is useful to first compare the employment trend figures.

Table 1 contains employment growth by nine major industries for the U.S., Minnesota, South Dakota, North Dakota, Iowa, Wisconsin (neighboring states to Minnesota), and Illinois, plus Texas, California, and Florida where employment is growing rapidly, and New York where employment is growing very slowly. The nine industries include: agriculture; mining, contract construction; manufacturing; transportation; wholesale trade; retail trade; finance, insurance, and real estate; and services. This list includes three industries not analyzed in subsequent sections as these industries are not footloose (i.e., they are tied to location-specific resources or markets), are tied to (inter)national trends more than the others, and are not likely to be influenced by the same set of factors as the other six.

Overall employment in Minnesota between 1973 and 1980 grew 35%, which was much faster than employment grew in the U.S. (22.1%). Moreover, employment growth in seven of the nine industries was more rapid in Minnesota than in the U.S. In all industries, except agriculture and mining, employment grew between 8% and 27% faster than the same industries in the U.S. Employment in contract construction and manufacturing grew much more rapidly in Minnesota than in the U.S. as a whole.

TABLE 1
Percentage Change in Employment by Major Industry, 1973-1980:
U.S., Minnesota and Selected States

| | U.S. | Minn. | S.Dak. | N.Dak. | Ia. | Wisc. | Ill. | Tex. | Cal. | Fla. | N.Y. |
|---|---|---|---|---|---|---|---|---|---|---|---|
| Total | 22.1% | 35.0% | 31.9% | 46.7% | 24.1% | 22.6% | 11.9% | 47.1% | 41.4% | 31.4% | 2.6% |
| Agriculture | 28.6 | 19.3 | -40.0 | 26.1 | 25.6 | 21.0 | 18.6 | 10.7 | 71.6 | 35.8 | 7.7 |
| Mining | 65.4 | 25.3 | 14.9 | 164.0 | -10.1 | 4.7 | 45.3 | 103.6 | 57.2 | 57.3 | 4.4 |
| Construction | 19.9 | 47.5 | 18.4 | 64.3 | 34.3 | 20.4 | 9.2 | 65.4 | 60.7 | 5.4 | -19.1 |
| Manufacturing | 7.0 | 25.1 | 43.7 | 62.2 | 13.3 | 11.0 | -4.4 | 35.6 | 31.2 | 24.2 | -8.6 |
| Transportation | 15.3 | 23.2 | 25.9 | 35.6 | 13.7 | 17.1 | 1.8 | 41.0 | 24.1 | 20.0 | -15.0 |
| Wholesale Trade | 23.5 | 34.5 | 44.1 | 53.1 | 51.4 | 32.9 | 13.5 | 43.5 | 37.4 | 29.6 | -3.3 |
| Retail Trade | 21.5 | 27.2 | 25.4 | 28.6 | 16.2 | 19.6 | 10.1 | 38.9 | 32.7 | 34.6 | -0.5 |
| Finance, Insurance, Real Estate | 27.6 | 38.3 | 32.2 | 46.4 | 34.6 | 32.2 | 29.5 | 39.5 | 51.0 | 26.7 | 12.7 |
| Services | 45.3 | 56.2 | 35.2 | 50.4 | 42.3 | 45.7 | 41.3 | 59.9 | 57.7 | 50.6 | 26.7 |

*Source:* U.S. Department of Commerce, Bureau of the Census, *County Business Patterns,* (Washington, D.C.: U.S. Government Printing Office, selected years).

Of the four neighboring states to Minnesota, total employment in North Dakota and South Dakota grew more rapidly than in the U.S. but only North Dakota had a growth rate that was greater than the rate in Minnesota. North Dakota had very strong employment growth relative to the U.S. in all industries except agriculture. With the exception of services, employment growth in the other eight industries was more rapid in North Dakota than in Minnesota.

Employment growth in South Dakota showed a more uneven pattern, but three industries—manufacturing, transportation and wholesale trade—grew faster in South Dakota than in Minnesota. With few exceptions, employment growth in each industry was higher in Minnesota than in the other three north central states.

Of the three states where total employment is growing rapidly, employment growth in Minnesota was higher than in Florida. Moreover, employment growth in Minnesota was higher than in Florida in all but three industries—agriculture, mining, and retail trade. Between 1973 and 1980 employment grew 47.1% and 41.1% in Texas and California, respectively. Employment grew faster in every industry (except agriculture in Texas) in these two states than it did in Minnesota. In Texas, mining is the most rapidly growing industry, and manufacturing grew at five times the national average compared to three and one-half times the national average in Minnesota. In California, much of the rapid, overall employment growth can be attributed to strong employment gains in agriculture, mining, and contract construction.

In sum, Minnesota had more rapid growth in total employment than the U.S. as a whole. In a few categories Minnesota did as well as the fast-growth states and in many categories its employment growth rates were higher than the corresponding rates of its neighboring states.

THE METHOD

To determine which factors help explain the differences in the growth rates reported in Table 1, a statistical model is employed. The technique statistically relates the employment growth rates of the forty-eight contiguous states from 1973 to 1980 to the set of potential explanatory variables or factors. For the sample chosen and within the set of factors chosen, a factor is said to be a significant determinant if it explains some of the observed differences or variance in the employment growth rate. A factor which does not help to explain or account for the differences observed in the states' employment rates is said to be insignificant.

Of the significant factors, some will explain or account for more of the differences in employment growth rates than others. These important significant factors will have larger elasticities, i.e., for any percentage change in these factors, the percentage change in employment growth rates will be larger than for significant factors with smaller elasticities. Thus, rather than simply ask if taxes matter, we ask, in this framework, are taxes a significant and strong determinant of employment growth rates?

As this study compares Minnesota to other states rather than comparing Minnesota's growth rate in 1976 to Minnesota's growth rate in 1980, the results are best interpreted as a test of Minnesota's competitive advantage (disadvantage) relative to other states, not as a test of which factors explain Minnesota employment over time.

Below is a description of each of the variables used in the analysis. A value for each variable was obtained for each of the forty-eight contiguous states.

## THE VARIABLES

### 1. The Dependent Variable

The dependent variable is the percentage change in employment between 1973 and 1980 in each industry. The industries examined are manufacturing, transportation, wholesale trade, retail trade, finance (actually, finance, insurance, and real estate), and services. Total employment, which is the aggregate of these six industries, is also examined. Total employment, thus, does not represent all employment as agriculture, mining, and contract construction have been omitted.

### 2. Potential Explanatory Variables (Factors)

The factors hypothesized to be important determinants of employment have a large number of dimensions to them. In what follows, these dimensions are represented using a large number of variables. For technical reasons, some of these variables are later dropped from the empirical work.

*Labor climate variables.*    Labor climate is measured using wage rates, union activity, labor availability, productivity and unemployment compensation benefits. The wage rate variable (WAGE) is the average hourly pay for manufacturing production workers in a state. This same wage rate measure is used for every industry analyzed. If the manufacturing wage rate is high, other industries will have to pay higher wages to attract, hire, and retain employees. Thus the manufacturing wage rate is expected to be indicative of the overall wage level in the state.

Union activity is measured using three variables: the percentage of the work force that unionized in 1976 (UNION), a variable equal to one if the state has a right to work law and zero otherwise (RTW), and the percentage of working time lost in a state due to union work stoppages (WSTOP). WSTOP is calculated using the average percentage of working time lost for years 1975, 1976 and 1977. The percentage change in the population between ages eighteen and forty-four (P1844) between 1965 and 1973 measures the growth in the prime working age population in a state.

The median education level in the state in 1976 is a measure of labor's inherent productivity (EDUCL). The level of unemployment compensation is measured as the average weekly basic unemployment insurance payment in 1976 (UI). Workers' compensation is another aspect of the labor climate that, due to a lack of data, is not represented among these variables.

*Energy.* Energy prices are difficult to measure. There are many energy types—electric, natural gas—and different tariff structures for user classes. One study which uses both natural gas and electric prices found electric prices to be statistically significant factors while natural gas prices were not significant determinants.[3] Thus, for this analysis the industrial average electrical bill for the 300KW - 600,000 KWH use class (ELEC) is used to proxy energy prices.

*Fiscal climate.* The fiscal climate in a state is difficult to capture with only a few variables—thus numerous variables are proposed to measure both the expenditure and the tax climate in a state. On the expenditure side, the education burden in 1977 (EDUCI) and the welfare burden (public welfare plus medicaid) in 1977 (WELI) are included in the regressions. These state and local expenditures from own-source revenues on each of these functions are measured as a percentage of state personal income.

On the tax side, a measure of the overall level of tax effort in the state is the first dimension of the tax burden used here. The ACIR measure of effort, which is an index of a state's effort relative to the national average of 100, is used to measure effort (TEFF). Higher effort implies higher taxes given the state's fiscal capacity. An effort index of 120 for example would imply that the overall level of taxes is 20% higher in that state compared to the average in all states. Because it is often stated that firms are concerned about fiscal trends as well as about the level of taxation, the percentage change in effort from 1967 to 1977 (PTEFF) is used in the analysis as well as TEFF in 1977.

Some policymakers and business representatives appear to believe that high nominal tax rates have detrimental effects on business' perception about a state. They argue that nominal rates matter even though the high nominal rates do not necessarily imply high taxes as taxable income in a state may be small due to, for example, generous depreciation allowances, deductibility of federal taxes, and a weighted apportionment formula for the state corporate income tax. The suggestion is that businesses do not look much beyond the nominal tax rate, and that these so-called "announcement effects" about nominal rates affect business location decisions. Others argue that businesses do look beyond the obvious nominal rate and instead consider effective rates of taxation when making employment change decisions. These two hypotheses are tested for two specific taxes—the corporate income tax and the personal income tax.

The highest nominal state corporate tax rate in 1976 (HCIT) measures the marginal tax rate on corporate income and is a measure of the announcement effect mentioned above. An alternative and more accurate measure of corporate tax burden is the ACIR's 1979 measure of the effective corporate tax rate or the ratio of corporate tax revenue to corporate tax capacity (EFFCIT).

High personal taxes may make it difficult for firms to attract employees to staff an expansion on-site or a new branch plant. To measure the so-called announcement effect the nominal state income tax rate for incomes of $50,000 or more (IT50) is used. An alternative that is a more accurate measure of personal income tax burden is the ACIR's effective tax rate—the ratio of taxes to income—for households at various levels of income. The measure is available for households with incomes of $25,000 or more or for households with income of $50,000 or more (EFFIT50). The two measures are highly correlated, and because the results are similar using either measure, only the latter is employed here.

Tax progressivity may also adversely influence employment growth if individuals do not have a strong preference for redistribution at the state level. The average 1977 effective tax rate for the personal income tax and the sales tax combined is calculated for the 90th percentile of income and the 10th percentile of income.[4] The difference between the effective tax rates in those two income percentiles is used as a measure of the combined progressivity of these two personal taxes (PROG). The greater the difference between the average tax rate at the upper end of the income distribution and the average tax rate at the lower end, the more progressive is the state's tax system.

Some researchers[5] argue that businesses may prefer states which rely more heavily on local tax sources because businesses may get more benefits from local governments than state governments and businesses can vary their tax bill within the state with a choice among several local governments. It is also argued that businesses may prefer states that make greater use of sales taxes, because, for various reasons, the sales tax is not as burdensome as the individual income tax or corporate income tax. To test these hypotheses, the local revenue raised from own sources as a percentage of state and local taxes (PCTLOC) in 1977-78 and sales tax revenues as a percentage of total state and local revenue in 1976-77 (SALETX) are included among the fiscal variables.

*Climate.* Temperature variations are used to measure climate. The average maximum daily temperature for every day in the month of July for the past thirty years in each state (MAXTEMP) is used to measure the heat extreme. A comparable measure of the average minimum temperature for every day in the month of January for the past thirty years in a state (MINTEMP) is used to measure the cold extreme. These variables are used to test whether firms and employees specifically avoid cold climates and prefer warmer climates.

*Market variables.* To measure the market potential in a state for final goods producers, and particularly for the retail trade, finance, and services industries, the population density in a state in 1973 (DENST) and the per capita income in a state in 1977 (PCI) are included in the equation. For many businesses, the relevant market area is either much smaller than a state (two mile radius) or much larger than a state (the world). For these firms, DENST, in particular, will not be a good measure of the market. It may instead act more like a regional variable, i.e., all high DENST states may be in the northeast. P1844, which was described above as a labor variable, may also represent a growing market for some industries, such as retail trade and services and thus is included in the equation.

*Agglomeration economies.* Firms in some industries may be strongly attracted to one another. Specifically, manufacturing firms often cluster in locations to take advantage of agglomeration economies (cost savings resulting from the spatial concentration of firms). (This argument, however, is probably more compelling at the local level than at the state level.) A high concentration of manufacturing in a state may also lead to employment growth in wholesale trade and transportation if manufacturing firms are a market for those industries. Thus, the percentage of total employment in manufacturing in 1973, the beginning of the time period examined, (PCTMFG) is included for these three industries.

The PCTMFG variable, like the DENST variable above, may have an alternative interpretation. PCTMFG may not be a good measure of the spatial concentration of manufacturing firms (after all, two states with 20% manufacturing could have very different spatial concentrations of those firms). It may instead measure the mix of the industrial base and as manufacturing is a slow growth sector relative to other sectors, a high PCTMFG would be expected to inhibit the overall growth of the state's jobs.

THE RESULTS: WHICH BUSINESS CLIMATE FACTORS AFFECT EMPLOYMENT GROWTH?

The extensive list of variables described above is used in an initial test for each industry (the results not reported here). The factors within each subgroup (e.g., labor climate, fiscal climate, etc.) were examined to check whether they are highly correlated with one another. If a factor was highly correlated with one or more factors in the subgroup, and it was always statistically insignificant in the initial test and not found to be statistically significant in other studies of location, it was dropped from the set of factors, and a preferred model was formulated. The final set of variables, those tested in the reported results, is listed in Table 2. It should be emphasized, that the same explanatory variables may not be statistically significant for all industries, and even the signs of some variables could differ between industries. For example, the sales tax may discourage

TABLE 2
Results for Percentage Employment Changes 1973-80: By Industry

| | (1) Total Employment | (2) Manufac- turing | (3) Transpor- tation | (4) Wholesale Trade | (5) Retail Trade | (6) Finance, Insurance, Real Estate | (7) Services |
|---|---|---|---|---|---|---|---|
| WAGE | -** | | | | -** | -** | -* |
| WSTOP | | | -* | | | | |
| EDUCL | | | | | | | |
| P1844 | | | | | | -* | |
| ELEC | -** | | -** | -** | -** | -** | -** |
| EDUCI | +* | | | | +** | +** | |
| WELI | | | | | | | |
| PTEFF | -** | -** | | | -* | | -** |
| EFFCIT | +* | | | | | | |
| EFFIT50 | | | | -** | -** | -** | |
| SALETX | | | | -* | | | |
| MAXTEMP | +** | +* | +** | +* | | | +** |
| MINTEMP | | | | | | | |
| PCTMFG | -** | -** | -** | -** | | | |
| DENST | | | | | -** | -** | |
| PCI | +** | | | | +** | +** | +** |
| $R^2$ | .85 | .73 | .75 | .63 | .69 | .75 | .62 |

*Source:* Staff Computations

  + :  The variable is positively related to employment growth (higher values of this factor contribute to employment growth).

  -:  The variable is negatively related to employment growth (higher values of this factor inhibit employment growth).

\* and \*\* indicate statistical significance at the 90% and 95% confidence levels, respectively. A blank indicates that the variable is statistically insignificant in the specific regression, i.e., it does not help explain the observed differences in employment growth rates for that industry.

wholesale and retail trade locations, but have no effect on manufacturing locations.

The equation using the announcement effect variables (IT50 and HCIT) instead of the effective rate variables (EFFIT50 and EFFCIT) generally had slightly less explanatory power (as evidenced by the lower $R^2$ of the equations) than the effective rate equations. Moreover, for the three industries in which the coefficient of the effective income tax variable is statistically significant and has the expected negative sign, the coefficient of IT50 in the counterpart announcement equation is either not statistically significant (retail trade) or has less statistical significance than in the counterpart effective rate equations (wholesale trade and finance, insurance, and real estate). Thus, the idea that firms and employees do not look beyond the nominal rates of taxation is rejected here and only the results using the conceptually more correct effective rates are reported below.

The results for percentage change in total employment for these industries and in each of the six industries are reported in Table 2. Displayed on the left side is the final list of factors that were tested for each industry. In the seven columns that follow, significant factors are indicated by one or two asterisks and a negative (positive) sign if the factor inhibits (enhances) employment growth.

For the six industries as a whole (column 1), higher wages, and energy prices had a negative and statistically significant effect on the percentage change in total employment. For fiscal variables, higher spending on education as a proportion of income appears to have had a positive statistically significant influence on employment growth. A higher percentage increase in tax effort discouraged employment growth and it was statistically significant. Surprisingly, a higher effective corporate income tax rate increased total employment growth but the factor was only statistically significant at a confidence level of 90%.

Employment growth was higher in states that have warmer climates as represented by the average maximum temperature for July variable and higher in states with a higher per capita income. Growth in total employment was also higher in states with a lower concentration of manufacturing. This finding supports the alternative hypothesis that this variable measures industry mix and not agglomeration economies. It illustrates that employment growth was spreading away from traditional manufacturing states.

For manufacturing (column 2), the signs were generally as hypothesized, but only PTEFF, MAXTEMP and PCTMGF were statistically significant. These coefficients show that an increase in relative tax effort reduced manufacturing employment growth and that employment growth was stronger in warmer climates, other things being equal. Again, the agglomeration economies story was not borne out by the results as manufacturing employment grew more slowly in states with higher concentrations of manufacturing employment.

The results for manufacturing in other research are not uniform across these studies. With one exception,[6] studies analyzing state level employment data generally do not find that wages or energy prices influence employment growth in manufacturing. At least two studies find that taxation influences manufacturing employment growth.[7] This study, however, in part confirms that increasing the relative level of taxation in a state reduces manufacturing employment growth.

For transportation (column 3), more work stoppages and higher energy prices reduced employment growth. The fiscal variables were not (individually) statistically significant. Transportation employment, like manufacturing, grew more quickly in warmer climates as the sign on the MAXTEMP variable shows. Transportation employment grew less rapidly in states with higher concentrations of manufacturing employment.

Higher energy prices adversely affected employment growth in wholesale trade (column 4). Higher effective personal income tax rates and a higher percentage of state and local revenue raised from sales taxation had a negative and statistically significant effect on wholesale trade employment. Wholesale trade also grew more rapidly in states with warmer climates and more slowly in states with high concentrations of manufacturing employment.

Higher wages and energy prices also adversely affected employment growth in retail trade (column 5). Three of the fiscal variables influenced employment growth in this industry. On the one hand, both a higher percentage increase in tax effort and a higher effective personal income tax rate reduced employment growth in this industry. On the other hand, higher expenditures on education as a percentage of income appears to have increased employment growth in this industry. For market variables, population growth in the 18-44 age cohort did not affect retail trade employment growth, and high population density adversely affected employment growth in this sector. Thus, population density may act as a regional variable instead of a market variable. Another market variable, per capita income, did positively influence employment growth in retail trade.

Higher wages, energy prices and, somewhat surprisingly, population growth in the 18-44 cohort reduced employment growth in the financial industries (column 6). The last result may indicate that the 18-44 cohort does not demand many financial services because they are still for the most part in the consumption phase of their life cycle.

A higher expenditure on education as a percentage of income had a strong positive affect on employment growth in the finance industry, and high effective personal income tax rates adversely affected employment growth in this industry. As in retail trade, employees in the financial industry are probably attracted to and deterred by, respectively, these aspects of the fiscal structure.

Population density in the state adversely affected employment growth in the finance industries, and per capita income had a strong positive influence on employment growth in this sector.

Higher wages and energy prices adversely affected employment growth in services (column 7), and larger increases in the relative tax effort in a state also had an adverse effect on employment growth in this sector. Warmer climates and stronger per capita income growth had a positive effect on employment growth in the services industries.

To summarize the results reported in Table 2 for total employment, wages, cost of electricity, education expenditures, trend in tax effort, warm climate,

TABLE 3
Elasticities of Percentage Employment Change with Respect to
Statistically Significant Independent Variables Reported in Table 6

| | Total Employment | Manufacturing | Transportation | Wholesale Trade | Retail Trade | Finance, Insurance, Real Estate | Services |
|---|---|---|---|---|---|---|---|
| WAGE | -1.12** | -1.08 | 0.28 | -0.45 | -1.05** | -1.34* | 0.51* |
| WSTOP | -0.08 | -0.23 | -0.16* | -0.03 | -0.05 | -0.01 | -0.04 |
| P1844 | 0.00 | 0.19 | 0.12 | 0.05 | 0.11 | -0.25* | -0.09 |
| ELEC | -0.84** | -0.68 | -1.10** | -0.72** | -0.91** | -0.73* | -0.49** |
| EDUCI | 0.72* | -1.09 | -0.69 | -0.49 | 1.43** | 1.94* | 0.31 |
| PTEFF | -0.06** | -0.14** | -0.05 | -0.03 | -0.05* | -0.04 | -0.04** |
| EFFIT50 | -0.10 | -0.07 | -0.01 | -0.33** | -0.23** | -0.25** | 0.03 |
| SALETX | .05 | 0.31 | -0.04 | -0.31* | -0.08 | -0.04 | 0.10 |
| MAXTEMP | 2.42** | 3.82* | 6.25** | 2.49* | 0.57 | 0.30 | 1.62** |
| PCTMFG | -0.85** | -6.60** | -0.64** | -0.58** | | | |
| DENST | -0.05 | | | | -0.11** | -0.09** | -0.01 |
| PCI | 2.36** | | | | 2.58** | 4.16** | 1.39** |

*Source:* Staff Computations
* and ** indicate that the factors defining the elasticity are statistically significant determinants at the 90% and 95% level of confidence respectively.

percentage of manufacturing and per capita income were significant determinants of employment growth. The retail trade and finance industries appear to also have been influenced by wages, cost of electricity, education expenditures, and per capita income but, unlike total employment, these industries were affected by the effective individual tax rate and population density of the state. The fiscal variables that were highly significant determinants in explaining employment growth in either the total employment category or one of the six industries that compose total employment were education expenditures, trend in tax effort, and the effective individual tax rate.

Table 2 indicates which factors were found to be significant in explaining the differences observed in employment growth rates. But to determine the relative strengths of these effects, the elasticities of the employment growth rates with respect to the significant explanatory variables must be calculated. Elasticity figures are reported in Table 3.

To interpret Table 3, note, as an example of a strong determinant, that the elasticity for WAGES in the total employment equation is -1.12. This implies that for a 10% decrease in a state's wages relative to the other states' wages, the employment growth rate would increase 11.2%. By contrast, the effect of DENST is much weaker. The elasticity figure for DENST in the finance equation (-0.09) indicates that a 10% increase in population density decreases employment in this industry by less than 1% (0.9%). The larger the elasticity (in absolute value) the stronger is that factor's effect on employment growth in a state.

For total employment, the elasticities indicate that the wage rate, electricity charges, expenditures on education, warmer climate, the concentration of manufacturing employment, and per capita income have the strongest effects on employment change. The elasticity of the percent change in employment with respect to EFFIT50 is relatively high for the wholesale trade, retail trade, and finance industries, but that of PTEFF is relatively low.

## INTERPRETATION AND IMPLICATIONS FOR TAX REFORM IN MINNESOTA

While the elasticity coefficients indicate the relative importance of a given percentage change in different variables on any state's employment growth, how an individual state such as Minnesota fared relative to other states depended on how that state compared to the other states regarding the factors determined to be significant (as indicated by * and ** in Table 2) and important (as indicated by large elasticities in Table 3). For example, if Minnesota had about average U.S. manufacturing wage rates, then, even though the elasticity of manufacturing wage rate variable is high, the wage rate variable would not have had much effect on the growth rate of Minnesota's employment relative to the U.S. average. Correspondingly, if Minnesota's increase in tax effort was 50% higher than the U.S. average, this variable would have played a significant role in determining the percentage of employment changes even though its elasticity was relatively small.

Table 4 reports the Minnesota figure used in the equations, the U.S. average figure and the elasticities for the statistically significant variables listed in Table 3. The figures for the effective corporate income tax rate are also reported simply because they are likely to be of interest. Just as the corporate income tax rate was found to be significant with a positive effect in this analysis, so other studies have found this variable to be significant with a negative effect. Thus, we have no confidence in its influence and no elasticity is reported.

It is interesting to note from the last column of Table 4 that Minnesota compared favorably in several categories. Wage rates were not out of line with the U.S. average; Minnesota spent more on education relative to the U.S. average; Minnesota had a per capita income that was 6.5% higher than the average; the percentage increase in the labor force was nearly 50% higher in Minnesota than the U.S. average; the state population density was much lower than the average; and the tax effort decline was greater in Minnesota than the U.S. average. It is readily apparent from these figures that Minnesota differed unfavorably from the U.S. average in terms of the effective individual income tax rate, the percentage of total revenue attributable to the sales tax, and the effective corporate income tax rate. Minnesota was at a competitive disadvantage relative to the U.S. average with respect to work stoppage, electricity costs, and temperature.

From Table 4 the elasticity figure for PCTMFG indicates that PCTMFG was a strong determinant of the relative employment growth rates for the states for total employment, transportation, and wholesale trade, and an even stronger determinant of the growth rate for manufacturing. The negative values imply that relative to other states, a higher percentage of total employment in manufacturing in 1973 in a state inhibits the state's employment growth rates. The last column of Table 4 indicates that Minnesota had a smaller share of its industrial base in manufacturing in 1973 than the average state. This below-average PCTMFG helps explain Minnesota's high growth rate relative to the U.S. average in total employment, manufacturing, transportation, and wholesale trade.

For total employment, wages, warm climate, and per capita income had the largest elasticities. Since Minnesota had above-average wages and below-average maximum temperature, these two factors inhibited Minnesota's employment growth. Minnesota had above-average per capita income so this factor contributed to Minnesota's employment growth relative to the U.S. average.

TABLE 4
Elasticities for the Significant Variables and Minnesota vs. the U.S. Average
for the Sample Period

| | Elasticity of Employment Change with Respect to the Explanatory Variables | | | | | | | | | |
| | Total Employment | Manufacturing | Transportation | Wholesale Trade | Retail Trade | Finance | Services | MN Figure | U.S. Average Figure | MN Figure as a percentage of U.S. Average |
|---|---|---|---|---|---|---|---|---|---|---|
| WAGE | -1.12 | | | | -1.05 | -1.34 | -.51 | $5.98 | $5.72 | 104.5 |
| WSTOP | | | -.16 | | | | | .21 | .16 | 131.3 |
| P1844 | | | | | | -.25 | | 27.38% | 18.33% | 149.4 |
| ELEC | -.84 | | -1.01 | -.72 | -.91 | -.73 | -.49 | $2563.00 | $2360.00 | 108.6 |
| EDUCI | .72 | | | | 1.43 | 1.94 | | 8.9% | 7.9% | 112.7 |
| PTEFF | -.06 | -.14 | | | -.05 | | -.04 | -5.0% | -4.3% | 116.3 |
| EFFIT50 | | | | -.33 | -.23 | -.25 | | 7.7% | 3.3% | 233.3 |
| SALETX | | | | -.31 | | | | 7.9% | 12.4% | 63.7 |
| MAXTEMP | 2.42 | 3.82 | 6.25 | 2.49 | | | 1.62 | 79.4 | 86.6 | 91.7 |
| PCTMFG | -.85 | -6.60 | -.64 | -.58 | | | | 28.35% | 29.7% | 95.5 |
| DENST | | | | | -.11 | -.09 | -.01 | 49.0 | 152.4 | 32.2 |
| PCI | 2.36 | | | | 2.58 | 4.16 | 1.39 | $7108.80 | $6674.70 | 106.5 |
| EFFCIT | | | | | | | | 7.9% | 4.1% | 192.7 |

*Source:* Staff Computations

The more interesting variables for our purposes are the fiscal variables. Even though PTEFF, the tax effort trend, was significant for four of the seven categories of employment, that the elasticity is very small and Minnesota's value for this factor did not vary a great deal from the U.S. average indicate that PTEFF had little if any effect on Minnesota's growth rate relative to the U.S. average. If it had any effect at all, its influence was positive as Minnesota's tax effort declined further in percentage terms than the U.S. average during the sample period.

Expenditures on education (as a percentage of personal income) were significant for three categories and the elasticities are relatively large. Since Minnesota spends 12.7% more than the U.S. average, this variable had a large positive effect on Minnesota employment growth rate relative to the U.S. rate.

The effective individual income tax rate variable was significant for three industries, but its elasticity is relatively small. For a 10% increase in this rate, the percentage decrease in the employment rate would be between 2.3% and 3.3%. This is a variable whose Minnesota value was much greater than the U.S. average, and thus, even though the elasticity is small, this factor probably had a strong negative influence on Minnesota's growth rate in wholesale trade, retail trade, and finance.

The variable representing the percentage of total revenue attributable to the sales tax was significant only for wholesale trade, and its elasticity is relatively small. But as Minnesota was far below the U.S. average on this variable, it contributed positively to employment growth in wholesale trade.

To summarize, many of the factors with the strongest effect on Minnesota's employment growth relative to the U.S. in 1973-80 were factors over which policymakers have little control. Such factors (see Table 4) include wages (in the categories of total employment, retail, finance, and services), maximum temperature (total employment, manufacturing, transportation, wholesaling, services), work stoppage (transportation), percentage change in labor force (finance), electricity costs (all but manufacturing), percentage of total employment in manufacturing (total employment, manufacturing, transportation, and wholesale), population density of the state (retail, finance, and services) and per capita income (total employment, retail, finance, and services).

The fiscal variables where Minnesota departed greatly from the U.S. average were the effective individual income tax rate (EFFIT50), the effective corporate tax rate (EFFCIT) and the share of total revenue attributable to the sales tax (SALETX). No conclusion can be made about the influence of EFFCIT, and SALETX was significant only for wholesale trade and its contribution to employment in that industry was probably not large. But EFFIT50 was significant in explaining growth rates in wholesale trade, retail trade, and finance and the elasticities, while small, are large enough to conclude that this factor inhibited growth in these sectors.

Minnesota did not vary a great deal from the U.S. average on the two fiscal variables of expenditures on education as a percentage of income (EDUCI) and the trend in tax effort (PTEFF). The elasticities for PTEFF are so small that the importance of this variable in explaining Minnesota's employment growth can essentially be ignored (except possibly for manufacturing where the elasticity is more than twice the elasticity obtained in the other three categories). The elasticities for EDUCI on the other hand were relatively large, particularly for retail trade and finance, and also to a lesser degree for total employment; thus we can conclude that Minnesota's above-average expenditures on education were important in explaining the relatively high employment growth rate for Minnesota from 1973 to 1980.

What do these conclusions imply for policy reform? With respect to tax levels, the results for EFFIT50 are relevant. It was a factor that was highly correlated with TEFF (overall tax effort) and effective tax rates are good measures of burden (unlike nominal rates). The results would indicate that, for at least some industries (wholesale trade, retail trade, and finance) a heavy tax burden was a deterrent to employment growth. Minnesota's employment growth in those three industries may benefit from a reduction in effective individual income tax rates.

To bring about such a reduction in individual income tax rates it may be necessary to decrease spending. The results here indicate that it would be unwise to let the burden of any expenditure decrease rest on education. Education expenditures relative to income had a positive effect on overall employment growth. It is interesting to note that another expenditure category, welfare, was not a significant determinant (either positive or negative) of employment growth rates in any of the industries.

Another means of decreasing the individual income tax burden, if not the overall burden, would be to change the mix of taxes to rely more heavily on sales taxes or local taxes. There was no strong evidence that the shares of total state and local revenue attributable to local taxes or to the sales tax had any effect on employment growth. Thus a shift to these taxes may have no influence on employment while the shift away from individual income taxes may have a positive effect.

The trend in overall tax effort appears to have only a small effect on employment growth. The effect is in the expected direction, i.e., a larger decrease in the overall tax effort increases employment growth rates.

The most recent figures available on overall employment growth rates indicate that, as in the previous time period, Minnesota outperformed all of its neighboring states and the U.S. average. From March 1983 to March 1984, rates for Minnesota and the U.S. average were 4.8% and 3.4% respectively. Do these encouraging employment numbers negate the results here? On the contrary, the results here indicate that Minnesota's lower electricity costs, lower population density, lower percentage manufacturing, and higher per capita income probably contributed to its relatively high employment growth rate. The more recent figures on fiscal variables indicate that Minnesota's employment growth (at least in the finance and trade industries) may have been even higher if, without cutting education expenditures, the overall tax level could have been decreased further or if, at least, the burden of the individual income tax could have been lessened.


## ENDNOTES

1. Alexander Grant and Co., *The Fifth Study of the General Manufacturing Business Climates of the Forty-Eight Contiguous States of America, 1983,* Chicago, 1984.

2. T. R. Plaut and J. E. Pluta, "Business Climate, Taxes and Expenditures, and State Individual Growth In the U.S., *Southern Economic Journal,* 1983.

3. D. W. Carlton, "The Location and Employment Choices of New Firms: An Econometric Model with Discrete and Continuous Endogenous Variables," *Review of Economics and Statistics,* 1983.

4. Daniel R. Feenberg and Harvey S. Rosen, "State Personal Income and Sales Taxes: 1977-83," a paper presented at the National Bureau of Economic Research Conference on State and Local Finance, Cambridge, June 1984.

5. Plaut and Pluta, "Business Climate."

6. V. Fuchs, *Changes in the Location of Manufacturing in the U.S. Since 1929* (New Haven: Yale University Press, 1962).

7. For a review of this literature, see Michael Wasylenko, "The Role of Taxes and Fiscal Incentives in the Location of Firms," in Roy W. Bahl, ed., *Urban Government Finance: Emerging Issues* (Beverly Hills: Sage Publications, 1981).

# 6

# The Tax System and
# Intergovernmental Linkages*

For most states, a systematic examination of state and local tax structure can proceed with only a brief reference to the state-local intergovernmental system. A study of Minnesota taxes, however, requires an explicit recognition and examination of the interplay between state-to-local aid programs and the Minnesota method of taxing property. This is true for two reasons. First, the bulk of the state's general fund expenditures are, in fact, pass-throughs of state revenues to local governments. Second, these tax/state-aid linkages have important implications not only for the overall level of Minnesota's taxes but also for their incidence (equity) effects.

Accordingly, the primary purpose of this section is to make explicit these linkages among the state aid programs. This provides the background for discussions in subsequent chapters that specifically deal with the issues of fiscal accountability among levels of government and the equity effects for Minnesota taxpayers.

The remainder of this chapter is divided into two parts. First, a brief overview of the Minnesota intergovernmental system is presented with comparisons drawn to the U.S. state/local system as a whole. The text then concludes with a detailed examination of the linkages among Minnesota's property tax relief devices and state-to-local aid programs.

## MINNESOTA AND THE U.S.[1]

Public services in the United States are provided by 82,688 governmental units, the vast majority of which are local. These units are distributed quite unevenly among the fifty states, with the number ranging from nineteen in Hawaii to about 6,464 in Illinois. Only five states have more units of government than Minnesota's 3,530.

Minnesota's above-average number of local governments does not necessarily imply an above-average reliance upon local government to finance local public services. In fact, this is not the case. Table 1 illustrates that local governments in Minnesota raised only 49% of their general

---

*This chapter was written by John Bartle, a consultant to the commission.

99

TABLE 1
Composition of State and Local Revenues
U.S. Aggregate and Minnesota, 1982-83

| Revenue Component | U.S. Aggregate | | | Minnesota | | |
|---|---|---|---|---|---|---|
| | Total | State | Local | Total | State | Local |
| | (Aggregate amounts in millions of dollars) | | | | | |
| Total revenue | 593,586 | 357,637 | 338,070 | 12,635 | 8,074 | 7,277 |
| General* | 486,878 | 290,456 | 298,542 | 10,664 | 6,841 | 6,522 |
| Intergovernmental | 89,983 | 72,704 | 119,399 | 1,766 | 1,509 | 2,955 |
| Own-source | 396,895 | 217,752 | 179,143 | 8,899 | 5,332 | 3,567 |
| Taxes | 284,585 | 171,440 | 113,145 | 6,106 | 4,320 | 1,786 |
| Property | 89,254 | 3,281 | 85,973 | 1,712 | 4 | 1,708 |
| General Sales | 64,890 | 53,639 | 11,251 | 997 | 992 | 5 |
| Income | 69,387 | 62,941 | 6,446 | 2,232 | 2,232 | — |
| Motor Fuel | 10,943 | 10,793 | 149 | 262 | 262 | — |
| Other | 50,113 | 40,785 | 9,327 | 903 | 829 | 74 |
| Current Charges | 62,625 | 23,182 | 39,443 | 1,497 | 582 | 915 |
| Miscellaneous | 49,685 | 23,130 | 26,555 | 1,296 | 430 | 866 |
| | (Percentage distributions by level of government) | | | | | |
| Total revenue | 100.0% | 100.0% | 100.0% | 100.0% | 100.0% | 100.0% |
| General* | 82.0 | 81.2 | 88.3 | 84.3 | 84.7 | 89.6 |
| Intergovernmental | 15.2 | 20.3 | 35.3 | 14.0 | 18.7 | 40.6 |
| Own-source | 66.9 | 60.9 | 53.0 | 70.3 | 66.0 | 49.0 |
| Taxes | 47.9 | 47.9 | 33.5 | 48.3 | 53.5 | 24.5 |
| Property | 15.0 | 0.9 | 25.4 | 13.5 | * | 23.5 |
| General Sales | 10.9 | 15.0 | 3.3 | 7.9 | 12.3 | 0.1 |
| Income | 11.7 | 17.6 | 1.9 | 17.6 | 27.6 | — |
| Motor Fuel | 1.8 | 3.0 | * | 2.1 | 3.2 | — |
| Other | 8.4 | 11.4 | 2.8 | 7.1 | 10.3 | 1.0 |
| Current Charges | 10.6 | 6.5 | 11.7 | 11.8 | 7.2 | 12.6 |
| Miscellaneous | 8.4 | 6.5 | 7.9 | 10.2 | 5.3 | 11.9 |

*Source:* Calculated from U.S. Bureau of the Census, *Governmental Finances in 1982-83* (Washington: Government Printing Office, October 1984). Table 5.

*Less than one-tenth of one percent.

revenue from own-sources in 1982-83. This compares with a 53% for local governments throughout the nation. In contrast, the local share of total state and local direct expenditures (which counts intergovernmental revenue as an expenditure of the recipient unit) is above average in Minnesota: 62.3% compared with the national average of 58.8%. The contrast between the local role in raising revenue and its role in spending for services is accounted for by three facts:

• A large percentage of total state government spending in Minnesota is for aid to localities (34.7% versus 29.8% nationally);
• Minnesota local governments derive no money from local income taxes and almost no money from local sales taxes, while local governments nationally raise 5.2% of their total revenue from these sources; and

- Property taxes account for 23.5% of local total tax revenue in Minnesota compared with 25.4% nationally.

## LINKAGES AMONG STATE AID PROGRAMS

In Minnesota there are several state aid programs to local governments, many of which interact with each other. Table 2 summarizes the discussion of this section, demonstrating how various programs are linked.

These linkages are of concern for four reasons. First, outlay reductions in one program that cause outlay increases in another make it harder to cut state spending. Second, there is a potential for certain state programs to work against each other. This will waste money and frustrate the accomplishment of the goals of each of the affected programs. Third, under current state property tax relief arrangements, certain types of property will receive large total credits. This will initially reduce the property tax burden on such property from what it would be without these credits. And fourth, the present system creates incentives for higher local public spending.

This discussion identifies two general types of interaction—automatic linkages and optional linkages. An automatic linkage means that a change in one program directly causes a change in the cost of another. In short, the two programs are inherently related. An optional linkage means that a change in one aid program may result in a decision by local officials, which in turn changes the cost of another aid program.

## AUTOMATIC LINKAGES

Several aid programs are related so that a change in the funding of one program will automatically cause a funding change in another program. There are three basic categories of these relationships: linkages among property tax relief programs; linkages among school foundation aid and classification ratios; and linkages between local government aid and levy limits.

### PROPERTY TAX RELIEF PROGRAMS

There are seven major programs that reduce a property-owner's tax. Five of these are credits which are subtracted from the tax bill a property owner receives. These include:

- *Agricultural School Credit (ASC).* Reduces the tax bill by between 10% and 29% for owners of agricultural homestead and nonhomestead property, timberland, and seasonal recreational property.

## TABLE 2
### Minnesota Linkages Among State Aid Programs - 1984

| PROGRAMS | INTERACTION | RESULT |
|---|---|---|
| **Automatic Linkages** | | |
| 1. THC and HC | Both affect taconite households. | Change in THC causes an opposing change in HC. |
| 2. ASC and HC | Both affect agricultural homesteads of greater than one acre. | Change in ASC causes an opposing change in HC. |
| 3. THC, HC, and ASC | All affect taconite agricultural homesteads greater than one acre. | Change in ASC causes an opposing change in both THC and HC; change in THC causes and opposing change in HC. |
| 4. NPC, WC, and ASC, HC. | NPC and WC reduces credits on other land. | Change in NP or WC may cause an opposing change in HC; change in ASC may cause an opposing change in NP or WC. |
| 5. HC and CB | HC subtracted from CB calculated. | Change in HC causes an opposing change in CB. |
| 6. TR and other credits | Credits affect net tax; TR is triggered by increases of over 28% in net tax. | Decreases in credits that are large enough can increase TR outlays. |
| 7. Foundation aid basic allowance/levy and property tax relief | Basic allowance and levy affect state aid share of school district revenue. Remainder is financed by school property tax levies, part of which are paid by property tax relief programs. | Change in the basic allowance levy change the division of school district revenue between foundation aid and local property taxes. Property tax relief outlays change with property tax changes. |
| 8. Classification ratios and foundation aid | Classification ratios partially determine local tax base which influences state foundation aid. | Change in classification ratio changes school district tax bases which cause an opposing change in foundation aid. |
| 9. Clasification ratios and property tax relief | Classification ratios determine taxable portion of property market value; property tax relief pays part of property tax. | Changes in classification ratios change property taxes which change property tax relief for certain types of property. |
| 10. LGA and levy limits | LGA received is subtracted from allowed levy limit. | Changes in LGA cause opposing changes in levy limits. |
| **Optional linkages** | | |
| 1. Levy limits and property tax relief programs | Levy limits control local levies; property tax relief programs pay part of local levies. | Changes in levy limits may affect local levies which will change property tax relief outlays. |
| 2. Direct aid to localities unrelated to levy limits (i.e., highway aid, welfare aid) and property tax relief. | Direct aids fund certain locally-administered programs; property tax relief programs pay part of local levies. | Changes in state aids may affect local levies which will change property tax relief outlays. |

*Source:* Minnesota Tax Study Commission (1984).

*Notes:*
| | |
|---|---|
| HC - Homestead Credit | ASC - Agricultural School Credit |
| THC- Taconite Homestead Credit | CB - Circuit Breaker |
| NPC- Native Prairie Credit | WC - Wetlands Credit |
| TR - Targeted Relief | LGA- Local Government Aid |

- *Homestead Credit (HC)*. Reduces total property tax paid on owner-occupied homestead property by 54% up to a $650 maximum.
- *Taconite Homestead Credit (THC)*. Reduces total property taxes on owner-occupied homesteads in "taconite relief areas" by either 66% up to $475, or by 57% up to $420.
- *Wetlands Credit (WC)*. Provides a direct credit to qualifying wetlands on all property owned (since wetlands are also tax-exempt). The credit equals .005 of the average market value of an equal acreage of tillable land in that jurisdiction.
- *Native Prairie Credit (NPC)*. Operates in the same manner as the wetlands credit. The credit equals .015 of the market value of tillable land.

These credits are subtracted from the gross tax bill in this order: ASC, NPC, WC, THC, and HC. The remainder is the net tax paid by the property owner. It is highly unlikely that a landholder could receive all of these credits. Most will only receive one.

There are two other types of property tax relief: the property tax refund (also known as the *circuit breaker*) and targeted relief. Both of these are granted in the form of a tax refund. These operate as follows:

- *Circuit Breaker (CB)*. Homeowners and renters may receive a refund for a portion of the property tax paid. The refund is primarily determined by income level, net property taxes (which, in turn, depend on the amount of the homestead credit), and
- *Targeted Relief (TR)*. Homeowners with increases of more than 20% in their 1985 net property tax may receive a refund for 100% of the net tax increase above 20%. This refund is phased out between income levels of $40,000 and $50,000. All homeowners in 1984 may receive a refund of 50% of the net tax increase above 10% if their net taxes exceed 2.25% of property market value. For taxes payable in 1985, TR will equal 50% of increases above 12.5% up to a $400 maximum, with no income restriction.

Linkages between these programs will have important budgetary and equity implications. Six linkages among property tax relief programs can be identified:

- Homesteads in taconite areas can receive both the THC and the HC. An increase in the HC directly reduces THC payments. At the current rates, $1 increase in the HC results in a decrease in the THC between 57 and 66 cents, subject to the credit maximum.
- The agricultural school credit (ASC) and the homestead credit (HC) in certain instances can both be credited against taxes on agricultural homesteads. The ASC applies to all qualifying land and property on an agricultural homestead except the dwelling, a garage, and one surrounding acre. The HC now applies to the entire acreage of qualifying

agricultural homesteads. Therefore only the HC applies to the dwelling and the first acre, but the ASC and the HC may then both apply to the same property on the rest of the land classified as a homestead. As a result, on agricultural homesteads larger than one acre, a decrease in the ASC will increase outlays for the HC, subject to the credit's limits. The actual increase in HC outlays will depend on the HC percentage and the portion of these households at the HC maximum. For every $1 decrease in the ASC that affects the HC, it is estimated that HC outlays will increase 28 cents.[2]

- For qualifying taconite agricultural homesteads, the ASC, THC, and HC can all apply. The linkage between the ASC and the THC is the same as that described for the HC and ASC. The reactions between the THC and the HC is explained above.

- The native prairie credit (NPC) and the wetlands credit must be applied against other property that is taxable. On the tax statement, these two credits are subtracted before the HC, so if either of these credits is applied against taxes on homestead property, they will reduce the amount available for the HC (and in taconite areas, the THC). The ASC is subtracted before the NPC and WC and will affect NPC and WC outlays when the full amount of these two credits cannot be taken.

- In using the circuit breaker, a taxpayer subtracts the homestead credit received before calculating the circuit breaker. Therefore, increases in the HC will automatically decrease the amount available for the CB. Between 1978 and 1981, outlays attributable to the homeowner's portion of the circuit breaker fell from $123.4 million to $54.1 million, partly due to increases in the HC.[3]

- Targeted relief (TR) is also tied to property tax credits. Outlays for TR may increase if other credits are reduced significantly. This will automatically occur, but only when the resulting increases in net property taxes exceed 20%. Therefore, the magnitude of the linkage depends on the particular change.

This discussion leads to three conclusions: (1) Outlays for these credit programs are determined in part by the order in which they are taken on tax statements; (2) A change in outlays for one credit may automatically cause an opposing change in outlays for other credits. This linkage is unlikely to cause the credits to work at odds with each other, but an attempt to reduce outlays in one program may be partially offset by increased outlays for another program; (3) As a result of the overlaps among these credits, certain property owners in particular situations will receive large total credits and may pay net property taxes that are substantially lower than those paid by other property owners.

## SCHOOL FOUNDATION AID AND CLASSIFICATION RATIOS

Foundation aid is a state aid program that ensures that school districts will have a basic revenue amount per pupil[4] ($1,475 for school year 1984-85) for a common basic tax levy (24 mills). Therefore, regardless of property wealth, districts receive a similar basic amount for a given tax levy, with the exception of districts "off the formula." Above the foundation aid basic amount, school districts may raise more revenue from a combination of local property tax levies and state aids.

There are three automatic linkages among school foundation aid, classification ratios, and property tax relief. They are as follows:

- Changes in foundation aid's basic revenue allowance and the basic tax levy both automatically affect property tax relief outlays. For instance, a decrease in the basic levy will reduce property taxes, and so reduce certain property tax relief outlays. In addition, such a change will also shift part of the burden of school finance from local property taxes to state aids. Similar shifts happen with changes in the basic revenue allowance amount. Because the foundation aid program mandates the division of a district's revenues between property taxes and state aids at any given level of a district spending, this linkage is automatic. It has been estimated that a $1 change in the basic levy induces an opposite change in state property tax credits equal to between 13 and 13.8 cents.[5]

- Classification ratios set the portion of a property's market value which is subject to taxation. In Minnesota there are several classification ratios for different types of property (chapters 16 and 17). Changes in classification ratios change a local government's base of taxable property. Since foundation aid is determined in part by district property tax base, such a change will affect the level of state aid to school districts. This linkage is automatic, although districts may react to these changes and set into motion other optional linkages.

- Changes in classification ratios on property receiving tax relief also create an automatic linkage. For example, lowering the classification ratio on homestead property will lower taxes on homesteads and so reduce outlays for homestead tax relief programs (HC, THC, TR, and CB). This impact may be reduced if local governments allow their mill rates to increase to compensate for the reduction in tax base. However, even if localities increase mill rates to compensate fully for the decreased taxable base, total taxes on homesteads will still be lower because the tax burden has been partially shifted to nonhomestead property.

## LINKAGES BETWEEN LEVY LIMITS AND LGA[6]

The overall state levy limitation applies to all counties and to cities with populations over 5,000, and limits the total property tax that can be levied. Certain levies can be excluded from the limitation. Local government aid (LGA) provides formula-determined grants to most cities, counties, and some towns in order to reduce property taxes. In calculating a jurisdiction's levy limit, the full amount of LGA received, a part of the taconite aids, and native prairie and wetlands reimbursements to counties are subtracted from the maximum allowable levy. To illustrate, a decrease in LGA of $1 directly results in a $1 increase in the levy limit. Whether or not changes in the levy limit translate into changes in levies depends on local action. That is an optional linkage and is discussed in the following section.

## OPTIONAL LINKAGES

Optional linkages among state aid programs result when changes in outlays for an aid program cause a local fiscal response which in turn induces a change in another state program. Unlike automatic linkages, optional linkages do not always cause changes in outlays for other programs.

For instance, a decrease in state welfare aid to a county will cause an increase in county property taxes, if the county decides to make up all or part of the reduction in program expenditures. In turn, this levy increase will cause an increase in state property tax relief. The end result is that state welfare aid has decreased, the county's tax levy is higher, and state property tax relief outlays also have increased. The net savings to the state is lower than the welfare aid reduction would indicate, as the cut has induced a rise in other state outlays. Of course, this is only one possible result. County officials could choose not to increase taxes and instead absorb the full amount of the aid decrease. In this case, property tax relief outlays will be unaffected and the reduction in welfare aid represents the net savings to the state.

This illustrates the difference between automatic and optional linkages among state aids. Automatic interactions happen directly and with certainty—no other party must act for the result to occur. An optional linkage requires action by some other party and so may not happen. As such, the impact of these linkages are much harder to identify because of the uncertainty involved. Further, different local units may react in much different ways. However, it is clear that such influences are an important factor in determining the net impacts of changes in state aid policies.

Two state programs are related in this way to the property tax relief programs: levy limits and direct state aids to localities.

### LEVY LIMITS[7]

Levy limits set the maximum permissible property tax levy for counties and cities. A local decision to increase property taxes in response to a levy limit increase will increase outlays for property tax credits and refunds except in the unlikely instance where all affected taxpayers are at their credit and refund maximums. If, on the other hand, local taxes do not change in response to levy limits, there will be no change in property tax relief outlays with other factors the same.

These effects will be strongest for cities or counties at their levy limits. In such a case, a levy limit decrease may force a locality to reduce its levy. This will then decrease property tax relief outlays. In the other direction, a levy limit increase may provide an opportunity to increase local revenues, and if so, would increase property tax relief outlays.

### DIRECT STATE AIDS TO LOCALITIES

Unlike LGA, some aid programs are not included in the levy limit. Two such programs are welfare aids and highway and street aids. In both cases, the aid is tied to local conditions like "approved highway aids" and "reimbursable costs" for welfare aids. However, changes in funding patterns may affect local property tax levies and, in turn, property tax relief outlays. This is an optional linkage since a local decision must occur for property tax relief outlays to be affected.

## CONCLUDING COMMENT

Four general conclusions can be drawn from this examination:

- None of the linkages described prevent any of the aid programs from achieving their stated objectives.
- The linkages are likely to frustrate the efforts of the budget cutters since a decrease in outlays for many of these programs will either directly or indirectly increase outlays for other programs. There is no case where these effects can be expected to overwhelm the initial budget cut; however, in many cases the compensating increases are significant.
- Property owners of certain types of property are likely to pay much less property tax than other owners of like-valued property. Whether or not the particular circumstances causing this result are justified is a policy question.
- A fourth conclusion—which is only suggested here, but for which, empirical evidence will be presented below (chapter 15)—is that the state "property tax relief" aids actually have the economic effect of stimulating a higher level of local government spending than would otherwise occur. Thus, the Minnesota system of linkages among state-to-local-aid programs and the tax system not only results in overly complex and

uncertain intergovernmental arrangements, but over time actually thwarts the basic goals that it was ostensibly intended to achieve.

## ENDNOTES

1. This discussion utilizes U.S. Bureau of the Census definitions of "revenue," "expenditure," and "intergovernmental aid." Thus, the numbers presented here will vary somewhat from data in the remainder of this and subsequent chapters that draw on Minnesota state sources. See U.S. Bureau of the Census, *Governmental Finances in 1982-83,* (Washington: Government Printing Office, October 1984), Tables 5, 13, and 17.

2. This was estimated as follows: for taxes payable in 1983, 52.4% of agricultural homesteads receiving the HC were not receiving the $650 maximum. Therefore, for every decrease in the ASC that affected the HC, 52.4% of agricultural homesteads would receive an increase in the HC equal to 54% of the change. The other 47.6% are already at the $650 maximum, and so will receive no more. The net effect in outlays then is 52.4% x 54% = 28.3%. This estimate is slightly overstated because the HC increase will push some homeowners to the $650 maximum, and only part of their increase will receive the 54% credit. The same method for the state as a whole gives an increase of 23.0% in HC outlays for decreases in other credits affecting the HC. For nonagricultural homesteads, this figure is 22.7%. Differences result from portions of households at the credit maximum. The source for HC payment distribution was: Minnesota Department of Revenue, *Property Taxes Levied in Minnesota (Taxes Payable in 1983),* pp. 196 and 203.

3. Legislative Auditor, *Evaluation of Direct Property Tax Relief Programs* (February 1983), pp. 84-85. These are actually figures that are also influenced by other factors. It is likely that the "pure" effect of the HC on the CB is greater than indicated since other factors, such as increased tax levies, were at the same time exerting an upward influence on outlays.

4. A district's pupil units are calculated as follows: nonhandicapped kindergarten students are weighted as 0.5 pupil units, handicapped kindergarten students and students in grades 1-6 are weighted as 1.0 pupil unit, students in grades 7-12 are counted as 1.4 pupil units, and an additional 0.5 pupil units are added for each pupil whose family receives AFDC.

5. Alan Hopeman, Legislative Analyst, Minnesota House of Representatives Research Department. Letter to Representative John Tomlinson, March 29, 1984.

6. The Minnesota Local Government Aid (LGA) program is analyzed by Michael E. Bell, "Minnesota's Local Government Aids Program," in *Staff Papers,* vol. 2 of the *Final Report of the Minnesota Tax Study Commission,* ed. Robert D. Ebel and Therese J. McGuire (St. Paul: Butterworth Legal Publishers, 1985).

7. Levy limits are discussed in chapter 17 of this volume.

# Part II

# Analysis of Revenues

# 7

# The Individual Income Tax Structure

## INTRODUCTION

In 1956, at the time of the last comprehensive study of the Minnesota tax system, only twenty-nine states levied an income tax on individuals. In 1984, forty states, as well as the District of Columbia, used such a tax. The average U.S. state derived 29% of their 1983 state tax revenues from the individual income tax.[1]

An income tax can be structured to achieve any combination of several goals—to raise revenue, redistribute income, or direct economic behavior. But any tax, no matter what its goals, necessarily represents a compromise among the criteria of a good tax.[2] Primary among these are equity, efficiency (neutrality), competitiveness, and simplicity. While Minnesota's personal income tax must be tested against all these measures, at the state level the simplicity aspects of taxation dominate the other criteria. The state, much more than the federal government, is limited in its ability to alter substantially the distribution of income or the direction of economic behavior. Because of its higher tax rates, the federal income tax is more likely to dominate a taxpayers' economic decisionmaking. Further, attempts to increase sharply the progressivity of the income tax, for example, could lead, at the extreme, to migration of higher-income taxpayers to states with less severe tax systems.

The complexity of an income tax is also fed by the complexity of the economy. To some extent, intricate economic transactions may require an intricate income tax. The federal income tax, however, has become sufficiently riddled with special exceptions to generate serious discussions and proposals for its reform and simplification. In addition, states like Minnesota that begin with some federal concept of a tax base, but attempt through their own tax to counter or enhance tax policies set at the federal level, introduce even more complexity into the system. In all cases, the benefits of attempting to achieve at the state level these other-than-revenue-raising goals are greatly minimized by the much stronger behavioral incentives and disincentives of the federal income tax code. An apt analogy is that of a small boat (a state income tax) following in the wake of a large ship (the federal code). Smooth sailing requires following along.

This analysis, then, is rooted in the view that simplification of the Minnesota income tax would be of enormous benefit to both the state and its taxpayers. In achieving this simplification, it is important to recognize that the distribution of the tax burden, and its degree of progressivity are quite separable from the definition of the tax base. To simplify the income tax is to simplify the derivation of the base; simplification may be most readily achieved by increasing conformity with the federal tax rules. Any distributional consequences of doing so can be remedied by adjusting the state's tax rates. This theme, in fact, drives the analysis of the deductibility of federal income taxes, the use and level of standard and itemized deductions, and Minnesota's allowance of a personal credit. Accordingly, each potential change must not be considered in isolation, but rather must be seen as an integral part of a major structural reform of the Minnesota personal income tax.

This chapter begins with a brief description of Minnesota's income tax structure and of the importance of the income tax to Minnesota revenues. The discussion then shifts to the issue of conformity to the federal income tax as a means of simplifying Minnesota's own tax. With an eye toward adopting federal taxable income or federal adjusted gross income as a starting point, this section presents arguments for and against retention or repeal of the modifications that currently exist in the Minnesota statute. Third, this chapter examines issues related to the distribution of the tax burden, including the tax treatment of the family and the use of credits for many purposes such as tax relief for lower-income persons. The final section summarizes three alternative income tax systems using "conformed" tax bases.

## BASIC STRUCTURE OF THE TAX

As of 1983, all single persons with gross income exceeding $2,800 and all married persons with gross income exceeding $4,100 must file a Minnesota income tax return. Table 1 delineates the computation of the income tax liability under the Minnesota system. Federal adjusted gross income (FAGI) is taken from the federal return (line 32 of form 1040) and adjusted to derive Minnesota gross income. An additional deduction is allowed from this gross base for federal income taxes paid during the year, to yield Minnesota AGI. A taxpayer may take either specific itemized deductions or a standard deduction against AGI to obtain Minnesota taxable income. Minnesota does not require that a taxpayer itemize on his federal return before he can itemize for state purposes. However, married taxpayers must both use the same method for taking deductions on the state return; if one spouse itemizes, so must the other. A progressive nominal rate structure ranging from 1.6% to 16.0% is applied to this tax base to determine before-credit tax liability. Both

TABLE 1
Computation of Minnesota Tax Liability
1984

Federal AGI

Add:
— federal deduction for two-earner married couples

— certain IRA, Keogh, SEP and public retirement plan contributions

— a portion of ACRS deductions not allowed by MN

— interest on certain state and local bonds and scholarship bonds from outside MN

— investment credit recapture

Subtract:
— interest on U.S. bonds

— unemployment compensation and social security benefits taxed at the federal level

— retirement pay exclusion

— certain other pension distributions

Minnesota Gross Income

Subtract: Federal Tax Liability
Minnesota AGI

Subtract:

Minnesota Standard Deduction    OR    Federal Itemized Deductions
(as adjusted, before ZBA)

Minnesota Taxable Income

Apply rates from 1.6% to 16%
Tax Before Credits

Subtract: Tax Credits

Minnesota Tax Liability

refundable and nonrefundable credits are subtracted from the tax to produce the final state tax liability.

ROLE OF THE PERSONAL INCOME TAX IN THE SYSTEM

Minnesota's personal income tax has been and continues to be a prominent element of the state's tax system. Through the 1970s and into the early 1980s it has contributed on average about 40% of the state's tax revenues, and about 22% of all state and local revenues. Its importance has steadily increased to reach 46% of state tax revenues in 1983. This is significantly greater than the 1983 average for all states of 29%, and is the highest of the neighboring states. Wisconsin is the second highest in the region; it relied on its personal income tax to provide 40% of state tax revenues in 1983.

Moreover, as a percent of state personal income, Minnesota's tax is relatively high. During the past decade Minnesotans have paid an average of 3.7% of their personal income in state income tax. In 1983, the rate jumped to 4.3%; while the rate of increase in personal income was down from 11% in 1982 to 5% in 1983, income tax revenues climbed 28%, compared to 11% a year earlier. The tax increase was due in part to an increase in the tax surcharge from 7% in 1982 to 10% in 1984 and in part to lower federal taxes in 1983. In terms of personal income, Minnesota's tax was third highest in the nation behind Delaware and Oregon. In terms of the most recent data on tax effort among the states, Minnesota ranked fifth highest, with an effort of 84.5% above the U.S. average.[3]

## CONFORMITY

As most taxpayers complete their federal income tax returns before beginning their state returns, their burden in filling out their state returns depends largely on the degree of conformity between the state and federal income tax laws. If there is a high degree of conformity, the state tax burden can be completed in thirty minutes or less. If there is little conformity, several hours, several evenings, or even several hundred dollars in accountant and attorney fees may be required to fill out the state tax return. In addition, because a taxpayer does not benefit from having already made computations under federal rules, a nonconforming state statute probably leads to an increased number of inadvertent taxpayer errors, and consequently to higher administrative costs. In the interest of reducing taxpayer compliance costs, inadvertent errors, and administrative costs, a strong case can be made for a high degree of conformity between state and federal income tax laws. It should be recognized, however, as was noted in the introduction, that there may be overriding considerations of equity or efficiency that would lead one to support major departures from the federal tax base.

There is one potential danger at this time of a state like Minnesota moving toward conformity: the federal income tax itself may be restructured significantly in 1985 or 1986 if the administration and the Congress enact measures to narrow the gap, now equal to 5% of GNP, between federal spending and revenues. If the federal government chooses some form of a consumption tax, the federal individual income tax may become a dumping ground for every legislator's favorite tax expenditure. On the positive side, any fundamental changes in (rather than substitutes for) the federal individual income tax will likely take the form of base broadening, thus increasing rather than threatening the potential state tax base. In fact, if state revenues were sufficiently increased by the base broadening of the federal reforms, Minnesota could lower its marginal tax rates.

CONFORMITY IN MINNESOTA

In 1961 Minnesota took a step toward conforming its income tax base to the federal tax base by adopting federal AGI, with certain adjustments, as the measure of Minnesota gross income (MGI). Since 1961, however, frequent changes to the internal revenue code and rejection of or only partial acceptance of those changes by the Minnesota Legislature, have substantially reduced the degree of conformity. In fact, the 1983 Minnesota income tax statute requires as many as forty adjustments to federal AGI to obtain MGI. Minnesota took a second step toward conformity in 1983 when, in lieu of its own list of more than twenty itemized deductions, it adopted itemized deductions as computed under the federal rules, though here, too, Minnesota requires some adjustments to the federal amount.

Table 2 reconciles federal AGI to Minnesota taxable income (line 10 of form M-1) for 1982, the latest year such data are available. Minnesota's taxable base is just less than 66% of federal AGI; only 17% of that gap is attributable to personal deductions. In essence, Minnesota's income tax base differs from the federal tax base in four important respects: (1) Minnesota's adjustments to FAGI, (2) its adjustments to federal itemized deductions, (3) its allowance of a deduction for federal income taxes, and (4) its personal

TABLE 2
Reconciliation of Federal AGI
to Minnesota Taxable Income
1982

| | ($ billions) | |
|---|---|---|
| Federal AGI | $34.4 | 100.0% |
| Two-Earner deduction | .2 | 0.6 |
| Other additions | 1.1 | 3.2 |
| Subtractions | (3.0) | (8.7) |
| Minnesota Gross Income | 32.7 | 95.1 |
| Federal Income Tax Deduction | (4.4) | (12.8) |
| Personal Deductions | (5.7) | (16.6) |
| Minnesota Taxable Income | $22.6 | 65.7% |

*Source:* Minnesota Department of Revenue (1984).

credit and standard deduction. The first three of these deviations are summarized below. A detailed discussion of each of these issues is provided elsewhere.[4]

## CONFORMITY TO THE FEDERAL BASE

*Adjustments to federal adjusted gross income (FAGI) and federal itemized deductions.* If conformity to the federal income tax, and in particular to federal taxable income is desirable, several changes to Minnesota's individual income tax are required. Table 3 summarizes the modifications to FAGI and federal itemized deductions that, arguably, may be most easily justified as candidates for elimination. The table shows the 1985 revenue impact under current law of eliminating each major modification. The other major deviation, the federal tax deduction, is discussed separately below.

From a list of twenty-three categories of adjustments to FAGI and federal itemized deductions identified, only two need to be retained on the basis of a state differing from the federal government. These are U.S. bond interest earned and state income taxes as an itemized deduction.

In the aggregate, the revenues lost from eliminating the additions will be offset by revenues gained from eliminating the subtractions, with only a slight net revenue gain of $13.3 million (Table 3). That is not to say, however, that the changes would be distributionally neutral. Clearly, some taxpayers would be winners, some losers.

Notwithstanding the issues associated with the personal exemption, standard deduction, and filing status, which are discussed in the next section, the acceptance of these recommendations would permit Minnesota to adopt federal taxable income as the starting point of its tax base. One number (line 37 of form 1040) could simply be lifted from the taxpayers' federal return. Again, whether to retain or repeal these modifications should not be decided on the basis of the one-year revenue estimates presented in Table 3; these merely give a sense of the magnitude of the gaps in the tax base. Once Minnesota chooses its tax base—primarily on the grounds of horizontal equity and simplicity (and by choosing conformity Minnesota implicitly trusts the federal government's choice of the tax base)—it can devise a rate schedule to yield the desired revenue and tax burden distribution, as is shown in the final section of this paper.

*Federal income tax deduction.* Minnesota is one of sixteen states that permit the deduction of federal income taxes in computing the state tax base. In Minnesota the deduction, which is taken against Minnesota gross income to obtain Minnesota AGI, is the single largest adjustment to FAGI, totaling $4.5 billion in 1982.

The case for state income tax deduction of federal income taxes paid is a difficult one to make. It rests on the definition and measurement of the appropriate tax base for a state level tax. If one accepts that the income tax base should be defined and measured in terms of a taxpayer's ability to pay taxes, gross income should include all sources and a deduction from income should be allowed only when it would produce a better measure of ability to pay. Theoretically this would require that benefits derived from public services be included in income and that taxes paid be allowed as a deduction.

TABLE 3
Modifications to FAGI and Federal Itemized Deductions
Calendar Year 1985 Revenue Impact

($ millions)

| Modification | Minnesota Revenue Gain[a] (Loss)[b] |
|---|---|
| Federal Adjusted Gross Income | |
| Two-Earner deduction | $ (57.5) |
| IRA, SEP, Keogh contributions | (74.3) |
| Employer "pick-up" contributions | (22.9) |
| Farm losses | (3.0)) |
| Investment credit recapture | (0.8) |
| ACRS | (13.0) |
| Other-state bond interest | (3.0) |
| Other additions | (33.5) |
| Total additions | $(208.0) |
| | |
| Pension exclusion | $ 113.5 |
| Military pay | 14.4 |
| Social security & railroad retirement benefits | 23.9 |
| Unemployment compensation | 11.7 |
| Other subtractions | 54.8 |
| Total subtractions | $ 218.3 |
| | |
| Total − FAGI | $ 10.3 |
| | |
| Itemized Deductions | |
| Charitable contributions | $ (4.5) |
| Education expenses | 7.3 |
| Adoption expenses | .2 |
| | |
| Total − Itemized Deductions | $ 3.0 |
| | |
| Net revenue impact of recommendations | $ 13.3 |

[a]Taxed by U.S., but not Minnesota.
[b]Taxed by Minnesota; not taxed by the U.S.
*Source:* Minnesota Department of Revenue.

Clearly, valuation of public services and assignment of that value to taxpayers is not feasible, and deduction of taxes may not therefore be appropriate.

One rationale for deduction of state taxes at the federal level is as a means of relieving some of the burden of tax overlapping which arises from two levels of government taxing the same base. But as there is no clear need for the same relief to be provided again at the state level, this rationale cannot be used to justify deductibility of federal taxes.

A second common argument that the commission received regarding the merits of maintaining the deductibility of federal taxes paid was that the level of one's federal tax bill is beyond the Minnesota taxpayers' control, and thus to disallow the deductibility amounts to a "tax on a tax." Again, the argument is not persuasive. Although it is certainly true that federal tax law is determined externally by Congress, to say that it is uncontrollable requires quite a leap of faith. Indeed, as evidenced by the large and robust financial planning industry, one could argue that particularly for persons with high incomes, the amount of federal tax paid is more subject to manipulation than most other expenditures. Indeed, at the very highest Minnesota income ranges, the effective rate is slightly more influenced by the effect of itemized deductions than federal deductibility.[5] As for the "tax on a tax" argument, it is useful to come back to an elementary principle of public finance: taxes are the prices paid for public goods. Thus, just as one buys a privately produced automobile, or vacation, or movie for personal use, one also buys a set of federally provided services (e.g., defense). Accordingly, there is no compelling reason for treating one of the services (all of which are part of society's preferences) specially unless some overriding social benefit (e.g., net job creation) is served.

There are several arguments against deductibility of federal taxes. First, as with any deviation from conformity, the deduction adds complexity to the state tax. A separate tax form is needed for computing the portion of federal taxes that may be deducted—only that portion which relates to income included in the Minnesota base. The instructions alone filled three pages in 1983.

Moreover, the interaction between the mutual deduction and the effective marginal tax rates is so abstruse that few taxpayers actually know the combined state and federal marginal tax rate they face. A state income tax increase caused, for example, by an increase in the marginal rate, in turn increases the state tax deduction on the federal return, thereby decreasing federal taxes; but the federal tax cut is diminished by the lower tax deduction on the state return and a higher state tax, which once again impacts the federal return. Agility with simultaneous equations appears to be a prerequisite to understanding the state tax. More importantly, however, though the revenue loss to the state caused by deductibility can be severe, the taxpayer realizes only a small reduction in effective combined federal-state taxes.

Second, because the deduction eliminates a significant portion of the tax base, it is one of the factors contributing to the unusually high level of nominal (statutory) income tax rates in Minnesota. A state with a smaller tax base simply requires higher nominal tax rates to yield revenue equal to a large-base/low-rate state, though effective tax rates—actual tax paid by the taxpayer per dollar of income—will be the same. Of course, other factors contribute to Minnesota's high tax rates, in particular the state's above-average reliance on the income tax as a source of revenue and the state's above-average overall burden. But these factors result in a high actual effective tax burden. In contrast, the deduction of federal income taxes only creates high nominal (statutory) rates, without changing the overall effective tax burden.

And finally, the state should question whether its policy of "reverse revenue sharing" with the U.S. Treasury is desirable or, for that matter, even intended. For that is a practical reality of the provision. When a state permits a deduction for federal taxes paid, it is in effect paying part of the Minnesotan's federal tax bill in the form of forgone state personal income tax revenues.

Table 4 shows an alternative statutory rate schedule for single persons that preserves the same revenue and tax burden distribution as the current Minnesota rate schedule, when applied to a Minnesota tax base that disallows the federal income tax deduction. Because the federal tax is progressive, Minnesota's federal tax deduction increases with income, and high-income taxpayers receive a proportionately greater deduction than lower-income taxpayers. The deduction thus causes the distribution of the state tax burden to be in effect less progressive than is apparent in its nominally progressive rate structure. In fact, as is clearly exposed in the rate schedule in Table 4 where the marginal rates begin decreasing at taxable income levels over $27,000, the result is a regressive tax at the upper end of the income distribution.

In considering the case for or against this deduction, the issues of tax burden discrimination and the tax base should be analyzed separately. If Minnesota were to disallow the deduction of federal income tax in the determination of its tax base, it could adjust the rate structure to produce any revenue yield and any burden distribution that it chooses, including the current ones, as shown in Table 4 where current revenue yield and the burden discrimination are maintained. Given this option, the federal deduction seems superfluous. Its elimination would facilitate taxpayer compliance and understanding, allow the application of lower nominal (statutory) tax rates, and permit the use of a rate structure that more clearly reflects the distribution of the tax burden.

TABLE 4
Alternative 1983 Minnesota Rate Schedule
for Single Persons
(No deduction allowed for federal income taxes paid)

| Income Over | But Not Over | Marginal Tax Rate | Current Law Marginal Tax Rate |
|---|---|---|---|
| 0 | 672 | 1.6% | 1.6% |
| 672 | 1,344 | 2.2 | 2.2 |
| 1,344 | 2,687 | 3.5 | 3.5 |
| 2,687 | 4,030 | 5.3 | 5.8 |
| 4,030 | 5,373 | 6.3 | 7.3 |
| 5,373 | 6,716 | 7.1 | 8.8 |
| 6,716 | 9,401 | 8.1 | 10.2 |
| 9,401 | 12,086 | 9.0 | 11.5 |
| 12,086 | 16,785 | 9.8 | 12.8 |
| 16,785 | 26,855 | 10.0 | 14.0 |
| 26,855 | 36,925 | 9.8 | 15.0 |
| 36,925 | 50,000 | 9.6 | 16.0 |
| 50,000 | 100,000 | 9.4 | 16.0 |
| 100,000 | | 9.2 | 16.0 |

*Note:* The above rate schedule is revenue neutral in FY 1983, based on the Minnesota Department of Revenue 1983 taxpayer sample, and has only minimal redistributional impact. For comparison, the brackets were kept as close as possible to Minnesota's 1983 rate schedule. No other adjustments were made to the tax base, except to eliminate the deduction of federal taxes.

## ISSUES OF TAX LIABILITY DISTRIBUTION ACROSS TAXPAYERS

### FILING STATUS

*Policy considerations.* Tax policy considerations of the income tax treatment of the family and the individual can be separated into three reasonable and generally accepted goals of equity: (1) an income tax should be progressive; (2) married couples with equal combined incomes should pay the same tax, regardless of the relative contribution of each spouse to the combined total; and (3) the tax should not penalize or subsidize marriage, i.e., two working persons who marry should not pay more or less tax simply because they married. These three goals are necessarily conflicting and, in general, no single tax system can achieve them all. For example, a progressive rate structure that taxes the family as a unit will make the tax of a combined income of $20,000 greater than the tax on two separate incomes of $10,000, each of which would be taxed at lower marginal rates, thus imposing a marriage penalty.

The federal income tax generally recognizes the family as the basic taxable unit, and thus emphasizes the achievement of equity among married couples with equal combined incomes. Under federal rules married persons must file a joint tax return for their aggregate income and they face a different rate schedule from single persons. Equity among couples, however, comes at the cost of neutrality with respect to marital status. It directly conflicts with goal three. Depending on the distribution of income within the couple, two persons who marry pay more or less than the combined tax of the two persons as singles. The so-called marriage penalty was only recently reduced by the enactment of a special deduction for two-earner families.

In contrast, Minnesota's income tax is, in general, directed at the individual taxpayer. Married persons may file joint, separate, or combined returns, and both singles and married persons are subject to the same rate schedule. A two-column combined return, which separately computes the tax for each spouse, is generally the most advantageous filing alternative for married persons. Because the tax is computed for each spouse, the couple gets two runs up the rate schedule; each bracket is used twice before moving on to the next highest tax rate. The more even the distribution of income between the spouses the lower the combined tax. This benefit creates an incentive to shift income to the lower-earning spouse when possible, by, for example, transferring ownership of income-producing property, adjusting partnership allocations, or altering salaries from a family-owned business.

By allowing income to follow the individual, regardless of marital status, Minnesota averts any marriage penalty. However, a horizontal inequity is created as two couples may pay substantially different tax bills depending on who earns the income. The differential between one- and two-earner couples can be large at levels of combined income in the middle brackets.

*Minnesota Options.*  Assuming that Minnesota chooses to have a progressive income tax, the ultimate realization of either of the other two equity goals hinges on a difficult policy question: does the state want to tax, and thus measure equity among individuals or households? The confusion in Minnesota's current treatment is perhaps reflected in its simultaneous use of a tax credit that attempts to help one-earner couples, but a filing system that helps two-earner couples. The state provides a $50 homemaker credit to any household that takes care of a dependent child. This suggests that the state wants to ease the tax burden of one-earner families relative to two-earner families.

The federal income tax represents a compromise among the goals, but it nevertheless remains rooted in the concept of the family as the taxable unit. The state has three basic options:

*1. Retain the Current System.*  The combined filing, emphasizing the individual as taxpayer, seems increasingly appealing in a world where the "typical family unit" is no longer typical. Marriages are less permanent, and less commonly a prerequisite to a two-adult, two-earner household. At the extreme this might call for mandatory separate filing.

Separate filing based on the individual as the taxpaying unit would, however, retain three problems. First, one-earner families would continue to pay a higher tax than two-earner families of equal combined income. However, an argument can be made that a tax liability differential, if not the large one that occurs under Minnesota's system, may be justified. The argument is that perhaps the one-earner household, which benefits from the efforts of a full-time homemaker (unmeasured imputed income) and does not incur the additional (often nondeductible) expenses of having two workers, does in fact enjoy a higher standard of living and a greater ability to pay taxes. In essence the two families do not have equal ability to pay taxes and therefore should have different tax liabilities. Note that at the federal level the two-wage-earner deduction addresses this problem to some extent.

The second problem with separate filing is that the incentive to shift income to the lower-earning spouse would remain. The steeper the range of bracket rates, the stronger the incentive. Because the federal tax, however, does not create such an inclination, it is possible that the state tax alone is not potent enough to motivate such shifting between spouses.

Third, and most important, as long as the federal government taxes the combined income of the couple, complexities are added to filing the Minnesota form. Taxpayers essentially must recalculate income for each spouse.

*2. Joint returns with income splitting.*   Minnesota could eliminate the tax discrepancies among couples with varying distributions of equal income and still avoid a marriage penalty by permitting couples to treat combined income as if it is equally earned by each spouse, regardless of who actually earns or owns the sources of income. This method of taxation carries the idea of the couple as an economic unit to the extreme. A couple would in effect face tax brackets twice the size of those applicable to a single person earning half as much. Instead of using a separate rate schedule for joint filers, the state could still use one rate schedule for both types of taxpayers and simply permit married persons to split their combined income equally in two. Under this system, if two people marry, their tax would go down or stay the same, depending on their relative contributions to combined earnings, but the tax would never increase. The maximum tax bonus from marrying would occur when a single person marries a nonworking spouse. This penalty on being single may be particularly unjustified when the cost savings (such as shared rent) that married couples realize by living together are acknowledged.

More than ten states incorporate an income-splitting concept into their income taxes. Moving from its current system to one of income splitting among married couples would, however, generate substantial revenue losses for Minnesota. Couples whose income split is more skewed than fifty-fifty would receive tax cuts relative to what they now pay.

*3. Compromise between Options 1 and 2.*   The first option equates tax liabilities among individuals, without regard to marital status, and thus couples with equal combined incomes but different income splits are treated differently. The second alternative equates tax liabilities among couples, and consequently imposes a penalty on being single. A marriage bonus occurs for any couple whose income split is not fifty-fifty. Minnesota could, like the federal government, engineer a compromise by having two rate schedules, one for married couples, one for singles. While acknowledging the family as the taxpaying unit the rate schedule for joint filers could be constructed to be neutral with respect to marriage for any given income split. That is, a separate rate schedule could be constructed such that the tax under the joint rate schedule for a couple whose income is split, for example, eighty-twenty would be the same as the total tax of those taxpayers with each member's tax liability separately computed under the single rate schedule. A couple whose income is more evenly distributed than is assumed in the joint rate schedule would be penalized (a marriage penalty) while a couple whose income is actually more skewed would benefit (a marriage bonus).

The advantages of this rate schedule over Option 2, which simply doubles the width of the brackets of the single schedule (preserving tax liability only for couples with a fifty-fifty split) are that the overall revenue loss is less, and it may be perceived as being more equitable as some taxpayers experience bonuses, others losses. The closer the income split assumed in the table is to the actual mean income split of all taxpayers, the lower is the aggregate revenue consequence of switching to joint returns and the smaller are the tax savings (losses) realized by most couples when they marry.

To summarize, if the appropriate unit is the individual, then Minnesota's system is designed reasonably well. If, instead, the couple (family) is determined to be the appropriate unit of taxation, the Minnesota system must be changed. In the final section, married couple rate schedules based on an eighty-eighty split of income are constructed and presented as policy alternatives.

## TAX CREDITS

Tax credits are an important tool for relieving unusual burdens for certain taxpayers. Minnesota's personal credit and low-income credit help to differentiate the tax treatment of families of different size (and the elderly or handicapped), and of lower-income persons. The low-income credit as currently formulated has several drawbacks. It is complicated, requiring a separate worksheet and a separate tax table in the income tax package. Also, because it is not indexed, the credit has not kept pace with the rest of the income tax structure and has become less effective as a source of low-income tax relief. Minnesota could elect to grant a credit similar to the federal earned income credit, or even a percentage of the federal credit. This conforming method would be a simpler means than the current method. In 1984 the state legislature did consider adopting one-half the earned income credit. Though the proposal was defeated, it was considered neither in conjunction with an enhanced standard deduction, nor in the context of a major reform.

Minnesota also grants a credit for taxes paid to another state or a Canadian province. This credit prevents the inequity of taxpayers paying state-level tax twice on the same income.

In contrast to these credits that are part of the structure of the Minnesota income tax, tax credits may also be used as a vehicle for delivering a variety of subsidies. In general, a substantial amount of income tax complexity results from using the income tax to encourage or subsidize economic activities. The government could grant a deduction for a particular type of expenditure, such as charitable contributions, and thereby encourage taxpayers to make contributions. But because deductions might have a tendency to appear unfair—they are generally only available to taxpayers who itemize, and their value increases with the bracket of the taxpayer— both Congress and state legislatures have turned to the income tax credit. Credits generate their own list of problems, however. First, all taxpayers must contend with the credit, either in the instructions, or as a line on the form, to determine their eligibility. Those who are not eligible may be left with the perception that somehow they have been cheated; that others got something they did not. Second, unless the credit is refundable, it is only useful to those with a tax liability. Refundable credits, on the other hand, cause otherwise nonfilers to file a return simply to get their refund, something tax administrators want to avoid.

Table 5 summarizes the other tax credits (other than the low-income credit, the personal credit, and the credit for taxes paid to other states) available to Minnesota taxpayers, all of which have been adopted since 1974. Each of these credits is designed to decrease the effective cost of the expenditures of a very narrowly defined group of taxpayers. In fact, none of these credits is claimed on even 10% of all returns.

The policy question is straightforward: could these subsidies more properly be made through direct cash grants? Use of credits to accomplish goals that are unrelated to equity criteria may be asking too much from the income tax. Minnesota may want to prune its list of tax credits back to those that may be required in the pursuit of equity. And, as pointed out in the discussion of the tax treatment of the family, Minnesota should avoid tax credits that are inconsistent with its income tax system as a whole.


## TAX ALTERNATIVES BASED ON CONFORMITY

In this section, three options to Minnesota's current system are presented. The common characteristic is that each increases the degree of conformity of Minnesota's personal income tax to the federal tax. The two major

TABLE 5
Credits To The Minnesota Personal Income Tax
1984

| | Estimated Calendar Year 1985 Revenue Cost (in millions) | Year Adopted | Percent of Returns Using the Credit in 1982 |
|---|---|---|---|
| Nonrefundable[a] | | | |
| Conservation Tillage | $0.4 | 1985 | b |
| Homemaker | 1.9 | 1978 | 2.9 |
| Political contribution | 6.0 | 1974 | 6.5 |
| Pollution control | 2.0 | 1979 | 0.1 |
| Residential energy | 9.3 | 1979 | 0.2 |
| Small business equity investment | 2.6 | 1983 | n/a |
| Refundable | | | |
| Dependent care | 15.1 | 1977 | 1.5 |

*Source:* Minnesota Department of Revenue

a    This table excludes three "structural," non-tax-expenditure credits: the low income and personal credits, which are considered separately in another section of this paper, and the credit for income taxes paid to another state.

b    The credit is not effective until 1985 and is not expected to apply to more than 250 to 350 taxpayers, or less than 0.02 percent of estimated 1985 returns.

n/a  Not Available

components of conformity, tax base conformity and taxpaying unit conformity, are incorporated into each.

If the arguments for defining the taxpaying unit as the individual are found to be compelling, Minnesota's method of filing could be retained while still conforming on the tax base. But simplicity considerations may be overriding. Without conformity on the taxpaying unit, the calculations required to define individual income for the Minnesota form can be very complex.

These three options are merely illustrative. The state could consider any number of rate schedules and modifications to the tax base. The three major options are:

*Option A:*    Flat rate tax on federal tax liability.

*Option B:*    Graduated rate structure on federal taxable income (married couple rate schedule based on eighty-twenty income split)

*Option C:*    Graduated rate structure on federal adjusted gross income (married couple rate schedule based on eighty-twenty income split)

*Option A.* A flat rate tax on federal tax liability would be piggybacked—administered and collected by the federal government—or it could be controlled by the state. A revenue-neutral shift from the current Minnesota tax to a single-rate tax levied on federal tax liability would require a state tax rate of 43.0%, based on estimated calendar year 1985 tax revenues. This tax is necessarily progressive. Under this option, for example, taxpayers with Minnesota AGI between $5,000 and $10,000 would pay approximately 3%

## TABLE 6
### Statutory (Nominal) Rates for Options B and C

Option B:   Federal Taxable Income as the Tax Base

| Singles | | Married Couples | |
|---|---|---|---|
| Size of FTI $ | Rate % | Size of FTI $ | Rate % |
| $    0 –  $ 4,000 | 0.0 | – $  5,000 | 0.0 |
| 4,000 –    6,000 | 4.0 | $ 5,000 –    7,500 | 3.2 |
| 6,000 –    9,000 | 7.0 | 7,500 –   11,250 | 5.6 |
| 9,000 –   12,000 | 9.0 | 11,250 –   15,000 | 7.2 |
| 12,000 –   15,000 | 9.5 | 15,000 –   18,750 | 7.6 |
| 15,000 –   18,000 | 9.8 | 18,750 –   22,500 | 8.6 |
| 18,000 –   21,000 | 10.0 | 22,500 –   26,250 | 8.8 |
| 21,000 –   24,000 | 10.1 | 26,250 –   30,000 | 8.9 |
| 24,000 –   28,000 | 10.2 | 30,000 –   40,000 | 9.6 |
| 28,000 –   32,000 | 10.3 | 40,000 –   45,000 | 9.7 |
| $32,000 and over | 10.4 | 45,000 –   60,000 | 10.1 |
| | | 60,000 –   75,000 | 10.2 |
| | | 75,000 –  120,000 | 10.3 |
| | | $120,000 and Over | 10.4 |

Total Revenue Raised: $2,114 million (CY 1985)

Option C:   FAGI as the Tax Base

| Singles | | Married Couples | |
|---|---|---|---|
| Size of FAGI $ | Rate % | Size of FAGI $ | Rate % |
| $    0 –  $ 4,000 | 0.0 | 0 – $  5,000 | 0.0 |
| 4,000 –    6,000 | 4.7 | $ 5,000 –    7,500 | 3.8 |
| 6,000 –    8,000 | 5.7 | 7,500 –   10,000 | 4.6 |
| 8,000 –   11,000 | 6.7 | 10,000 –   13,750 | 5.4 |
| 11,000 –   14,000 | 7.7 | 13,750 –   17,500 | 6.2 |
| 14,000 –   19,000 | 8.2 | 17,500 –   23,750 | 7.5 |
| $19,000 and over | 8.6 | 23,750 –   30,000 | 7.8 |
| | | 30,000 –   40,000 | 8.0 |
| | | 40,000 –   55,000 | 8.2 |
| | | 55,000 –   70,000 | 8.4 |
| | | $70,000 and Over | 8.6 |

Total Revenue Raised:   $2,117 million (CY 1985)

of their gross income in tax, compared to about 11% for taxpayers with original MAGI over $50,000. Consequently, tax increases are generally experienced by higher-income taxpayers. In aggregate, taxpayers in the lower brackets would also have some tax increase relative to current law, primarily because of the loss of the low-income credit and certain subtraction modifications. The state could compensate for this impact by providing some simplified form of low-income tax credit, and, for example, a credit based on taxable retirement income.

*Options B and C.* Table 6 outlines a graduated tax on federal taxable income (line 37 of form 1040) and another on federal adjusted gross income (line 32). The federal personal exemption is incorporated in each in place of Minnesota's current personal credit. Even with tax base conformity, the state retains control of its zero bracket amount, which is set here at $4,000 for single persons ($5,000 for married couples filing jointly).

The rate schedules for the two federal tax bases were designed to raise virtually equivalent amounts of revenue and to be progressive. Note that the nominal rates are lower with the broader federal base, FAGI. The rate schedules for married couples are based on eliminating any marriage penalty or bonus for couples with income splits of eighty-twenty. All other couples will experience either bonuses or penalties.

In Table 7, the resulting effective tax rate for the options B and C, are compared to the effective rates resulting under current law. It is evident that the choice of tax base has little to do with the amount of revenue raised or the distribution of the burden. Any level and distribution can be achieved through rate structure adjustments once a tax base has been chosen.

To design a simple, well-understood individual income tax system, conformity to some federal base and, possibly, to the federal definition of

TABLE 7
The Distribution of the Burden:
Average Effective Tax Rates for Current Law,
Option B, and Option C

| Original Minnesota | Taxes as a % of MGI | | |
|---|---|---|---|
| Gross Income Class | Current Law | Option B | Option C |
| $    0 –    5,000 | 0.4 | 0.6 | 0.6 |
| 5,000 –   10,000 | 1.8 | 1.4 | 1.4 |
| 10,000 –   20,000 | 4.0 | 3.4 | 3.3 |
| 20,000 –   30,000 | 5.3 | 4.6 | 4.5 |
| 30,000 –   40,000 | 6.0 | 5.1 | 5.1 |
| 40,000 –   50,000 | 6.4 | 5.5 | 5.5 |
| 50,000 –  100,000 | 6.9 | 6.1 | 6.2 |
| $100,000 and over | 6.5 | 6.5 | 6.5 |
| Overall | 5.5 | 4.8 | 4.8 |

the taxpaying unit, is probably desirable. Horizontal equity may also be enhanced by such a change and any degree of vertical equity, i.e., progressivity, can be accomplished in the rate structure.

## RECOMMENDATION

### INDIVIDUAL INCOME TAX REDUCTION AND SIMPLIFICATION

- To address the fact that Minnesota's individual income tax is overly complex, the commission recommends that the Minnesota tax base conform to federal taxable income.
- Because the deduction for federal taxes paid results in a regressive, unstable, complex tax, the commission recommends that this deduction be eliminated.

(The commission recognizes that, even if, on average, taxpayers are held harmless or are benefited by these changes, some individual taxpayers will pay more. This result will occur, since under the previous definition of Minnesota's tax base, some individuals had zero or negative Minnesota taxable income and thus paid no Minnesota taxes. Under the new definition, some of these taxpayers will have taxable income and be required to pay taxes in Minnesota. Also, those individuals who, within their income class, had a relatively large deduction for federal taxes paid, may pay more.)

- The commission recommends that Minnesota conform to federal filing status, adopting the federal definition of the taxpaying unit which is the married couple (the family). This change will result in a simpler tax system and thus reduced taxpayer compliance costs. It also results in equal treatment for married couples with equal combined incomes (horizontal equity based on household income). The commission recognizes that marriage neutrality is lost by this change.
- To avoid excessive use of the tax system to accomplish goals other than raising revenue and redistributing income, the commission recommends that the fuel tax credit and the small business equity credit be eliminated. The commission recommends that the homemaker credit be eliminated since under federal filing status the credit is no longer necessary. The commission recommends retention of the political contribution credit, the dependent and child care credit, the residential energy credit, and the low-income credit because they are effectively targeted. For simplicity, the design of these credits should conform closely to the corresponding federal credits.
- To design an individual income tax that will contribute to a fair, simple, neutral, competitive Minnesota tax system, the commission recommends an income tax reduction of approximately 20% which is distributed so as

to concentrate the tax cuts in the lower- to middle-income brackets while ensuring that all brackets experience declines in their effective rates. This added progressivity of the income tax is explicitly recommended in order to use the income tax as the vehicle for offsetting the added regressivity of the commission's property tax proposal. In making this recommendation, the commission stresses that the sum of the burdens of the income tax, property tax, and sales tax results in a reduction of the effective tax rates for Minnesota taxpayers across all income classes. This recommendation clearly illustrates the point that by making the property tax more explicit and redesigning the mix and structure of the big three (income, sales, and property) taxes, Minnesota can preserve its commitment to distributing the tax burden according to ability to pay, set in place a tax system that removes the built-in incentives for higher local government spending (e.g., removal of the property tax credits) and further promote overall job growth (through the general reduction in personal income tax burdens and lower property taxes on commercial/industrial property.)

• The commission is neutral regarding the issue of the tuition, transportation, and nonreligious textbooks deductions. This decision stems solely from the fact that due to U.S. constitutional considerations, no other remedies (e.g., credits, direct expenditures) are available to the state.

## ENDNOTES

1. U.S. Department of Commerce, Bureau of the Census, *State Government Tax Collections,* 1983. Table 3.

2. The six criteria (goals) adopted by the commission are presented in chapter 1.

3. For a discussion, see chapter 4 on "Minnesota Fiscal Comparisons" in this volume. Minnesota's 1982 tax-effort index for the personal income tax is 184.5, where the U.S. average equals 100.0. Four states have higher taxes: New York (213.5), Oregon (197.9), Delaware (189.1), and the District of Columbia (185.0).

4. Sunley, Emil M. and Mary M. Walz, "Simplification of Minnesota's Personal Income Tax," *Staff Papers,* vol. 2 of the *Final Report of the Minnesota Tax Study Commission,* ed. Robert D. Ebel and Therese J. McGuire (St. Paul: Butterworth Legal Publishers, 1985).

5. Data supplied by the Minnesota Department of Revenue shows that as taxpayers move through the very high Minnesota adjusted gross income (MAGI) brackets (beginning at $100,000) the Minnesota effective rates increase and then decline (at a MAGI $1 million and above) at about the same rate under the two scenarios of (a) current law except elimination of federal deductibility and (b) current law except itemized deductions. In fact, the power of itemized deductions in lowering effective rates is slightly greater than that of federal deductibility.

# 8

# Indexation of the Individual Income Tax

## INTRODUCTION

In 1979, Minnesota enacted a form of tax indexing, a mechanism whereby the major items of the individual income tax code that are stated in fixed dollar terms (the personal credit, maximum amount of the standard deduction, and the tax bracket boundaries) are annually adjusted to allow for inflation. The fundamental idea behind tax indexing is to prevent non-legislated increases in tax burdens: those that result solely from inflation, automatically increasing peoples' tax burdens even though their real incomes—income adjusted for inflation—have not risen proportionately.

Unlike some other indexing states, Minnesota first adopted indexing in a relatively comprehensive way.[1] However, in recent years, the tax law has become so convoluted in the attempt to accomplish other policy objectives that Minnesota cannot now be said truly to have tax indexing. Indeed, in applying the commission's goals of simplicity, equity, and accountability, a case can be made for either moving back toward a "clean" measure or of scrapping the idea altogether.

This chapter is organized in two sections. The first, the "Statement of the Problem," provides a discussion of the effect of the interplay between inflation and a progressive individual income tax as a way of laying out the issues. The second section, "Indexing in Minnesota," describes how indexing operates in Minnesota.

## STATEMENT OF THE PROBLEM

Under stable (noninflation) price conditions and economic growth, the yield of a progressive personal income tax increases more than proportionately as income increases and the burden is distributed among taxpayers in accordance with legislated criteria of tax equity. However, during periods of increase in the general price level of the magnitude we have recently been experiencing in the United States, the personal income tax may change its legislated character.[2] With inflation, nonlegislated tax increases occur that produce an arbitrary redistribution of the tax burden. Concomitantly, real tax revenues to the state grow more rapidly than personal incomes, thus potentially generating a larger public sector. As a result, inflation creates a situation that subverts intended legislative tax policy and, as a result, poses a set of policy choices that differ from those in a world of relative price stability.

To illustrate how inflation can lead to automatic tax increases, consider a married Minnesota taxpayer, who is part of a family of four, and had a 1983 income (wages only) of $15,000. The taxpayer files a joint federal return, then moves to the Minnesota return using both the 10% standard deduction and the personal credit ($68 per person in 1983).[3] Under these conditions, the family's Minnesota income tax bill comes to $754, giving an effective tax rate (tax due divided by current income) of 5.0%. (See Table 1).

Now, assume that the economy experiences an inflation for the next four years of 7% per year and that the taxpayer's income just keeps pace with inflation—that is, the family's before-tax real income (purchasing power before taxes) is maintained. As Table 1 shows, the taxpayer's nominal or money income rises to $19,662—a 31% increase—just enough to maintain a constant real income before taxes. But, the tax bill rises by nearly 67% over 1983 levels and, as a result, the effective rate jumps by 1.4% from 5.0% to 6.4%.

Why, with no change in real income, might the relative increase in the Minnesota tax bill be twice that of nominal income? Because in this example two key code provisions—the personal credit and the tax bracket boundaries—were eroded in terms of their real (constant dollar) value.* As a result, the taxpayer's after-state-tax income is actually reduced from $14,246 in 1983 to $14,307 between 1983 and 1987.

INDEXATION: EFFECT ON THE TAXPAYER

Full indexing eliminates this automatic-inflation, progressive-income-tax spiral. Under an indexed system, the fixed-dollar provisions of the tax code (the personal credits, the maximum amount allowable under the standard deduction and the income tax brackets) are increased each year by the rate of inflation as measured, for example, by the consumer price index (CPI).[4] With indexing, incomes that increase at the rate of inflation are no longer automatically subject to higher effective tax rates and thus, the taxpayer's real income (purchasing power) after taxes remains unchanged.

What would have happened had the taxpayer's income increased faster than inflation, say by 10% per year to $21,961 by 1987? Under an indexed

---

* In lieu of itemizing deductions, one may claim a standard deduction equal to 10% of Minnesota AGI up to a maximum of $2,250. This maximum is not reached in this example. Were the taxpayer constrained by the maximum, the increase in effective rates would have been even greater than provided in this illustration.

system, the increase up to the inflation induced amount—i.e., up to $19,662—would be held harmless in terms of effective tax rates. However, the difference of $2,299 (i.e., $21,961 minus $19,662) would be subject to a higher effective tax rate as the taxpayer moved into a higher income tax bracket. But note—only that portion of the taxpayer's increase in real income was subject to the higher tax bracket amounts. There was no automatic inflation tax and thus, after taxes, the family still has a higher purchasing power in 1987 than 1983.

Conversely, had the taxpayer's nominal income failed to keep pace with inflation—i.e., to have risen to less than $19,662 by 1987, full indexation would result in a lower effective tax rate.

PUBLIC SECTOR EFFECT

The discussion above focuses on taxpayer burden. But, what about the other player in the game—i.e., the Minnesota government? The answer is

TABLE 1
Inflation Induced Tax Changes[a]
(Change In Minnesota Income Tax Burden For A
Hypothetical Family of Four Assuming a 7% Annual
Average Rate of Inflation and Constant Real Income)

|  | 1983 | 1985 | 1987 |
|---|---|---|---|
| Minnesota Gross Income | $15,000 | $17,174 | $19,662 |
| Less: Federal Taxes Paid | 1,018 | 1,166 | 1,334 |
| Minnesota Adjusted Gross Income | 13,982 | 16,008 | 18,327 |
| Less: Standard Deduction | 1,398 | 1,601 | 1,833 |
| Minnesota Taxable Income | 12,584 | 14,407 | 16,494 |
| Tentative Tax Due | 1,026 | 1,265 | 1,530 |
| Less Credits | 272 | 272 | 272 |
| Total Tax Due | 754 | 993 | 1,258 |
| Effective Tax Rate[b] | 5.0% | 5.8% | 6.4% |
| Percent Increase In Nominal Income (1983 base) | --- | 14.5% | 31.1% |
| Percent Increase In Nominal Tax (1983 base) | --- | 31.7% | 66.8% |
| Real Income After State-Tax (1983 dollars) | $14,246 | $14,132 | $14,037 |
| Real Income After State plus Federal Tax (1983 dollars) | 13,228 | 13,114 | 13,021 |

Source:    Staff Calculations.

[a]Assumes federal income tax is indexed.

[b]Current year tax due divided by current year income.

that unless a progressive income tax is fully indexed, the government automatically reaps windfall tax revenues with the legislature never even having to discuss the topic. The equation is quite simple: without indexing, as the taxpayer's effective tax rises and thus his/her after-tax income falls, the extra real dollars paid by the taxpayer end up in the state treasury. In the example in Table 1, the taxpayer's loss of after-tax income of $209 ($14,246 minus $14,037) between 1983 and 1987 went to the Minnesota treasury.

## EQUITY

There is more to the problem of the interplay between inflation and a progressive income tax than the fact that tax burdens automatically rise in the absence of indexation. Tax burdens not only rise, but they do so in an arbitrary and inequitable manner.

General price level increases, which result in corresponding increases in taxpayer income, subject larger portions of the income to highest applicable marginal (and, therefore, effective) tax rates. In addition, the effect on various taxpayers is not uniform; taxpayers move from one marginal rate bracket to another unevenly because the brackets vary in width. The bracket effect is greatest for persons whose taxable income rises through ranges where tax brackets are narrow and the increases in marginal tax rates are relatively the largest. In general, in Minnesota, the bracket effect is larger for the low- and lower-middle-income groups than for the higher-income groups.

Distortions in income tax liabilities across income classes stemming from inflation are not limited to those created by the gradual movement into higher tax brackets. If incomes increase from inflation while the personal credit remains unchanged, there is an increase in the proportion of total income subject to tax. The concomitant increase in tax liabilities will be greatest for those families with low income and many dependents. In short, not only is the term *bracket creep* (often used to describe the problem of an unindexed tax) incorrect, since it ignores other items of a tax code defined in fixed dollar terms, it is also misleading because it implies that the nominal graduated rate structure makes a tax progressive. Even if the Minnesota tax had a flat rather than a graduated rate structure, as long as it had a fixed-dollar personal credit (or personal exemption or standard deduction) it would qualify as a progressive tax.

## POLITICAL ACCOUNTABILITY

Politics is, or ought to be, about choice. Pressures for higher spending—education, highways, welfare, economic development programs—make the choices difficult and, at times, even unsavory. If current taxes do not cover spending plans, the legislature must consider either tax increases or spending cuts.

What can be said for indexing is that it promotes honesty. What full indexing requires—and it is as simple as this—is that if the legislature wants to reap the benefits from the inflation tax, it has to meet and vote to do so. Indexing does not lower taxes, and it does not create revenue shortfalls. It simply forces a governor and a legislature to make choices openly.

Conversely, what makes the repeal or lesser use of indexing or (as discussed below with respect to the Minnesota law) so attractive to some is that it obscures and confuses one of those choices: raising taxes. Without indexing, increases will occur again and again, automatically and irreversibly. As one commentator has put it:[5]

"[the legislative body] assumes that it cannot be accused of doing what it cannot seem to be doing. This seems dishonest because it is."

The fundamental point bears repeating: indexing does not require that taxes be lowered. It only requires that if taxes are to be raised, the legislature must do so visibly.

## INDEXING IN MINNESOTA

As noted above, Minnesota does not now have what one could truly call tax indexation. At first glance it certainly has something that looks like indexing. There is, for example, an inflation adjustment factor that may be applied to the personal credits, standard deduction maximum, and the tax bracket boundaries. But a closer look at the system reveals that the system is not only complex, but that the complexity works in a manner that

- results in an inflation adjustment unrelated to generally accepted measures of ability to pay;
- tends to favor the government at the expense of the individual in his/her role as taxpayer;
- provides a political escape hatch whereby the inflation tax is automatically triggered as fiscal choices become increasingly difficult; and
- creates problems for tax administrators.

### THE MINNESOTA ARITHMETIC AND ABILITY TO PAY

Because Minnesota law permits one to deduct federal income taxes in computing Minnesota adjusted gross income (MAGI), in a period of inflation (and an indexed federal tax), MAGI will grow more slowly than inflation. Why? Because the taxes permitted for purposes of federal deductibility are growing faster than inflation. Accordingly, state law requires the commissioner of revenue estimate an adjustment factor used to "gross up" MAGI—i.e., one designed to undo the fact that federal taxes paid are deductible. The results are arbitrary and capricious.* This is true for two reasons. First, it shows a basic inconsistency in the income tax law: on the one hand, the legislature has said federal deductibility is desirable; on the other hand, through this adjustment factor it takes part of it away. One could argue that either federal deductibility is or is not appropriate policy. If it is, the adjustment factor should go. If it is not, federal deductibility itself can be eliminated and the adjustment factor is not needed.

Second, the adjustment factor frustrates equity. This is so because the effect of the factor is to define the tax base for the individual so that it is neither federal nor Minnesota adjusted gross income, both reasonable measures of ability to pay. Instead, the tax base for the individual is a value related to some average federal tax bill, something that for many taxpayers is unrelated to past or present ability to pay.

MINIMIZING THE POWER OF INDEXATION

In the first part of this chapter, the point was made that what makes indexation attractive from both an equity and accountability viewpoint is that it isolates the taxpayer from automatic increases in effective tax rates as money (rather than real) income increases. All that is required to accomplish this for Minnesota (or any state) would be to index all tax code items that are stated in fixed-dollar limits by a measure of price level change—e.g., the CPI.

This would, quite simply, keep the taxpayer even with the personal income tax, regardless of whether his/her real income rises, falls, or stays the same over time. For example:

• if real income stays the same, the effective tax rate stays the same;
• if real income increases, the effective tax rate increases on that portion of the taxpayer's income that rose in excess of the rate of inflation; and
• if real income falls (inflation outpaces earning power), the taxpayer's effective tax rate falls.

Minnesota law, however, is designed so that the state treasury wins regardless of the change in income. That is, it generates added real tax revenues as Minnesotans' real incomes rise (this is as it should be); but its real revenues do not fall if the taxpayers' real incomes fall.

---

* The adjustment factor applies whether inflation occurs or not. Thus, any change in federal taxes will be compensated for by the adjusted factor.

This special feature is the result of a 1980 law (effective 1981) provision that the inflation adjustment for purposes of indexing shall be the lesser of the growth in the CPI or the percentage increase in Minnesota gross income between the previous year and the current tax year. The result is that the indexation is not symmetrical. If taxpayers' real incomes rise faster than the CPI, the CPI is used (as it would under true indexation), and the taxpayers and the government share in those gains. But, if the CPI rises faster than average Minnesota income—i.e., real income across the state falls as inflation outpaces rises in nominal (money) incomes, the taxpayers' effective tax rates are not permitted to fall, since now the inflation adjustment is based on the lower nominal income level. The result is that effective tax rates rise and after-tax purchasing power declines while the government's share of total income automatically rises. And, because this occurs automatically, the legislature never has to meet. In short, this complexity raises more than an issue of simplicity. That the inflation-induced increases in tax revenue can be obtained without ad hoc political action is in opposition to the commission's goals of equity and accountability.

POLITICAL ESCAPE HATCH

Finally, there is a third special feature of the Minnesota tax law that minimizes the power of indexation. As a result of laws enacted by the 1982 legislature, if by September 15 of the calendar year the commissioner of finance determines that receipts will be insufficient to fund appropriations, which include a $250 million budget reserve, this triggers a full or partial suspension of any indexation (inflation adjustment). Taxes are automatically allowed to rise in order to maintain the appropriations and the reserve. Again, the legislature neet not meet.

SIMPLICITY IN TAX ADMINISTRATION

The complexity in the tax law creates difficulties for tax administrators. This is particularly true regarding the subtle issue of what the legislature means by "average gross income" for Minnesota for purposes of computing the lesser of the growth in CPI or average income. The law requires that the "best available data sources and reasonable forecasting procedures be used."[6] This requires a decision on forecasting techniques, judgments regarding behavior of income and filer growth, a guess as to where Minnesota is in the present business cycle (which, in turn affects income and number of filers) and "numerous assumptions about the relationship between Minnesota and U.S. statistics on employment and income."[7] With all this administrative complexity and uncertainty, which must be sorted out annually, it is not clear that the intent of even the 1982 amendments are being achieved.

## RECOMMENDATION

### COMPLETE INDEXATION OF THE INDIVIDUAL INCOME TAX

The commission not only recognizes that inflation brings increases in real income tax revenue and introduces distortions in tax equity, but also that taxpayers may not readily perceive the automatic real tax increase that occurs from the inflation-personal-income-tax interplay. The commission finds that the current indexing scheme in Minnesota is so convoluted that Minnesota's individual income tax cannot honestly be referred to as an indexed tax. This is particularly true because of the use of the lesser of the consumer price index or average Minnesota income for purposes of making an inflation adjustment to the personal credits, standard deduction, and tax bracket boundaries, and the provision that permits any form of indexation to be suspended by the commissioner of finance in a period of fiscal stress.

Accordingly, the commission recommends that in order to achieve the goals of equity, accountability, and certainty in taxation, personal income taxes should not be allowed to increase automatically as a result of inflation, but rather as a result of overt legislative action. This requires that unless the legislature convenes to suspend indexation for any one year, the Minnesota personal credits, standard deduction, and tax bracket boundaries be indexed annually by the full amount of the consumer price index or some generally accepted measure of price level change. In order to enhance the goals of political accountability and tax equity, the legislature should repeal the provision that permits the commissioner of finance to suspend indexation.

## ENDNOTES

1. The inflation adjustment was based on 85% of the percentage increase in the consumer price index for consumers in the Minneapolis-St. Paul metropolitan area. An excellent analysis and discussion of indexation in Minnesota is provided in Research Division, Minnesota Department of Revenue, *Income Tax Indexing,* A Report to the Governor and the Minnesota Legislature, Report 128 (May 1982). See especially the analysis by Daniel A. Salomone, p. 85-91.

2. *U.S. Council of Economic Advisors, Economic Report of the President, Washington, D.C., 1984.*

3. Additional personal credits for the blind, deaf, and quadraplegic are also indexed. The homemaker credit and credit for political contributions are not indexed.

4. Other possible price index measures are possible. The CPI is adopted since it is generally understood and widely accepted as an inflation measure. A discussion of this topic is provided in *Income Tax Indexing,* p. 28ff. Minnesota applies the Minneapolis - St. Paul Consumer Price Index for Urban Consumers (CPI-U).

5. Robert J. Samuelson, "Indexing Hypocrisy," *National Journal.* February 19, 1983. p. 384.

6. Salomone, *Income Tax Indexing,* p. 87ff.

7. *Ibid.*

# 9

# The Minnesota Estate Tax

## INTRODUCTION

The estate tax in Minnesota is a type of tax called a transfer tax. Transfer taxes are taxes on property left by individuals to their heirs (taxes on the transfer of wealth from one person to another). Many kinds of such taxes have been devised over the years. If the transfer occurs during the transferor's life, the tax is designated as a *gift tax*. If the transfer occurs on the death of the transferor, the tax is designated as a *death tax*. There are two major kinds of death taxes: the *inheritance tax* and the *estate tax*.

The inheritance tax is defined as a tax levied upon the privilege of receiving property from the deceased, while the estate tax is levied on the privilege of transferring property at death. Under an inheritance tax, a separate tax is computed on the value of each transfer. Characteristically, the amount of each transferee's share that is exempt from tax and the rates of tax for different classes of transferees will vary depending on the relationship of the transferor to the transferee. To illustrate, under the former Minnesota inheritance tax, a legacy of $25,000 to a child would have an exemption of $6,000 and be taxed at a rate of 2%, producing a tax liability of $380. But the tax on a like gift to a nephew had an exemption of $1,500 and a rate of 6%, resulting in a tax of $1,410. The sum of the separate taxes on each gift becomes the inheritance tax for the entire estate.

Under an estate tax, the value of the decedent's gross estate is determined, certain deductions and exemptions are subtracted, and the result is the taxable estate. A rate schedule uniform to all estates is then applied to the value of the taxable estate. Once the tax is determined, certain credits are subtracted to produce the actual amount of tax due.

Transfer taxes have been criticized by those who believe that such taxes discourage individuals' incentives to work and save. But, in deciding whether and how hard to work and save, the effect of income taxes is probably much more important than the potential disincentive inherent in transfer taxes.

As bequests and gifts add to an individual's (the recipient's) economic well-being and ability to pay, many would argue that such transfers should simply be incorporated under the income tax by including gifts and inheritance in the recipient's taxable income. Income averaging could be

141

used to moderate the impact of the graduated rate structure of the income tax. This alternative method of taxing transfers, however appealing, has never been seriously considered at the federal or state level.

Perhaps the strongest justification for transfer taxes is as a means of redistributing wealth. Unequal distributions of wealth, even more than unequal distributions of income, violate generally accepted notions of economic justice and equal economic and political opportunity. If redistribution is the only legitimate goal of transfer taxes, the administration of such taxes is possibly best left to the federal government as any attempt by a state to affect strongly its own distribution of wealth will be exacerbated by migration of this highly mobile set of residents.

Despite the appeal of transfer taxes, very little revenue is raised from these taxes at the federal level. It may be that the preference for wealth equalization is not strong in the U.S. Also, even though taxes on the transfer of wealth are difficult to justify at the state level (except as an easy source of revenue), all states, except Nevada, levy some type(s) of transfer tax. Many state taxes are designed to mitigate the competitive (migration) effects and most are not a significant source of revenue.

Because Minnesota conforms closely to the federal estate tax and because many states' estate taxes have a special relationship to a credit allowed on the federal tax, the federal estate tax is briefly described in the next section. The next section provides a description of Minnesota's estate tax and last section discusses the resulting policy implications.


## THE FEDERAL ESTATE TAX

The federal government imposes both an estate tax and a gift tax on wealth transfers, but only the former is described here. The gross estate consists of all property owned by the decedent at the time of death, including stocks, bonds, real estate, and mortgages. Insurance owned by the decedent is also part of the gross estate, as are all gifts in excess of the annual exclusion within three years from death. To arrive at the taxable transfer, the following deductions are allowed from the gross estate: funeral expenses, estate settlement expenses, debts, legal fees, charitable bequests, and an unlimited deduction for property passing to a surviving spouse.

The estate tax rates (which have been unified with the gift tax rates) begin at 18% on the first $10,000 of the taxable transfer and rise to 55% on any amount over $3,000,000. There are three credits that can be taken against the tax liability figured by applying these rates to the taxable transfer. In addition to a credit for any gift tax paid, two other credits that have an important impact on Minnesota's (as well as other states') estate tax are allowed. First, a credit is allowed for state death taxes paid (any type of death tax to any state) up to a limit equal to 80% of the federal tax liability imposed by the 1926 federal tax rate schedule. This seemingly arbitrary maximum has been in place since 1926 even as the federal rate structure has varied a great deal in the intervening years. Second, a credit is allowed for both estate and gift tax purposes, called the unified credit, which is set at $96,300 for 1984 and is scheduled to increase to $192,800 by 1987. The unified credit effectively exempts the first $325,000 of taxable estates in 1984 and will exempt the first $600,000 of taxable estates by 1987.

The credit for state death taxes paid was established to discourage interstate competition. A state would not have to fear outmigration of residents in response to a state death tax if the entire state burden could be used to decrease the federal burden dollar for dollar. With this credit, a resident could not decrease his or her total transfer tax burden by moving to a state with no death taxes. Death tax revenues of the states were thus protected from interstate competition by the federal government's picking up the bill. Many states have designed their estate taxes so that the state liability is equal to or limited to the value of the federal credit for state death taxes paid. When a state limits the total of its death taxes to the federal credit, this form of taxation is called a "pure pick-up tax."

## THE MINNESOTA ESTATE TAX

In 1979, the Minnesota inheritance and gift taxes were repealed and replaced with the Minnesota estate tax. The gross federal taxable estate is the basis for the computation of the Minnesota tax. The value of non-Minnesota property is subtracted from this base as are various exemptions and deductions.

Minnesota conforms to federal law by allowing an unlimited deduction for property transferred to a spouse (the marital deduction) and by exempting a certain amount of the value of the estate where the amount is equal to the effective exemption at the federal level brought about by the unified credit. Thus, for 1984 the maximum estate deduction is $325,000 and will be $600,000 by 1987.

Despite this high degree of conformity to the federal estate tax base, there are a few items in which Minnesota varies from federal law. For example, employee benefits are exempt under Minnesota law but not under federal law.

In 1984, a five-step graduated rate schedule applied to the Minnesota taxable estate beginning at 8% on the first $75,000 and rising to 12% on any amount over $875,000. By 1987, these rates will be compressed to 10% on the first $100,000 of taxable estate, 11% on the next $500,000, and 12% on any remainder.

The tax liability calculated by applying the rates above to the Minnesota taxable estate will not necessarily be the amount of tax due from the taxpayer. The Minnesota estate tax payable is the greater of (a) the amount calculated under the estate tax schedule or (b) the federal state death taxes credit. Thus, the Minnesota estate tax is actually bounded by the pick-up tax. The tax liability on any given estate will be at least the pick-up amount.

Notice that under this system whereby the pick-up tax is the minimum Minnesota liability, some estates will pay a higher total federal-plus-state estate tax liability in Minnesota than they would pay in those states whose estate taxes are limited to the federal-state death taxes credit or pick-up (at least with respect to those estates whose Minnesota liability is greater than the federal credit). There is no systematic evidence, however, that Minnesota's estate tax has had a negative impact on the migration of elderly citizens. Recent data from the census bureau indicate that the net outmigration of persons aged 65 and over has not been appreciably different from the net migration rate of Minnesota's overall population.

Due in part to the yearly increase in the amount of the estate deduction, by 1988 Minnesota's apparent competitive disadvantage will virtually disappear as the federal credit will be the effective tax for all estates in Minnesota except those ranging in size from approximately $1,250,000 to $2,500,000. Based on 1983 estimates, there will be approximately seventy-five returns in this category out of a total 350 expected returns. Thus, for most taxpayers, the calculation of tax liability based on Minnesota taxable estate using the Minnesota rate schedule will be superfluous.

As noted above, very little revenue is raised under the estate tax at either the federal or state level. In 1982, Minnesota raised $24,393,000 from its transfer taxes which represents 0.64% of total state taxes. Of this $24 million, over $17 million was raised under the estate tax. In 1983, the estate tax yielded close to $11 million. By contrast, if Minnesota had employed a pure pick-up tax in 1983, the revenue yield would have been nearly $9 million. Because of the estate deduction and the unlimited marital deduction, by 1987 the difference between the revenue yield of a pure pick-up tax and the current Minnesota estate tax will be insignificant.

## IMPLICATIONS FOR POLICY: AN EVALUATION OF THE MINNESOTA ESTATE TAX

Because of the small amount of revenue generated by the tax and the nature of the tax, the criteria of certainty and accountability are not applicable in an evaluation of Minnesota's estate tax. The efficiency (neutrality) criterion is probably not violated by the tax since there is little evidence that the federal tax, let alone the less onerous state transfer tax, discourages work effort or savings.

Vertical equity as represented in this context by the redistribution of wealth is potentially enhanced by federal and state transfer taxes in general, and, thus, by Minnesota's estate tax. The amount of redistribution effected by the tax is probably not large, however, as evidenced by the small amount of revenue raised. In 1982 Minnesota's total estate tax liability as a percentage of the value of all Minnesota gross estates was 1.5%. The lack of revenue raised and lack of redistribution effected both at the federal level and at the state level are attributable to the generous deductions, exemptions, and credits allowed estates and inheritances.

There is no evidence that Minnesota's estate tax violates the commission's competitiveness criterion. Minnesota could completely eliminate any such competitive concern by either eliminating its estate tax or adopting a pure pick-up tax. The former option accomplishes nothing that cannot be accomplished with the latter option, and the former would result in a revenue loss to the state. Under the pure pick-up tax, a state simply claims part of the tax liability (tax revenue) that the estate would have paid to the federal government. Given the similarity of the states' transfer taxes and given the lack of evidence with respect to whether the minor differences in these taxes affect migration, the competitiveness criterion is probably not as relevant in evaluating this tax as common perception would lead one to believe.

The final criterion by which Minnesota's estate tax must be judged is simplicity. The current structure is easy to comply with and administer, primarily because the tax conforms quite closely to the federal estate tax. Determining Minnesota tax liability does require an additional set of calculations, though, and for many estates these calculations are superfluous as Minnesota liability will equal the federal-state death taxes credit.

Thus, although the current system scores well on the simplicity criterion, a pure pick-up tax is yet simpler and the revenue yield would be only slightly less than the revenue yield of the current Minnesota estate tax. It is worth mentioning that the change to a pure pick-up tax might have a symbolic effect—a message would be conveyed—that Minnesota is interested in encouraging its elderly to stay in Minnesota.

The only drawback of a pure pick-up tax appears to be the fact that the Minnesota estate tax would be completely tied to the federal tax. The federal government could, as part of its concern for federalism and the preservation of the state revenue base, substantially increase the amount of the state death-taxes-paid credit, in which case, the revenue available to the states would be automatically increased. At the other extreme, the federal government could eliminate the credit or the estate tax altogether. Recent years have seen a movement for the total elimination of federal death taxes, and legislation for this purpose has been introduced every year since 1981. In the unlikely event of repeal or adoption of the federal state tax, if the pure pick-up tax were in effect, all death tax collections would cease. In that event, Minnesota would want to reevaluate the purpose of transfer taxes and consider a return to a simple tax not unlike its current estate tax.

## RECOMMENDATION

### ADOPT A PURE PICK-UP TAX

The commission finds that the Minnesota estate tax conforms closely to the federal estate tax and is thus very easy to comply with and administer. All estates valued at $325,000 or more are subject to the Minnesota estate tax at rates of 10%, 11%, and 12%. The federal estate tax allows a credit for state death taxes paid, with an upper limit on the size of the credit. Many states define their death taxes to be equal to the limit of the federal credit. This form of state death taxation is called a pure pick-up tax. If Minnesota were to adopt a pure pick-up tax, the revenue loss would be minimal (especially in future years), the process of filing Minnesota estate taxes would be even simpler than under current law, and any competitive disadvantage relative to other states would be eliminated.

Accordingly, the commission recommends that Minnesota adopt a pure pick-up tax equal to the federal deduction for state death taxes paid. The result would enhance the competitiveness and ease of taxpayer compliance with the tax law with only a small loss of revenue.

# 10
# General Sales and Use Tax

## INTRODUCTION

A sales tax is a tax on part of the disposition of income (consumption, not savings) rather than a tax at the source of income. A sales tax can be either general or selective in its application. A general sales tax would apply to a broadly defined, though not totally comprehensive, consumption base. A selective sales tax would only be applied to an individual consumption good. Selective and general sales (and use) taxes can be and often are used simultaneously.[1]

A general sales tax will not be comprehensive because some items are excluded as a result of the administrative difficulty of including some consumption goods (e.g., imputed rent), decisions by policymakers to attempt to reduce the regressivity of the tax (e.g., excluding food purchased for home consumption), and attempts by policymakers to encourage the consumption of goods thought to be socially desirable (e.g., prescription drugs).

The sales tax may be calculated as a percentage of the sales price, in which case it is referred to as an ad valorem tax. Alternatively, the tax may be a fixed amount per unit of product, that is, a unit tax. The first is a tax on the value of sales while the second is a tax on the quantity.

A general sales tax requires the ad valorem approach. In addition to certain efficiency advantages, the ad valorem approach is preferred to the unit tax because the unit tax might cause producers to adjust units in which their product is sold to avoid part of the tax. This would reduce the built-in revenue flexibility of the sales tax, since it would not be sensitive to rising prices.

The sales tax structure Minnesota chooses can be judged against the several goals presented in chapter 1. Revenue productivity is, of course, one of these. However, it is generally agreed that at least four others should be given particularly close attention when judging the structure of the sales tax. For now, these other criteria are simply introduced along with some illustrations of the Minnesota policy issues involved. These issues are examined in greater detail toward the end of this chapter.

EFFICIENCY OR NEUTRALITY

Does the tax minimize unintended interference with private decisions? There are three major implications of this objective as applied to the sales tax. The first is that the sales tax be designed in such a manner that the amount of the tax constitutes a uniform percentage of the selling price. One way to accomplish this goal is to structure the sales tax so that it impacts the consumer at the final (retail) stage of production and distribution, and not at the intermediate stages of resource extracting, manufacturing, and wholesaling. This minimizes the likelihood of "tax pyramiding"—the taxation of the same commodity at more than one stage of production.

Two traditional state/local rules for minimizing tax pyramiding are to exempt from the sales tax those goods and services that either become a physical ingredient or that are directly used in the production of a taxed final product. Minnesota's practice of taxing the purchases of capital goods and building and construction materials thus becomes a major concern.

A second major problem for a state sales tax concerns changes in consumption patterns induced by differential tax rates among commodities that compete for consumers' purchases. A sales tax can lose its neutrality in either of two ways. One way occurs when the sales tax is imposed on a narrow subset of consumer goods and services. The result is that consumers will be induced to substitute, to some degree, exempt goods for taxable goods. For Minnesota, which among the forty-six sales tax states (including D.C.) has the fifth most narrow retail sales tax base, this looms as an important problem.[2]

The third way the Minnesota sales tax loses neutrality is by combining use of a narrow tax base with its high-tax-state stature, relative to all but one of its neighboring states (Wisconsin). Consumption patterns may be influenced by different tax rates among jurisdictions. If some jurisdictions do not tax a commodity as heavily as competing areas, consumers will be induced to transfer some purchases from the higher- to the lower-tax jurisdictions. Thus, when examining its own general sales tax policy, Minnesotans must also consider the possible effects on its retail sector of getting too far out of line with its neighbors. Since Minnesota has a higher statutory tax rate than any of its border states but a narrower base, this suggests that consideration should be given to a lower rate for broader base tradeoff. Unfortunately, for Minnesota such a tradeoff is not readily achieved given the facts that (a) relative to all but one border state (Wisconsin), Minnesota is a higher-tax state and therefore "needs" the tax dollars (at least in the short run) and (b) the retail portion of the sales tax is the one tax handle for which Minnesota has some excess capacity (see chapter 4). Minnesota's tax effort is far above most of its neighboring jurisdictions with respect to the other major state revenue source, the income tax. Thus, in order to finance a given flow of expenditures, the state may have to rely more heavily on the sales tax at retail despite the likely border effects.

## VERTICAL EQUITY ("GRESSIVITY")

The traditional criticism of the sales tax from an equity point of view is that the distribution of the tax burden between income classes is regressive. This occurs because the lower the income the larger the percentage of that income that is spent on consumer activity. In contrast, as incomes increase, people are able to save more (consume less) of their income and thereby pay relatively less in sales tax.

If the desired policy is to reduce the regressivity of the sales tax, there are three approaches to be considered. The first is to provide an "over-the-counter" exemption for certain consumption goods that take a larger percentage of consumers' budgets as income falls (e.g., food). The second is to tax broadly goods and services, but provide an income-related tax credit that offsets a portion of the sales tax liability for lower-income families. A third approach, which is a variant of the second, is to package a broad retail sales tax with a personal income tax structure that offsets the sales tax regressivity through rate reductions in the low-income classes.

## HORIZONTAL EQUITY ("EQUAL TREATMENT OF EQUALS")

The equity criterion applied to a broad-based sales tax also asks whether families in equal economic circumstances (e.g., income) pay equal amounts of taxes. Families in the same income class will pay different amounts of sales tax if total consumption varies between equal income families, or if the consumption of taxable goods varies within income classes.

As was true for neutrality, the goal of horizontal equity is most likely to be achieved by adopting a broad tax base. That Minnesota's sales tax is almost entirely levied on goods and not services provides a classic case of horizontal inequity. That a Minnesota consumer is subject to the sales tax when buying shampoo for home use but then is exempt from the tax when going to a hairstylist is just one illustration. Similarly, a purchased watch is taxed, but watch repair is not. And so it goes.

## EASE OF ADMINISTRATION AND TAXPAYER COMPLIANCE

The two operational criteria for tax simplification require that the tax be established in such a manner that administration can be made effective at reasonable cost, and compliance difficulties and costs for the taxpaying firms (collecting units) be minimized. Once again, the preference is for a tax structure that promotes uniformity rather than for a tax base that is narrowly designed.

## STATUTORY AND INSTITUTIONAL CHARACTERISTICS

Minnesota enacted its retail sales tax in 1967 and became one of the last three of the forty-six states to adopt such a levy. Although, as already noted, it has one of the highest nominal sales tax rates of the forty-six states, Minnesota's tax base is one of the most narrow in the nation. The specific statutory and institutional characteristics of the tax are summarized below:

### STATUTORY RATE

The general statutory rate is 6% of the taxable base. The state also applies a reduced rate (4%) to farm machinery and special tooling. Capital equipment is also subject to this reduced rate, but only by refund, and only if the equipment is for new business plants or plant expansion.

### TAX BASE

The tax applies to gross receipts from the retail sales, use, storage, or consumption in Minnesota of tangible personal property. Taxable sale includes, beyond ordinary commodity transactions, the transfer of information and directions via computer software, renting, producing, fabricating, printing, or processing tangible personal property, preparing or serving meals and drinks, admissions to amusements and athletic events, furnishing transient lodgings and related services, furnishing electricity, gas, water or steam, local exchange telephone service and intrastate toll service, cable and similar television services, producers' capital equipment, and building construction materials.

### STATUTORY EXEMPTIONS

Major exemptions from the tax base include food for home consumption, prescription and nonprescription medicines, clothing and wearing apparel, motor fuel, residential heating fuel (through the months from November through April), and virtually all services to persons.

### INSTITUTIONAL EXEMPTIONS

The law also exempts charitable, religious, or educational institutions if the property purchased is used in performing charitable, religious, or educational functions, sales to any senior citizens' groups or associations organized for nonprofit purposes, and property sold to a tax-exempt organization for nonprofit use.

TAX YIELD

The history of the Minnesota sales and use tax reflects substantial growth, from $113 million in fiscal 1968 to $1,388 million (estimated) in fiscal 1985. That growth has somewhat exceeded that experienced by other tax sources, and at present accounts for 25% of state tax collections.

A comparison of Minnesota's 6% statutory rate with other states[3] suggests that Minnesota is at the top of the state sales tax ranking. Indeed, only seven states (including the District of Columbia) are at or above the Minnesota tax rate level. But, as was discussed above in the chapter on "Minnesota Fiscal Comparisons," statutory rates can be quite misleading regardless of which tax one examines. Although a high rate may have an initial "announcement effect," the relevant tax policy variables are effective tax rate and tax effort. These latter two measures explicitly bring in some interstate common denominator of tax capacity (e.g., the representative tax system) measure.

Once this adjustment of a common denominator among states is introduced, Minnesota is found to rely less heavily on sales taxes—i.e., make a lower tax effort—than the average of other states. As the evidence above (chapter 4, Table 9) indicates, Minnesota sales tax effort is about 76% of the average U.S. state. Another fact, which is also revealing, is that in terms of effort, Minnesota relies more than twice as much on the personal income than it does on the sales tax.

In sum, because of its unusually narrow base, Minnesota relies less heavily on the general sales tax than the typical state using the tax. The high total tax effort of Minnesota may suggest that greater reliance should be placed on the sales tax for revenue purposes. Whether, in fact, more intensive utilization of the sales tax by Minnesota is desirable on tax policy grounds (and if so, how) is the primary focus of the remainder of this chapter.

INTERSTATE COMPARISON OF TAX BASE COMPONENTS

State sales taxes typically apply to retail transactions—that is, sales to the final consumer. However, coverage of consumption expenditures by individuals is far from complete in Minnesota as well as in other states. Detailed comparisons across states for several major expenditure categories are provided in a companion technical report.[3] Patterns that are important to note include:

- *Food Exemption.* Like Minnesota, twenty-eight states (including the District of Columbia) exempt purchases of food for at-home consumption. Although such an exemption complicates both compliance with and administration of the tax, the exemption does relieve a portion of the regressivity of the tax. An alternative direct approach, the refund of sales tax paid through a credit or rebate structure, is used in only eight states.

- *Prescription Medicine.*  As of 1985 all but two states (Hawaii and New Mexico) will exempt prescription medicine. The exemption is usually justified on the grounds that it reduces regressivity while at the same time it does not overly complicate compliance or administration.
- *Nonprescription Medicine.*  Minnesota is only one of nine states (plus the District of Columbia) that extend the medical products exemption to nonprescription items. This exemption leads to difficult interpretation problems regarding what is and is not to be included on the exempt list.
- *Clothing.*  Minnesota is one of only five states that exempt clothing (plus Connecticut, which exempts only childrens' clothing). Few states have seriously considered copying the exemption. Each of Minnesota's neighboring states taxes clothing.
- *Items Subject to Selective Sales Taxes.*  Many states exempt items subject to selective sales taxes (especially motor fuel, cigarettes, and alcoholic beverages). This treatment has no logical position; if an item appropriately bears the extraordinary tax burden of a special excise, there is no reason to relieve that burden in the general tax structure. Furthermore, the special exemption complicates compliance and administration. Although states almost always extend sales tax coverage to alcoholic beverages, they do not regularly tax cigarettes and gasoline. Ten states tax motor fuel and thirty-six tax cigarettes. Minnesota exempts motor fuel and taxes cigarettes. Alcohol is subject to an 8.5% rate.
- *Residential Fuel and Electricity.*  Fewer than half the states tax residential fuels and electricity. In Minnesota and Wisconsin exemptions are based on time of year. Maine exempts only a portion of electricity purchased, and two states (Tennessee and Utah) apply lower rates to the purchases.
- *Services.*  Few states have extended their sales taxes broadly to services; Minnesota is one that taxes services the least.[4,5] Only six (including South Dakota and Iowa) have taxed services broadly, but the remaining states apply the tax only to services specifically noted in the law. Minnesota and twenty-one other states tax utilities, admissions, and transient lodging services as part of their general sales tax.

BUSINESS INPUTS

Although Minnesota conforms with a majority of states in exempting raw materials used or consumed in agricultural and industrial production (e.g., fuels, chemicals, packaging products, feeds, seeds) and production of personal property intended to be ultimately sold at retail, it levies the sales tax at a reduced rate (4%) on farm machinery and fully taxes sales of supplies and equipment owners, sales of building materials to contractors and subcontractors, and computer software. As already noted, capital equipment may be subject to a 4% rate. This treatment of business inputs tends to put Minnesota out of line with its border states. Iowa (fully) taxes farm machinery at 3%; South Dakota levies a (partial) rate of 3%, and Wisconsin exempts farm machinery.

## EVALUATION OF ALTERNATIVE TAX BASES

Comparing the general sales tax and alternative tax base structures compels one to make judgments regarding the tradeoffs among the various normative goals of tax policy. The primary issues with respect to the Minnesota sales tax pertain to the size (breadth) of the taxable base. Once the tax base is extended, the rate arithmetically "falls out," given the desired revenue yield.

There are two general issues of tax base size in Minnesota. The first is whether the current tax base should be broadened to include items currently tax exempt: food for home consumption, new clothing, services, prescription and nonprescription medicine, gasoline, or some combination of two or more of these. An equally important concern is whether the current tax base should be narrowed by providing exemption for two types of business purchases of real capital (equipment and machinery, building construction materials and farm machinery).

Table 1 provides a summary of the components of the tax base broadening/narrowing alternatives that were considered by the commission. A more detailed listing is available in the manual of *Standard Industrial Classification* codes published by the U.S. Office of Management and Budget.

Laying out these statutory changes only begins the debate. What one needs to know in order to make an informed policy judgment is the effect these changes will have on the revenue, productivity, equity, efficiency and administration characteristics of the tax. These topics are examined next.

### REVENUE AND EQUITY

The revenue productivity and equity implications of the current sales tax base and its alternatives are presented in summary form in Table 2, which provides the following information:

Column 1 shows the FY 1985 dollar and percentage changes that would occur, assuming the various tax base changes listed on the left side of the table. The addition of food adds the single largest amount to revenues. Gasoline, business services, and clothing follow in that order. The exemption of purchases of capital (including building construction materials) would decrease the existing sales tax base by 15.9%.

Column 2 provides an estimate of what the statutory rate of the sales tax would be if the base changes shown are made, and if the total tax collections are kept at an "equal yield" level (in the case for FY 1985, at $1,388.2 million). These rates will, of course, reflect the revenue gains in the revenue change column. Again, the revenue power of taxing food or some combination including food is clear.

Column 3 provides an indicator of the overall vertical equity ("gressivity") of the sales tax. The numbers shown, which range from 0.635 to 0.588, indicate whether or not payments from a sales tax would increase more or less rapidly than income. The lower the index the greater the regressivity from the tax. The index for the current Minnesota base equals 0.611. This means that a family with income 10% higher than another would bear a sales tax higher by only 6.11%. Thus, the base is regressive (as

TABLE 1
Summary of Tax Base Components
For Various Retail Sales Tax Bases

---

*Current Base Plus Food for Home Consumption.* The current Minnesota tax base includes candy, soft drinks and bottled water, retailer prepared sandwiches and packaged foods; ice cream cones, ice, gum, and vendor machine foods. The option was to add general groceries.

*Current Base Plus Clothing.* The present tax base includes furs, jewelry, blankets, towels, notions, billfolds, athletic, sporting, and recreational articles. Now added are new clothing and wearing apparel in general.

*Current Base Plus Services to Persons.* Services are now generally excluded from the tax base except for delivery service charges incorporated into the selling price of taxable tangible property and photographic studios. Now added are personal services (laundry and dry cleaning, beauty/barber shops, funeral services), and miscellaneous repair services (auto, radio/television/phonograph, reupholstery and furniture, welding, and air conditioning).

*Current Base Plus Business Services.* Legal, architectural, engineering, business, advertising, and accounting services are added to the current base.

*Current Base Plus Gasoline.* Motor fuels for automobile, aviation, and special transportation are now considered taxable. Motor fuels are now taxed by Minnesota as part of its selective sales tax system.

*Current Base Less Capital Goods.* At present, the sales tax base includes capital equipment and machinery and construction materials. The alternative tax bases examined included exemption for all business (including farming) purchase of capital (equipment and machinery and construction materials).

incomes rise, relative tax burden falls). As this column shows, the prospects for improving that performance are not great: the regressivity index for all current consumption (the broadest base) is 0.588, or somewhat more regressive (MR in Table 2) than the current system. Of the alternatives considered, expansion of the base to clothing would reduce regressivity, but only very slightly, and expansion to clothing and services would leave the regressivity index virtually unchanged. Although these overall indexes of regressivity are not available for all the tax base options shown in the left column, it is possible, by comparing how the indexes change as one component is added to or deleted from a tax base, to generally rank each option as more regressive (MR) or less regressive (LR) than the current base. Thus, it is clear that while taxing food is the engine for revenue enhancement, it also adds more than the other changes to the regressivity measure. This may suggest why broadening the base to food alone (and, for example, at the same time exempting services and/or clothing) is often politically difficult to achieve.

Column 4 provides a checklist of another important tax policy consideration, horizontal equity—the extent to which otherwise equal families (i.e., equal incomes) pay different effective tax rates. Since the surest way to achieve horizontal equity of a consumption tax is to avoid discriminating among consumers on the basis of whether they happen to have preferences for taxed vs. nontaxed items, the tax policy solution is to tax on as broad a base as possible. It follows that because the present Minnesota tax base is so narrow, all of the alternatives shown lead to improvements in horizontal equity; and, finally

Column 5 shows the dollar amount by which total collections from the Minnesota personal income tax would be reduced (the state income tax offset) as a result of the fact that higher sales tax payments will increase the amount of deductions taken on itemized tax returns.[6]

There are three ways to improve the vertical equity of the general sales tax. The first, and most common, is to provide for over-the-counter commodity exemptions as Minnesota now does for food, prescription drugs, and laundry and dry cleaning. However, as Table 2 shows, the amount of the regressivity that is alleviated is not great, and thus the question arises: is there another way to address the vertical equity goal without incurring large revenue losses from the exemptions?

In terms of a direct on-the-spot (time of purchase) solution, the answer to the preceding question is no. Accordingly, the practical alternative is to make up for the sales tax regressivity by including a progressive tax elsewhere in the revenue system. For Minnesota, as for any state, the major tool for effecting this goal is the personal income tax, which can be designed to accomplish this result in two ways:

• Enact a progressive tax rate structure and leave it at that. What evidence

TABLE 2
Sales Tax Alternatives
Minnesota, 1985

| | 1 | | 2 | 3 | | 4 | 5 |
|---|---|---|---|---|---|---|---|
| | FY 1985 Gross Revenue $ Millions | Implications (% change) | Equal Yield Rate | Vertical Equity:* Overall Regressivity | Index | Horizontal Equity | Offset: Additional Revenue Lost to Personal Income Tax ($ millions) |
| Current Base | $1,388.2 | --- | 6.0% | R | .611 | | -0- |
| Current Base *Plus* | | | | | | | |
| Food | 259 | 18.7 | 5.1 | MR | .555 | + | $ 7.6 |
| Clothing | 132 | 9.5 | 5.5 | LR | .624 | + | 3.9 |
| Services to Individuals | 54 | 3.9 | 5.8 | MR | | + | 1.6 |
| Business Services | 172 | 12.4 | 5.4 | LR | | + | 5.0 |
| Food & Clothing | 391 | 28.2 | 4.7 | MR | .569 | + | 11.4 |
| Clothing & Services (Ind) | 186 | 13.4 | 5.3 | same | .611 | + | 5.2 |
| Food, Clothing & All Services | 617 | 31.6 | 4.2 | MR | .568 | + | 12.8 |
| Gasoline | 169 | 12.2 | 5.3 | LR | .627 | + | 4.9 |

(table continued on next page)

| | | | | | | | |
|---|---|---|---|---|---|---|---|
| Clothing, (Ind) | | | | | | | |
| Services, Gasoline | 355 | 25.1 | 4.8 | LR | .623 | + | 10.4 |
| Clothing & Gasoline | 301 | 21.7 | 4.9 | LR | .635 | + | 9.0 |
| Nonprescription Medicine | 10 | .7 | 6.0 | LR | | | |
| All Current Consumption | --- | | --- | MR | .588 | + | |
| Current Base, Exempt all Capital (Equipment & Machinery and Construction Materials) | -221 | -15.9 | 7.9 | LR | | | |
| Current Base, Exempt Construction Materials | - 78 | - 5.6 | 6.6 | LR | | | |
| Clothing and Personal Services; Exempt Materials | | | | | | | |
| Construction | + 108 | 7.8 | 5.6 | LR | | | |

Source:　Minnesota Tax Study Commission.

*R (Regressive); MR (more regressive); LR (less regressive)

we have is that Minnesota does, indeed, do this more than most states. A recent ACIR study, which compares tax burdens among fifty cities—the largest city in each state—shows that Minneapolis residents face among the most progressive of income (and total) taxes;[7] or

- Add to the personal income tax a special tax credit that is specifically designed to offset (fully or partially) sales tax regressivity. The rationale of this sales tax credit is straightforward. Rather than provide over-the-counter exemptions to all consumers of an exempt item (e.g., food, whether it be hot dogs or lobsters) and thus lose the sales tax revenues from low- and high-income consumer activity alike, retail sales could be taxed very broadly, and at income tax time, a refund could be provided in the form of a tax credit targeted only to low- or low- and middle-income groups. Thus, unlike the exemption, which provides tax relief to consumers regardless of income, the credit is restricted to certain taxpayer classes.

These differences can be illustrated as follows. The typical Minnesota family that has an income of $35,000 spends about 8% of their income (or $2,800) on food for home consumption. If that were taxed, this family would pay $168 in sales taxes on food. In contrast, the family with a $7,000 income pays about 16% or $1,120 on food. With food taxes at 6%, this family's tax bill is $67. Although the dollar amount of tax paid by the lower-income family is less than that of the higher-income one, the burden (tax as a percent of income) is clearly regressive—it is about twice as much for the $7,000 family.

Now assume that a special sales tax credit of $45/dependent were granted as part of the income tax, and that this credit was available only to those earning $25,000 or less. The $7,000 income family qualifies and, in effect is refunded the taxes it paid on the first $750.00 ($45 divided by 6%) of food consumed by each dependent. If this is a three-member family, the first $2,250 of groceries becomes sales tax free.

Who pays for this refund? The people above $25,000 (in this example) who fail to qualify for the credit. However, note that the Minnesota treasury also gains. Here, for example, rather than losing $303 in taxes from both families through over-the-counter exemption for all food, the state's tax loss is limited to $135 ($45 multiplied by three dependents).

In its policy deliberations, the commission examined several options for combining a broader sales tax with a variable vanishing credit (the tax relief amount declines as income increases). One of these options, extending the base to food for home consumption in conjunction with a liberal tax credit ($88.7 million) is presented in Table 3. As the table illustrates, the credit is a highly flexible policy instrument. Depending on the size of the credit amount, it is possible to reduce the net tax burden for the lowest-income groups.

The credit vs. exemption choice has other features requiring brief comment. First, the credit is also superior to the commodity exemption approach on horizontal equity grounds. Even though families may have equal incomes, their consumption patterns (preferences) will vary by characteristics such as family size, age, race, housing, tenure, and urban vs. rural residence.

The credit approach also tends to be superior to the current Minnesota over-the-counter method on the grounds of taxpayer compliance. Unlike the credit, the exemption creates more paperwork for retailers, since separate records are required for taxable vs. exempt sales. For example, if a supermarket sells chicken roasted on a rotisserie on the premises, the sale is taxable. However, baked products prepared and sold by the supermarket are exempt on the basis that they are for home consumption. One eats the chicken in the store's parking lot and takes the doughnuts and milk home?

The major advantage the exemption has over the credit has to do with taxpayer ease. The over-the-counter exemption requires practically no consumer effort—the tax relief is given at the checkout counter. The credit, however, requires the consumer either to fill out an income tax form or make a special disclosure of annual family income. One possible result of these added procedures is that some of the people in the very low income groups for whom this relief is primarily intended would be lost in the process.

TABLE 3
Expand Sales Tax to Food at 6% and
Provide a $88.7 Million Variable Sales Tax Credit, FY 1985

| Minnesota Gross Income Class | Food Tax Paid Per Dependent | Credit Per Dependent | Net Added Tax (+) or Rebate (-) | Food Tax Only | |
|---|---|---|---|---|---|
| | | | | Effective Rate before Credit | Effective Rate after Credit |
| Less than $3,000 | $29 | $45 | $-16 | 3.4% | |
| 3,000 — 3,999 | 38 | 45 | - 7 | 1.5 | |
| 4,000 — 4,999 | 40 | 45 | - 5 | 1.3 | |
| 5,000 — 5,999 | 42 | 40 | 2 | 1.2 | < .1% |
| 6,000 — 6,999 | 40 | 40 | 0 | 1.0 | 0 |
| 7,000 — 7,999 | 53 | 40 | 13 | 1,3 | .3 |
| 8,000 — 9,999 | 55 | 40 | 15 | 1.1 | .2 |
| 10,000 — 11,999 | 57 | 40 | 17 | 1.0 | .3 |
| 12,000 — 14,999 | 51 | 40 | 11 | .8 | .2 |
| 15,000 — 19,999 | 50 | 30 | 10 | .7 | .3 |
| 20,000 — 24,999 | 44 | 30 | 14 | .6 | .2 |
| 25,000 and above | 49 | 0 | 49 | .5 | .5 |

*Exhibit* ($ millions)
Additional Sales Tax Revenue at 6% $259
Additional Sales Tax Revenue at 5% 216
Cost of Credit $89

*Source:* Minnesota Tax Study Commission

EFFICIENCY

*Rate differentials at Minnesota's borders.*    Loss of sales along the border of the state can be the result of its neighbors applying a lower statutory sales tax rate. For high price items, purchasers may buy in the lower tax rate area, even though they incur travel costs to do so. Vendors in higher tax rate jurisdictions must face reduced customer traffic, or they must reduce pretax prices, provide greater service, or make other accommodations to compensate for the tax disadvantage.

The border circumstances in Minnesota are complicated because the taxation of business purchases and the narrow consumer portion of the Minnesota tax means that, along a given border, some Minnesota merchants will be selling at a competitive advantage, while others will be at a disadvantage; and, the state has international as well as state boundaries. Furthermore, an inadequate amount of data hinders estimation of the border effect: the high Minnesota rate, compared to its neighbors, began after the most recent (1977) census of retail trade, so its distortion does not appear in that data.

In order to provide some answers to the border loss problem, the commission compared sales activities in Minnesota's border counties with similar activities in interior counties.[8] Despite the complexities of the analysis, the commission found that the higher Minnesota sales tax rate (5% in 1982, compared with 3% in Iowa and South Dakota and 4% elsewhere) did reduce sales levels. Apparel store sales, a category generally exempt in Minnesota but taxed in surrounding states, were higher on the borders, possibly the result of purchases by out-of-state customers. In total, the high statutory tax rate appeared somewhat to discourage retail activity along the state's border.

*Retail services to business.*    The imposition of the 6% sales tax on business services has several special merits: it looks like a good revenue producer (Table 2); however one should be warned that these numbers assume that the size of the tax base will not change (decrease) once the tax is imposed. Also, it can be justified on both grounds of vertical equity (probably progressive) and, certainly, according to horizontal equity.

There are, however, some practical problems respecting business services that cause more concern than other retail sales activities. First, some problems of tax enforcement and administration would be created. Some service firms (especially the professional firms with out-of-state offices) could avoid the tax rather easily by billing from the non-Minnesota offices. This practice could lead to serious questions about the reliability of the Table 2 revenue estimates regarding this particular tax base component. Moreover, taxing services to business would require Minnesota revenue officials to make cumbersome case-by-case determinations of what part of a firm's total receipts were actually attributable to Minnesota sources and thus to taxation. When the Washington, D.C., study commission faced the same issue, the professional firms were quite blunt: if they did not have out-of-state billing facilities already in place, they would legally establish them.[9] Minnesota firms could be expected to react in a similar manner.

Second, if Minnesota were to enact such a tax, it would put a 6% wedge between prices of Minnesota firms and non-Minnesotans in the same business. Clients from out-of-state who buy computer services are likely to be more footloose in their purchasing choices than are purchasers of apparel, food, or personal services.

The result is that on practical fiscal expediency grounds, the practice of taxing all business services may be self-defeating.

*Capital purchases.* The sales and use taxation of purchases of capital equipment has a major plus: it is a prodigious revenue producer. Moreover, the tax may in part be shifted to nonresidents in their role of consumers of Minnesota-produced products or as factory suppliers to Minnesota firms.

However, the equity and competitiveness characteristics of the tax law as it now exists must be considered as negatives for tax policy:

First, the incidence is capricious. Depending on the market conditions under which the taxed firm operates, the tax may either be paid by shareholders (which would add to the overall Minnesota tax progressivity to the extent the Minnesotans are shareholders) or, the more likely case, by the final consumer (in which case the nonexported portion has a regressive effect for Minnesota). Moreover, because the tax is levied prior to the retail stage, tax pyramiding results for nonvertically integrated operations.

Second, when one considers the high statutory rate and the fact that most states substantially exempt purchases of capital equipment from the sales tax, Minnesota runs the great risk of providing a disincentive to employment growth. And, given Minnesota's high statutory rate on capital purchases, the problem is of genuine concern. This is so because the announced rate of 4% on equipment "purchased for new or expanding *industries*" can be misleading. The lower (4%) rate applies only to capital equipment used by the purchaser or lessee for manufacturing, fabricating, or refining a product to be sold at retail, and it must be purchased for the establishment of a new or the physical expansion of an existing facility in the state. Still taxed at the 6% rate is "machinery or equipment purchased or leased to replace machinery or equipment performing substantially the same function in an existing facility; repair or replacement parts or machinery or equipment used to extract, receive, or store raw materials."[10]

Moreover, the law provides that the tax on all equipment and machinery be initially taxed at 6%. Then, the purchaser is to file a refund claim with the revenue department for the 2% overpayment. No more than two refund claims may be filed per year. Given the narrowness of this partial exemption and the relatively high Minnesota statutory rate, the disincentive to economic growth must be considered. Nevertheless, it does not necessarily follow that the best tax policy is complete exemption. As is discussed in the following chapter, there is an optional taxation argument that some sales taxes should be levied at different rates. For example, if the rate on all capital were 2%, Minnesota would still generate about $100 million in revenues and minimize the likely negative growth effects.

*Tax administration and compliance.*    It is difficult to see how the process of taxing at one rate (6%) and then refunding to a lower rate (4%) with a limit of two refunds per year serves either the goals of simplicity in tax administration or tax compliance. Rather, the legislature has placed both revenue officials and taxpayers in a game of hide-and-seek. In short, Minnesota has opted for complexity over simplicity, with little observable gain.

REVENUE STABILITY

One of the goals of this commission is to promote certainty and predictability in the Minnesota state/local tax system. All the intentions to provide a well-designed package of public goods and services can be thwarted if the financing of these public expenditures is so uncertain as to make their delivery uncertain. Accordingly, state and local governments must employ a mix of taxes, some of which will exhibit automatic revenue responsiveness over the business cycle and others that will provide a more stable or steady source of revenues as economic conditions change. The state, however, has two major revenue sources: income (personal and corporate) and sales. The income taxes tend to be "income elastic" over the business cycle—i.e., their revenues automatically grow faster (slower) than the economy in times of economic expansion (recession). This is not an undesirable characteristic for a tax system, if it is balanced by reliance on other tax sources that tend to exhibit less income elasticity or stability. In order to achieve this balance, most states turn to taxes on a stable part of the economy—consumer expenditures.

This is where the Minnesota system has a problem. Although it utilizes a sales tax, it is unusual in that it is narrowly based on the public component of spending, viz, retail sales, and broadly based on one of the most volatile parts of the economy, capital purchases. The result is that the Minnesota treasury automatically tends to look very healthy in periods of growth (its FY 1985 $1 billion surplus was in part due to this upward revenue elasticity); but it can be very vulnerable during an economic downturn.

Of course, no tax system can be so finely tuned to hit the cycle just right. There will always be a need for ad hoc tax adjustments. But if an economy is to maintain its competitiveness as well as provide a smooth flow of public services over time, elements of revenue stability are needed.

Minnesota has at least two ways it can achieve these goals. The first is to make its sales tax more stable over the business cycle. This can be accomplished by either broadening the tax base to those spending activities that tend to be relatively unresponsive or inelastic over time (e.g., clothing and food for home consumption) and/or reduce its reliance on the more volatile elements of the tax base (e.g., purchases of capital equipment).

Regarding the first of these options, the evidence for Minnesota is what one would expect on a priori grounds. Data on behavior of personal consumption expenditure for various periods between 1975 and 1982 support the view that the stability of the Minnesota sales tax would be enhanced if food and/or clothing were added to the base.[11]

A second means of enhancing the revenue stability of the state tax system would be to adjust the intensity to which Minnesota relies on its income taxes vs. a broadened retail sales tax. Although there is no scientific evidence on the quantitative nature of how the overall responsiveness of the Minnesota fiscal system would change if the state traded some income tax revenues for sales tax revenues, the a priori conclusion is rather clear: at least some move toward consumption taxes and away from income taxes is merited.

## TAX ADMINISTRATION AND COMPLIANCE

Some aspects of sales tax administration have already been discussed above. As a general rule, the expansion of the sales tax base ranks high on administrative considerations since the administrative problems of determining what is and is not an exempt item would be reduced. One example regarding food has already been mentioned. There are many more possible. Similarly, taxing all new clothing would eliminate "linedrawing" problems that now exist (e.g., taxable asbestos vs. nontaxable apparel clothing; exempt bathing suits vs. taxable athletic recreation suits).

Finally, a comment on the idea of a lower (e.g., 2%) rate on business inputs is appropriate here. The use of differential rates can lead to very cumbersome problems for revenue officials and taxpayers alike. The "optimal tax" argument is theoretically attractive, but if multiple rates are introduced into the sales tax as routinely as they have been in the Minnesota (classified) property tax, the system may become too complicated to understand and too unwieldy to administer fairly. The lower 4% rate on farm machinery sales already creates special administrative and compliance problems since it requires that the retailer make special computation adjustments on the sales and use tax return.

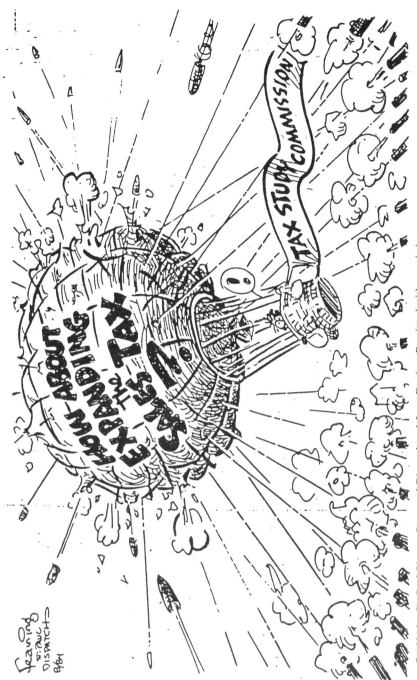

# RECOMMENDATION

## BROADENING OF THE GENERAL SALES AND USE TAX BASE

The commission has found that due to the narrowness of its base, the sales tax results in an unstable source of revenue for the state, and it can contribute to budget uncertainty during times of economic fluctuation. The narrow base also can pay widely different sales tax bills (and thus bear widely different shares of the state tax burden) by making different personal consumption decisions.

In order to mitigate these problems, the commission recommends that the sales tax base be extended to include new clothing and personal services. The stability, certainty, and equity of the sales tax are greatly enhanced by this change. And, the distribution of the sales tax burden is no more regressive under this broader base than the distribution under Minnesota's current narrow base.

While the commission recognizes that the stability and equity goals could largely be achieved if, as a result of this base broadening, the sales tax rate were lowered to an equal yield amount, it nevertheless concludes that the present rate of 6% should be maintained. New revenues can be used to reduce the burdens of other Minnesota taxes, which unlike the sales tax, are utilized much more heavily in this state than in the other states with which Minnesota must compete for jobs. A heavier reliance on the sales tax combined with reduced pressures on these other taxes will result in a tax mix in Minnesota that more closely approximates the tax mix of the average state.

# ENDNOTES

1. States that levy a sales tax also levy a use tax. The use tax applies at the same rate as the sales tax when one purchases a taxable item for storage of use or consumption in Minnesota without paying the sales tax. The use tax includes in its base (a) items purchased outside Minnesota, (b) items initially purchased exempt for resale but then taken out out of inventory for business or personal use; (c) purchased exempt for use in agricultural or industrial production but then put to taxable use; and (d) sales-taxable items purchased from a Minnesota seller who does not collect the sales tax. Special sellers and consumer's use-tax forms are provided by the revenue department. The problem with a use tax is in its enforcement. Although a revenue department can with relative ease search out buyers of large items such as boats and airplanes, auditing for less expensive items is so costly it is rarely pursued. In order to make this problem less severe Congress must enact legislation that requires vendors to collect use tax for states in which they have more than some minimum amount in annual sales.

2. Daniel R. Feenberg and Harvey S. Rosen, "State Personal Income and Sales Taxes: 1977-1983," a paper presented to the National Bureau of Economic Research Project on State and Local Finance, Cambridge, Massachusetts, June 1984.

3. For state-by-state detail, see John L. Mikesell, "Retail Sales and Use Taxation in Minnesota," *Staff Papers,* vol. 2 of the *Final Report of the Minnesota Tax Study Commission,* ed. Robert D. Ebel and Therese J. McGuire (St. Paul: Butterworth Legal Publishers, 1985).

4. Minnesota taxes the value of producing, fabricating and processing—i.e., "fabrication labor." Examples of fabrication labor of products used for final consumption include furniture upholstery making, matting and/or framing of art, taxidermy, engraving, custom sawing, cutting or milling charges by a sawmill, woodworking shop or lumber yard, reproducing copies of typed or printed matter on paper stock (and collating and assembly), pipe cutting and drilling holes in bowling balls. Minnesota Statutes section 297A.01, subdivision 3(b).

5. U.S. Advisory Commission on Intergovernmental Relations (ACIR), *Significant Features of Fiscal Federalism* (1982-83 ed.), Table 46, Washington, D.C., 1984.

6. These reductions in income tax revenues involve moving from a calendar year to the next fiscal year. For example, the sales tax that is paid on CY 1985 is taken as a deduction on personal income taxes filed and collected in FY 1985.

7. Michael Lawson, *Tax Burdens for Families Residing in the Largest City in Each State,* 1982, ACIR Working Paper, (Washington D.C.: U.S. Advisory Commission on Intergovernmental Relations, 1984).

8. Mikesell, "Retail Sales and Use Taxation."

9. Michael E. Bell and Robert D. Ebel, *Financing An Urban Government* (Washington, D.C.: The District of Columbia Government 1978), Chapter 12.

10. Minnesota Department of Revenue, *Sales and Use Tax Changes,* June 1, 1984.

11. From 1975 to 1978 the rate of increase in the Minnesota sales tax base declines while spending for clothing and food nearly doubles. From 1979 to 1980, the sales tax grew by 2%, while food plus clothing grew five times faster. In the 1981-82 period, the current sales tax base declined by 4%, yet food and clothing expenditures increased by 4%. Data provided by William A. Blazar, from *National Income and Product Account* data. (November 1984).

# 11

# Selective Sales Taxes

In addition to employing a general sales and use tax, state/local governments employ a range of special narrowly-based taxes on consumption. In Minnesota the list includes the motor vehicle excise tax, motor fuels tax, alcoholic beverage tax, cigarette and tobacco taxes, and mortgage transfer and deed taxes. These taxes along with motor vehicle license (registration) fees, road tolls, transient accommodations taxes, and (borrowing an idea from neighboring South Dakota) taxes on the sale of controlled substances are the subject of this chapter.

These taxes can be treated as selective sales taxes. The first step in analyzing them is to lay out the rationale for such levies and then to evaluate them against the normative criteria for judging the performance of state/local taxes. Accordingly, this chapter begins with a summary of the statutory provisions of the taxes, including data on their revenue performance over time and Minnesota vs. U.S. comparisons. Following this descriptive section, the chapter takes a look at the rationale for selective sales taxation and then proceeds to a tax-by-tax analysis.

## DESCRIPTION OF THE MINNESOTA SYSTEM

### STATUTORY PROVISIONS

A summary of the statutory features of Minnesota's major selective sales (including motor vehicle license or registration tax) is presented in Table 1. The first of these taxes, the motor vehicle excise tax, is applied when a vehicle is first required to be registered to operate on Minnesota streets and highways. Although the tax is statutorily different from the general sales tax (since it is levied regardless of the age or of evidence of an actual arms-length sale), it is essentially in lieu of the retail sales tax.[1] The remaining taxes are, however, properly classified as selective sales levies and are examined as such. The first two of these (motor fuel and vehicle license) are considered together in one class (highway user taxes) as are the two real estate levies (mortgage registry and deed transfer taxes).

Revenue yields for each of these levies are provided in Table 2. Taken together they account for approximately 18% of total Minnesota state and

TABLE 1
Minnesota Excise and Licenses Taxes:
Rates, Bases, and Disposition, 1984

| Tax | Base | Rates | Disposition |
|---|---|---|---|
| Motor vehicle excise tax | Selling price of any vehicle required to register in Minnesota | 6 % | To be transferred from the general fund to special funds |
| Motor fuels tax | Gallons used in highway vehicles and aircraft | Gasoline and special fuels: $.17 per gallon for highway, $.05 per gallon for avaiation. Gasohol: $.15 per gallon | Highway fuels: 99.25% to Highway User Tax Distribution Fund; .75% to Dept. of Natural Resources. Aviation fuels: State Airports Fund |
| Motor vehicle license tax (registration) | For cars and pickup trucks; base value of vehicle adjusted for age. For trucks and buses: gross vehicle weight | For cars and pickup trucks: $10 plus 1.25 percent of base value but not less than $25 after 1-1-85. For trucks and buses: statutory schedule with tax varying by weight, age, and use | Highway User Tax Distribution Fund |
| Alcoholic beverage tax | Alcoholic beverages manufactured or received for sale in Minnesota | $.04 to $1.16 per liter for wine and distilled spirits; $2.00-$4.00 per barrel for beer. Also, tax of 2$1/2$% of retail sales price of liquor and beer with more than 3.2% alcohol | State general fund |
| Cigarette tax | Cigarettes and little cigars sold in Minnesota | $.18 per pack of 20 | State general fund: 89%; Natural resources: 5$1/2$%; Natural Resources Acceleration Account: 5$1/2$% |
| Tobacco products tax | Tobacco products other than cigarettes | 20% of wholesale price | State general fund |
| Mortgage registry tax | Principal amount of debt secured by mortgage of any real property in Minnesota | $.15 per $100 of principal | State general fund: 95%; Counties general funds: 5% |
| Deed transfer tax | Any transfer of real estate by deed, instrument, or writing | $2.20 plus $1.10 for each $500 of considertion in excess of $1,000 | State general fund |
| Lodging tax (may be imposed by any city) | Sales of transient lodging accommodations | Up to 3% | 95% must be used to promote tourism |

Source: Minnesota Department of Revenue.

local taxes. Although direct percentage comparisons with U.S. total must be made with caution due to the varying classifications of these taxes by the U.S. Census Bureau, Minnesota is about at the average of all states in terms of percentage reliance, though above the U.S. tax effort (chapter 4) in this category.

The relative importance of excise and license taxes declined significantly over the twenty-five years from 1957 to 1982. As shown in Table 3, the four main categories of selective sales taxes—motor vehicle, motor fuel, alcoholic beverage, and cigarette and tobacco products—accounted for 40.5% of tax revenues in 1957, but only 17.0% in 1982. Column 6 of Table 3 shows how the 1957-82 growth rates of these taxes compare with the growth rate of all taxes collected by the state: each grew more slowly than all taxes, with the tax on alcoholic beverages showing the least growth.

Revenue growth for selective sales tends to be relatively slow because inflation directly increases the tax bases of and dollar revenues from income, retail sales, and ad valorem excise taxes. In contrast, during periods of inflation, revenues from per-unit taxes (cigarette, motor fuel, and alcoholic beverages) grow less rapidly than other tax revenues unless tax rates are increased frequently.[2] Although inflation often triggers the legislature to enact rate increases, there is typically a lag between the inflationary impetus and the tax rate increase, especially when the rate of inflation is rapid and/ or unexpected.

TABLE 2
Revenue from Selected Sales and License Taxes,
Fiscal Years 1981-1984

| Taxes | FY 1981 Amount $000 | FY 1981 % of total taxes | FY 1982 Amount $000 | FY 1982 % of total taxes | FY 1983[a] Amount $000 | FY 1984[b] Amount $000 |
|---|---|---|---|---|---|---|
| Motor vehicle excise | 87,083 | 2.56 | 103,767 | 2.72 | 122,597 | 170,900 |
| Motor fuels | 232,871 | 6.86 | 259,351 | 6.81 | 263,445 | 315,000 |
| Motor vehicle licenses | 140,845 | 4.15 | 152,889 | 4.01 | 176,919 | 187,400 |
| Alcoholic beverages[c] | 55,803 | 1.64 | 55,465 | 1.46 | 53,336 | 54,302 |
| Cigarette and tobacco | 88,629 | 2.61 | 88,958 | 2.33 | 85,435 | 84,253 |
| Mortgage registration | 8,561 | .25 | 10,448 | .27 | 10,721 | 28,900 |
| Deed transfer | 8,514 | .25 | 7,508 | .20 | 8,860 | |

*Sources:* Data for 1981 and 1982 are from Minnesota Department of Revenue, Research Office, *Minnesota Tax Handbook,* August 1982, and addendum, September, 1983. Data for 1983 and 1984 have been provided by personnel at the Minnesota Department of Revenue and Minnesota Department of Transportation.
[a]Total collections for 1983 and 1984 not available to compute percentage shares.
[b]Estimated.
[c]Amounts do not include the 5 percent additional retail sales tax imposed on on-sale liquor from May 1, 1982 through June 30, 1983, nor do they include the 2 1/2 percent retail sales tax on both on-sale and off-sale liquor that has been levied since July 1, 1983.

TABLE 3
Changing Importance of Excise and
License Taxes, 1957-1982

| Tax | Revenue from indicated tax as percentage of all state tax revenues | | | | | Percentage change in revenues 1957-1982 |
|---|---|---|---|---|---|---|
| | 1957 | 1960 | 1970 | 1980 | 1982 | |
| | (1) | (2) | (3) | (4) | (5) | (6) |
| Motor vehicle excise and license | 12.45 | 12.25 | 6.40 | 6.86 | 6.66 | 633 |
| Motor fuel | 17.64 | 16.62 | 12.11 | 5.91 | 6.64 | 415 |
| Alcoholic beverages | 5.67 | 4.58 | 3.38 | 1.66 | 1.43 | 246 |
| Cigarettes and tobacco products | 4.71 | 6.22 | 4.90 | 2.64 | 2.30 | 569 |
| All four tax groups | 40.47 | 39.66 | 26.79 | 17.05 | 17.04 | 476 |
| All state taxes | 100.0 | 100.0 | 100.0 | 100.0 | 100.0 | 1,271 |

*Source:* Tax data are from Office of the Legislative Auditor: *State and Local Government Finances in Minnesota: A Review of Trends in Revenues and Expenditures, 1957-1982,* November 1983. GNP deflator is from U.S. Department of Commerce, Bureau of Economic Analysis.

[a] *1982 revenue/4.22 (1957 revenue), where 422 is the 1982 value of the GNP deflator for state and local purchases with 1957 value = 100.*

INTERSTATE COMPARISONS

All states levy taxes on gasoline, cigarettes, and alcohol. Table 4 shows that Minnesota's rates on these products exceed those levied in most states. They exceed the median rates, and with one exception of the cigarette tax in Wisconsin, they also exceed the rates of surrounding states (Illinois, Iowa, North Dakota, South Dakota, and Wisconsin). Although Minnesota's per-unit gasoline (motor fuel) tax is among the highest in the nation, it is not greatly out of line since one-half of the states levy a tax of 13 cents per gallon or more. Moreover, unlike eleven other states, Minnesota does not levy additional sales or gross receipts taxes on motor fuels.

Minnesota and most other states also tax other motor fuels: diesel, liquified petroleum gas (LPG), and gasohol. And, like a majority of other states, Minnesota taxes diesel and LPG (when used in highway vehicles) at the same rate as gasoline (17 cents per gallon), while taxing gasohol at a lower rate (2 cents per gallon lower until June 30, 1985, and 4 cents per gallon lower from July 1, 1985, through June 30, 1992). Table 5 summarizes current practice in the taxation of these fuels.

TABLE 4
State and Federal Excise Tax Rates,
January 1, 1984

|  | Gasoline (cents per gallon) | Cigarettes (cents per pack) | Distilled spirits (dollars per gallon) |
|---|---|---|---|
| Minnesota | 17 | 18 | 4.39 |
| Illinois | 12[a] | 12 | 2.00 |
| Iowa | 13 | 18 | b |
| North Dakota | 13 | 18 | 4.05 |
| South Dakota | 13 | 15 | 3.80 |
| Wisconsin | 16 | 25 | 3.25 |
| Federal[c] | 9 | 16 | 10.50 |
| Median rate, all states | 13 | 15 | 2.75 |
| Highest rate, all states | 18 | 26 | 6.50 |
| Lowest rate, all states | 5 | 2 | 1.50 |
| Number of states using tax | 51 | 51 | 33 |

*Source:* Federation of Tax Administrators, *Tax Administrators News,* January, 1984 and Advisory Commission on Intergovernmental Relations, *Significant Features of Fiscal Federation, 1982-83,* Washington, D.C., 1984.

[a]Will increase to 13 in July 1985.

[b]State monopoly on retail sales, 66 percent markup on sales of spirits.

[c]Recent legislation increased the federal tax on diesel fuel used by trucks from 9 to 15 cents per gallon, while reducing the federal highway-use taxes on heavy trucks. Cigarette taxes will decrease as previously scheduled to 8 cents per pack on September 30, 1985; distilled spirit taxes will increase on that date to $12.50 per gallon.

## CONCEPTUAL FRAMEWORK

### RATIONALE

There are four jurisdictions that are generally offered to support selective sales taxes:

- *Beneficiary Charge.*   If the use of a product can be easily and directly associated with the receipt or use of government services, this tax on the product or service can serve as a type of beneficiary or user charge. Taxes on motor vehicles and motor fuels, which are earmarked for highway use, are often viewed in this manner. An interesting implication of this benefits-received view is that selective sales and license taxes can be designed to achieve simultaneously the two goals of efficiency and equity in taxation, two goals often in conflict with one another with respect to other forms of taxation.
- *Full Accounting for Social Costs.*   If the private market system operates in a manner that causes the price one pays for a commodity to fail to take into account all the costs associated with its use, an inefficient allocation of resources results. In order to correct for (or at least minimize) this

inefficiency, taxes can be added to the market price in order to force buyers to take into account the full social costs of their private decision to use the product and/or reduce the use of that product. The classic case for such special sales taxes are those levied on pollution activities. Also, taxes on alcohol and tobacco products are sometimes rationalized that their use generates costs for members of society other than the users. For example, alcohol use can lead to automobile accidents that damage persons other than the users. Similarly, the costs of treating heart attacks, emphysema, and lung cancer caused by smoking are borne in part by nonsmokers as they pay taxes to support private and public health care. Note, however, that it does not follow that the revenues from such taxes should be earmarked to pay for the damage (e.g., through specific health programs or campaigns) caused by this failure of the market to account fully for all costs of consumption or production of a product.

• *Sumptuary.* Some taxes are imposed to discourage fully the use or consumption of a particular commodity. Such "sumptuary" taxation intentionally interferes with consumer choice on the ground that consumption of the taxed commodity is socially undesirable for moral or other reasons. This justification is frequently used to justify the introduction of tax policy as one tool in the control of drug trafficking.

• *Minimizing Interference with Consumer Decisions.* As is indicated from the above discussion, the use of special consumption-based taxes places an added emphasis on the distortion of economic decisions. In some cases, such as for the full accounting for social costs and the sumptuary rationales discussed above, these distortions or interferences with the market system are considered desirable. Usually, however, it is the goal of

TABLE 5
Differential Taxation of Motor Fuels,
January 1, 1984

| | Number of states in which the fuel is:[a] | | | |
|---|---|---|---|---|
| Fuel | taxed at same rate as gasoline | taxed at lower rate than gasoline | taxed at higher rate than gasoline | not taxed[b] |
| Diesel | 38 (MN) | 0 | 12 | 1 |
| LPG | 36 (MN) | 8 | 0 | 7 |
| Gasohol | 23 | 23 (MN) | 0 | 5 |

*Source:* Federation of Tax Administrators, *Tax Administrators News,* January, 1984.
[a]Includes District of Columbia.
[b]Wyoming levies a fee of 1.1. mills per ton-mile in lieu of a gallonage tax on diesel fuel and LPG.

tax policy to raise revenues while at the same time minimize interference with the private (e.g., consumer) decisions. Economists have investigated the properties of a tax system designed to achieve this goal. The conclusion of the optional taxation literature most relevant to this discussion is that the tax goal of minimizing unintended interferences with consumer decisions of a tax is achieved by taxing most heavily those goods having demands that are relatively insensitive to small changes in price—i.e., those goods with the most "price-inelastic" demands. To put it another way, certain narrowly-based sales taxes are targeted to "pluck the feathers of the chicken that squawks the least."

## WHO PAYS? IMPACT VS. INCIDENCE

In describing how the burden of a tax is distributed, it is important to distinguish between tax impact (the initial distribution of tax liabilities) and tax incidence (the distribution that prevails after all adjustments to the tax have been made). The process that generates a difference between impact and incidence is called tax shifting.

The impact of selective sales taxes is in most instances on sellers, but it is widely agreed that these taxes are shifted to buyers. When buyers are final consumers, there is no further shifting and the taxes are distributed among households (consumers) in proportion to their expenditures on the taxed products. When buyers are businesses (for example, fuel purchased by trucking companies), the taxes add to the businesses' costs and are likely to be shifted to the consumers of the products that the businesses are producing or distributing. The degree to which these taxes can be fully shifted to consumers is a function of the seller's specific market situation. Here, the primary determinant is the number of other sellers who are also in the market and who are offering a close substitute product. The less the availability of these substitute commodities, the more easily the seller can pass on the tax. For example, gasoline retailers near the Minnesota border may not be able to shift fully the gasoline tax if the retailers across the border are subject to a lower tax, in which case Minnesota's border gasoline retailers may face a highly price-elastic demand. Allowance is made for this possibility in the current law. The tax rate on gasoline sold by retailers within seven and one-half miles of the border is set so that it cannot be more than 3 cents per gallon above the rate levied in the neighboring state. By similar reasoning, the incidence of motor vehicle license taxes is on households. License taxes on vehicles owned and used by households cannot be shifted, while license taxes on vehicles used by transport operators add to their costs and are therefore likely shifted in part to consumers of transported products.

In short, the incidence of selective sales taxes is largely on households, even though these taxes are collected from and initially paid by sellers of cigarettes, alcoholic beverages, motor fuels, vehicles, and transportation services. And, the burden of these taxes is generally regressive. As noted above, households bear these taxes in proportion to their expenditures on the taxed products, and in the case of the commodities discussed here, spending as a percentage of income increases as income itself decreases. Figure 1 graphically depicts this inverse expenditure-income relationship for consumers in the north central states for gasoline, alcohol, and tobacco products. With spending as a percentage of income on the vertical axis and income on the horizontal, the downward slope of the figures shows the regressive pattern of these expenditures. Thus, it follows that a tax on these items will tend to be distributed in a similar pattern. The figure shows that the tax regressivity for motor fuel taxes is likely to be greatest for persons with incomes below $16,000 per year and then level off (but not quite to proportionality) after that. In contrast, the graph flattens out much faster for tobacco products and alcoholic beverages.

## HIGHWAY TAXES

### THE PRESENT STRUCTURE

Most highway administrators and user groups agree that some adjustments will have to be made in the next few years to increase the amount of revenues generated from highway taxes (primarily gasoline taxes and motor vehicle licenses) in order to pay for rising costs of roadway maintenance. The primary reason for these adjustments stems from the fact that as big trucks get bigger and heavier, road damage increases. Clearly, someone will have to pay if roads are to be maintained. Accordingly, this next discussion looks at the issue of Minnesota's method of highway financing. It begins with an evaluation of the present structure and then proceeds to examine a major reform, which is now used in eight states and is being considered at the federal level, a weight-distance tax. Following is a discussion of several less sweeping alternatives available to Minnesota.

With the exception of the motor vehicle excise tax, all of Minnesota's taxes on motor vehicles and motor fuels are earmarked (or dedicated) for transportation purposes. Furthermore, under present law, motor vehicle excise taxes will be fully transferred by FY 1992 from the state general fund to the highway user tax distribution fund (75%) and the transit assistance fund (25%). Thus, Minnesota's taxes on motor vehicles and motor fuels are appropriately regarded and evaluated as user taxes, applying primarily to the operation of highway vehicles in Minnesota.

In evaluating Minnesota's motor fuel and motor vehicle taxes, two questions are central:

• Are the taxes distributed equitably among and within highway user classes?

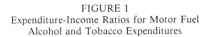

FIGURE 1
Expenditure-Income Ratios for Motor Fuel
Alcohol and Tobacco Expenditures

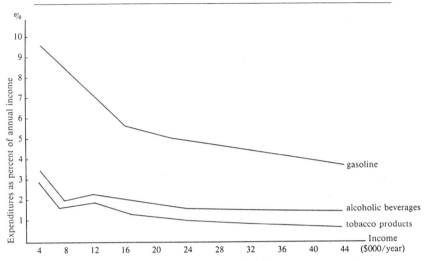

*Source:* U.S. Department of Labor, Bureau of Labor Statistics, *Consumer Expend
Survey: Diary Survey,* 1980-81, Table 9, p. 40. Data are for urban consumer units, North
Central region.

• Is the distribution of taxes among various classes such as to encourage efficient development and use of the state's transportation system?

Equity in highway-user taxation is framed in terms of the "benefits received" criteria. This requires that taxes be distributed according to cost generated—relatively high tax burdens on users that generate relatively high costs and conversely. Thus, fairness is assessed by comparing the distribution of taxes among users with the distribution of user generated costs.

Efficiency also requires that highway users pay taxes that correspond to the costs that they generate. That is, highway taxes should accurately signal costs to users. When they do, individuals and businesses will use and demand provision of highways only when they are efficient (cost-effective) modes of transport. Thus, when taxes understate costs, inefficiently large highway systems will be demanded; conversely when taxes overstate costs, too little investment will be made in roadways.

*Estimating Costs.* Having established these two criteria, the practical question arises as to how to estimate the costs for highway use. Based on the premise that a vehicle generates cost in (a) proportion to the distance it travels, and (b) increasing as axel weight increases, the U.S. Department of Transportation has recently (1982) estimated the per-mile costs of various classes of vehicles. These "cost responsibility" estimates are provided by vehicle type in column 1 of Table 6. The data show that on a per-mile basis, the heavier the load the larger the per-mile cost—i.e., where cost refers to damages that require road repairs. These cost responsibility numbers show that automobiles rank lowest at 47 cents per mile while the "big rigs" are eleven to fifteen times that. In short: heavy vehicles do more damage more quickly than light ones. A recent report by the U.S. General Accounting Office considered that the heaviest rig—an 80,000 pound, five-axle truck—weighs about as much as twenty automobiles but has the same impact on an interstate highway as 9,600 cars.

At first glance, Minnesota's highway tax system appears to be a fairly satisfactory system of taxing highway users according to cost responsibility. *Motor vehicle license* tax payments depend on weight and other vehicle characteristics (age and use), but not distance traveled. The license (registration) tax for automobiles and pickups are based on value. Farm vehicles generally pay a lower tax than nonfarm vehicles. *Fuel tax* payments depend on miles traveled and miles per gallon. Therefore, with this two-part system of taxation, which is typical of most states, users of Minnesota highways do pay taxes that are roughly related to vehicle weight and miles traveled.

However, the system has serious limitations from both equity and efficiency perspectives. Since fuel tax rates are the same for all vehicle types, the per-mile user tax varies among vehicle types and weights only to the extent that miles per gallon vary. Therefore, fuel tax payments can closely approximate cost responsibilities only if there is a close correspondence between fuel consumption per mile and costs generated per mile. But such is not the case. As Table 6 also shows, fuel consumption increases as vehicle weight increases, but costs generated per mile traveled increase more rapidly, so that fuel tax payments decline as a proportion of cost responsibility (see column 3). The result is that when between-class comparisons are made, lighter vehicles pay a larger share of their cost than heavier vehicles. And within classes the lighter members of the class overpay relative to the heavier members. In economic jargon, there are cross-subsidies occurring.

This aspect of fuel taxation (underpayment by relatively heavy vehicles and overpayment by relatively light vehicles) is clearly inequitable, if cost responsibility is the accepted basis for assessing equity. Furthermore, it provides inefficient signals to highway users, leading to overuse by heavier vehicles and an excessive demand (expressed through the political process) for highways that will handle the heavier vehicles.

Minnesota's license tax rates, shown in Table 7, increase with vehicle weight. This tax therefore helps to correct the between-class equity problem

TABLE 6
Estimated Cost Responsibility, Fuel Consumption,
and Tax Payments, by Vehicle Class[a]

| Vehicle class | Cost responsibility (cents/mile) | Fuel consumption (miles/gallon) | Fuel tax payments as proportion of cost responsibility[b] |
|---|---|---|---|
| Automobiles and Motorcycles | .47 | 18.0 | 1.06 |
| Pickups and Vans | .56 | 13.6 | 1.32 |
| Single-Unit Trucks less than 26,000 pounds | 1.09 | 7.7 | 1.07 |
| Single-Unit Trucks 26,000 pounds and above | 2.64 | 6.3 | .55 |
| Combination Trucks less than 50,000 pounds | 3.36 | 5.6 | .48 |
| Combination Trucks 50,000 to 70,000 pounds | 4.07 | 5.5 | .40 |
| Combination Trucks 70,000 to 75,000 pounds | 5.49 | 5.3 | .31 |
| Combination Trucks 75,000 and above | 7.29 | 5.3 | .23 |

*Source:* U.S. Department of Transportation, *Alternatives to Tax on Use of Heavy Trucks, Report to Congress,* January, 1984. Cost responsibility is from Table III-3; fuel consumption is derived from column 1 of Table III-4.

[a]Estimates of cost responsibility are for federal highway program of $12.8 billion in fiscal year 1985. For each vehicle class, average operating characteristics are assumed.

[b]Assumes federal fuel tax rate of 9 cents per gallon.

discussed above. Indeed, between-class inequity could in principle be eliminated by setting license tax rates so that each vehicle class taken as a whole pays fuel plus license taxes equal to its cost responsibility. But within-class inequities would remain because vehicles that travel fewer miles than the class average would pay taxes in excess of the costs they generate while vehicles that travel more than the average would underpay; high-mileage users would be subsidized by low-mileage users.

More important, because it is stated as a fixed fee, the license tax does not change the additional (marginal) tax costs of highway use, which are determined by the fuel tax rate and miles per gallon. Consequently, imposing a license tax based on vehicle weight and type does not solve the efficiency problem that arises when the per-mile fuel tax does not accurately reflect the highway costs generated by an additional mile of travel. That is, a license tax does not reduce the incentive for inefficient overuse of the highway system by relatively heavy vehicles.

*Revenue adequacy.* Table 8 shows that from 1970 through 1982 Minnesota highway user tax revenues did not increase as rapidly as the operation and maintenance cost index published by the U.S. Federal Highway Administration. Stated differently, these revenues fell 21% in real terms or purchasing power. The state's ability to finance maintenance and/ or expansion of its highway system from user taxes clearly diminished over this period, and in this sense revenues were inadequate. Whether revenues have been inadequate in a broader and more absolute sense must be based on judgments about the amount that Minnesota should be spending on highways and how that spending should be financed.

One consequence of the relatively slow growth of user tax revenues has been increased reliance on other revenue sources, primarily appropriations from general funds; this pattern of change is common to Minnesota, its neighbors, and the U.S. as a whole. Also, revenues appear to be insufficient to fund construction and reconstruction needs to be identified and defined by the Minnesota Department of Transportation.[3]

Revenues grew more slowly than costs primarily because motor fuel tax rates did not increase in line with costs. Tax rates increased only 86% while costs increased 178%. Thus, the apparent inadequacy of the system could have been remedied by ad hoc tax rate increases. Of course, such increases require legislative action and, therefore, are typically imposed only with a lag. This lag is well illustrated by the fact that the 143% increase in the fuel

TABLE 7
Minnesota License Tax Base Rate Schedule

| Total gross weight in pounds | Base rate |
|---|---|
| 0- 1,500 | $    15 |
| 1,501- 3,000 | 20 |
| 3,001- 4,500 | 25 |
| 4,501- 6,000 | 35 |
| 6,001- 9,000 | 45 |
| 9,001-12,000 | 70 |
| 12,001-15,000 | 105 |
| 15,001-18,000 | 145 |
| 18,001-21,000 | 190 |
| 21,001-17,000 | 270 |
| 27,001-33,000 | 360 |
| 33,001-39,000 | 470 |
| 39,001-45,000 | 590 |
| 45,001-51,000 | 710 |
| 51,001-57,000 | 860 |
| 57,001-63,000 | 1,010 |
| 63,001-69,000 | 1,180 |
| 69,001-73,280 | 1,320 |
| 73,281-78,000 | 1,520 |
| 78,001-81,000 | 1,620 |
| plus $50 for each ton or fraction thereof in excess of 81,000 pounds. | |

The license tax for each category and age of truck is calculated as a fraction of this base rate as specified in Minnesota Statutes, Section 168. Only two other states, Oklahoma and North Dakota, consider age in setting license taxes.

tax rate from 1970 to 1984 was not sufficient to offset the 178% cost increase that occurred over the shorter 1970-82 period. That is, the fuel tax rate has increased more slowly than the cost index, even when allowance is made for the recent sharp increase in the rate (from 13 cents in 1982 to 17 cents in 1984).

Over the next decade, revenue adequacy will be enhanced by the deduction of motor vehicle excise tax revenues to the highway user tax distribution fund. But conditions that characterized the past decade—rising maintenance and operation costs and relatively static fuel consumption— seem likely to persist. Indeed, from FY 1984 through FY 1990, fuel tax revenues are forecast to decrease slightly, given current tax rates. A slight increase in other traditional user tax revenues is forecast, but the rate of increase is likely to fall short of the rate of inflation. Thus, future increases in fuel and license tax rates seem likely. Barring such increases or the implementation of a weight-distance tax, an increasing fraction of revenues will be obtained from taxes that are not closely related to highway use.

TABLE 8
Increases in Highway Costs, User Tax Revenues,
and Tax Rates, 1970-1984

| Item[a] | Percentage increase: | |
|---|---|---|
| | 1970-1982 | 1970-1984[b] |
| Index of federal highway maintenance and operation costs | 178 | n.a. |
| Fuel tax rate, Minnesota | 86 | 143 |
| Fuel tax rate, federal | 0 | 125 |
| Minnesota highway user tax collections[a] | 120 | 169 |
| Gasoline, taxable gallons, Minnesota | 1 | 5 |

*Sources:* Index of highway costs from Federal Highway Administration, *Highway Statistics, 1982.* User tax collections and gasoline gallons from Minnesota Department of Revenue publications and personnel.

[a]Motor fuel and motor vehicle license tax revenues.

[b]Data for 1984 are estimated.

## THE WEIGHT-DISTANCE TAX

*Equity and efficiency.* The equity and efficiency goals of taxation could both be enhanced if Minnesota replaced its present two-part (motor fuel plus license tax) system with a weight-distance on trucks. This tax is basically a mileage tax, with the tax rate per mile of travel on public highways an increasing function of gross vehicle weight. Equity and efficiency would be achieved if the per-mile tax rate for each vehicle class were to approximate closely the costs generated when a vehicle of that class travels a mile on public highways. At present, eight states—Arizona,

Arkansas, Idaho, Kentucky, New Mexico, New York, Ohio, and Oregon—
have weight-distance taxes. In addition, Wyoming and Colorado have a ton-
mile tax, which is similar.[4]

Table 9 illustrates the difference between the weight-distance tax and the
two-part user tax employed by Minnesota and most other states. The
comparison, which is for an 80,000 pound, gross vehicle weight, five-axle
combination, also illustrates the equity and efficiency problems of the two-
part Minnesota system. Cost responsibility for this type of vehicle is
estimated at 2.224 cents per mile empty and 17.14 cents per mile fully
loaded. The example is constructed on the assumption that vehicles of this
class are fully loaded for 60% of their miles and empty for the remainder,
giving an average cost responsibility of 11 cents per mile.

As column 2 of Table 9 shows, the weight-distance tax per mile is the same
regardless of miles traveled, and thus the marginal tax levied per mile (the
tax for each additional mile traveled) is equal to the estimated cost
responsibility per mile. Thus, the weight-distance tax is fair in that it charges
each vehicle for the costs that it generates whether it is a low-mileage or a
high-mileage vehicle, provided that it has the assumed sixty-forty ratio of
fully loaded to empty miles. Vehicles with a higher ratio of loaded to empty
miles underpay, while vehicles with a lower ratio overpay.

From an efficiency perspective, a tax is ideal if it confronts users with a
tax per mile that accurately reflects the additional costs generated by an
additional mile of travel. The weight-distance tax does not fully measure up
to this ideal because it does not vary with load.[5]

TABLE 9
Comparison of Weight-Distance and Two Part Tax System, 1982

| Thousands of miles traveled per year | Cost responsibility $ per mile (1) | Tax payments, $/mile[a] | | |
|---|---|---|---|---|
| | | Weight-distance tax (2) | $1,620/year plus $.17/gallon (3) | $4,000/year plus $.17/gallon (4) |
| 10 | .11 | .11 | .194 | .432 |
| 20 | .11 | .11 | .113 | .232 |
| 40 | .11 | .11 | .073 | .132 |
| 50 | .11 | .11 | .065 | .112 |
| 70 | .11 | .11 | .056 | .090 |
| 90 | .11 | .11 | .050 | .077 |
| 100 | .11 | .11 | .049 | .072 |

*Source:* Estimates of cost responsibility are from Federal Highway Administration, *Final
Report on the Federal Highway Cost Allocation Study,* May, 1982.

[a]Columns 3 and 4 for Minnesota assume vehicle average 5.25 miles per gallon and therefore
pay fuel taxes of $.0324 per mile. The $1,620 is the fee that now applies in Minnesota.

Column 3 shows the tax per mile for the present two-part Minnesota system. At present, the 80,000 pound, five-axle vehicle pays a registration fee of $1,620 per year and a fuel tax of 17 cents per gallon. With this tax scheme, vehicles that travel less than 20,871 per year overpay (they pay user charges that average more than 11 cents per mile), while vehicles that travel more than 20,871 miles underpay.[6] This same conclusion—that the vehicles in a given class that travel less overpay and therefore subsidize the group that travels more—would be exacerbated if the Minnesota license fee were to be increased (see column 4). Thus, the two-part system is inherently inequitable in that it always charges low-mileage users more per mile of roadway.

Moreover, note that if one ignores the between-class cross-subsidy, the two-part system in Minnesota is also deficient from an efficiency perspective, since it imposes a marginal tax per mile of only 3.24 cents, far short of the 11 cents per mile cost responsibility.

*Tax yield.* As the above discussion indicates, equity and efficiency considerations are of primary importance in discussions of selective sales taxation. Having established these two arguments for a weight-distance tax as a replacement for the present Minnesota system, two other practical issues arise: first, what is the proper yield or level of the tax, and second, can such a tax meet the criteria for ease of administration and taxpayer compliance.

The issue of level or yield is discussed first. Once one accepts the premise that highway taxes are essentially user fees and that cross-subsidies among users should not be continued, it follows that the annual yield of the weight-distance tax should be set to cover the total annual damage costs. This "correct" level has not been estimated here, in part because it would entail a major survey to learn the incidence of the use by type of vehicle on all of Minnesota's roadways. Accordingly, for present purposes, it is necessary to proceed with the discussion of the pros and cons of this tax vis-a-vis the several other options, on the assumption that if a switch to weight-distance is made, the switch will be made only after an appropriate state agency (e.g., the Minnesota Department of Transportation) carries out a thorough study regarding the highway damage costs associated with various vehicles. If it turns out that the elimination of the present tax subsidy that now accrues to the heavier and more traveled vehicles would cause some unintended outcomes such as reduced employment, the state has two choices: either indefinitely continue some (perhaps the current) amount of subsidy on a vehicle class basis with the subsidy to be made up out of the general fund, or provide for a subsidy that gradually vanishes over some transition period (e.g., two to three years). Regardless of which choice is made, if an equal yield substitution is made, the result will be increased efficiency and equity in highway tax policy and enhanced fiscal accountability since the subsidy will be direct and explicit rather than, as presently structured, under the veil of cross-subsidies.

From the point of view of smaller and less driven vehicles, the result will be an elimination of the implicit payments to the heavier vehicles and a reduction in relative highway tax burdens.

*Administration and compliance.*    Assuring accurate reporting of miles traveled on public highways is the key administrative problem and cost in weight-distance taxation. Reporting methods range from self-assessment, in which case operators report mileage as recorded by their odometers, to automated systems that utilize sealed meters. Such meters are now in use by larger carriers in the U.S., and they have been used for taxing purposes in other countries.

Experience in Oregon, which has employed a weight-distance tax since 1949, attests to the feasibility of administration of the tax and relative ease of taxpayer compliance. Oregon relies on self-reporting, with the administrative agency maintaining a separate account for each trucking firm.

Total administrative costs, which include a share of the overhead costs of the Oregon Public Utility Commission (the administering agency) as well as audit and collection costs, are estimated at 5% to 7% of gross receipts. Compliance appears to be very satisfactory, with collections estimated to be 95% of taxes due.

Moreover, the information that motor carriers must report to comply with Oregon's weight-distance tax is typically available from records that they keep for other purposes. Interstate carriers must file periodic reports in most states (including Minnesota) giving number of miles traveled, in total and in the specific state, and the gallons of fuel purchased in the state. They must also supply detailed information on their operations to state and federal income tax administrators. Thus, the recordkeeping and reporting costs directly attributable to Oregon's system appear to be minimal.

One final note, if a weight-distance tax were adopted as a full or partial replacement for the present two-part system, there are still two reasons to maintain some license (registration) fee: first, it clearly aids in administration and regulation; second some highway costs are fixed (overhead) costs and thus not affected by additional use (e.g., drainage systems and right-of-way acquisition).

DIESEL DIFFERENTIAL

A less bold alternative to weight-distance type proposals is a "diesel differential" levy whereby diesel gasoline is taxed at higher rates than nondiesel fuel as a way of differentially taxing heavy trucks, the main buyers of diesel. Twelve states currently tax diesel at a rate higher than gasoline, with rate differentials ranging from 1 cent to 3 cents per gallon. Among nearby states, both Iowa and Illinois have diesel differentials of 2.5 cents per gallon. Adoption of a diesel differential by Minnesota would have the following advantages:

- *Revenues* would increase by approximately $3 million per penny increased. Thus, if Minnesota were to meet Iowa's 2.5 cents per gallon, highway revenues would rise by $7.5 million. Of course, an alternative would be to use these extra dollars to reduce the motor fuel tax on smaller vehicles such as automobiles and pickups, thereby maintaining an equal yield of motor fuel revenues.
- *Equity and Efficiency* between vehicle class improvements could occur if some (or all) the revenues from the diesel differential were used to reduce license fees on smaller and lighter vehicles. However, equity would not be served if the higher diesel rate were used to finance a net reduction in license taxes on heavier vehicles.
- *Ease of Administration and Compliance* is achieved if the differential is simply reflected in the pump price. In contrast, attempts to differentiate among vehicles at the pump could be most cumbersome.

The diesel differential also has several disadvantages:

- *Equity and Efficiency* violations would remain because as vehicle weight increases, the costs generated by highway use rise much more rapidly than does fuel consumption. For example, doubling the diesel rate to 34 cents per gallon would result in a per-mile fuel tax for fully loaded 80,000-pound vehicles of only 6.5 cents, well below current estimates of the cost that such a vehicle generates per mile of travel. Therefore, a diesel differential would reduce but not eliminate the undertaxation of heavy vehicles relative to light vehicles.
- *Tax Enforcement* problems would be aggravated because diesel oil ostensibly purchased for tax exempt nonhighway uses can be diverted to use in highway vehicles. A higher tax on highway use of diesel would increase the incentive for such diversion. Enforcement would be facilitated—but administration made more difficult—by collecting the tax on diesel from distributors on all sales, and then having nonhighway users file for a credit upon application.

### INDEXING MOTOR FUEL TAXES

Until the late 1970s, states increased fuel tax rates only through periodic legislative action. However, in response to the rapid inflation of the late 1970s and early 1980s, eleven states and the District of Columbia have enacted (as of January 1984) mechanisms for administratively adjusting fuel tax rates in response to one or more indexing factors. Three of these states and eight others levy sales or gross receipts taxes on fuel purchases, in addition to the gallonage tax. Among neighboring states, Illinois currently levies a sales tax as well as a gallonage tax on fuel purchases. And indexing will become effective in Wisconsin in 1985.

Indexing on the basis of highway costs keeps the real value (purchasing power) of user contributions for the financing of highway services from eroding during periods of inflation. It is also desirable on equity and efficiency grounds because it prevents a decline (such as occurred in 1974-80) in the real user-tax payment for highway repair.

If Minnesota had indexed its motor fuel tax rate on the basis of operation and maintenance costs since 1960, the state would have a fuel tax rate that is at least 4 cents higher than the current 17 cents per gallon, and be generating additional revenues of about $74 million for FY 1985. This estimate takes into account that at 21 cents per gallon, Minnesota would be somewhat of an outlier in motor fuel rates (18 cents is now the highest) and thus that some gasoline sales would be reduced.[7]

A decision to recommend indexing should address the question of "Which index"? Several indexes are available, including the consumer price index (CPI), retail price of fuel, wholesale price of fuel, the U.S. Federal Highway Administration operation and maintenance cost index, and sales of taxable fuels. States utilizing indexing typically restrict the range over which tax rates may vary in response to index changes.

During periods of rapid inflation, indexing on the basis of operation and maintenance costs assures that revenues grow as rapidly as costs if fuel consumption is either static or increasing. However, this same result is not as likely to be achieved with indexing based on other factors such as the CPI or the wholesale and retail prices of fuel. These indexes often move independently of operation and maintenance costs.

Ohio and Michigan are the only states that at present index on the basis of operation and maintenance costs; Wisconsin will index on this basis beginning April, 1985. Ohio and Michigan also use a second factor, taxable sales, to which tax rates are inversely related—when taxable sales (gallonage) falls, the tax rate increases. This two-part indexing mechanism is superior to other mechanisms if the objective is to prevent the purchasing power of fuel tax revenues from falling during periods such as the late 1970s and early 1980s, when highway costs were increasing in dollar terms and rising fuel prices were curtailing fuel consumption.

### INDEXING LICENSE TAXES

Minnesota's motor vehicle taxes are partially responsive to inflation in that registration fees for automobiles and pickup trucks are based on dollar value. That is, revenues from license taxes on automobiles and pickups increase when the rate of inflation increases, although less than proportionately. In contrast, revenues from truck and bus registrations, which are based on age, weight, and use, are not sensitive to the inflation rate. License taxes could, like fuel taxes, be fully indexed to operation and maintenance costs or some other measure of inflation, and the arguments pertaining to indexing fuel taxes would also hold for indexing license taxes.

## DEDICATION OF MOTOR VEHICLE EXCISE TAX

Fourteen states currently dedicate some or all of their motor vehicle sales and use tax revenue to a road or highway fund. On July 1, 1984, Minnesota began dedicating a part of its motor vehicle excise tax revenues to the highway users tax distribution fund (HUTDF) and the transit assistance fund; the fraction dedicated will reach a maximum of 75% to the HUTDF and 25% to the transit fund in FY 1992.

Dedication of motor vehicle excise tax revenues to HUTDF has been supported as an offset to the failure of traditional user tax revenues to keep pace with highway costs and funding needs. However, as shown above, this failure can in large part be attributed to the fact that the legislature has not adjusted fuel and license tax rates in response to inflation. Thus, the dedication of motor vehicle excise tax revenues to the HUTDF is essentially a decision to substitute general tax revenues for per-unit motor fuel and license tax revenues.

Motor vehicle excise taxes are paid by highway users and in that very general sense they are user taxes. However, the amount of tax paid does not vary directly with highway mileage, and more important, it is only loosely connected to costs generated by highway use. The motor vehicle excise tax is therefore far from an ideal user tax and the transfer of excise tax revenue to the HUTDF can be viewed as the use of general purpose revenue for highway financing that continues the subsidy of the big rigs.

An alternative to dedicating motor vehicle excise tax revenue to the HUTDF would be to follow the lead of ten other states and include fuel purchases in the retail sales tax base and dedicate the resulting sales tax revenues to the HUTDF. The advantage of this alternative is that the sales tax on fuel is more directly related to highway use than is the motor vehicle excise tax.

## TOLLS

Another method of financing highway costs is the use of highway tolls. Since tolls assess a fee for the use of a particular road, they provide a mechanism for bringing highway taxes closer to the costs resulting from use of the highways. Most highway costs are not specific to a particular road. For instance, pavement damage costs are incurred on all roads, and taxes funding this cost need not distinguish between different roads. However, certain costs may be uniquely associated with a particular road. For instance, a toll may be appropriate where a road or bridge requires particularly high costs to allow vehicles to reach certain places. Similarly, a congested urban highway can create costs for users in terms of their time lost due to the road's crowded condition. Again, a toll could signal to motorists the full costs of additional crowding at that time. Such a toll could ensure that only those who valued the time saved at or above the cost of the toll would drive on the road then and decrease crowding to the appropriate level.

The advantage of tolls suggests an accompanying disadvantage. Tolls are ill-advised on roads that cannot be uniquely differentiated. For instance, it would be bad policy to assess a congestion toll on one road that runs alongside and to and from the same places as another nontolled road. Traffic would simply be diverted from the toll road to the free road for no good reason. Similarly a toll on a road or bridge not requiring expensive building costs might also divert traffic or lead to under use of the road or bridge.

Tolls also have the disadvantage of having high administrative costs and may, to some degree, impair highway safety. Further, states are restricted from assessing tolls on completed federal interstate highways.

Because of the particular characteristics of Minnesota's highway needs, tolls do not appear appropriate for widespread adoption. Minnesota does not have any especially dense urban areas that might call for congestion tolls, nor do there appear to be any needs for roads or bridges that are extraordinarily expensive. Nevertheless, the idea should not be rejected outright. In the right circumstances—where the user and the service received are clearly identifiable and the roadway is easily differentiated from other roadways—tolls provide an equitable and efficient means of at least partially financing highway costs.

## ALCOHOL AND TOBACCO TAXES

Minnesota's selective sales taxation of alcohol and cigarette products, while certainly less complex than highway taxation, has a similar feature: the taxes are levied on a per-unit method.[8] As Table 1 indicates, cigarettes are taxed at 18 cents per pack, and alcoholic beverages are taxed on a per-liter (wine and distilled spirits) and per-barrel (beer) basis. Tobacco products other than cigarettes are taxed on an ad valorem basis of 20% of wholesale price.

The result of this per-unit approach is that the real value of these taxes has fallen; the burden of the tax on the sale of a pack of cigarettes or a gallon of liquor or beer is about 60% less than it was in 1972. As shown in Table 3, these taxes account for a small and shrinking share of state revenue.

### EQUITY AND EFFICIENCY

Excise taxes on alcohol and tobacco products are regressive in their incidence (Figure 1). Nevertheless, they continue to be used, presumably because they are seen as serving other purposes. In particular, they may:

- Reduce the use of the taxed products, often seen as desirable on two grounds: use is unhealthy for the user; and users impose costs on others (e.g., automobile accidents caused by intoxicated drivers and publicly financed treatment of health problems resulting from the use of alcohol and tobacco).
- Force buyers to recognize full costs associated with use, regardless of whether the full costs discourage use.
- Facilitate regulatory activity aimed at controlling the availability of alcoholic beverages and tobacco.

Equity is (roughly) served because the external social costs that tobacco and alcohol users impose on others, including other users, are reduced. This is true even if the taxes do not affect the amount of alcohol and tobacco used if one views the tax as a compensation for the cost users impose on others. This compensation effect is easily arrived at when tax revenues are dedicated for programs that make restitution for bodily and property damages caused by intoxicated persons or treat health problems associated with alcohol and tobacco use. *But the compensation is no less real if excise tax revenues are used for general government purposes; in this case, compensation takes the form of relatively lighter overall tax burdens for persons who make relatively little use of alcohol and tobacco.*

Efficiency is promoted in two ways. First, efficiency is promoted because the taxes serve as stand-ins for external costs that would otherwise be ignored by individuals as they make decisions about alcohol and tobacco use. Stated differently, in the absence of taxation (or some other deterrent to use), there would be "overuse" of the products because individuals would not give full weight to the costs that their use imposes on others.

Second, because these taxes are on products that exhibit relative price-inelasticity, the tax minimizes interference with consumer behavior (i.e., the excess burden of the tax is minimized).

This second efficiency argument deserves a bit more comment, however, since there is evidence that not all smokers react to price in the same way. Specifically, there is evidence that at least for teenagers, the price response may be significant. Indeed, Minnesota teenage smoking appears to be so sensitive to price that an increase of 1% in Minnesota cigarette prices would actually cause an even greater (1.4%) decrease in cigarette consumption.[9]

The evidence of whether a similar differential impact exists for alcohol consumption is not available. Thus, the only conclusion here is that demand for alcohol is generally unresponsive to price change. A 1% increase in the Minnesota tax on distilled spirits would reduce consumption by only about 0.6%.[10] Demand for beer tends to be even less responsive to price changes, while wine is more responsive.

From available evidence about price elasticities, it seems fair to conclude that Minnesota's excise taxes reduce consumption of distilled spirits and cigarettes, but the decrease is not large in relation to total consumption of these products. Whether these relatively small reductions produce equity and efficiency gains that justify the use of regressive taxes cannot be determined with the information available. At a minimum, they preclude a firm verdict against excise taxes on either equity or efficiency grounds. Such a verdict would seem to require solid evidence that the external costs associated with alcohol and tobacco use generate small equity and efficiency losses relative to the equity loss associated with the use of regressive taxes.

## TAX YIELD

As noted, the importance of taxes on tobacco (particularly cigarettes) and alcoholic beverages is shrinking due to the automatic inflation erosion of the tax rates. This erosion, in turn, is the result of the failure of the legislature to act often enough in making periodic rate adjustments. In short, there is a similar choice: allow inflation to continue to erode real tax rates as Minnesota has been permitting in recent years; or recommend some automatic upward rate adjustment mechanism.

If the latter approach is taken, there are two possible ways to go:

*Indexation.*   The first is to index automatically the per-unit cigarette and alcoholic beverage taxes by an inflation measure such as the CPI. To be sure, taxes would increase. If tax rates had been indexed in 1972 to the CPI, the tax on cigarettes today would be 44 cents per pack, the tax on distilled liquors would be $10.80 per gallon, and the taxes on beer would be $4.92 per barrel for low beer and $9.84 for strong beer. If this inflation adjustment were made for 1984's expected 4% rate of inflation, the revenue yield on cigarette taxes would increase by approximately $2.3 million (to $86.5 million) and on alcoholic beverages by about $9 million (to a total of $55.2 million).

The effect of indexation of the tax base would be influenced by the tax actions of other states. If tax rates in other states were not adjusted upward in response to inflation, whether by indexation or by frequent legislative changes, then Minnesota's indexation would continuously push up its rate relative to those of other states. The incentives to bootleg and to drive across the border to purchase the taxed commodity would thereby be increased, and any response to those incentives would mean fewer taxable sales in Minnesota. Accordingly, if it were eventually determined that Minnesota taxes were getting out of line over time, the index could be suspended on an ad hoc basis. On political accountability grounds, an ad hoc suspension of indexation, however, may be preferable to the present system of no indexation, since it requires an explicit legislative decision to not raise rates. Inflation erodes the tax base with no explicit legislative debate on the topic.

If Minnesota adopted such a "full disclosure" procedure by indexing, it would be the first state to do so.

*Ad valorem taxation.*   If alcoholic beverage and cigarette tax revenues were placed on an ad valorem rather than a per-unit basis (as Minnesota now does for tobacco products other than cigarettes) the same effect of indexation would be achieved, with the added merit of easier administration and enhanced taxpayer understanding. Legislatively, it would be a very simple matter to accomplish—just recast the 18 cents per pack of cigarettes in terms of a current percentage of value and enact that rate.

These advantages notwithstanding, only Hawaii employs an ad valorem tax on cigarettes and alcoholic beverages. The main disadvantage of the ad valorem approach is that it would prevent inflation-induced erosion of revenues only to the extent that prices of the taxed commodities increase as rapidly as prices in general. Over the past fifteen years, cigarette and alcoholic beverage prices have not done so.

## TRANSIENT LODGING TAXES

Six Minnesota cities (Duluth, Bloomington, Minneapolis, Rochester, St. Cloud, and St. Paul) levy 3% taxes on sales of transient lodging. Legislation passed in 1983 allows any city at present not imposing a transient lodging tax to levy such a tax for promoting tourism. The rate may not exceed 3% and 95% of the revenue must be earmarked for tourism. To date, only Winona, Mankato, and Moorhead have levied a tax under this legislation. At present, local transient lodging taxes are levied in thirty states.

### RATIONALE

There are a number of justifications for taxing transient accommodations at a higher rate than the general sales tax. First, visitors generate costs which must be borne by residents. Therefore, not only can special tourist taxation be justified, based on the incremental variable costs attributed to their presence, but also any additional capacity costs incurred by the local jurisdiction. It is not unreasonable to assume that the provision of services by the local jurisdiction is greater than might otherwise be necessary because of the visitors' presence.

The second justification is one of fiscal expediency. Since the tax is on nonresidents, it provides a way to lower the taxes paid by Minnesotans. Though perhaps a bit cynical, this export feature is at the heart of many states' tax levies.

Finally, there are two revenue productivity arguments that can be advanced in support of the tax. First, the demand for transient accommodations tends to be relatively insensitive to small changes in price.

The demand is relatively price-inelastic. Thus, according to the economists' optimal taxation theories, the tax is well suited for a higher rate.

The second revenue argument is based on the fact that the expenditures of transients on hotel/motel and other tourist related services tend to be income-elastic. That is, as the incomes of persons in the (national or regional) economy grow over time, family expenditures for travel and tourist services tend to increase by even greater amounts. Thus, a tax on these visitor-related expenditures automatically tends to grow as the economy grows, thereby reducing the need for legislative action to enact rate and/or base changes.

## YIELD

A state-level tax would be an alternative or supplement to local taxes. As an alternative, it would prevent the inequity that arises when cities do not levy a transient accommodations tax, but nevertheless benefit from tourism taxes and programs of their neighbors. As a supplement, it could apply in all cities or only in those cities that do not levy a local transient lodging tax. Funds could be returned to the cities from which they originate. The estimated yield of a 1% state-level transient lodging tax is $2 million per year.[11]

## EFFICIENCY

Would a 1% tax discourage visitors? Because of the price-inelasticity, there would be little effect. This is particularly clear if put in terms of the

TABLE 10
Mortgage Registry and Deed Transfer Tax Rates
Minnesota and Selected States

| State | Deed transfer tax per $500 consideration | Mortgage registry tax, per $100 of principal debt |
|---|---|---|
| Minnesota | $1.10 | $ .15 |
| California | .55[a] | none |
| Illinois | .25 | none |
| Iowa | .55 | none |
| Michigan | .55 | none |
| New York | .55 | 1.00 |
| North Dakota | none | none |
| South Dakota | .50 | none |
| Texas | none | none |
| Wisconsin | 1.50 | none |

*Source:* Minnesota Department of Revenue, *Minnesota Tax Handbook,* August 1982.
[a]City or county option.

marginal effect of the tax. For example, at the downtown St. Paul Holiday Inn a room for two costs the users $86 per night, maximum. This assumes no discounts (e.g., conventions) and that the charge is not being written off as a business tax deduction or as a reimbursable expense. Add another 1% per night tax, and the price rises by 86 cents. That is about half the price of a beer in the lounge.

## EQUITY

Available data on household consumption patterns show that expenditures on hotel and motel lodging increase roughly in proportion to income, and they increase more rapidly than total consumption expenditures as income increases. Hence, the incidence of a tax on sales of transient lodging is proportional to progressive in respect to income, and thus satisfies the ability-to-pay criterion.

## EARMARKING

As noted, present legislation now permits taxes on transient accommodations if earmarked for tourism promotion. It is difficult, however, to make such a user-cost link. If the argument for earmarking is that tourism promotes the general welfare (e.g., jobs), then general fund expenditures make sense, not special funding. Similarly, the often heard argument that the tax is justified only if visitors benefit by receiving a special set of lodging-related services loses its power once one considers that residents also pay taxes but are generally only indirectly compensated for these through the general expenditure process.

## ADMINISTRATION

Only the Minneapolis and Rochester taxes are collected and administered by the state revenue department; the other cities administer their taxes locally. Administration and collection costs would likely be reduced if the latter taxes were collected by the state as it collects the state sales tax.

## MORTGAGE REGISTRY AND DEED TRANSFER TAXES

Minnesota levies a mortgage registry tax on the principal amount of any debt that is secured by mortgage of real property situated in the state. The rate is 15 cents per $100 of principal. It levies a deed transfer (real estate transfer) tax on each transfer of real property by deed, instrument, or writing. The tax is $2.20 for the first $1,000 or less of consideration plus

$1.10 for each additional $500. The mortgage registry rate has remained unchanged since 1945, the deed transfer rate since 1967. Table 10 compares tax rates in Minnesota with its neighbors and selected other states.

Because they depend on the value of the real estate that is transferred or mortgaged, these taxes are not simply fees for recording mortgages and property transfers. They were originally imposed for revenue purposes, a point made clear in the opinion upholding the constitutionality of the mortgage registry tax:

> There are good and sufficient reasons why a special method should be devised for the taxation of this kind of property. It is a notorious fact that the owners of securities in the forms of bonds and notes have not been in the habit of paying their proportionate share of the taxes. This has been due in a measure to the ease with which the existence of such property can be concealed from the tax officials. But when the owner of a note takes a mortgage on real estate as security, and places it upon the public records, he exposes his ownership—at least, his ostensible ownership—and enables the assessor to reach him.*

This 1908-reasoning does not hold up very well in today's fiscal environment. Although it may be true that owners of intangible property evade taxes, that is an income enforcement and not a property or sales tax issue. Moreover, since intangible property (and the transfer thereof) is exempt under Minnesota statutes, there is no clear horizontal equity (treatment of like activities) justification for taxing the transfer of real property.

This leaves us with two possible justifications: administrative ease (as the court notes, the papers are indeed publicly recorded) and administrative cost-recovery. Regarding this second point, there is a case for a cost-of-service tax, but no case based on real estate value.

Finally, one should note that the mortgage registry tax is essentially a tax on loan transactions, and, as such, it is borne by borrowers and/or lenders. Similarly, the deed transfer tax is borne by buyers and/or sellers of real estate. Data for making a systematic estimate of the incidence of these taxes are not available. But the taxed transactions are engaged in predominately by persons in the middle- and upper-income strata or their agents. Hence, the taxes are likely to range from proportional to progressive in their incidence; they are vertically equitable. Again, however, horizontal equity is not satisfied since equally-valued property ownership varies among persons of a given income level.

In Minnesota, both mortgage registry tax and deed transfer tax rates are high relative to many of the states; however, whether the level of these two taxes impedes efficient operation of the real estate and mortgage markets has not been examined here.

---

* Mutual Benefit Life Ins. Co. v. County of Morrison, 104 Minn. 179, 182-83, 116 N.W. 572, 574 (1908).

## TAXES ON CONTROLLED SUBSTANCES

In view of the recent concern regarding the "new crime" (1970s-1980s) of drug trafficking, two states have enacted selective sales and license fees on the sale of marijuana and other controlled substances. Arizona has a dealer license fee of $100, an excise tax of $10 per ounce on marijuana and a $125 per-ounce tax on controlled substances. South Dakota takes a harder line approach: license fees are $500 for marijuana and $1,000 for controlled substances. Marijuana sales are taxed at $50 per ounce and controlled substances at $5,000 per ounce. These taxes are administered by requiring that a tax stamp be affixed to each parcel sold, and requiring each dealer to have a valid license.

There are three justifications for these tax laws:

- *Supports System of Law.* The taxes create another way to prosecute drug dealers: they can be charged with tax evasion in addition to current criminal statutes on the drug trade.
- *Horizontal Equity.* The levies address one part of a growing problem, the tax evasion occurring in the underground economy. It does not follow that because activities are illegal they have no economic impact and their participants should therefore be preferentially treated vis-a-vis persons who engage in legal and taxable market transactions; and
- *Sumptuary.* As long as the dealing in these controlled substances is illegal, one can presume that the economic objective is sumptuary (and, thus not a revenue producer).* Although a Minnesota tax on controlled substances would surely not eliminate drug dealing within the state borders, it would send out signals to prospective dealers to trade elsewhere.

There are two additional features of the taxes that must be recognized. The first is, that if the Minnesota drug trade is large, the taxes may have some negative employment effects. In some states where marijuana production is a significant industry (e.g. Hawaii, particularly on Hawaii and Maui) this has been a major policy concern.

Second, since drug trafficking is illegal, there is a civil liberties issue regarding the rights of one to be protected against self-incrimination. Accordingly, Arizona and South Dakota provide that persons who voluntarily comply with the tax law may do so confidentially. Given the (laudable) zeal with which the Minnesota Department of Revenue enforces

---

* Actually, revenue yields may not be trivial. Arizona officials estimate that in 1982, if the tax had been levied on the then confiscated amount of marijuana, cocaine, heroin, and hashish, the state would have raised $10 million. In the first ten months of the tax system, $380,000 of assessments have been levied and $30,000 collected.

nondisclosure laws, one can conclude that this taxpayer confidentiality would be maintained in this state.

## RECOMMENDATIONS

### AGAINST EARMARKING OF GENERAL TAX SOURCES

The commission agrees upon these findings about the procedure of earmarking state tax revenues:

* In Minnesota, approximately 14% of tax revenues were earmarked in 1981. These revenues in large part went for expenditures on highways and aids to taconite areas.
* Since 1967, there has been a major decrease in the share of tax collections that are earmarked. However, it cannot be demonstrated that this has had an effect on the functional distribution of expenditures. This pattern is similar to but more pronounced than the national average.
* Earmarking may enhance efficiency if a tax acts as a user charge for a particular service.
* Earmarking reduces budgetary flexibility and can remove portions of the budget from regular review.

Therefore, the commission recommends that the practice of earmarking revenues to specific expenditures be avoided except in the clear user charge case. All other revenues should be deposited in the general fund. The legislature may then do what they are elected to do, namely choose how to allocate funds among competing programs. This will make fiscal decisions more explicit and will enhance political accountability.

### MAINTAIN SPECIAL FUND DEDICATION OF THE MOTOR VEHICLE EXCISE TAX

The scheduled dedication of motor vehicle tax revenues to the highway and transit funds is a response to the failure of traditional highway user tax revenues to keep pace with funding for infrastructure maintenance and transportation planning. Part of this funding problem can be addressed by building in responsiveness in the motor fuel and license fee structure. However, additional funding from the motor vehicle excise is warranted in recognition that the benefits of a well maintained, integrated transportation system has general benefit to Minnesotans regardless of where they live or work.

### MAINTAIN THE REAL VALUE OF HIGHWAY FUEL AND LICENSE TAX REVENUE

Highway user tax revenue has not grown as rapidly as highway maintenance and operation costs, primarily because fuel and license tax rates have not been addressed as rapidly as inflation has driven up highway costs. Specifically, from 1970 through 1982, the purchasing power of user tax revenues fell 21%. The highway system revenues from user taxes clearly diminished over this period, and reliance on other revenue sources, primarily appropriations from the general fund, increased. This pattern of change was common to Minnesota, its neighbors, and the U.S. as a whole.

Accordingly, the commission recommends that the state implement a system of variable tax rates under which fuel and licenses would be increased automatically when highway costs, as measured by the federal operation and maintenance cost index, increase. This could be done by either indexing present per-unit taxes or moving from a per-unit to an ad valorem tax on motor fuel.

## MAINTAIN THE REAL VALUE OF ALCOHOL AND CIGARETTE TAXES

The commission finds that Minnesota's per-unit excise taxes on cigarettes and alcoholic beverages are being steadily eroded by inflation. Although these taxes are by their nature regressive, they serve three important purposes. They improve efficiency by increasing the cost of smoking and drinking which have adverse social impacts. Because the consumption of these goods for most people is not sensitive to price, these taxes minimally interfere with consumer decisions and satisfy the goal of tax neutrality. Teenagers are an exception to the general unresponsiveness of cigarette consumption to higher prices; teenage smoking is significantly reduced by the cigarette excise tax.

Accordingly, the commission recommends that the current per-unit taxes on alcoholic beverages and cigarettes should be replaced with ad valorem taxes that initially will produce an equal revenue yield. If the federal excise tax on cigarettes should decrease in the future (as is presently scheduled), Minnesota should increase its tax by an equal amount.

## PERMIT THE LOCAL OPTION TO TAX TRANSIENT ACCOMMODATIONS

The commission finds that the transient accommodations tax is a source of revenue that also meets the goals of efficiency (minimization of distortions in consumer behavior) and equity in taxation. However, it also concludes that, since localities vary in their ability to attract and tax lodging guests, the decision whether to utilize this tax should be a local, not a state, decision.

Accordingly, the commission recommends that the state leave this tax policy to local government units. The issue of whether to tax and, if a tax is levied, to earmark proceeds, is a local one. The state should not require that these tax revenues be earmarked for the benefit of the tourism industry.

### STATUS QUO RELATING TO THE MORTGAGE REGISTRY AND DEED LEVIES

The commission finds that the primary justification for the mortgage registry tax and deed transfer levies stem from the ease of administration and, to a lesser extent, revenue productivity. Accordingly, the commission recommends that these taxes be maintained.

### SALES TAXATION OF CONTROLLED SUBSTANCES

The commission views with concern the growing problem of untaxed activities in the underground economy of illegal drug traffic. Accordingly, both to correct for the inequities resulting from the de facto exempt taxation of the sale of controlled substances and to recognize a time honored fiscal tool—a sumptuary tax—as an aid to law enforcement efforts, the commission recommends that Minnesota follow South Dakota, Arizona, and Florida and levy steep license fees on drug dealers and selective sales taxes on the sales of controlled substances. In making this recommendation, the commission explicitly recommends that the revenue department insure the confidentiality of information voluntarily provided by dealers of controlled substances.

## ENDNOTES

1. The selling price is net of any trade-in value of another vehicle. In the case of a gift or sale at nominal value, the value of the tax is determined by guidelines of the average value of similar vehicles. Vehicles purchased for resale by a dealer or for use of a dealer (dealer plates) are exempt. Minnesota Statutes, Section 297B-02.

2. The effect of inflation of the real value of gasoline tax revenues is an excellent example of this general problem. The manner and pattern of recent rate increases clearly show the lagged adjustment of rates to inflation. For an analysis of recent changes in gasoline taxation see J. H. Bowman and J. L. Mikesell, "Recent Changes in State Gasoline Taxation: An Analysis of Structure and Rates," *National Tax Journal,* Vol. 36, No. 2, June 1983, pp. 163-182.

3. Minnesota Department of Transportation, *State Transportation Programs in Minnesota,* January 1, 1984, pp. II-3 through II-6.

4. U.S. Department of Transportation, *Alternatives to Tax on Use of Heavy Trucks,* Report to Congress, January 1984, pp. VI-8 through VI-13 and VII-10 through VII-11. For discussion of weight-distance tax options and administrative issues, see also John Merriss and Loyd Henion, "Oregon's Weight-Distance Tax: Theory and Practice," a paper presented at the 24th Annual Meeting of the

Transportation Research Forum, Washington, D.C., November 3-5, 1983; and Loyd Herrion and John Merriss, "An Equity Assessment of Federal Highway User Charges," a paper presented at the 63rd Annual Meeting of the Transportation Research Board, Washington, D.C., January 16-20, 1984.

5. Type of roadway traveled would also influence cost responsibility. A ton-mile tax, currently used by Colorado and Wyoming, does not allow for load differences, but doing so greatly complicates compliance and administration.

6. A weight-distance tax could, of course, be based on a different loading assumption. For example, assuming that vehicles are always fully loaded would mean a tax rate of 17 cents per mile, and all but fully loaded vehicles would be overcharged.

7. These estimates are derived from Thomas F. Pogue, "Minnesota Highway User Taxes: Issues and Alternatives," in *Staff Papers,* vol. 2 of the *Final Report of the Minnesota Tax Study Commission,* ed. Robert D. Ebel and Therese J. McGuire (St. Paul: Butterworth Legal Publishers, 1985).

8. This section focuses only on the selective sales component of these taxes. One should note, however, that sales of tobacco products are taxed the same as other consumer purchases under the retail sales tax (6%) and alcoholic beverages are taxed at a higher rate of 8.5%.

9. Elasticity estimates by Carolyn Allmon, Minnesota Department of Revenue. See also E. Lewit and D. Coate, "The Potential for Using Excises to Reduce Smoking," *Journal of Health Economics,* Vol. I, 1982, pp. 121-145.

10. Estimate by Mark Misukanis, Minnesota Department of Revenue.

11. Estimate provided by the Minnesota Department of Finance.

# 12
# The Corporate Net Income Tax

## INTRODUCTION: PURPOSE AND SCOPE

This chapter focuses on the major general business tax employed by Minnesota—the corporation income tax (enacted in 1933). Many of the comments and issues here apply as well to the bank excise tax (1944). The chapter has three purposes:

- to analyze Minnesota's corporate income tax in relation to the entire Minnesota tax system;
- to compare the Minnesota tax to the corporate income taxes in other states and to the federal tax on the income of corporations; and
- to evaluate the tax on several criteria including equity, efficiency, and simplicity.

In the next section the rationale for the taxation of corporations is presented with particular attention paid to the implications of having a more open economy at the state level than the national level. A third section contains a description of Minnesota's tax and presents data on the revenue yield of the tax. Section four contains comparisons of the Minnesota tax to the tax in other states in terms of the law and the revenue yield. Several issues specific to the taxation of corporate income at the state level are discussed in the final part of the chapter. The analysis in the earlier sections leads to conclusions about the reasonableness and effectiveness of the tax and to implications for tax reform which are presented in the final summary section.

## RATIONALE FOR TAXING THE INCOME OF CORPORATIONS

It is important to realize that ultimately people, not institutions such as business firms, pay taxes. A tax on the income of corporations is a tax that is paid by the corporations' shareholders, wage earners, property owners, and/or customers. To justify a tax on the income of corporations, then, one must justify the tax as it affects those who actually pay it.

One rationale for the corporate income tax is that it acts as a device for protecting the base of the individual income tax. Without it, certain types of corporate source income, in particular, unrealized capital gains (retained earnings) escape taxation. The result is that individuals can hide income within the corporation and the tax base is subject to erosion.

A corporate income tax is, nonetheless, an imperfect means of getting at this source of income. The retained earnings are taxed at the rate applied to corporate income which is not related to the circumstances of the potential taxpayers (the shareholders). Also, it may result in the double taxation of dividends since they are taxed under both the corporate income tax and the individual income tax. An additional problem occurs if the tax is not, in fact, paid by shareholders in the form of reduced corporate source income (reduced dividends and retained earnings), but is instead shifted—passed on—to the factors of production in terms of lower wages or rents or on to consumers in the form of higher prices. Then the corporate income tax does not even imperfectly accomplish its goal of plugging this tax loophole. The individuals who benefit from this source of income do not, in fact, pay the tax.

A second rationale for a corporate income tax is the argument that a state is entitled to tax all income earned within its borders by residents or nonresidents. Since a state is an open economy, income is likely to leave the state. Thus, the income must be taxed at its source. This rationale would seem to argue for taxing immobile factors rather than the elusive income.

A final rationale for the corporate income tax is based on the benefit principle. Corporations receive corporation-specific benefits from government services such as roads, police and fire protection, sewage treatment, and education for their workers. The benefit principle implies that the taxes paid should be related to the value or cost of the benefits received. It is not at all clear that the net income of a corporation is related to the value or cost of the services rendered. In reality, corporate income tax is likely to be a capricious wage or sales tax rather than a tax on corporate source income.

To summarize, each of the justifications for the taxation of corporate income at the level of the corporation has its flaws. Eventually, all taxes are paid by individuals and it is impossible to determine with certainty who actually pays the corporation income tax. Nevertheless, many states have corporate income taxes, and the remaining sections of this report describe and analyze the effects of Minnesota's corporate income tax.

## DESCRIPTION OF THE MINNESOTA CORPORATE INCOME TAX

### TAX STRUCTURE

To define the corporate income base, Minnesota begins with the federal definition of taxable income before certain deductions. Several items are added to and subtracted from this federal base. Some of these adjustments are made with the intention of defining a state's net income as opposed to a national net income. Other adjustments to the federal base are items where Minnesota has chosen not to conform for purposes other than determining the state's share of various income sources. Briefly, unlike the federal government, Minnesota taxes a fraction of the contributions made to non-Minnesota charities, certain types of interest, state income tax liabilities, a part of the federal accelerated cost recovery system (ACRS) depreciation deduction, and domestic international sales corporations (DISC) income. And, unlike the federal government, a fraction of the long-term capital gains and the foreign dividend gross-up are not part of the Minnesota tax base.

If the corporate taxpayer does all of its business in Minnesota (a 100% Minnesota corporation), a two-tiered tax rate schedule is applied to the net taxable income defined above to determine its tax liability. The rates are 6% on the first $25,000 and 12% on the remainder. For multistate corporations, the share of total net income that Minnesota can tax must first be determined. In Minnesota, formula apportionment is used to make that determination. The formula depends on three factors: property, payroll, and sales, and on the ratio of each of these factors in Minnesota to the total (for the corporation if nonunitary, for the unitary group if unitary) for each factor everywhere. In determining its Minnesota apportionment percentage, the corporation can choose to give each of the factor ratios equal weight (an arithmetic average) or it can weight the property and payroll ratios at 15% and the sales ratio at 70%.

In Minnesota, a multistate corporation is required to file as part of a unitary group if, between the corporate members of the group, there is "unity of ownership, operation, and use," i.e., if the corporations, in a significant way, act as one business entity. Minnesota is a domestic unitary state since only corporations created or organized in the United States can be included in the unitary group. The income of the members of a unitary group is combined and then formula apportionment is used to apportion the Minnesota share of the income to the various corporate members, the taxpaying units. The two-tiered tax rate schedule is applied to each member's apportioned base.

Minnesota corporations that have no out-of-state payroll, property, or sales can elect to be considered as members of a unitary group. This will be advantageous for the taxpayers if one of the members has a net operating loss. Filing under the unitary method enables the group to take the loss currently rather than having to carry the loss forward to future tax years or backward to previous tax years.

REVENUES

In recent years, revenues from corporate taxes have provided about 4% of total state and local general revenue (see Table 1). One measure of the burden of a tax is the share of state personal income taken up by the tax. This share has been around 1% in recent years and was even smaller in 1981 and 1982.

In 1982, the corporate income tax as a major tax category was the least important tax in terms of revenue as it provided the smallest share of total state and local revenue. This low reliance on corporate income taxes in Minnesota mirrored the average for the states (see Table 2). To summarize, for Minnesota and most other states, the corporate income tax provides only a moderate amount of revenue and the burden relative to other Minnesota state and local taxes is quite low.

## COMPARISONS OF STATE CORPORATE INCOME TAXES

Forty-five states and the District of Columbia tax corporations on some measure of net income. Michigan deviates from net income by employing a consumption-type, value-added tax base. The five states without a corporate income tax are South Dakota, Texas, Nevada, Washington (which uses a gross receipts tax), and Wyoming. Virtually all states that impose a corporate income tax use the federal definition of taxable corporate income as a starting point for calculating state corporate income.

Significant additions and deductions are made to the definition of federal taxable income by nearly all states in order to establish a base that is appropriate for a state. Additions and deductions are also used by the states to provide incentives to certain business activities that reflect state, rather than federal, policies.

The two most common additions to federal taxable income are income taxes, including state, local, and foreign taxes; and various forms of federally exempt interest income. Most states also use a modified form of the federal net operating loss deduction. Minnesota's base is typical in these regards.

Minnesota is atypical in that it allows a less generous treatment of fixed and capital assets by not conforming to federal law on ACRS depreciation, depletion, and amortization deductions. In addition, Minnesota is one of only three states to add DISC net income to the definition of taxable corporate incomes.

The three most common subtractions from the federal definition of taxable income are the portion of wages for which the corporation claimed the federal jobs tax credit and therefore could not deduct from federal gross income; interest on U.S. obligations and securities; and an adjustment for the foreign dividend gross-up (taxes paid by the foreign corporations who pay the dividends). Minnesota is one of only eleven states that does not allow the interest deduction for U.S. obligations and securities, and it is the only state that provides a deduction for 60% of long-term capital gains.

TABLE 1

Revenue From Minnesota Net Corporate Income Tax* In Absolute,
As a Share of Total State and Local General Revenue, and
As a Share of Total State Personal Income; For Selected Years

|  | Corporate Net Income Tax Revenue (thousands) | Corporate net Income Tax Revenue as a Share of Total General Revenue | Corporate Net Income Tax Revenue as a Share of Total Personal Income |
|---|---|---|---|
| 1982 | $325,295 | 3.4% | .75% |
| 1981 | $331,718 | 3.8% | .83% |
| 1980 | $381,217 | 4.7% | 1.06% |
| 1977 | $258,095 | 4.3% | 1.05% |
| 1976 | $196,436 | 3.6% | .86% |

*Source: Government Finances,* Series No. 3 and No. 5, for various years, U.S. Department of Commerce, Bureau of the Census; and *Significant Features of Fiscal Federalism,* 1982-83 edition, Advisory Commission on Intergovernmental Relations.

*Net corporate income tax revenues include revenues from the taxation of financial institutions (the bank excise tax).

TABLE 2

Percentage Distribution of State and Local General Revenue,
1982, Minnesota and U.S. Average

|  | Minnesota | U.S. Average |
|---|---|---|
| Federal Aid | 18.2% | 19.1% |
| Property Taxes | 14.4% | 18.0% |
| General Sales Tax | 9.1% | 13.3% |
| Individual Income Tax | 16.0% | 11.1% |
| Corporate Income Tax | 3.4% | 3.3% |
| Other Taxes | 11.5% | 12.7% |
| Interest Earnings | 6.4% | 5.6% |
| Charges and Misc. | 21.1% | 16.9% |

*Source:* See Table 1.

STATUTORY TAX RATES

Twenty-nine states and the District of Columbia use a flat rate corporate income tax and seventeen use a graduated rate system. Alaska's corporate income tax rates are the most steeply graduated, with nine steps to a top rate of 9.4% on net income in excess of $90,000.

The average of the top nominal tax rates is 7.5%. Minnesota's top rate is 12%, which is the highest rate in the nation, equaled only by Iowa. The average level of net income at which the top rate applies is approximately $200,000 for the seventeen states with a graduated tax. Minnesota's top tax rate applies to all net income in excess of $25,000. Thus Minnesota's corporate tax combines the highest top rate applied at a relatively low level of taxable income.

## TAX CREDITS

Nearly all states use tax credits that are ostensibly intended to encourage certain business activities. The two most common categories are credits for alternative energy or conservation investments; and credits to reward job creation, especially in economically depressed areas (typically called enterprise zone credits).

There is, however, a wide variance in the number of credits allowed by the states. The number of credits allowed ranges from Colorado with more than a dozen credits that include virtually every form of alternative energy technology and conservation investment to New Jersey which provides no credits. Minnesota, in addition to a few minor credits, has tax credits for the following activities: new research and development expenditures, small business investment, and investment in pollution control equipment.

## TREATMENT OF UNITARY COMBINATIONS

Fourteen states, including Minnesota, require unitary combination of groups of related corporations. Of these, ten states define the unitary group on a worldwide basis and four limit the group to domestic corporations. Nine states and the District of Columbia provide an option for unitary treatment, four use worldwide, and six domestic combinations. Twenty states do not allow unitary treatment of related groups of corporations.

## APPORTIONMENT FORMULAS

The standard formula for determining the proportion of business income that should be allocated to a state is the simple (arithmetic) average of three factors: percentage of total property in the state, percentage of total sales occurring in the state, and percentage of total payroll paid in the state. Thirty-seven states plus the District of Columbia use the simple average of these three factors. Iowa is the only state apportioning income based solely on the proportion of total sales occurring in the state (although Missouri allows this as an option). Colorado allows corporations to choose the simple average of the three factors or the average of two factors, sales and property.

Six states use a weighted average of the three factors: Wisconsin, New York, Massachusetts, Florida, Connecticut, and Minnesota. All of these except Minnesota weight the factors as follows: property 25%, payroll 25%, sales 50%. Minnesota allows corporations the option of using either the three-factor simple average or apportioning using the following factor weights: property 15%, payroll 15%, sales 70%.

To summarize, while Minnesota's tax base is similar in most respects to other states that use a corporate income tax, Minnesota applies the highest tax rate at a net income level that is lower than average. Minnesota allows an average number of tax credits and is one of only fourteen states requiring unitary treatment of related corporations. It is one of only three states that give corporations a choice of apportionment formulas and the only state to offer 70-15-15 factor weights.

## RELIANCE ON CORPORATE INCOME TAXES

Interstate differences in corporate tax bases, rates, credits, and income allocation schemes all contribute to differences in the states' reliance on corporate income taxes as sources of revenues. On average, the fifty states raised 3.3% of total state and local revenues from corporate income taxes (including bank excise taxes).

Minnesota closely resembles this national average, receiving 3.4% of its revenues from corporate income taxes. Alaska has highly profitable oil and gas producing corporations that contribute to its corporate income tax revenues, giving Alaska the highest percentage of its total taxes from this source at 11%. Connecticut's corporate income taxes are 5.7% of total revenues, second highest in the nation. Of the states with fully operating corporate income and bank excise taxes, West Virginia receives the smallest fraction of its total revenues from these taxes, 1.0%. (It should be noted that West Virginia levies a gross receipts tax on businesses in addition to its corporate income tax.)

Corporate income tax revenue as a percentage of total state personal income gives an indication of the burden of the tax. On average, corporate income taxes represent 0.62% of total state personal income. The corporate income taxes of Alaska and New York represent the highest fraction of state personal income, 11.36% and 1.17% respectively. West Virginia and Indiana have the lowest corporate tax effort of states with fully operating corporate income and bank excise taxes, representing 0.21% and 0.23% of personal income respectively. Corporate income taxes in Minnesota represent 0.75% of personal income. Minnesota's corporate taxes as a fraction of personal income rank ninth among the fifty states and the District of Columbia.

In sum, although Minnesota's corporate income tax burden is somewhat above average, it is well below the highest states. Furthermore, Minnesota's fraction of total revenues from corporate income taxes is very close to the national average. Minnesota's overall reliance on corporate taxes is moderate in comparison to most states.

## ISSUES CONCERNING STATE TAXATION OF CORPORATE INCOME

### APPORTIONMENT OF THE TAX BASE

Because many of the corporations doing business in Minnesota are multistate corporations, some means of determining how much of the corporation's income is to be taxed by each state must be devised. The amount of income allocated to each state should reflect the income generated by the corporation's operations in that state.

## SEPARATE ACCOUNTING VS. FORMULA APPORTIONMENT

One means of dividing a corporation's income among several states is separate accounting. Under this method, the corporation determines, for each state, the value of gross sales, the cost of goods sold, wages, etc. Thus, by determining the revenue generated in each state and the costs associated with generating the revenue in each state, the corporation allocates its total net income across the states.

The primary problem with separate accounting is that, for many items transferred between divisions in a corporation, there is no easily determined market price. For example, consider a corporation composed of two divisions, one which makes flour that is then "sold" to the other division to make biscuits, a final consumer product. What is the price? The cost to the biscuit manufacturing division of the flour? Is it the cost actually incurred by the flour-making division? Is it the price of flour in the supermarket? If the flour division also sells to other customers, other flour product manufacturers, the price quoted to these customers would be a reasonable arms-length price. But often the sole purpose of a division is to produce an intermediate product for another division.

The determination of these transfer prices between divisions of the corporation is important because the amount of income allocated to any one state will vary with the level of the transfer prices. In the example above, suppose that the flour division is located in a high-tax-rate state, say, Minnesota, and the biscuit division is located in a low-tax-rate state, say, Texas. By setting a very low price (value of gross sales) for the flour, one that just covers the cost of manufacturing the flour, the net income associated with the flour division would be zero and the net income associated with the biscuit division would be relatively high given the low cost of the flour. Thus, no income is allocated to Minnesota and no taxes are paid to the high-tax state even though it is clear that the operations in Minnesota contributed in a significant way to the income earned by the operations in Texas.

Because the transfer prices are set by the corporations, and the states have limited means to audit these figures, separate accounting can be used purposefully to avoid paying taxes by manipulating the income associated with one division.

This potential for tax avoidance would appear to be especially strong for vertically integrated corporations, i.e., corporations composed of many divisions, each at a different level of the production process, each transferring intermediate products to another division with the last division in this vertical string selling a final, finished product. But the potential for manipulation of income is also present for horizontally integrated corporations. The overhead costs of services provided by the corporation for all divisions, services such as advertising, accounting, managerial staff, patents, financing, and marketing can be allocated to certain divisions in order to effect a result similar to the example above.

## FORMULA APPORTIONMENT

Because of this potential for manipulation, which is related to the taxpayer difficulty of determining transfer prices and costing services provided by the corporation for all divisions, most states have abandoned separate accounting as a means of apportioning the income of multistate corporations. Instead, almost all states use some form of formula apportionment. Under formula apportionment, the presence of a corporation in a state is determined by the amount of payroll, property, and/or sales in the state. The state's share of the corporation's total of these three factors determines the state's share of the total net income of the corporation.

Formula apportionment eliminates the potential for the manipulation of income across states through transfer pricing. It is a well-defined, easy to understand method of allocating a corporation's income among the various states in which it operates.

Formula apportionment does have its problems. Because the states use different formulae, and because the determination of nexus in a state is not equivalent to having one of the factors in the state, what is referred to as "nowhere-income" (income not taxed by any state) can result, as can the double taxation of income (this is a form of double taxation distinct from the double taxation of dividends). Nowhere-income is only a problem if there is some presumption that every dollar of income must be taxed by some state.

An example. Suppose a corporation has one-half of its payroll, one-half of its property, and two-thirds of its sales in a state that uses an arithmetic average formula; five-ninths of the corporation's income is apportioned to the state. The corporation's remaining payroll, property, and sales are in a state that uses a sales-only formula so that one-third of the corporation's income is apportioned to this state. In total, eight-ninths of the corporation's income is apportioned to one or the other state, one-ninth escapes taxation.

Because states employ different formulae, it is theoretically possible that double taxation will occur, i.e., that more than 100% of the corporation's income will be apportioned to the states. If in the example above, the sales fractions are reversed between the two states, two-thirds of the corporation's income is taxed in the sales-only state and four-ninths of total income is taxed in the state with the arithmetic formula. Ten-ninths, more than 100%, of total income is taxed in one state or another.

A corporation can respond to the incentives inherent with the possibility of nowhere-income and double taxation. Corporations can choose locations for new operations that result in nowhere-income and can avoid locations that produce double taxation. If this is easy to do, the potential results of the process of apportioning income across states are simply a subset of the results that corporations can effect by responding to differing rates and formulas. These tax-induced incentives (distortions to economic behavior) are discussed in detail in the section on the economic effects of the tax.

### DOMESTIC UNITARY

Just as formula apportionment arose as a solution to a potentially large tax loophole, so the unitary definition of the business entity (the firm) is viewed as a solution to another means by which corporations could transfer income to avoid paying state corporate income taxes. Without a unitary definition of the firm, which combines closely related affiliated corporations, a corporation could potentially manipulate transfer prices of goods and services passed between affiliated corporations located in other states to avoid paying taxes in high-tax-rate states. Separate accounting is the culprit in both cases, in one case between divisions, in the other between affiliated corporations.

One can find a unitary definition of the firm appealing without having to invoke potential tax avoidance behavior on the part of corporations. Unitary is simply a method of defining the business entity, the firm. Four vertically integrated divisions within one corporation compose the same economic entity as four vertically integrated affiliated corporations operating under one parent corporation. Tax policy should treat these two firms the same. The corporate structure of the firm should not in and of itself, unless it affects the profitability of the firm, effect the tax liability of the firm (or the tax rules that govern it).

The problem for the design of a tax system that is neutral with respect to corporate structure is that the tax-paying unit is the corporation, a legal designation; it is not the firm or the business entity, an economic designation. Because of this fact, the corporate structure of the firm will affect tax liability. To avoid paying taxes, the four-division corporation, frustrated by the substitution of formula apportionment for separate accounting, could reorganize into four affiliated corporations. The income associated with any one of the corporations would again be a determination for the corporations using separate accounting. Through a judicious choice of transfer prices for intermediate goods passed between the corporations or through costing of joint services provided by one corporation (the parent) to all four corporations, the income allocated to the corporation in the high-tax-rate state could be small and the amount allocated to the corporation in the low-tax-rate state could be large.

Thus, to treat seemingly identical firms the same, regardless of their corporate structure, and to close a second tax loophole resulting from the corporation and not the business entity being the taxpaying unit, unitary formula apportionment is a solution. Unitary defines the income of the business entity (the unitary group) and formula apportionment is used to apportion the unitary group's combined income not only across the states but across the members (the corporations) of the unitary group.

The economic distortions caused by formula apportionment that will be discussed below are the same whether the unitary definition of the business entity is used or the business entity is defined to be the corporation. Essentially, as a brief preview, formula apportionment results in incentives, not present under separate accounting, for taxpayers to open operations or expand in low-tax-rate states. Without unitary, these operations are called divisions. With unitary, these operations are called corporations.

*The definition of a unitary group.*    A major problem with defining the business entity for tax purposes as a unitary group is the definition itself. Which affiliated corporations should be members of the same unitary group? If the rationale for unitary is based on the opportunity for manipulation of income across corporations, only corporations whose interactions and common control would facilitate this type of income transfer should be in the same unitary group. This leads to a definition that is close to how one would ideally define the business entity (the firm) as an economic unit.

Joint ownership and a flow of intermediate products between two corporations would seem to form a unitary group. But how much ownership is needed for control—50%? 80%? And how strong a flow—most of a corporation's products? Any amount? One set of managers for the two corporations would probably justify a finding of "unity of operation" but does the contracting out of advertising services from the same advertising agency by the two corporations constitute "unity of use"?

These are difficult questions, which lead to two related problems for the taxpayer. First, taxpayers often complain that, under unitary, affiliated corporations can be pulled into the group so that part of their income is allocated to states that have contributed little or nothing to the generation of that income. Second, if different states use different definitions for a unitary group, tax compliance may be difficult and costly. With differing unitary group definitions, a corporation may not know whether it is in a unitary group in Minnesota, a different unitary group in California, and no unitary group in Florida. The problem is that, even if each state's law is reasonably easy to understand, it is a part of the tax code that is open to interpretation.

To summarize, if the definition is too restrictive, there is a danger that truly related corporations will not be brought into the unitary group and tax avoidance will be possible. This is a problem for the tax collector. If the definition is too all encompassing, there is a danger that truly unrelated corporations will be brought into the unitary group. The distortions to the taxpayers' bills may be large and unjustified causing a problem for the member corporations.

*The Minnesota definition of a unitary group.* The Minnesota statutes define a unitary business as follows: "Business activities or operations carried on by more than one corporation are unitary in nature when the corporations are related through common ownership and when the trade or business activities of each of the corporations are of mutual benefit, dependent upon, or contributory to one another, individually or as a group." In order to be more precise, the description continues to state that if there is common ownership, defined as more than 50% of the voting stock, any one of three factors can lead to a determination of a unitary business: "horizontal type of business" (corporations whose products or services are in the same line of business), "steps in a vertical process" (corporations who provide intermediate products or services for one another), and "strong centralized management" (executive officers of one corporation involved in determining policies of the other corporations).

The Minnesota definition does appear to be clear and reasonably concrete. It may, however, be too broad. Whether it leads to corporations being combined when they are not economically related, and thus could not possibly manipulate income through transfer prices and costing of joint services, cannot objectively be determined a priori for all cases. Some states do use a more restrictive definition of a unitary group that requires 80% ownership, which is one of the rules used to determine a consolidated group at the federal level. Using this standard brings an element of conformity at least with the federal law into the definition, at the risk of missing important, economically related affiliates.

Regardless of whether the Minnesota law is acceptable to taxpayers and tax administrators alike, one of the major compliance problems is differences in the laws across the states. No unilateral change on Minnesota's part can alleviate this problem.

In terms of the ultimate effect of unitary on tax revenue for the state or on tax liability of a corporation, the results are ambiguous. For the state, more or less income may be pulled into the state while the state's share of the factors certainly will not increase. Examples can be easily found of corporations whose tax liability in a state will decline under unitary and those whose liability will increase. In general, if the corporations that are pulled into the state in a unitary group are more (less) profitable than the taxpaying corporation in the state, then that corporation's tax liability is likely to go up (down).

# ECONOMIC EFFECTS OF STATE CORPORATE INCOME TAXES

## EQUITY

Whether a state corporate income tax is horizontally and vertically equitable will depend on who ultimately pays the tax. Since any version of the equity criterion compares tax burdens of individuals (the ultimate taxpayers), the equity of the corporate income tax can only be evaluated in light of the incidence of the tax.

*If the tax is not shifted.* If the tax is paid by the shareholders in terms of a lower after-tax rate of return, less after-tax income to be reinvested or distributed, the presence of the tax whether at the state or national level is not likely to create horizontal inequities. This is the case because the individuals who chose to become shareholders in the corporation could have chosen another portfolio if a preferred one were available. If the opportunities of investors are equal, we expect them to choose portfolios with the same expected returns. One portfolio may include stock in corporation A and the other may not, but no horizontal inequity results because of the differential taxation of the potential items in the portfolio. Purchasers of the stock will take the tax into account when determining whether to include the stock as part of their portfolios.

The fact that retained earnings are all taxed at the same corporate rate can lead to vertical inequities, however, if individual income tax rates differ from the corporate rate. For example, if the corporate income tax rate is less than the individual rate, an individual with a significant amount of corporate-source income in the form of unrealized capital gains may pay less in taxes than an individual with less income all of which is noncorporate-source income. This can result because the individuals have different abilities to save (because their incomes are different) and savings are taxed differently than income used for current consumption.

*If the tax is shifted.* In fact, corporate income taxes may not be paid by shareholders. Instead, the burden of the taxes may be shifted to consumers and the factors of production in the form of lower wages, lower rents, and higher prices. Shifting is potentially more likely to occur at the state level than the federal level since after-tax rates of return must be the same across the states for investment to occur in all of the states. Investment will not occur in a state where the after-tax rate of return is lower than can be earned elsewhere. Thus, the fact that investment occurs in a high-tax-rate state may be evidence that the tax is being shifted and the burden is being borne by consumers, wage earners, and/or landowners.

To summarize, the equity of the tax must be judged in light of the incidence of the tax. The incidence of the tax (who actually pays the tax), however, is difficult to know precisely. But the resulting burden is likely to be capricious and inequitable as individuals with different occupations and consumption patterns, but equal incomes, will pay different amounts in taxes.

A neutral (efficient) tax should have two characteristics. First, if the tax is to be a benefits tax, which is arguably the most tenable rationale for state corporate income taxes, the tax payment should relate to benefits received. Second, the tax should not affect economic decisions in an unintended, significant way. The extent to which economic decisions are changed in order to avoid paying the tax should be small.

*Benefits tax.* A state corporate income tax is likely to be a poor approximation to a benefits tax. This is true for two reasons. First, as argued above, the services that are provided to corporations by the state and local governments are not likely to be related to the net income of the corporations. Two corporations could have very different net incomes (one even a zero or negative income) and yet cost the state the same in terms of the services provided. A better base for a benefits tax might be the property value of the corporation or the payroll of the corporation or some combination of the two. (As corporations do pay property taxes they may already be paying for benefits received (provided).

Second, because businesses other than corporations benefit from state services, there is no compelling reason to apply this approximate benefits tax to only the corporate form of the business enterprise. Proprietorships and partnerships are taxed as individuals under the individual income tax only. They are thus not subject to two different taxes (one on individuals and one on the business of an individual) as are the owners of corporations. In summary, a state tax based on corporate income is not a good approximation to a benefits tax, and by this criterion is inefficient.

*Distortions to economic decisions.* Several distortions to economic decisions may result under a state corporate income tax based on formula apportionment. Whether or not corporations actually respond to the potential incentives and disincentives is not known with certainty. The remainder of this section is a discussion of two types of decisions that are likely to be affected.

Under formula apportionment, firms in high-tax-rate states will have an incentive to open operations (whether divisions or mergers with other corporations is not relevant) in low-tax-rate states, not because the after-tax rate of return is higher in the low-tax-rate state (we argued above that they must be the same), but simply to avoid paying taxes to the high-tax-rate state. By opening operations in low-tax-rate states, the apportionment factor ratios in the high-tax-rate state drop, those in the low-tax-rate states rise, and the overall tax liability of the corporation falls. More of the corporation's total overall income, not just the income associated with the new investment, is apportioned to the low-tax-rate state when new operations are added in the low-tax-rate state. This is different from the result under separate accounting where only the taxes associated with the new investment are affected.

Minnesota's unequally weighted formula will have an effect on the type of investment or type of corporation that is encouraged or discouraged by different tax rates. For example, a corporation in Iowa, a high-tax-rate state, has a stronger incentive to locate its retailing divisions in low-tax-rate states than to locate property and payroll in low-tax-rate states because of the heavy weight put on sales in Iowa. In other words, Iowa's formula is conducive to exporting corporations. A similar statement could be made regarding Minnesota's emphasis on the sales factor, were it not that Minnesota businesses can choose the equally-weighted, three-factor formula.

Under unitary a merger can result in similar beneficial tax consequences. A highly profitable corporation in a high-tax-rate state has an incentive to merge with a less profitable corporation in a low-tax-rate state. The tax liability of the combined group will be lower than the sum of the tax liabilities of the two corporations filing separately in their home states. To illustrate this possibility, consider a corporation with income of $500,000 located in a high-tax rate state (say, 10%). A corporation with equal property, payroll, and sales factors earns income of $100,000 in a low-tax-rate state (say, 6%). Before the merger, the tax liabilities are $50,000 and $6,000 for a total of $56,000. After the merger the combined income of $600,000 is apportioned equally across the two states so that $300,000 is taxed by each state. The total tax liability of the unitary group is $48,000 ($30,000 + $18,000). Thus, unitary formula apportionment results in tax-induced incentives for mergers between corporations with different profit margins located in states with different tax rates.

Under separate accounting, each new investment decision stands on its own. High-tax-rate states may be avoided if the tax cannot be shifted; such avoidance assumes that taxes paid elsewhere will not be affected. There is no tax-induced incentive to merge with a corporation in another state. Under formula apportionment, tax liability in every state in which the corporation has nexus will be affected when a new division is opened or a merger is accomplished. The total tax liability of the corporation will be lower if these new operations open in low-tax-rate states. Because it distorts economic decisions by providing incentives for firms in high-tax-rate states to open operations in low-tax-rate states, formula apportionment is a source of inefficiencies.

The second type of inefficiency resulting solely from formula apportionment is that the tax acts like a set of taxes on payroll, property, and sales. When a firm increases its payroll, property, or sales in the state with no change in income, the taxes owed in the state increase. Since tax liability increases when factors increase, the tax is based on the factors. These implicit factor taxes will differ across firms. More profitable firms will have higher tax rates on each factor since their tax liabilities are greater. Because the implied tax rates differ across firms, all firms do not face the same tax-inclusive costs of investment. Less profitable firms will be better able to increase payroll, property, and sales because the implied tax rates associated with such behavior are lower. The result is an inefficient use of resources as the tax-inclusive prices of the factors do not reflect the true resource costs of the factors.

To summarize, a state corporate income tax is likely to be inefficient because it does not approximate a benefits tax, it distorts decisions concerning where to open new operations, and the implied factor taxes will differ across firms leading to inefficient uses of resources. A state corporate income tax is likely to be inequitable since, regardless of who actually pays the tax, the resulting burdens may differ across seemingly like individuals and may not vary with income in a fair manner.

Whether these potential distortions are a cause for concern depends on whether firms actually respond to the incentives and disincentives identified. The tax-induced incentive for firms in high-tax-rate states to open operations in low-tax-rate states may not be strong because state corporate income taxes are, in general, relatively low and do not vary a great deal. The other inefficiencies and the inequities result even if tax rates and formulas are the same in all of the states. Empirical evidence on the severity of these distortions or the incidence of the tax is practically nonexistent, so concrete conclusions about the tax based on its economic effects cannot be made.

## SUMMARY AND IMPLICATIONS FOR TAX REFORM

The Minnesota state corporation income tax is unusual for two reasons. First, Minnesota's current top rate of 12% is the highest in the country. Due to certain provisions in the law, the effective rate paid by many corporations will be lower, especially for multistate corporations. Also, the rate will vary across corporations as their operations vary across the states. For example, the effective marginal tax rate for new investment in Minnesota by a corporation with no sales in Minnesota is $(.15)(.12) = .018$ (the property weight times the statutory tax rate).

Second, Minnesota is one of only three states that allow multistate corporations a choice between two apportionment formulae. If a corporation's sales ratio (fraction) is less than the average of the corporation's payroll and property ratios, it will be to the advantage of the corporation (and to the disadvantage of Minnesota's revenue) to choose the sales-dominant formula instead of the arithmetic-average formula.

Minnesota's corporate income tax is based on taxing the business entity. The business entity (firm) may be a corporation composed of one or many divisions, or it may be a unitary group composed of one or many affiliated corporations. As already mentioned, the income of multistate corporations is divided among the states using a three-factor formula for apportionment rather than separate accounting. Combining the income of a unitary group of corporations carries this reliance on formula apportionment to the division of income among corporations.

The potential for corporations to avoid paying taxes through the manipulation of income by setting transfer prices and costing shared services is a strong theoretical justification for formula apportionment based on a unitary definition of the income base. There is little empirical evidence, though, of the extent to which corporations actually do (or did in states that are now unitary but previously were not) transfer income to their affiliates or divisions in low-tax-rate states. The court cases concerning the oil companies are specific examples where such behavior was evidenced. Disclosure and auditing problems make the gathering of systematic evidence very difficult, if not impossible.

Taxing the firm (the business entity) rather than an operation within the firm is appealing strictly in terms of common sense and economics. That is, the corporate structure of the firm, if it truly acts as one business entity, should not affect the way the firm is perceived by tax administrators or corporate managers.

It would seem that unitary formula apportionment has the weight of rational, fair taxation on its side. Unless clear evidence to the contrary is presented, this form of state corporate income taxation is probably the best available. Refinements to either the unitary definition or the apportionment formula in Minnesota may be able to be justified, however. For example, Minnesota could go to a tighter definition of a unitary group such as the definition of a consolidated group. Or Minnesota could simplify the process of filing by requiring only one return for the unitary group (this change may have already been adopted). The state may want to change the apportionment formula to encourage or discourage certain types of corporations to open operations in Minnesota by putting a heavier weight on one factor or another.

Although unitary formula apportionment may be the most reasonable way to tax the income of corporations at the state level, there are compelling reasons to believe that any state corporate income tax, no matter how well designed, will be inequitable and inefficient. If the tax is shifted in the form of higher prices or lower payments to the factors of production, the ultimate burden will not be paid by the shareholders, but by consumers, wage earners, and landowners. Further, the distribution of this burden may well be capricious, satisfying neither horizontal nor vertical equity.

The tax is inefficient for two reasons. It is an imperfect benefits tax since the value or cost of the public services that benefit the corporation is unlikely to be related to net income. Also, the tax distorts economic decisions, decisions as to where to open new operations and decisions as to where factors will be employed, since the implied factor tax rates vary across firms.

The tax is theoretically inequitable and inefficient, but there is little empirical evidence about the extent of these distortions. As state corporate income taxes are relatively low, even if they differ from one another, the incentives are probably weak and the distortions are probably not great.

The incentives for Minnesota corporations to open operations in low-tax-rate states can be completely eliminated by lowering Minnesota's rate. But there will be revenue consequences and the benefits of such a change are difficult to measure.

Eliminating the corporation tax would preclude the complexities involved in taxing multistate operations with a state tax, eliminate the distortions to economic decisions, potentially eliminate the inequities of the tax, and solve the problem of attempting to rationalize the tax as a benefits tax. The tax could possibly be replaced with a tax on some aspect of the corporation which more closely proxies benefits received. An explicit tax on the factors of production or sales would not be affected by the corporation's actions in other states, and any degree of equity could potentially be affected. A question that would still need to be addressed is why only the corporate form of the business entity is taxed.

It is difficult to rationalize state corporation income taxes, as they are likely to be inefficient, inequitable and complex. But, if a tax on the net income of corporations in Minnesota is to be continued, the tax, in order to enhance simplicity, fairness and efficiency, should be based on unitary formula apportionment, it should conform as much as possible to the federal tax and other states' taxes, and, possibly, the rate should be lowered if the distortions to economic decisions are perceived as being large.

## RECOMMENDATIONS

### GENERALLY MAINTAIN THE STATUS QUO RELATING TO THE CORPORATE NET INCOME (PROFITS) TAX

Minnesota's top nominal corporate net income tax rate (12%) is the nation's highest. However, the combination of its alternative weighted apportionment formula for multistate businesses and the state's extensive use of direct taxes on individuals causes Minnesota to exhibit only average reliance on general business taxes when the state is compared to the nation as a whole.

Two problems the commission found were (1) the tendency to treat financial institutions different from nonfinancial businesses, and (2) some dissatisfaction with Minnesota's use of domestic unitary combination for purposes of apportioning the income of multistate businesses. Accordingly, after examining the two foregoing issues along with a proposal for reduction of the nominal tax rate, the commission generally recommends the status quo with respect to the corporate net income tax, and specifically that the state subject both financial and nonfinancial corporations to the same corporate income tax in order to enhance simplicity and neutrality; and in order to have a simple, competitive, and fair corporate tax, domestic unitary combination be retained and worldwide unitary combination continue to be rejected.

## FUTURE CONSIDERATION OF A GENERAL BUSINESS ACTIVITIES (VALUE ADDED) TAX*

The commission has carefully weighed the pros and cons of the value added tax as a permanent part of the Minnesota fiscal system and finds that the tax may be well suited for future use as part of the general business tax structure. This will be particularly true if, in the near term, the state is unable to reduce reliance on that part of the retail sales tax that behaves as a "turnover levy"—the tax on capital purchases.

Nevertheless, the commission finds that at present, there are other, more pressing, tax policy concerns facing the state. Accordingly, the commission recommends that the basic nature of the state general business tax structure not be modified, and that the net income (profits) approach be maintained. This recommendation does not preclude future consideration of a value added tax.

---

* The commission also examined the alternatives of a gross receipts tax and the value added tax. The analysis regarding the other forms of general business taxation are presented by Robert D. Ebel, "The Value Added Tax," *Minnesota Tax Journal,* 1:10 (Spring 1985): 193-204.

# 13

# Taxation of Insurance Companies

United States insurance companies earned $75,939 million in premiums for life and health insurance in 1982, of which $1,379 million was in Minnesota. Earned premiums for property and casualty firms in Minnesota were $2,054 million during 1980. Annuity considerations and other insurance would add greatly to this amount indicating that the industry is a substantial economic force in Minnesota. Any industry generating so much economic activity is a prime target for taxation. That is particularly true of an industry which is already regulated by the state, and where the industry is dominated by foreign firms. (A foreign firm is one chartered in the U.S. but outside of Minnesota, domestic firms are those chartered in the State of Minnesota.) Given these characteristics of the insurance industry in Minnesota, and in every state, it is not surprising that the industry is subject to taxation through a variety of special levies, which raised over $76 million for Minnesota state government during 1982. That figure fell to $70 million in 1984.

## THE MINNESOTA INSURANCE INDUSTRY[1]

The Minnesota insurance industry can be divided into property/casualty and life/health firms. Some basic differences arise between these categories of firms, and these differences create difficulties in evaluating the firms in a single study. The differences are reflected throughout the analysis that follows. To summarize:

- *Life insurance* is frequently sold through long-term contracts. Because of this, the firms must maintain reserves to meet future liabilities, and this situation complicates analysis of the firms and calculation of their income. Life insurance companies tend to price their products nationally, except for large group policies, which are experience rated. Life and health insurance is provided by 509 firms (domestic, foreign, fraternal, and domestic nonprofit health companies, see Table 1). Foreign firms earn 79.2% of direct life premiums. Foreign firms are less dominant in providing accident and health insurance; Blue Cross and Blue Shield receive over five times more premiums than the next largest insurer. Six of

TABLE 1
Minnesota Insurance Industry, 1982

| Type of Company | Number[a] | Total Assets[b] (Thousands) | | | Direct Earned Premiums[c] (Thousands) |
|---|---|---|---|---|---|
| Property/Casualty | | | | | |
| Domestic property and casualty | 53 | $ 5,687,834 | | | $ 358,750 |
| Foreign property and casualty | 498 | 209,920,529 | | | 1,755,981 |
| Township mutual | 129 | 55,419 | | | 30,492 |
| Life Firms | | | Life | Accident and health | Annuity considerations |
| Domestic life insurers | 26 | 9,662,835 | 98,773 | 78,978 | 132,806 |
| Foreign life | 425 | 553,083,065 | 618,672 | 597,372 | 213,879 |
| Domestic fraternal | 9 | 2,375,944 | 25,199 | 1,748 | 34,609 |
| Foreign fraternal | 46 | 8,746,312 | 38,362 | 6,371 | 10,165 |
| Domestic nonprofit health service plan corporations | 3 | 110,758 | | 337,811 | |
| Other | 3 | 4,385 | 574 | 713 | |

Source: Minnesota Department of Commerce, "Fiscal Year 1983 Annual Report Supplement on Insurance Companies Authorized to do Business in Minnesota."
[a]Number of companies licensed in Minnesota.
[b]Assets are the companies reported assets, and not necessarily assets in Minnesota.
[c]Direct earned premiums in Minnesota.

the largest eight life insurers are foreign firms. Minnesota Mutual Life and Northwestern National Life are the biggest domestic life insurers. At least five domestic mutual and thirty-five foreign mutual firms operate in Minnesota and the remainder are stock companies.
* *Noncancellable health insurance* is comparable to life; and
* *Property/casualty* firms generally operate with shorter term contracts and their income is more easily measured. This distinction within the industry is less significant than it was several years ago. Property/casualty firms are finding that litigation can often extend their liabilities well into the future, while life companies are selling more insurance with shorter term contracts. Unlike life companies, property/casualty companies set rates based on experience in the area.

There are 680 firms licensed to sell property and casualty insurance in Minnesota, including domestic, foreign, and town mutual insurers (domestic, nonprofit, and generally small companies) (Table 1). Foreign chartered companies receive a dominant share of premiums paid in

Minnesota, collecting 81.9% of premiums in 1982. Seven of the ten largest companies are foreign, led by State Farm Mutual Automobile Insurance Company. The St. Paul Fire and Marine Insurance Company is the largest domestic property and casualty insurer and fifth largest insurer in the state.

The property and casualty industry can be further divided into stock and mutual firms. The stock firms are owned by shareholders who choose to purchase an ownership share in the firms, regardless of whether the firms' products are also consumed. Those firms which do not have mutual ownership are stock companies. Mutual companies are owned by policyholders, each of whom acquire ownership in the company when they buy a policy. There are at least fifty-six foreign mutual firms, seventeen domestic mutual companies, and 129 township mutual companies.

## LEGAL STRUCTURE FOR TAXATION OF INSURANCE COMPANIES IN MINNESOTA:

Insurance firms are directly or indirectly taxed by nearly every levy imposed by Minnesota state and local governments, including sales, property, and corporate income taxes. The intent here is to focus only on the state taxes and fees levied on insurance corporations.

### PREMIUM TAX

The major tax that impacts on insurance companies is the gross premium tax. Use of premium taxes as a base for insurance companies was first begun in 1824 when New York taxed the agents of foreign corporations. This tax, which is statutorily levied in lieu of all other taxes except those on real property, is paid annually at a rate of 2% on gross premiums less return premiums. A return premium is a dividend applied to payment of premiums and any portion of premiums returned after cancellation or termination of a policy. Reinsurance premiums and annuities are exempt from the tax.

The tax is collected on most insurance premiums paid by Minnesota residents to companies licensed to operate in Minnesota. Certain companies are exempt, including nonprofit health insurance, fraternal insurance, ocean marine insurance, and domestic mutual property and casualty companies.

### CORPORATE INCOME TAX

The gross premium tax is levied in lieu of other taxes, but this limitation does not apply to the corporate income tax because it is regarded as an excise. Insurance corporations are generally subject to the income tax in the same manner as are other corporations and at the same 12% tax rate. There are, however, three major differences in the way the tax is imposed on insurance corporations:

- *Definition of Taxable Corporate Income.* One is that under the Minnesota corporate profits tax, taxable incomes for the insurance companies are determined using the definitions established in the United States revenue act of 1936. Companies generally find this troublesome because major revisions in insurance taxation occurred nationally in 1959 and again in 1984. Thus, the calculations for Minnesota are distinct from those necessary for tax purposes in other states and nationally. There is also a lack of consensus as to how to interpret and implement the basic steps in an out-of-state tax law and this is complicated further because some of the annuity and universal life products available today did not exist in 1936. Compliance costs are increased and administration is made more difficult by the use of the 1936 code.
- *Apportionment of the Tax Base.* Insurance companies are treated in Minnesota so that the income for multistate corporations is apportioned to Minnesota according to the percentage that its gross premiums bear to total gross premiums. Other corporations use a three-factor formula including sales, property, and employment. Special provisions of the three-factor formula allow corporations to weigh sales heavily so the apportionment formulas may be only nominally different in practice.
- *Credits for Premiums Taxes Law.* Credits allowed for insurance companies generally preclude them from paying any state corporate income tax. The most important credits are for the taxes paid on a premium basis except for the firemen's relief surcharge (see below).

OTHER TAXES

The *Fire Marshall's Tax* is an additional levy on premiums applicable to fire insurance, and is set at a rate of 0.5%. For policies that partly cover fire hazard and partly cover other liabilities, the tax base is approximated as a certain percentage of premiums. For example, comprehensive automobile insurance is presumed to be 19% fire coverage.

A *Fireman's Relief Surcharge* is imposed on fire insurance premiums paid for property located in cities of the first class—Minneapolis, St. Paul, and Duluth. The surcharge rate is 2% and the surcharge base is the same as for the Fire Marshall's Tax. Revenues from the surcharge are used to help finance police and firemen's relief associations. Legislation allows a similar surcharge to be imposed in second class cities whenever their firemen's relief association trust funds fall below $50,000.

The *surplus lines tax* is levied on Minnesota brokers for insurance coverage written to Minnesotans but provided by firms which are not licensed to do business in Minnesota. Surplus line companies are only allowed to write insurance when no coverage is available from a Minnesota licensed insurer. The tax is imposed at a rate of 3% on premiums less cancellations. As in many states, the tax rate is higher than the premium tax rate. The inability to levy retaliatory taxes against surplus lines taxes is an important reason for the higher rate.

*Ocean marine* companies are taxed on the basis of taxable underwriting profits rather than gross receipts (premiums). The tax is levied at a 5% rate.

### RETALIATORY TAXES

Retaliation by one state for the insurance taxes in another is a unique part of the overall insurance tax structure. This type of tax was first imposed by the State of Massachusetts in 1832 and has spread to forty-seven states. A U.S. Supreme Court opinion in 1944, which held that insurance business could be considered to be in interstate commerce, would have eliminated retaliatory taxes. But the McCarren-Ferguson Act of 1945 indicated the regulation and taxation of insurance firms was in the public interest and permitted retaliatory taxation to continue.

Retaliatory laws come into play whenever taxes (including charges, fees, and assessments) on Minnesota domestic firms operating in another state are higher than those which Minnesota would impose on a comparable firm from that other state when it operates in Minnesota. Specifically, to measure retaliation, a foreign firm must calculate the tax for which it is liable in Minnesota and the tax that it would pay on the same basis as a foreign firm operating in its home state. For each tax, the firm must pay the higher of these two calculations. If the taxes it would pay as a foreign firm operating in its home state exceed its Minnesota liability, the firm pays the amount in excess of the Minnesota liability as a retaliatory tax to Minnesota. All revenues collected by Minnesota under the retaliatory tax must, by definition, be paid by foreign firms.

### FEES

The most significant fee paid by life insurance companies is the valuation fee. This charge is only collected from domestic life insurance companies and at a rate of 1 cent per $1,000 of life insurance in force. The revenues are intended to cover the auditing costs for the domestic life companies, though the collections significantly exceed that amount. Also, the costs of examining firms will not be proportional to insurance in force, so the base for this fee is questionable.

Fees of $15 for township mutual fire insurance companies and $30 for other companies are assessed for filing their annual report. A number of other fees and assessments are also collected.

## GROSS RECEIPTS VERSUS INCOME TAXATION

As discussed above, the basis for taxation of noninsurance firms is corporate profits, while insurance companies are taxed predominantly through premiums-based taxes. Insurance companies are also liable for the corporate income tax, but since premium tax payments are a credit against the state corporate income tax, few insurance firms incur any income tax liability and little revenue is generated. Corporate income taxes for foreign and domestic insurance companies are imposed by relatively few states, and since the tax is a low-revenue generator, it could be viewed as a nuisance tax. As noted below, however, it is one potential way that annuity income can be taxed.

- *Simplicity.* A major attribute of premium taxation is simplicity, as ease of compliance and administration is fostered. The base is premium revenues received by the firm with relatively few adjustments or deductions, and the base is simply multiplied by a flat rate to yield the tax liability. The ease is particularly apparent in comparison with the alternative income taxation, which requires a definition of income. Such a definition is complicated for insurance companies by the need to measure future liabilities, something particularly difficult for the life companies.
- *Revenue Certainty (Stability).* Revenues are probably the strongest reason for using premium taxes. Premium receipts are likely to be much more stable than insurance company income, so the revenue flow is more consistent and predictable. Further, insurance companies are perceived as large sources of available funds and, as noted above, since they are frequently foreign based, they are easy targets for taxation.
- *Neutrality (Efficiency).* The major potential disadvantage of gross receipts taxation for insurance firms and income taxation for other industries is that tax neutrality can be violated as industries are taxed unevenly. Tax neutrality exists when taxes are imposed so that no distortions are created in the way economic resources are allocated. Taxes that alter the decision of whether to insure, how much to insure, or by which company to insure will violate tax neutrality. As taxes distort these and other decisions, the likelihood is increased that the private sector will employ too few resources in heavily taxed industries and too many resources in lightly taxed industries. A later section of the chapter will be devoted to examining the effect on neutrality of the current tax structure and the use of gross receipts taxation.

A shift away from a premium-based tax structure and towards an income-based structure should be considered only with very careful study. Issues such as impacts through retaliation and the way tax burdens would be reallocated would need to be recognized. Finally, policymakers must remember that the premium base has been used for many years, and the effects on economic activity are in place as the firms and consumers have adjusted accordingly. On the other hand, rapid shifts in the structure of the financial industries may require evenness of tax treatment across these industries.

## CONTRIBUTION TO MINNESOTA REVENUE NEEDS

Insurance taxes are not prominent in the overall scheme of Minnesota's state and local revenue system. The $70 million of revenues (taxes plus fees) for 1984 accounted for only 1.4% of total state collections, and just over 1% when local taxes are taken into account. Nevertheless, for at least two reasons the issues inherent in the taxation of insurance are of particular interest. First, because of special institutional characteristics of the industry, several key issues of public finance, particularly with respect to the equal-treatment-of-equals criteria, are revealed. The second (and related) reason stems from the special nature of the taxation of insurance. The reliance on a gross receipts base and the presence of retaliatory taxes are both likely to come under increasing scrutiny in an era of financial deregulation characterized by the growth of tax exempt activities (e.g., self-insurance plans) and increased competition for the insurance dollar from other financial institutions.

Accordingly, an examination of the taxation is clearly warranted, and the appropriate way to begin the analysis of the issues is to lay out the characteristics of the four major types of revenue devices.

*The gross premium tax* generates nearly all of the tax revenues from the insurance sector. In 1984 the premiums levy accounted for $73.7 million, or nearly 97% of total insurance corporation taxes and fees collected. Revenue from the gross premiums tax increased more than six fold from 1963 to 1982. Another measure of the growth in premiums tax is the long-run income-elasticity, the percentage change in tax revenues divided by the percentage change in personal income. The premiums tax had an elasticity over the past two decades of 1.10, meaning that revenues grew somewhat faster than personal income. The elasticity was only 0.77 during the 1971 to 1981 time period, possibly evidencing some slowdown in premium relative to income growth. Shifts in the industry towards purchase of term rather than whole life insurance and toward self-insurance would partially account for the slowdown.[2]

*Corporation income tax* payments are the next largest category of collections from insurance companies, amounting to $3.6 million or 5.3% of taxes paid by insurance firms in 1981. Income taxes are relatively limited because premium tax payments are a credit against income tax liabilities. However, the insurance portion of the Minnesota corporate income tax with an income elasticity of 1.5, has been the fastest rising component of insurance taxes and has increased dramatically from the negligible $39,000 collected in 1964.

*The other insurance taxes,* fire marshall, surcharge, and valuation fees, totalled $2.6 million in 1982, though it should be noted that several other fees and assessments are not included in these statistics. The fire marshall's tax is the largest one included and has increased at approximately the same rate as the premium tax. The surcharge reported here was collected from the three first class cities of Duluth, Minneapolis, and St. Paul.

*The valuation fee* is a relatively small revenue generator, but it is important for other reasons. Only domestic life companies pay the fee, so it is significant to this particular group of firms. Also, the tax is levied on insurance-in-force, not premiums. The shift towards term insurance has led to more rapid growth in insurance-in-force than in premiums, so valuation fee collections have accelerated since 1971.

## NEUTRALITY IN MINNESOTA INSURANCE TAXATION

Three major areas where tax neutrality can be violated by the Minnesota insurance tax structure are considered in this section. One is the intra-insurance-industry effect of exemptions from taxation for certain types of insurance, which can lead to unequal allocation of resources within the industry. A second is interindustry differences that arise from alternative bases employed for taxing insurance and other industries. Finally, differences in taxation of the insurance industry across state lines are examined. This can influence retaliation costs and decisions about where to locate insurance firm headquarters.

### INTRA-INSURANCE-INDUSTRY DISTORTIONS[3]

Tax neutrality would require that all insurance activity be taxed the same, regardless of the legal structure of the insurer. Several significant exemptions from taxation are permitted in Minnesota, based on the status of the insuring entity. Blue Cross/Blue Shield, fraternal insurers, and domestic property/casualty mutual insurers are the major groups that are exempt from taxation. Health maintenance organizations, annuities, and self-insurance are also untaxed. Each of these categories is discussed below regarding the cost for exemption, the justification for exemption, and conclusions as to whether exemption is appropriate.

### BLUE CROSS/BLUE SHIELD[4] ($4.8 MILLION REVENUE LOSS TO MINNESOTA)

Blue Cross and Blue Shield were originally introduced as nonprofit corporations during the Great Depression. The intent was to make low-cost health care available to a wide range of people by spreading the risks across a community of individuals. Exemption from taxation was based on the fact that the "Blues" provided substantially different coverage than did other insurers, including some charitable services. Also, the exemption was undoubtedly designed to permit reduced premiums.

The Blues have grown to be the dominant provider of health insurance in Minnesota. During CY 1982 direct written premiums for Blue Cross and Blue Shield totaled $311,511,000; Bankers Life Company, the second largest provider of accident and health insurance (as measured by premiums), received $56,232,000 in the same year. In fact, Blue Cross and Blue Shield received 30.5% of all premiums paid for accident and health insurance. The premium tax revenue lost to Minnesota through exemption of the domestic nonprofit health service plan corporations, of which Blue Cross and Blue Shield are predominant, amounted to about $4.8 million in 1982. Since the Blues are domestic corporations operating only in Minnesota, there would be no retaliation caused by a tax on them.

Does the original structure and purpose of the Blues remain sufficiently intact so that continued exemption can be justified? Tax neutrality would indicate that insurance provided by the Blues should be taxed unless a substantial public interest would be served by no taxation. Otherwise, the tax works to raise the relative costs of profit-seeking firms and places these firms at a competitive disadvantage vis-a-vis the Blues.

An equity concern also develops when insurance is taxed under certain types of legal structure and not others. To the extent that the tax is shifted to the consumer through increased premiums, some consumers pay the tax while others are able to avoid it. Thus, because people with the same ability to pay taxes and the same purchases of insurance could pay different taxes, there are horizontal inequities.

At present, twenty states use gross receipts taxation for Blue Cross/Blue Shield insurance, so that taxation of these plan in Minnesota would be far from unique. Rates range from a low of 0.33% on Blue Cross and Blue Shield in North Carolina to a high of 2.5% on Blue Cross in neighboring South Dakota. Fourteen states impose the same rates on Blue Cross/Blue Shield and other domestic health insurance companies. Three states collect a fee based on the number of contracts in force.

A decision to tax the Blues in Minnesota would likely need to go together with reconsideration of regulations which influence their operations. Nonetheless, the conclusion of a recent study in Illinois was ". . . that the advantages obtained through HCSC's (the Illinois Blue Cross/Blue Shield Corporation) special nonprofit status are no longer valid."[5] No overriding public interest would be served by continued exemption of the Blues from taxation, despite some differences in the way the Blues operate. The authors determined that they had begun to perform substantially as an insurance carrier and thus, should be subject to taxation and other legal conditions as a domestic mutual insurance company.

A possible counter argument could be that the Blues are nonprofit corporations, and, as such, should be exempt from taxation. This argument is only potentially supportable if the premiums tax on health insurance is meant as a surrogate for the corporate profits tax. Even then, the effects of imposing a tax on the nonprofit Blues must be balanced against the distorted tax neutrality from taxing other types of health insurance. If the premiums tax is meant to be paid by consumers, or in any event is generally shifted to consumers, then the tax is not on profit, and the fact that the Blues are nonprofit should not preclude collection of a gross premiums tax. It should also be noted that the tax is imposed on many mutual companies.

## HEALTH MAINTENANCE ORGANIZATIONS ($7.6 MILLION REVENUE LOSS)

The issues relating to the taxation of HMOs parallel those above for the Blues. Both are nonprofit health providers that compete with for-profit operations, and both plans have a substantial insurance (risk factor) element.

A past justification for the tax exemption of HMOs in Minnesota has been that this is consistent with legislative policy to eliminate barriers to their development. A counter argument—that rapid HMO growth has been achieved, and is now making difficult the growth of competing activities (including untaxed hospitals and clinics)—should also be considered.

## FRATERNAL BENEFICIARY ASSOCIATIONS ($1.4 MILLION REVENUE LOSS)

Nine domestic and forty-six foreign fraternal insurers operated in Minnesota during 1982. The fraternal insurers are usually affiliated with religious, ethnic, or occupational groups and sell insurance to members. Life insurance premium receipts were $63.6 million and accident and health insurance premiums were $8.1 million. The Lutheran Brotherhood and AID Association for Lutherans dominated as they collected 68% of the premiums. The fraternals are specifically exempted from payment of premiums taxes at a revenue loss to Minnesota of $1.4 million.

The effects on tax neutrality that result from exempting the fraternals are similar to those described above for the Blues. A 2% wedge is placed between the costs borne by fraternals and those by profit-seeking insurers. Though it may be somewhat difficult to shift the tax on life premiums, the tax puts the profit-seeking firms at a competitive disadvantage.

## DOMESTIC MUTUAL PROPERTY/CASUALTY INSURERS ($3.9 MILLION REVENUE LOSS)

Domestic mutual property and casualty companies are subject to the Fire Marshall's tax, and domestic township mutual insurance companies are exempt from taxation. Exemption has been based upon the mutual status of the insurers, a status that means that the policyholders are owners of the companies and any profits are returned to the policyholders. Concern that the larger stock companies (particularly coming from out-of-state) would drive the smaller mutuals out of business is another justification for tax exemption.

There are twenty domestic mutual property and casualty insurers in Minnesota, which together had total premiums of $195.5 million in 1982. This accounts for 9.1% of the total Minnesota property and casualty market share (a decline of almost 1% since 1978). If the domestic mutual companies were subject to the 2% premiums tax, they would have paid $3.9 million; as it was, they paid only $0.6 million in taxes during 1982. This represents $3.3 million in foregone revenues. The 129 domestic township mutual companies are generally smaller, collecting in 1982 a combined $30.5 million in premiums. The domestic township mutual insurers would have paid $0.6 million if subject to the premiums tax.

Two practical points arise with respect to the taxation of Minnesota domestic mutuals under the premiums tax. First, in some categories (e.g., auto) the industry is characterized by price leadership by the most cost efficient of the insurance carriers, State Farm. Thus, some local firms argue that the 2% tax would not be easily shifted, thereby placing them at a competitive disadvantage. In this context, the policymakers must determine if it is in the public interest to subsidize the inefficient operation. If so, one way to accomplish this would be to continue the exemption from the premiums tax, but subject domestic mutuals to the net income tax (which is a path other states have chosen in order to partially close the domestic mutual loophole).

The second point (which furthers the argument for an income tax as a compromise between tax exemption and premiums taxation) is that at present the major property and casualty insurers in Minnesota are all exempt from the premiums (but not income) tax in their home state. This includes three Illinois firms (State Farm, Allstate, and Illinois Farmers) and one from Wisconsin (American Family). These foreign mutuals are, however, subject to both the Minnesota premiums and corporate net income taxes.

## SELF-INSURANCE ($10 MILLION REVENUE LOSS)

Many large business firms choose to self-insure, that is, they choose to bear the consequences of risk by setting up their own insurance plans for their employees. These self-insurance programs may be either administered by existing insurance carriers (in Minnesota, Northwestern National Life is by the far the largest firm that performs this role) or done in-house. In either of these cases, there is no premium paid and thus no tax.

The most frequent choices for self-insurance are those for which one can reasonably predict the probability of a loss and where there is no real exposure to catastrophe, viz, programs for workers' compensation, and employee health and welfare benefit plans, and property/casualty risks.

The basic economic activity is the same, whether self-insurance or purchased insurance is employed, so it is difficult to determine a different taxpaying capacity in these two instances. With insurance purchased through a carrier, the premium tax is paid only because a particular type of transaction occurs, not because it taxes the economic activity. The situation is comparable to that in which a firm pays sales tax if it buys a computer from a dealer, but no sales tax is paid if the firm makes the computer. Similarly, firms are encouraged to include self-insurance activities as part of their operations.

The issues relating to self-insurance are becoming progressively important ones as the frequency of such programs increases. To summarize:

*Neutrality (Efficiency).* Again, neutrality is a major concern not only from a tax policy perspective but from a political one as well—namely, that taxable insurance carriers are, quite simply, losing business. It is a problem for the taxable firm to compete against the untaxed. In short, self-insurance is the very kind of innovation that requires the attention of a tax study commission charged with looking to the future.

*Administration.* Proposals to include self-insurance plans in the premiums tax base present a practical and potentially very difficult problem that leads to the conclusion that probably the only real possibility of extending the premiums tax to self-insurance plans is to do it only for those that provide worker compensation benefits.

In the case of self-insurance plans, the insurance is often funded by means of union trust funds (usually set up as a result of union and management bargaining) or some similar employer trust operation. Theoretically, these plans should not be difficult to define and tax. For example, regarding health plans, nearly every self-insurer establishes something like a premium for the purpose of determining their employees' contribution toward the cost of their health coverage. It simply is the sum of 1) claims paid, 2) claims reported and unpaid, 3) an estimate for unreported claims, and 4) the cost of any stop-loss insurance plus administrative costs. It could be made the responsibility of the self-insurer to determine a premium or cost of their plan. There would be a tendency by self-insurers to undervalue unreported claims and administrative expenses, but for taxation purposes their estimate would be adequate.

Technically it could be done. But now, enter the federal government. Congress, through the enactment of the employee retirement income security act of 1974 (ERISA) has enacted a comprehensive regulatory scheme governing provision of employee benefits. As a part of that overall statutory scheme there is preempted ". . . any and all state laws" that would (among other goals) tax the bulk of employee benefit plans. This appears to be true even if a state attempts to tax only benefits paid.[6] The result is that unless Congress changes ERISA (which many inside and outside the industry are urging), most self-insurance plans are probably outside the state tax base.

*Revenues.*    Measuring the premium tax dollar loss from self-insurance is very difficult since public records are not kept on premiums paid. The one exception is workers' compensation. The Minnesota Department of Commerce has identified 118 firms that are self-insuring workmen's compensation with an estimated $92.1 million in premiums that would have been paid in 1981 without self-insurance. Generally only large firms self-insure workers' compensation as only four firms had less than $10,000 in potential premiums and twenty-seven had more than $1.0 million. In excess of $1.8 million in premiums were lost from self-insurance of workers' compensation.

## ANNUITY CONSIDERATIONS

Minnesota is one of twenty-eight states that does not levy a tax on annuity considerations. However, Minnesota could potentially tax profits that insurance firms earn from annuities through the corporate income tax. Only three states and the District of Columbia tax annuity premiums at the same rates as foreign and domestic insurance, and the trend has been towards declining taxation of annuities. Between 1959 and 1973, seven states repealed their annuity tax and thirteen reduced the tax in some manner.

Minnesota's insurance firms reported receiving $391.5 million in annuity premiums in 1982, and an argument could be made to tax these along with other insurance. Yet several strong arguments can also be made against taxation of annuities. One is that insurance firms must compete with other financial institutions which are not subject to an annuities tax but are subject to the corporate income tax. A 2% premiums tax on annuities would be a large percentage of the administrative fee for annuities and would place the insurance firms at a competitive disadvantage.

Premiums taxation of annuities could also harm domestic Minnesota firms as they seek to do business in other states. As previously noted, most states either leave annuities untaxed or subject them to light taxation. Retaliation could occur against the out-of-state operations of domestic Minnesota firms because of a tax on annuities in Minnesota.

Above it was noted that insurance firms pay very little in corporate income taxes, but are subject to taxes levied on both state income and premiums base. One reason to continue corporate income taxation for insurance firms is that it is a way to retain some taxation of annuity income. Shifts that are currently occurring in the types of products offered by financial institutions support the need to retain the corporate income tax on insurance firms.

## INTERINDUSTRY TAXATION

Differential taxation across industries can violate tax neutrality, particularly if the differentials exist between or within industries that are in competition among themselves. Insurance firms compete directly with banking, savings and loans, and stock and real estate brokerage industries, and relatively high taxes on the insurance industry would be expected to shift economic activity from it to another industry. Tax equity would also suggest that tax rates should be the same for all industries, unless the benefit principle could be used to justify different burdens.

### MEASURES OF INTERINDUSTRY TAX NEUTRALITY

Evaluation of tax neutrality involves comparing tax burdens across industries, and comparison requires an accepted basis. The ideal denominator for comparing business taxes is value added, the sum of the payments to all the private factors of production. Then, the ratio of tax payment to the denominator provides a "tax cost" measure of the relative importance of the tax to the total costs of the enterprise. Unfortunately, the value-added data for the Minnesota insurance sector is not now available.

However, an alternative (though less satisfactory) measure, net income (profits), is available from a sample of property/casualty and a sample of life companies that was drawn for this report. It was necessary to collect information from the sample of property/casualty and life companies in order to obtain the best information on income and other data about the insurance industry.

Comparison of taxes relative to income must begin with a definition of taxable income. Definitions as provided by Minnesota tax law are acceptable for industries other than insurance. Since taxable income for insurance firms is defined using 1936 definitions, it is not possible to compare burdens across industries directly without recalculating income for every firm. Thus, for the current purpose, life companies' income as reported for federal taxes is chosen as the definition of income. This income figure is apportioned to Minnesota by multiplying it by the percentage of the company's premiums in Minnesota. Property and casualty companies income is defined as net income from the Minnesota corporate income tax return.

TAX IMPACT ANALYSIS

Taxes relative to corporate income are presented in Table 2 for life and property/casualty insurance and several other industries for the years 1978 through 1982. Five years of data are provided in order to avoid the problem of an aberrant year. Both 1981 and 1982 are probably unusual years for the insurance industry because of the slow economy. Also, modified coinsurance agreements, which were in effect during the time the U.S. government negotiated a new insurance tax law, led to insurance incomes being understated.

A consistent pattern holds for 1978, 1979, and 1980. Insurance firms taxes are a higher percentage of income than are those paid by other industries, even when insurance company taxes are defined to include only the premiums tax. Life insurance firms in the sample paid between 13.6% and

TABLE 2
Taxes Relative to Income for Selected Years
(percentages)

|  | 1978 | 1979 | 1980 | 1981 | 1982 |
|---|---|---|---|---|---|
| Life Insurance Sample[a] | | | | | |
| Premium taxes | 15.1 | 13.6 | 17.1 | 25.9 | 25.2 |
| All insurance taxes[b] | 18.4 | 18.2 | 24.7 | 40.3 | 36.1 |
| All insurance taxes for firms with positive income | 16.1 | 16.8 | 21.3 | 33.7 | 26.3 |
| Property/Casualty Sample[a] | | | | | |
| Premium taxes | 43.6 | 48.8 | 52.6 | 51.1 | 117.4 |
| All insurance taxes[c] | 49.5 | 55.3 | 60.2 | 59.6 | 142.0 |
| All insurance taxes for firms with positive income | 45.2 | 55.3 | 58.3 | 59.6 | 86.8 |
| Banking and Bank Holding Companies[d] | 12.0 | 12.0 | 12.0 | 12.0 | N/A |
| Security and commodity brokers, dealers, exchanges and securities | 12.1 | 12.1 | 12.1 | 12.1 | N/A |
| Total Corporate Taxes, All Industries | 11.2 | 11.2 | 11.2 | 11.2 | N/A |

*Source:* Insurance tax sample and *Minnesota Corporate Income Tax,* Minnesota Department of Revenue, selected years.

N/A = not available.

[a]All firms reported in the appendix may not have been used every year. Data omissions were responsible for some exclusion. Property/casualty mutual companies may not be required to calculate income, so they are excluded.

[b]Includes premium and corporate income taxes and life insurance valuation fees.

[c]Includes premium, income, fire marshall, firemen's relief, and ocean profits taxes and second injury fund.

[d]Includes corporate income and bank excise taxes.

17.1% of income in premiums taxes. Property/casualty firms paid between 43.6% and 52.6% of income in premiums taxes. Insurance companies are certain to pay a generally higher percentage of income through premiums taxes than would occur through the corporate income tax because the premiums tax is a credit against the income tax and few firms have an income tax liability to pay. Other industries including those directly in competition with the insurance industry, pay approximately 11% of income in taxes. This contrasts with an average effective rate of 9.9% on noninsurance corporate business in Minnesota.

When all insurance taxes are included, the percentages of taxes to income are even greater. The sample of insurance firms used for this analysis appeared to be those with the greatest income, because their income tax liability after the premiums tax credit is relatively high compared with that paid by all insurance firms. This may have the effect of exaggerating the percentage of all taxes relative to income. Also, the definitions of income are not always comparable across industries, and this can distort the analysis.

Domestic life companies will tend to pay higher taxes than the foreign companies because only the domestic companies pay the valuation fee, though there is a tendency for foreign firms to pay greater corporate income taxes.

Property/casualty firms appear to pay much higher percentages of income in taxes than do life companies. However, because property/casualty firms can more easily shift the premiums tax to consumers, a study of ultimate incidence rather than initial impact would find that the differentials between the two parts of the insurance industry would be much smaller.

In summary, the insurance industry pays higher taxes relative to income than those paid by other industries. The effect is to put the life industry at a disadvantage relative to other direct competitors such as banks, savings and loans, and security firms.

## INTERSTATE TAX DIFFERENCES

The basic insurance tax structure is similar across state lines, though some differences do exist, particularly in such instances as whether corporate income, Blue Cross and Blue Shield, and annuities are taxed. Considerable diversity does exist in the tax rates.

Differences in insurance tax structures are important for two reasons. Retaliation is the more important, as Minnesota domestic insurance firms will be penalized when they operate in other states if the insurance taxation is too high at home or if the structure is too different. Also, overtaxation can potentially influence the location of insurance firms. This need not be a major concern because firms will make location decisions infrequently. The 1978 District of Columbia Tax Revision Commission Study did note, however, that the Acacia Insurance Company made a decision to locate in northern Virginia rather than the District of Columbia in order to avoid retaliation by other states because of the D.C. annuity tax.

STATE TAX STRUCTURES

State-by-state comparisons by type of insurance activity are adequately detailed in the volume of technical papers provided to the commission, and can be summarized with respect to Minnesota as follows:

- Minnesota's 2% premium tax rate is the mode (rate with the greatest frequency) across the United States. Twenty-four states and the District of Columbia tax foreign life and health insurance at 2%, and sixteen states plus D.C. tax domestic life and health at 2%.
- Twenty states (including Minnesota) and D.C. tax foreign property/ casualty companies, and sixteen plus D.C. tax domestic property/ casualty companies, at 2%.
- There is a tendency to tax insurance provided by foreign companies more heavily than that provided by domestic companies. Only two states tax foreign life and health premiums at less than 2%, but twenty-two tax domestic life lower than 2%, and a similar pattern holds for property/ casualty taxation. It should be noted that in many cases of low premium taxes, an income tax is imposed on domestic corporations. Foreign and domestic corporations can also lower their rates in various states by holding certain percentages of their assets in the state.
- There is a slight tendency to tax property/casualty insurance more heavily than life insurance. This probably results because the tax can be more easily shifted by property/casualty companies to consumers.
- Only sixteen jurisdictions, including D.C., tax annuity considerations received by foreign companies and fifteen tax annuity considerations received by domestic corporations. Foreign corporations are frequently subject to higher annuity tax rates.
- Nineteen states tax some form of corporate income earned by insurance companies, although few states actually impose the tax on all forms of insurance income. Only domestic companies are liable in seven of these states. Six states allow the income tax as a credit against the premium tax, or vice versa, so there is little duplication of payments. In most of these instances, the liability will arise from the premiums tax because its payments will exceed the income tax liability.

MINNESOTA TAXES RELATIVE TO NEIGHBORING STATES

Taxation of the insurance industry relative to other industries was described above. An alternative way to evaluate the level of Minnesota's insurance taxes is to compare them with other states. Because of the differences in tax rates and structures, the appropriate method of comparison is based on the overall tax structure. The approach adopted here was to calculate the tax burdens that would be imposed by other states on the firms included in the sample described above. Iowa, North Dakota, South Dakota, and Wisconsin, the states surrounding Minnesota, were used for this purpose.

The tax structures were simulated to the maximum extent possible. The detailed credits and tax structures could not always be replicated, but the results are representative of tax differences across states in the region.

Life insurance company taxes for the sample are shown in Table 3 as a percentage of their Minnesota burden. As noted above, the income taxes paid in Minnesota by the sample of firms are higher than would be expected from a random sample of Minnesota firms, so this may slightly lower the relative values listed for other states in the table. Nonetheless, the findings are that the firms paid higher taxes to Minnesota than they would have paid to the surrounding states except for South Dakota. Minnesota's taxes are higher because of its income tax (Wisconsin has an income tax for some domestic companies) and the valuation fee. South Dakota's taxes are higher in 1982 because the annuities tax was included in the calculation. Data were not available to include the annuities tax in earlier years.

Property/casualty company taxes relative to Minnesota are listed in Table 4. Taxes are higher in Minnesota than in every other state except South Dakota. The premiums tax rate is higher in South Dakota, leading to their exception, but the difference in tax levels is never greater than 6.6%.

## RETALIATORY TAXATION

Retaliatory taxes were first imposed in Massachusetts in 1832 and exist in all but five states today. Retaliatory taxes are paid by a Minnesota domestic firm to another state whenever a foreign firm operating in Minnesota would pay higher taxes to Minnesota than a Minnesota domestic firm would pay in the state where the foreign firm is domiciled. Foreign firms operating in Minnesota pay retaliation to Minnesota whenever the reverse is true, although Minnesota calculates retaliation on the basis of each separate tax and fee. The retaliatory taxes are calculated by first determining the taxes the Minnesota domestic firm would pay on the comparable business done in the foreign state (the amount the Minnesota firm would be taxed if it were a foreign insurance corporation doing business in Minnesota). The tax liability for the Minnesota firm, using the foreign state's tax structure, is then subtracted from the determination of Minnesota taxes on the domestic firm. If the result is positive (meaning the Minnesota taxes are higher than the foreign state's) the difference is paid in retaliatory taxes, in addition to

TABLE 3
Neighboring States Life Insurance Taxes
Relative to Minnesota

| | 1978[a] | 1979[a] | 1980[a] | 1981[a] | 1982[a] | Premium Tax Rates Domestic | Foreign |
|---|---|---|---|---|---|---|---|
| MINNESOTA | 100.0 | 100.0 | 100.0 | 100.0 | 100.0 | 2 | 2 |
| Iowa[b] | 80.5 | 73.5 | 68.6 | 63.5 | 70.0 | 2 | 2 |
| North Dakota[c] | 51.2 | 46.7 | 43.7 | 40.4 | 44.4 | 2 | 2 |
| South Dakota | 97.4 | 88.9 | 83.3 | 77.0 | 105.3[d] | 2.25 | 2.5 |
| Wisconsin | 86.9 | 79.4 | 73.6 | 68.2 | 73.6 | 2 | 2 |

[a]Values are taxes which would be imposed in each state relative to those actually paid by the sample of firms in Minnesota.
[b]Does not include the franchise tax which is a maximum of $3,010 per firm.
[c]Accident and sickness premium rate is 0.5%.
[d]Includes annuity tax because data was not available for earlier years.

TABLE 4
Neighboring States Property/Casualty Taxes
Relative to Minnesota

| | 1978[a] | 1979[a] | 1980[a] | 1981[a] | 1982[a] | Premium Tax Rates Domestic | Foreign |
|---|---|---|---|---|---|---|---|
| MINNESOTA | 100.0 | 100.0 | 100.0 | 100.0 | 100.0 | 2 | 2 |
| Iowa[b] | 85.8 | 85.6 | 85.5 | 85.1 | 81.1 | 2 | 2 |
| North Dakota | 42.9 | 42.8 | 42.7 | 42.0 | 40.5 | 1 | 1 |
| South Dakota | 106.1 | 106.0 | 106.6 | 106.2 | 102.1 | 2.25 | 2.5 |
| Wisconsin | 96.0 | 93.1 | 92.0 | 92.6 | 87.2 | 2 | 2 |

[a]Values are taxes which would be imposed in each state relative to those actually paid by the sample of firms in Minnesota.
[b]Does not include the franchise tax which is a maximum of $3,010 per firm.

other taxes due to the foreign state. If the result is negative, the Minnesota firm pays taxes due under the foreign state's tax laws with no retaliation.

PROTECTION OF THE DOMESTIC INDUSTRY

Retaliation has generally been justified as a means to protect domestic firms against unfair discrimination when operating in other states. The basic result of the system of retaliation across the U.S. is not protection. In fact, domestic firms can be trapped in a no-win situation when pressure arises for greater insurance tax revenues. If taxes for foreign firms rise, it costs the domestic firms large increases in retaliatory taxes to other states. The alternative, raising taxes only for domestic firms, reduces the competitive position of the domestic firms in Minnesota.

Further, retaliation is not structured to cause equal treatment of domestic and foreign firms in other states. If structured to achieve this result, retaliation would become effective whenever a state discriminated against foreign firms. Instead, retaliation is triggered when taxes are higher in a foreign state. The structure of retaliation causes states to move towards taxes that are in line with those imposed in other states, rather than equal taxes for domestic and foreign firms within every state.

The basic impacts of retaliation are to reduce each state's flexibility in taxing the insurance industry and in holding down state insurance taxes. Indeed, the insurance industry lobby has been the primary source of support for the U.S. legislation that keeps state regulation of the industry and retaliation in place. Attempts in every state to increase insurance taxes are met by the concern within the domestic industry that retaliation would create severe penalties if tax rates were increased. This concern tends to encourage uniformity of tax treatment across states for insurance firms.

Most states include all taxes on insurance companies in determining retaliation, though a few states, including Minnesota, retaliate on a tax-by-tax basis. This latter form of retaliation causes even greater pressures for uniform tax treatment. Particularly, the item-by-item retaliation discourages any state from creating an insurance tax structure that looks radically different from other states. If a state creates a different structure, it encourages insurance firms to develop subsidiaries that are domiciled in other states in order to avoid retaliation.

A strong argument can be made in favor of eliminating retaliation across the nation. No action by an individual state would overcome the difficulties created by retaliation, but there are some ways Minnesota could lessen its effects: viz,

- Provide domestic firms a credit against premium taxes for increased retaliatory taxes caused by any rise in Minnesota insurance taxes. Based on the findings below, the credit would probably eliminate the Minnesota tax liability of many domestic companies so the revenue loss would be substantial.
- Enact reciprocal legislation wherein Minnesota would agree not to retaliate against firms from other states if those states would do likewise regarding Minnesota firms. At least two states (New York and Massachusetts) enacted similar legislation in the 1970s. The effect of such legislation in Minnesota would probably be limited because there is unlikely to be a significant trend to such legislation; and
- A shift by Minnesota from the line-by-line form of retaliation to retaliation based on the overall tax structure of other states.

## RETALIATION COSTS TO MINNESOTA FIRMS

An increase in Minnesota insurance company taxes would result in higher tax payments for Minnesota domestic companies in every state where Minnesota insurance would then be higher. Since premiums within Minnesota are generally a small share of a large domestic firm's total premiums, the retaliatory taxes paid in other states will often dwarf their increased payments to Minnesota.

The retaliation costs to domestic firms from a 1% increase in the premiums tax rate was used to demonstrate the sensitivity to a tax increase. Each domestic firm represented in the sample was asked to estimate its costs in terms of retaliation for a 1% premiums tax increase. Eleven life insurance companies and nine property/casualty companies provided the required information.

Domestic property/casualty companies in the sample would pay an additional $1,096,904 in premium taxes (based on 1982 premiums) with a 1% increase in the premium rate. Retaliation costs paid to other states would be $12,534,891, meaning that it would cost these firms $11.42 in taxes paid to other states for every $1 paid to Minnesota.

Life companies would not be affected as dramatically, but the basic result remains. Firms in the sample would pay $774,925 in additional premium taxes with the rate increased. Retaliation costs would be $5,732,164 or $7.40 per $1 paid to Minnesota.

The sample tends to be dominated by large firms with significant business outside the state of Minnesota, so the relative retaliation costs reported here may exceed those which would occur if all domestic companies were included in this experiment. Nonetheless, it is clear that a higher insurance tax rate in Minnesota would result in much greater increases in retaliatory taxes paid to other states than Minnesota would receive from the domestic firms.

## RECOMMENDATIONS

### STATUS QUO RELATING TO THE INSURANCE PREMIUMS TAX BASE

The commission concludes that because of federal law prohibiting state taxation of self-insured health plans, eliminating the present tax-exempt status of certain health insurance carriers (e.g., Blue Cross and Blue Shield, health maintenance organizations) would be counterproductive since it would encourage the growth of self-insurance. This would penalize smaller employers who cannot afford to establish self-insurance plans. Accordingly, the commission recommends retaining the status quo relating to the premiums tax on health insurers.

The commission also concludes that the nonneutrality violations of the exemption of fraternal and domestic and township mutuals are minor, and that little would be accomplished by including these types of insurers in the premiums tax base. Accordingly, it recommends for the continued exemption of these firms from the premiums tax base.

## UPDATING THE CORPORATE NET INCOME TAX LAW RELATING TO INSURANCE COMPANIES

Although the revenues generated by the corporate net income tax on insurance companies are not large at present ($5.2 million in 1984), the commission concludes that for two reasons the state should maintain the tax. First, since some insurance companies earn taxable income by servicing self-insurance plans, which are not subject to the premiums tax, the income tax indirectly taxes some of these otherwise exempt activities. Second, over the longer term, tax neutrality (uniformity) is likely to be enhanced by the net income tax as the state is forced to adjust to rapid changes that are occurring in the insurance business (e.g., new types of insurance and insurance products).

Accordingly, the commission recommends that the corporate income tax be maintained as well as the status quo permitting taxable firms to deduct their premiums tax payments in computing their tax liability.

The major problem with Minnesota's corporate tax on insurance carriers is that it is based on 1936 statutes. This not only unnecessarily adds to the overall complexity of the entire tax structure, it also makes resolution of legal disagreement difficult since there is little non-Minnesota case law available for resolving disputes. Accordingly, the commission recommends that the corporate net income tax relating to insurance companies be rewritten to reflect present industry circumstances and to take advantage of tax law improvements in other states.

## FOR RECIPROCITY AGREEMENTS RELATING TO RETALIATORY INSURANCE TAXATION

The commission finds that retaliation serves no public purpose, but rather, it is a device that limits the state's flexibility to design its own insurance tax structure. Recognizing, however, that a unilateral decision not to retaliate against foreign firms will only result in net losses to the treasury, the commission recommends that Minnesota enact legislation whereby this state would agree not to retaliate against firms from other states that enact similar legislation.

## ENDNOTES

1. For a detailed background and analysis, see William F. Fox, "Insurance Taxation in Minnesota," in *Staff Papers,* vol. 2 of the *Final Report of the Minnesota Tax Study Commission,* ed. Robert D. Ebel and Therese J. McGuire (St. Paul: Butterworth Legal Publishers, 1985).

2. Much of the decline in the elasticity can also be attributed to the choice of 1981 as the final year (made because personal income data were available through 1981), because premium revenue growth was so weak in that year when the economy was hovering near recession.

3. Estimates are provided by Fox, "Insurance Taxation."

4. The other domestic nonprofit health service plan corporations, Delta Dental of Minnesota and Minnesota Vision Services Plan, Inc., are also untaxed and the substance of the arguments would apply to them as well.

5. Terry Stoica, *et al,* "Blue Cross/Blue Shield: A Case for Removal of Its Special Status in Illinois Law," Illinois Department of Insurance, May 1982.

6. A 2.75% annual tax on benefits paid imposed by Connecticut was struck down on the basis of ERISA in 1978 by the United States District Court in *National Carriers Conference Committee vs. Heffernan* (D.C. Donn. 1978 454F Supp. 914). A similar decision was made in 1980 in Minnesota in *St. Paul Electrical Workers Welfare Fund, A Trust, et. al. vs. Michael Markman,* Commissioner of Insurance, State of Minnesota, U.S. District Court for the District of Minnesota.

# 14
# Taxation of Minerals

Minnesota imposes three special taxes on the mining of iron ore and taconite: the taconite production tax, the occupation tax, and the royalty tax.[1] These taxes respectively replace an ad valorem property tax on taconite and taconite processing facilities, a corporate income tax on mining net income, and a special income tax on royalties received in connection with the exploration and extraction of iron ore and taconite. Taconite companies are not liable for local property taxes on taconite mining property (the ore deposit, mine, and concentrating plant), nor are they subject to Minnesota's corporate income tax.

This chapter examines Minnesota's separate system of mineral taxation from several perspectives, including the historic rationale for using special taxes on mining, how that rationale has changed over time, and the advantages and disadvantages of the existing tax structure.[2] It then analyzes two important policy issues facing the state:

1. The effect of existing mineral taxes on the economic health of the mining industry; and,
2. The treatment of mineral tax revenues for purposes of determining state aids for property tax relief.

At the outset, it should be noted that although taconite production has long been the major economic activity in northeastern Minnesota, the tax revenue collected from this activity is relatively small in comparison to total state tax revenues. In 1983, the three major mineral taxes generated $78 million or about 2% of total state tax collections in that year. However, the bulk of this money ($67 million) represents in lieu of property tax dollars and is therefore returned to local governments, residential property owners, and other mandated parties on the Iron Range. Less than 15% of the total mineral tax revenue is available for expenditures outside the Iron Range.

## HISTORICAL PERSPECTIVE

The conventional rationale for the separate treatment of minerals in a tax system stems from the special character of the mineral resource, i.e., it is a "gift of nature" whose value reflects not only the labor and capital invested in its recovery, but the natural scarcity of the resource. The value of the latter factor is often deemed to be far in excess of the former. Because the mineral resource may be regarded in some unspecified manner and degree as the natural heritage of the people, it may be argued that government, through its tax system, should recapture some portion of this excess value for the benefit of present and future generations. This natural heritage argument has frequently been used to justify taxing mineral extraction at heavier levels (through higher tax rates and/or additional taxes) than other types of private business activity. While this same theory could be extended to other gifts of nature, such as farmland, timberland, and water power sites, minerals have been differentiated on the grounds that the private mining activity forever diminishes the value of the resource, i.e., a mineral deposit is a wasting asset.

In the late 1800s, the objective of Minnesota's mineral tax policy was to encourage the development and growth of the mining industry. In an effort to keep taxes relatively low, the state levied a special tonnage tax on the extraction of natural ore in lieu of the ad valorem property tax. This tax was later appealed and replaced by the property tax, which at that time applied uniformly to all types of property. It was not until 1913 that the natural heritage rationale first found expression in Minnesota. In that year, the legislature enacted a property classification system in which mined and unmined iron ore was valued at its "full and true value" (other property classes were valued at one-third of full and true value) and assessed at a higher ratio to such value (50%) than any other class of property. By the 1920s, a growing public opinion that mining companies were reaping large profits from Minnesota ores led to the adoption of the occupation and royalty taxes, which were levied in addition to the ad valorem property tax.

This same pattern was later repeated with the mining of taconite. In order to encourage the development of the taconite industry, taconite ore and processing facilities were exempted from the property tax in 1941, and taxed instead under a production tax that was imposed at the rate of 5 cents per ton of production. Later, after substantial private investment in taconite processing facilities had occurred, the tax rate was steadily increased to provide the people of Minnesota (through its public sector) with a greater share of revenues from their "natural heritage."

Today, the slackening demand for steel and the enormous losses of the U.S. steel industry have effectively diluted the potency of the natural heritage principle. Current economic conditions suggest that there is little or no excess value (i.e., value in excess of that earned through the investment of labor and capital) accruing to mining companies from the production of taconite. Minnesota's continuing use of special mineral taxes is now related to reasons of administrative feasibility (simplicity) and efficient resource use (neutrality).

# TACONITE PRODUCTION TAX

## TAX STRUCTURE

Enacted in 1941, the taconite production tax is a per-unit tax on the volume of production (tonnage) from taconite mines. It is levied in lieu of the local ad valorem property tax. From its initiation at 5 cents per ton, the tax rate now stands at $2.04 per ton (subject to annual adjustment by a price index). This rate is applied to a three-year average of production. In 1983, the tax generated about $67 million from a taxable base of 25.2 million tons. In 1979, when the industry was at full capacity (about 60 million tons), the tax yielded revenues of $89 million. This illustrates how the averaging method adds stability to the tax base during a period of declining production (i.e., revenues decline less sharply than production).

## DISTRIBUTION OF REVENUES

Consistent with its role as a substitute for the property tax, the proceeds of the taconite production tax are returned to the Iron Range and distributed by statutory formula to all cities, towns, and school districts, irrespective of whether the local taxing jurisdiction contains an active mine. Since 1969, a portion of production tax revenues has also gone to the taconite homestead property tax relief account, which funds a special homestead credit program for owner-occupied homes and farms on the Iron Range. Since 1977, some money has also gone to two special funds—the taconite environmental protection fund and the northeastern Minnesota economic protection trust fund. They are used to finance environmental and public works projects (e.g., abandoned mine reclamation, water pollution treatment facilities, sewer and water, libraries) and industrial development in the region.

## ANALYSIS OF CURRENT TAX STRUCTURE

The advantages of the production tax are simplicity and neutrality. The only information required to administer the tax is the number of taxable tons produced per year. In comparison, an ad valorem property tax on mineral property involves determining the market value of underground ore reserves. Typically, market value is derived by estimating the present value of the future income streams that can be generated from the development of the resource. This requires estimating many unknown factors, such as the size and quality of the ore deposit, the cost of future ore extraction, and future mineral prices. Because of the difficulties involved in accurately estimating these factors, most states have moved away from property taxation. Moreover, an ad valorem tax on mineral property creates an incentive to accelerate the mining schedule in order to "mine out from under the tax," thereby encouraging the rapid depletion of the mineral resource. Because the production tax only taxes the ore at the time of extraction, it is neutral with respect to the rate of ore recovery. It also ensures that all mines are liable at the same tax rate, regardless of location.

The production tax, however, has one major disadvantage—an unstable revenue base. Its collections are responsive to demand in the U.S. steel industry for domestic ore. If demand is weak, as is currently the case, the subsequent cutback in production will lead to declining revenues just as local governments face more severe financial pressures to assist an unemployed populace.

## OCCUPATION TAX

### TAX STRUCTURE

Enacted in 1921, this tax closely resembles a business net income tax in that mining companies are allowed to deduct certain costs from the ore value in order to reach the taxable value of production. The tax is payable in lieu of the corporate income tax and in addition to the taconite production tax.

The base of the occupation tax is the value of iron ore at the mouth of a Minnesota mine. Because there is no published market price for ore at the mouth of the mine, its value must be approximated rather than directly set by the market. It is determined by deducting a mining company's costs of beneficiation[3] and transportation from the Lake Erie price for iron ore. In order to arrive at the taxable value of the ore, additional deductions are allowed, e.g., amortized development costs, mining costs, depreciation on plant and equipment, royalties payable by a nonowner operator, and a production tax allowance. In this manner, the occupation tax base approximates the net income from mining.

Originally levied at a rate of 6% of value, the statutory rate on taconite mining is currently 15%. Due to the presence of substantial tax credits, however, the effective rate of the tax is far below the statutory rate. Of greatest significance is the labor credit for high cost ores, which allows a specified percentage of labor costs to be credited against the occupation tax liability. This credit reduces the tax to a net effective rate of 6.75% and all eight taconite producers are presently taxed at that effective rate.

Taconite occupation tax revenues peaked in 1979 at $23.8 million on 55.3 million tons of production. This represents an average tax of 44 cents per ton. In contrast, taconite occupation tax revenues totaled about $6.2 million in 1982 with production tonnage at 23.4 million, or an average tax of 14 cents per ton. The reduction in revenue reflects the higher per-unit costs associated with operating taconite plants at levels substantially below capacity, the reduced production tonnage, and the affect of credits due from overpayments made in previous years.

## LIMITATION ON TAXATION

Since 1964, the burden of the occupation tax has been limited by statutory and constitutional (the taconite amendment) provisions, such that the sum of occupation, royalty and excise (general sales) taxes payable by taconite-producing companies in any of the next twenty-five years cannot be increased so as to exceed the greater of: (a) the amount of those same taxes payable under the laws of 1963; or (b) the amount that would be payable if taconite firms were taxed under the corporate income and excise tax laws applicable to manufacturing. Unless extended by legislative action, this constitutional limitation is scheduled to expire in 1989.

## DISTRIBUTION OF REVENUES

Stemming from the natural heritage argument that led to its adoption, all proceeds from the occupation tax are constitutionally mandated to go to the state—50% to the general fund, 40% to elementary and secondary education, and 10% to the University of Minnesota.

## ANALYSIS OF CURRENT TAX STRUCTURE

The advantages of the occupation tax were also related to administrative convenience and efficient resource use. All taconite producers in Minnesota are either wholly or jointly owned by the major U.S. steel and iron ore companies. Their production is sold at market price to their controlling owner or partnership under long-term contracts. The Lake Erie (market) price for iron ore is established by the few independent producers that operate in the lake states; therefore, this price is based on a very small number of true arms-length transactions. Under these conditions, the determination of the net incomes (profits) of taconite producers for purposes of corporate income taxation is extremely difficult. Thus, from a tax enforcement standpoint, the base of the occupation tax—the value of the ore at the mouth of the mine less certain statutory deductions—is an acceptable substitute for taxable net income.

Because it is a tax on net taxable value, the occupation tax does not effect a producer's decision as to the timing, quantity, and quality of the ore extracted. Therefore, it does not create an incentive to accelerate production in order to mine out from under the tax. And, to the extent that it is levied at the same rate as that on net income from other types of business activity, the occupation tax is neutral with respect to investment in the mining sector, neither encouraging nor discouraging it.

Like the production tax, the major criticism of the occupation tax is its instability, i.e., revenues fluctuate with changes in production costs and mineral prices. Because its revenues are a very small percentage of total state revenues, these fluctuations do not create undue hardship on the state budget during years of decline.

## EVALUATION OF REVENUE PRODUCTIVITY

### OCCUPATION TAX

Given current economic conditions on the Iron Range, it is unlikely that taconite producers would show a profit for purposes of corporate income taxation. Therefore, it is likely that, at present, the state is receiving at least as much (if not more) revenue from the occupation tax than it would if taconite producers were taxed under the corporate income tax. With prospects for the future of Minnesota taconite uncertain, the existing occupation tax appears to be a good compromise between a corporate income tax and a severance tax on gross sales, both of which are difficult to administer when there are few market transactions from which prices for the taconite product can be obtained. The deduction of certain expenses from the Lake Erie value of iron ore makes the tax responsive to the economic conditions of mining firms, while continuing to provide the state with a moderate amount of revenue when times are bad. Further, the existing tax rate (in relation to the Lake Erie value of iron ore) is low enough that it is unlikely that significant resources are being diverted from mining to other investments due to tax considerations.

The major problem with the occupation tax is its administrative complexity and compliance costs. For example:

- The labor credit no longer serves a useful purpose since all producers now qualify for the maximum credit. Elimination of this credit and the consequent reduction of the statutory tax rate from 15% to 6.75% would eliminate the administrative burden of keeping records and auditing labor costs for both the mining industry and the state. For purposes of consistency, this same change should also be made to the royalty tax.
- The limitation on taxation imposed by the taconite amendment is administratively cumbersome in that it calls for the combined occupation, royalty, and excise tax liability to be calculated under three sets of tax laws (laws of 1963, laws of 1974-83, and the corporate income tax laws) before the final liability can be determined (the lesser of the three amounts). It also inappropriately makes the state Constitution the repository of specific tax law instead of broad, long-term goals and principles. The occupation tax should be codified only in the statutes and payable according to current law without a "shadow" net income (profits) tax test.

PRODUCTION TAX

The taconite production tax is by legislative intent a substitute for ad valorem taxes on mines, concentrating plants, and ore reserves in northeastern Minnesota. This interpretation of the production tax has been tested in the courts numerous times, and was recently reaffirmed in a ruling of the Minnesota Supreme Court. Thus, when evaluating this tax, one should look for consistent treatment of the revenue raised by the production tax with that which might have been obtained through a property tax. In terms of the equivalency of their collections, it appears that taconite producers are paying somewhat higher taxes under the production tax. Because the base of the property tax—market value—would be determined according to the income approach to value, and given present conditions of global overcapacity in the steel industry and declining demand for domestic ore, taxable property values would likely be low (reflecting the low expectations for future profits).

The somewhat higher burdens imposed by the production tax may be merited. It allows for regional sharing of production tax revenues on the Iron Range, which reduces tax rate disparities among local units of governments and therefore distributes the benefits and costs of the region's economic circumstances across all those affected. Moreover, given the present and future public costs associated with mining activities (particularly the cessation thereof), there appears to be a continuing need to dedicate some portion of production tax revenues for environmental and economic development purposes.

## MINERAL TAX POLICY ISSUES

The remainder of this chapter addresses two important policy issues for mineral taxation in Minnesota:

1. Would changes in the production or occupation tax encourage additional production and thereby assist the recovery of the state's taconite industry?
2. Are production and property tax revenues treated in like manner for purposes of determining state aids for property tax relief?

TAXES AND THE ECONOMIC HEALTH OF THE TACONITE
INDUSTRY

Mineral taxes present an unusually clear-cut problem for Minnesota tax policy, i.e., given the substantial cutback in taconite production over the past few years, would a reduction in taconite taxes encourage additional production in the mining industry? This study concludes that the net result of a tax cut would probably be a loss to the state treasury since both short- and long-run decisions to operate or close taconite plants depend more on the demand for domestic steel than on tax considerations. For example:

- To the extent that the occupation tax is levied at the same rate as that on net income from other sources, it is unlikely to have any impact on plant closings in either the short or long run. Even if its rate is slightly higher (lower), the occupation tax is still unlikely to influence a decision to keep operating or to shutdown, since its rate on a per-ton basis is less than 1% of the delivered price for iron ore.
- The reduction of the production tax would not sufficiently lower the price of Minnesota taconite so as to increase its demand significantly; thus, it would not help the Minnesota mining industry to enlarge its market share. Even the complete elimination of the tax is not likely to make Minnesota ores competitive at Pittsburgh or at east coast steel mills. Ores from Australia, Brazil, Labrador, Quebec, Liberia, and Venezuela can be delivered to eastern seaboard locations at substantially lower costs than can Minnesota taconite.[4]
- All eight Minnesota taconite plants sell nearly all their output to the major U.S. steel and iron ore companies. These companies are obliged, under long-term "take-or-pay" contracts, to cover their taconite mine's production expenses, even if they cannot use the output. During the 1970s, they spent an estimated $2.5 billion to expand their taconite production capacity and to bring their plants into compliance with pollution control laws. The subsequent slowdown in the domestic demand for steel has not only left the steelmakers with excess iron ore capacity, but also with an obligation to service the debt used to finance the expansion.

Their decision to keep operating or to shut down is complicated by several practical considerations such as: (a) the terms of their partnership agreements; (b) their obligation to assume the debt of their taconite firms in the event of closure; and (c) the difficulty of selling their interest in a mine when the market is plagued with excess capacity. These factors are likely to outweigh the tax considerations of the shut down decision.

## EQUAL TREATMENT OF PRODUCTION TAX REVENUES

Minnesota's use of the production tax in lieu of the property tax creates a complex interplay between production tax distributions and state aids for purposes of property tax relief. The goal of equal treatment of equals requires that for purposes of computing state aids, revenues received from the taconite production tax should be treated in the same manner as revenues received from the property tax. In analyzing the relationships between the production-tax-supported taconite homestead credit and the state-paid homestead credit, this study finds that for purposes of determining state aid for property tax relief, production tax revenues are not treated as are property tax revenues elsewhere in Minnesota. Moreover, current practices place an upward pressure on state spending, and therefore on state revenue-raising. Specific findings are:

- The 1984 legislative action that reversed the order in which the taconite homestead credit and state homestead credit are subtracted from gross residential property taxes on the Iron Range has the effect of increasing that portion of the total property tax reduction paid for by the state homestead credit and decreasing that portion paid for by the taconite homestead credit (with no change in tax relief to the Iron Range homeowner). In short, the effect is to use state general fund revenues to help pay for special property tax relief on the Iron Range.
- At present, the special property tax relief that is provided to homeowners and farms on the Iron Range is not limited to the available production tax revenue in the property tax relief account. Instead, this account has an open and standing draw on the economic protection trust fund. In a period of low growth or declining production tonnage, the revenues generated by the production tax are likely to be insufficient to fund the mandated annual increase in the level of property tax relief. This may necessitate the use of the statutory draw down at a time when using the fund for economic development purposes is more important than ever. Although the change in the subtraction sequence for the taconite homestead credit alleviated this fiscal pressure, it did so at a cost to all state taxpayers.

## RECOMMENDATION

### SIMPLIFICATION AND ACCOUNTABILITY OF MINERALS TAXATION

The commission concludes that a reduction in occupation and production taxes is unlikely to encourage additional production and thereby assist a recovery in the state taconite industry. It therefore restricts its recommendations to actions that will simplify the tax structure and improve the political accountability of Minnesota's system of mineral taxation.

With respect to the occupation and royalty taxes:

- The commission recommends eliminating the labor credit and lowering the current statutory rate (15%) to the current effective rate of 6.75%. This enhances simplicity (all firms are now taxed at the effective rate) and neutrality (a potential penalty to those firms that lower their labor costs is removed). The commission also recommends lowering the statutory rate of the royalty tax (15%) to its present effective rate of 6.75%, consistent with the occupation tax rate.

- The state Constitution should define broad, long-term goals and principles, rather than be a repository for specific tax law. Therefore, the commission further recommends that the taconite amendment be allowed to expire in 1989, and thereafter, the occupation tax should be based on statutory law and adjusted so that its burden is similar to that imposed on net income (profits) from other business sources.

With respect to the production tax:

- The commission recommends maintaining the existing statutory rate and base, including the scheduled phaseout of the iron content escalator.
- The commission did consider abolishing the production tax and replacing it with an ad valorem property tax on taconite and taconite processing facilities. Although this alternative might provide Iron Range local governments with a more certain revenue source (particularly in uniform tax treatment of mineral and commercial/industrial property), it was rejected because it would add considerable complexity to the tax system (mineral property is valued according to the income approach, whereby the present value of future net income streams must be determined). It would also produce low taxable values because of the present global overcapacity in the steel industry and low demand for domestic ore, and substantially alter the existing shared tax base of Iron Range local governments.
- As part of its recommendation to eliminate the present complex system of property classification and multiple property tax credits and, in its place, adopt a three class/no credit system, the commission recommends abolishing the taconite homestead credit and distributing those production tax revenues directly to Iron Range local units of government. This eliminates using state general fund monies to provide special property tax relief to Iron Range homes and farms.

    At present, the financing of the taconite homestead credit is not explicit. The credit, which provides property tax relief to Iron Range residential and farm property owners above and beyond that available through statewide property tax relief programs, is partially funded by state general fund monies. In addition to violating political accountability, the credit places upward pressure on state spending since its maximum automatically increases each year.


## ENDNOTES

1. This paper is a shortened version of a more detailed report which examines the economic status of Minnesota's Iron Range in addition to an analysis of mineral

taxation. The larger report, "Minnesota Taxation of Minerals," was presented to the commission by Lisa A. Roden, September 12, 1984.

2. In addition to taconite, Minnesota has other ore bodies (copper-nickel, semitaconite, and gold) that, if developed, would be subject to the state's special mineral taxes and/or the local property tax. This report does not address tax policy in relation to the development of these resources.

3. Beneficiation (or concentration) is the process of separating particles of iron ore from the surrounding rock and compressing such particles into pellets for shipping.

4. For further discussion and empirical analysis, see Lisa Roden, "Minnesota Taxation of Minerals." A recent U.S. Congressional Research Office analysis puts the 1981 variable cost of production of one ton of iron ore pellets (exclusive of acquisition cost of the resource) at $18 per ton in Brazil and $30 per ton in the U.S. When transport costs are added in and the Brazilian government subsidy to its industry is eliminated, the variable cost of a ton of Brazilian pellets delivered to Chicago is about $30.50; and for U.S. pellets, about $40.50.

# 15

# Overview of the Property Tax

## INTRODUCTION

The property tax, although the largest state/local tax nationally, is the second most important source of tax revenue in the Minnesota state/local fiscal system. While the state no longer levies a property tax,[1] local governments generated $1.7 billion[2]—95.6% of their tax revenue—from the property tax in FY 1983. In an effort to hold down property tax burdens, the state allocates nearly 35% of its total expenditures to direct and indirect property tax relief programs.[3] Property tax issues, therefore, were an integral part of the commission's work, and they were among the most complex and controversial issues faced during these deliberations.

This overview chapter treats several key aspects of property taxation, including what role the tax plays in financing state and local governments, what types of property are included in the tax base, what administrative arrangements are used in estimating tax base values and setting tax levies, and on whom the tax burden falls. Because this overview sets the stage for several other chapters that take up specifics of the Minnesota system, the treatment here tends to be somewhat general and comparative rather than Minnesota-specific.

Subsequent chapters deal in detail with Minnesota property tax law and assessment administration, property tax relief, and the distribution of the tax burden. The discussion on property tax relief is further divided into direct and indirect categories; direct relief is provided through adjustments of individual tax bills—usually in a manner that changes the relative as well as absolute scope of the bills for various properties (i.e., classification, credits, and refunds)—while indirect relief reduces the overall property tax levy (i.e., local government aids and levy limits).

## FINANCING ROLE OF THE TAX[4]

Property taxation has long been the dominant feature on the state/local fiscal landscape in the United States. In FY 1983 it yielded $89.3 billion to state and local governments. This amount, equal to 31.4% of state and local tax revenue, made property taxation the largest of the state and local taxes.[5]

It also is the only one of the three basic forms of taxation—income, sales, and property—that is in use in all fifty states and the District of Columbia.

STATE AND LOCAL ROLE

The dominance of the property tax, however, is becoming less over time. Between 1960 and 1980, for example, the tax fell from 32.5% of all state/local general revenue to 17.9% (Table 1). In part, this decline reflects the sharp increase in federal aid over the period. However, a similar drop in the relative significance of the property tax is revealed even when we ignore federal aid, and express property tax revenue as a percentage of state/local, own-source general revenue (Table 2). By this measure, property taxes fell from 37.7% to 22.8% of state/local, own-source revenue between 1960 and 1980. Other state and local taxes, user charges, and other nontax revenue sources simply have grown more rapidly than the property tax.[6]

The decline has been sharp, not only for the state/local governments as a group, but also for Minnesota and each of its contiguous states (Iowa, North Dakota, South Dakota, and Wisconsin—Tables 1 and 2). In fact, the financing role of the property tax in the Minnesota state/local fiscal system has fallen even more rapidly than in the nation as a whole. Property taxes as a percentage of total Minnesota state/local revenues declined from 37.6% in 1960 to 16.4% in 1980—falling from 115.7% of the national average in 1960 to only 91.6% of the national average by 1980 (Table 1). Similarly, the share of total state/local, own-source revenues generated by the property tax has fallen from 115.1% of the national average in 1960 to 89.9% in 1980.

It is important to stress, however, that the property tax has declined only in relative terms. The per capita figures in Table 3 document the growth in absolute amounts over the same period for which Tables 1 and 2 show relative decline. In Minnesota, per capita property taxes increased from $117 in 1960 to $324 in 1980—an increase of 177%. Nationally, per capita

TABLE 1
Property Tax as a Percent of State/Local
General Revenue, Selected States, 1960-80

| State | 1960 | 1965 | 1970 | 1975 | 1980 |
|-------|------|------|------|------|------|
| MINNESOTA | 37.6 | 36.3 | 25.1 | 18.6 | 16.4 |
| Iowa | 37.5 | 39.9 | 33.5 | 25.6 | 22.1 |
| North Dakota | 30.0 | 26.6 | 25.8 | 16.2 | 14.1 |
| South Dakota | 36.2 | 34.5 | 33.6 | 26.4 | 21.9 |
| Wisconsin | 40.3 | 34.8 | 31.9 | 24.6 | 19.9 |
| U.S. Average | 32.5 | 30.8 | 26.1 | 22.6 | 17.9 |

Source: U.S. Bureau of the Census, Statistical Abstract of the United States, Washington D.C., Government Printing Office, various editions.

TABLE 2
Property Tax as a Percent of State/Local
Own-Source General Revenue, Selected States
1960-80

| State | 1960 | 1965 | 1970 | 1975 | 1980 |
|-------|------|------|------|------|------|
| MINNESOTA | 43.4 | 42.5 | 29.8 | 23.2 | 20.5 |
| Iowa | 44.3 | 46.2 | 39.1 | 31.9 | 27.4 |
| North Dakota | 38.2 | 33.0 | 31.7 | 20.6 | 18.2 |
| South Dakota | 45.5 | 45.8 | 42.8 | 36.5 | 30.6 |
| Wisconsin | 45.1 | 38.5 | 36.1 | 30.1 | 25.2 |
| U.S. Average | 37.7 | 36.2 | 31.3 | 28.5 | 22.8 |

property taxes increased from \$91 in 1960 to \$302 in 1980—an increase of 232%. Per capita property taxes in Minnesota have declined from 129% of the national average in 1960 to 107% in 1980. During this period, Minnesota's per capita property taxes grew at a slower rate than did all those of its neighbors, except North Dakota.

The Table 3 data show that, on nominal terms, per capita tax bills increased nearly threefold over the past two decades. This is, at first glance, quite startling. But, once one recognizes that those figures build in an income period of rapid inflation, a somewhat different conclusion emerges. Indeed, Table 4 shows that once one deflates the per capita property tax burdens (that is, eliminates the effect of the inflation over the 1960-80 period), in real terms per capita tax burdens in Minnesota not only have fallen, but have fallen significantly, when compared to the U.S. average and neighboring Iowa, North Dakota, and Wisconsin.

Finally, a look at the real per capita burden changes for just the 1975-80 period reveals that Minnesota's tax burden continues to fall and remain below that of all its neighbors, other than South Dakota; however, this recent decline is less than half what has occurred for the nation as a whole.

TABLE 3
Per Capita State/Local Property Taxes,
Selected States, 1960-80

| State | (Dollars) | | | | | Percent Change 1960-80 |
|-------|------|------|------|------|------|------|
| | 1960 | 1965 | 1970 | 1975 | 1980 | |
| MINNESOTA | 117 | 158 | 171 | 231 | 324 | 176.9% |
| Iowa | 109 | 155 | 213 | 263 | 360 | 230.3 |
| North Dakota | 113 | 140 | 219 | 267 | 351 | 210.6 |
| South Dakota | 105 | 123 | 175 | 192 | 269 | 156.2 |
| Wisconsin | 114 | 140 | 221 | 271 | 361 | 216.7 |
| U.S. Average | 91 | 118 | 168 | 242 | 302 | 231.9 |

*Source:* See Table 1.

TABLE 4
Per Capita State/Local Property Taxes,
Selected States, 1960-80

| | (Real Dollars)* | | | | | Percent change 1960-80 | Percent change 1975-80 |
|---|---|---|---|---|---|---|---|
| State | 1960 | 1965 | 1970 | 1975 | 1980 | | |
| MINNESOTA | 131.9 | 167.2 | 147.0 | 143.3 | 131.3 | - 0.5% | - 8.4% |
| Iowa | 122.9 | 164.0 | 183.1 | 163.2 | 145.9 | + 18.7 | -10.6 |
| North Dakota | 127.4 | 148.1 | 188.3 | 165.6 | 142.2 | + 11.6 | -14.1 |
| South Dakota | 118.4 | 130.2 | 150.5 | 119.1 | 109.0 | - 7.9 | - 8.5 |
| Wisconsin | 128.5 | 148.1 | 190.0 | 168.1 | 146.3 | + 13.9 | -13.0 |
| U.S. Average | 102.6 | 124.9 | 144.5 | 150.1 | 122.4 | + 19.3 | -18.5 |

*Source:* See Table 1 and *Economic Report of the President,* February 1984, Table B-52, p. 279.
*1967 was used as the base year. The Consumer Price Index for all items was the index card.

## ROLE IN LOCAL FINANCE

Local governments derive about three-fourths of their taxes from the property tax. This amounts to about 48% of local, own-source general revenue, a figure matched in Minnesota in FY 1983 (Table 5), but only with the help of a substantial, one-time gain from a change in the tax collection cycle. Even so, Minnesota is the only state among its neighbors where the property tax accounts for as small a share of local, own-source general revenues as the average for the nation as whole. One might conclude, therefore, that the Minnesota Miracle, that group of innovative property tax relief initiatives undertaken in 1971 by the governor and state legislature, is a success story in terms of its goal of reducing dependence on property taxes for funding local services.

TABLE 5
Property Taxes as a Percent of Local Own-Source
General Revenues by Type of Government, 1982

| | Local Total | County | City | Townships | School Districts | Special Districts |
|---|---|---|---|---|---|---|
| MINNESOTA | 47.9 | 58.3 | 25.4 | 81.1 | 75.3 | 13.9 |
| North Dakota | 55.7 | 57.7 | 21.9 | 100.0 | 81.3 | 49.4 |
| South Dakota | 62.3 | 62.1 | 30.9 | 66.0 | 86.5 | 4.8 |
| Iowa | 60.2 | 57.8 | 39.2 | — | 82.0 | 37.8 |
| Wisconsin | 64.1 | 41.0 | 58.8 | 62.7 | 86.5 | 12.0 |
| U.S. Average | 48.0 | 45.8 | 32.2 | 75.8 | 79.7 | 14.4 |

*Source: Governmental Finances in 1982-83,* U.S. Department of Commerce, Bureau of the Census, Government Printing Office, Washington, D.C., October 1984. Table 23.

The property tax, however, is not equally important to all types of local governments; nor are all types of local governments given equally significant ranks in the division of the property tax. As tables 5 and 6 indicate:

- Nationally, independent school districts derive a larger portion of their own-source general revenue from property taxation than does any other type of local government. In Minnesota, only townships derive a larger share of their own-source revenue from the property tax than do school districts. However, the share of school district, own-source revenue coming from property taxation in Minnesota is well below the national average (75.3% in 1982-83 versus 79.7%). Alternatively, the share of the property taxes in Minnesota raised by school districts exceeds the national average share for school districts: 47.3% of property tax revenues in Minnesota went to schools in 1982-83, compared with 43.5% nationally (Table 6);
- School districts in neighboring states raise a larger share of property taxes than do school districts nationally or in Minnesota, and they are more dependent on property taxes as a source of revenue than are school districts nationally or in Minnesota;
- Counties in Minnesota raise an above-average share of property tax revenues—29.0% in 1982-83, compared with 22.5% nationally—(Table 6). At the same time they place a well-above-average reliance upon the tax for own-source revenue—58.3% compared with 45.8% nationally—(Table 4); and
- Municipalities in Minnesota, like school districts, are below the national average in both respects. Counties, cities, and school districts account for 95% of property tax revenues in Minnesota compared with 91% nationally.

TABLE 6
Percent Distribution of Property Taxes Raised by
Each Level of Government, 1983

|  | County | City | Townships | School Districts | Special Districts |
|---|---|---|---|---|---|
| MINNESOTA | 29.0 | 19.2 | 2.0 | 47.3 | 2.5 |
| North Dakota | 23.5 | 12.7 | 3.9 | 56.1 | 3.8 |
| South Dakota | 19.3 | 14.7 | 2.3 | 63.5 | 0.3 |
| Iowa | 26.5 | 22.8 | — | 50.6 | 0.1 |
| Wisconsin | 16.2 | 33.1 | 2.4 | 47.9 | 0.4 |
| U.S. Average | 22.8 | 24.4 | 6.4 | 43.5 | 2.8 |

*Source:* See Table 4.

## THE TAX BASE

The property tax can be either general or selective in its application. A general tax applies broadly to all types of property and treats the various types uniformly. A selective tax, by contrast, is levied only on certain types of property.

For the last several decades, property taxation in the United States has become increasingly a tax on real property. The importance of personal property, both tangible and intangible, has dwindled substantially. The changes have been motivated by both practical and philosophical considerations. Intangibles are very difficult for the assessor to locate and, assuming success in discovering such properties, often difficult to value. Moreover, noting that intangibles—particularly stocks, bonds, mortgages, and the like—are merely claims on real and tangible properties that also are generally part of the tax base, many have argued that the taxation of intangible property constitutes an undesirable form of double taxation.

Taxation of tangible personal property also has declined, again for both administrative and philosophical reasons. Given the movable character of many forms of tangible personal property—e.g., inventories and railroad cars—tax avoidance often is relatively simple. Moreover, the tax, particularly as applied to inventories, is perverse in its effect: it rises when inventories rise (generally during an economic downturn). Popular and political unwillingness to take the administrative steps necessary to discover and list household personal property in general, together with the difficulties inherent in valuing such items, resulted in many states exempting such property; where it remains legally taxable, enforcement and compliance often are quite lax. Many states exempt at least some types of

TABLE 7
Percent Distribution of Net Assessed Property Values*
Subject to Local General Property Taxation, by Major
Category of Property, Selected States, 1976

| State | Total | State Assessed | Locally Assessed Total | Locally Assessed Real | Locally Assessed Personal |
|-------|-------|----------|-------|------|----------|
| MINNESOTA | 100.0 | 5.2 | 94.8 | 94.4 | 0.4 |
| Iowa | 100.0 | 8.4 | 91.6 | 85.5 | 6.1 |
| North Dakota | 100.0 | 9.1 | 90.9 | 90.9 | — |
| South Dakota | 100.0 | 7.0 | 93.1 | 71.9 | 21.1 |
| Wisconsin | 100.0 | — | 100.0 | 84.9 | 15.1 |
| U.S. Average | 100.0 | 7.1 | 92.9 | 80.6 | 12.2 |

*Source:* 1977 Census of Governments. Volume 2, U.S. Department of Commerce, Bureau of the Census, U.S. Government Printing Office, Washington, D.C., November 1978, Table 2.
*Net assessed values are gross values less partial exemptions, such as homestead exemptions. Wholly exempt properties are excluded from gross assessed values.

agricultural personal property, and even more exempt motor vehicles, often for political reasons rather than administrative considerations.

By 1981, complete exemption from the local property tax was accorded these major categories of tangible personal property by the number of states shown for each:[7] motor vehicles, thirty-one; household personal property, thirty-four (up from twenty-eight just two years before); agricultural personal property, seventeen (up from twelve in 1979); business inventories, twenty-two; and other commercial and industrial property, eight. These numbers include eight states[8] that exempted all tangible personal property— up from five states in 1979. As a result of these trends, the personal property share of locally assessed taxable property declined nationwide from 15.7% in 1961 to just 9.6% in 1981.

The data in Tables 7 and 8 reveal that in Minnesota and its neighboring states—even more than nationally—the practice of eliminating personal property from the tax base has been dramatic. In 1976, locally assessed personal property was 12.2% of net assessed property values nationwide; however, Minnesota and North Dakota had essentially eliminated personal property[9] from their net tax base, while South Dakota and Wisconsin had personal property shares that exceeded the national average by 73% and 23.8%, respectively. By 1981, all the states in the area had personal property shares of net tax base less than the national average, with Minnesota, North Dakota, and South Dakota essentially exempting all personal property.

## REVENUE STABILITY

The responsiveness of property tax revenue to economic growth, when such growth is measured by income growth (i.e., the income elasticity of the

TABLE 8
Percent Distribution of Net Assessed Property Values
Subject to Local General Property Taxation, by Major
Category of Property, Selected States, 1981

| State | Total | State Assessed | Locally Assessed Total | Locally Assessed Real | Locally Assessed Personal |
|-------|-------|----------------|-------|------|----------|
| MINNESOTA | 100.0 | 6.0 | 94.0 | 93.8 | 0.2 |
| Iowa | 100.0 | 8.3 | 91.7 | 87.3 | 4.4 |
| North Dakota | 100.0 | 7.0 | 92.8 | 92.8 | — |
| South Dakota | 100.0 | 5.6 | 94.4 | 94.4 | — |
| Wisconsin | 100.0 | — | 100.0 | 96.1 | 3.9 |
| U.S. Average | 100.0 | 5.6 | 94.4 | 84.8 | 9.6 |

*Source:* 1982 Census of Government, Volume 2, Table 3.

revenue), depends upon (1) the responsiveness of real estate market values to economic growth and (2) the ability of the local assessing jurisdiction to capture changing market values through the assessment process.[10] A stable tax typically will generate revenues that change relatively more slowly than income—i.e., revenue is income inelastic.[11]

In general, depending on assessment procedures and the extent to which increased market values are reflected in the property tax base, the property tax is characterized as being a "unitary elastic revenue source."[12] If a jurisdiction relied totally on the property tax as a source of revenue, it would continually face a fiscal gap as the economy grew because the demand for services is income-elastic, but property tax revenues are not. The resulting fiscal gap would create constant pressure on local officials to increase the property tax rate. Alternatively, to the extent a jurisdiction diversifies its revenue structure by deemphasizing the property tax in favor of more income responsive revenue sources—e.g., an income tax—this problem becomes less critical.

## EQUITY CRITERIA FOR DISTRIBUTING THE TAX BURDEN

The property tax, in part, is consistent with both the ability to pay and the benefit principles of taxation. From the standpoint of ability to pay, the case for a property tax rests largely upon imperfections in the taxation of income. The preferred measure of income is a very comprehensive one. Comprehensiveness is desirable to promote neutrality (economic efficiency); if there is no escape from the tax, the tax is not a factor in economic choices. This requires that all contributions to income—whether in the form of money income, imputed income (i.e., nonmonetary benefits, such as the value of housing services from owner-occupied housing), or increases in assets values—be taxed alike. But this is not standard income tax practice, in part for practical reasons. Whenever the flow of benefits from property totally or partially escapes income taxation, equity (implementation of the ability to pay approach) and efficiency concerns require that the asset which creates the benefits be subject to the property tax. The value of the asset is taxed because it represents the capitalized value of the stream of benefits.

An example may help to illustrate this notion. Suppose that Warren and O'Leary each have wages of $30,000 and assets of $100,000; the only difference is the form in which they hold their assets. Warren owns the $100,000 home in which she lives, while O'Leary has a $100,000 bank account. Both assets generate benefits, and an ideal income tax of the sort discussed above would tax both benefit streams equally. In practice, however, O'Leary's bank account yields interest payments that are subject to income taxation, while Warren's house provides her with a nonmonetary

stream of housing services that are not subject to income taxation. This difference in income tax treatment produces a horizontal inequity that can be redressed by property taxation.

In general, the foregoing reasoning suggests that the case for property taxation (or for relatively high property taxes) is strongest in the case of owner-occupied residences, the benefits from which completely escape income taxation. The inequity from the failure to tax the imputed value of owner-occupied housing services is exacerbated by the allowance of deductions from other income of the costs of generating these tax-exempt benefits—i.e., property taxes and mortgage interest.

Many argue that the property tax also is consistent with the benefits principle of taxation. Here the point is that property tax revenues tend to be used to finance local government expenditures—police, fire, sewer, water, etc.—that are site oriented services benefitting local property owners, and thereby increasing the value of their properties.

This argument, however, implicitly assumes that the benefits are distributed across properties in proportion to their property tax liabilities (and under the usual standard of tax uniformity, this implies benefits are distributed across properties in proportion to market value). This, in turn, implies that expenditure benefits are, in fact, capitalized in (add to) the value of the properties. Thus, the property tax on two homes of equal value and in receipt of equal service benefits must, for equity under the benefits principle, be the same. Any tax nonuniformities tend to depart from the theory underlying the benefits-received case for the property tax, as they cause tax shares to diverge from benefit shares. Nonuniformities can arise from either extralegal differences in tax treatment (e.g., assessment error) or intentional differences (e.g., classification which exempts homeowners from a portion of the tax with no comparable break for rental properties.)

The assumptions underlying the benefits principle may not be true for all goods and services provided by local government. For example, the direct benefits of education are not likely to be distributed across all properties in proportion to property taxes, but rather according to the number of public school children in the household. This does not suggest, however, that property owners without children in public school should be exempt from the school portion of their property tax. Why? Because public education not only provides direct private benefits to those attending school, but also provides some indirect benefits to those living in the community. To the extent there are such community-wide benefits, it follows that everyone in the community should contribute to funding local public education.

## WHO PAYS THE PROPERTY TAX?

Each year property owners pay local governments an amount equal to their net property tax liabilities. This transfer of funds—from property owner to the local government—represents the initial burden of the property tax. However, the property owner may be able to shift all or part of the net property tax to others through changes in the prices of things sold and/or purchased. This tax shifting may be either forward to users or backward to suppliers. The ability of the property owner to shift the property tax will depend upon both the type of asset taxed and market conditions. The type of asset is important because the mechanism by which shifting occurs is supply reduction, and the feasibility of this differs across asset clauses. In any event, the ultimate burden (incidence) of the property tax is likely to differ frequently from the initial burden.

It is important at this juncture to clarify some of the language used here and in subsequent property tax chapters. When discussing the distribution of the tax burden, or the incidence of the tax, the tax liability is expressed in relation to income. Alternatively, if the concern is with the tax liability in relation to the value of the property, the appropriate concept is the effective tax rate. The following example illustrates these concepts. From the example it is clear that even though the effective tax rate is increasing (from 0.5% to 0.8%) as income and home value rise, the tax liability relative to income is declining (from 1.7% to 1.0% of income). This tax would be regarded as a regressive tax when measured against income. But some ambiguities are present.

| | | CASES | | |
|---|---|---|---|---|
| | | A | B | C |
| INCOME | | $11,250 | $32,500 | $60,000 |
| VALUE OF HOME | | 40,000 | 62,500 | 70,750 |
| Tax Levy, No Relief | | 1,227 | 1,922 | 2,373 |
| Less: Deductibility | | 162 | 512 | 828 |
| Classification | | 475 | 586 | 534 |
| Homestead Credit | | 318 | 444 | 423 |
| Circuit Breaker | | 83 | -0- | -0- |
| Equals: | Net Tax | $ 189 | $ 380 | $ 588 |
| Tax Burden | $\dfrac{\text{Net Tax}}{\text{Income}}$ | 1.7% | 1.2% | 1.0% |
| Effective Rate | $\dfrac{\text{Net Tax}}{\text{Home Value}}$ | 0.5% | 0.6% | 0.8% |

In particular, the ratios of net tax to income and to home value are affected significantly by the treatment of income tax deductibility of property taxes, a provision that many may wish not to consider as a property tax feature. While ignoring deductibility does not change the basic patterns across the three cases—as income and home value rise, the net tax still falls as a percentage of income and still rises as a percentage of home value. But in the tax-to-income comparison, the gap narrows to a ratio of high-to-low of 1.3:1 rather than 1.7:1; and in the tax-to-value comparison, the gap widens to a ratio of high-to-low of 2.2:1 rather than 1.6:1.

|  | CASES | | |
|---|---|---|---|
|  | A | B | C |
| $\dfrac{\text{Net Tax Before Deductibility}}{\text{Income}}$ | 3.1% | 2.7% | 2.4% |
| $\dfrac{\text{Net Tax Before Deductibility}}{\text{Home Value}}$ | 0.9% | 1.4% | 2.0% |

Is deductibility a property tax feature or an income tax feature? Both sets of numbers may be useful, but in different circumstances. If dramatic income tax simplification of the sort often proposed in recent years were to be adopted, deductibility could be ended, or at least limited, without touching the property tax; from this perspective, it seems preferable to treat deductibility as a feature of income tax, not of property tax. Under current law, deductibility is a fact of life that helps shape the distribution of any state or local property tax increase or reduction.

The question of tax incidence is a very important consideration in shaping tax policy. Many states have adopted property tax relief policies, at least in part on the basis of a belief that the tax is quite regressive. Since the last major Minnesota tax study and the advent of the Minnesota Miracle, however, professional opinion on the distribution of property tax burdens has undergone significant change. The basis for the change is outlined below, and the upshot is that most economists now believe that the property tax is substantially less regressive than previously was believed.

The entire tax, whether imposed initially on business or not, ultimately becomes a burden on people (i.e., it reduces their real incomes). The question is whether the burden falls on people in their role as consumers of business products, in their role as suppliers of factors of production, or in their role as the owners of the taxed properties. The answer no doubt is that it falls on all these activities, with differences in market conditions determining which activity bears the heaviest burden.

The property tax base includes a variety of property types—land, improvements, and personal property. The assumptions about the potential for shifting that portion of the property tax falling on each component differ.

The supply of land is considered to be fixed. As a result of the fixed supply of land, potential users need bid no more for the land than they did before the imposition of the property tax. Indeed, since the owners of the land must pay the tax, the increased tax will lead prospective land buyers to offer less after the increase than before because the higher annual tax payment—to the extent it does not increase services to the property—reduces the net return to land ownership. In this case, therefore, the initial and final burden coincide and fall on the owners of land at the time of the tax increase.

The tax on improvements and tangible personal property owned by business is more complicated. Because the supply of improvements, unlike that of land, is not fixed over time, shifting of the tax is possible. But the nature of any shifting—forward to consumers or backward to resource suppliers—and the degree to which it occurs will depend upon the nature of the product and resource markets. Therefore, the outcome is uncertain and may vary across properties. According to the traditional view, the property tax on improvements is shifted forward in the form of higher rents. The property tax is viewed as reducing the rate of return on capital improvements, thereby slowing the rate of investment in taxed capital (e.g., new structures, rehabilitation, and maintenance). This restriction on supply will continue until the after-tax rate of return is equal to the rate of return existing before the imposition (increase) of the tax. Therefore, rents will increase by the amount of the tax and the property tax on the improvements will be shifted forward to the renter.

The renters or users of the improvements, in turn, may be able to shift the tax either forward or backward. The ability of the business to shift that portion of the property tax falling on improvements and personal property depends on 1) the market structure of the industry, 2) the availability of substitutes for the product, and 3) the degree of influence the firm has in determining factor input prices.

As opposed to this traditional view of property tax incidence, a new view starts from the premise that there is some level of property taxation that is common to all types of property and all jurisdictions. The analysis treats this portion of the tax as a uniform general property tax. For this level of tax, the initial and ultimate burdens against coincide and fall on the owners of capital since all forms of capital are subject to a uniform rate and there is no nontaxed sector to which capital can be shifted.

The second dimension of the new view of property tax incidence is an analysis of the effects of that portion of the tax which is not universal—i.e., a tax applied at different rates for different property types (e.g., commercial vs. agricultural properties) and/or in different jurisdictions. It is argued that, in response to these tax differentials, resources shift from high- to low-taxed sectors in an effort to maximize the after-tax rate of return, much as in the traditional analysis. The standard new view analysis, however, assumes a fixed supply of capital in the aggregate; as this capital moves around in response to tax differentials, therefore, the net return on all capital is reduced by the tax (whereas the traditional analysis suggests capital out-migration will take place until the after-tax return equals the before-tax return).

The differential tax rate feature of the new view can also be presented in a spatial context. In this case the differential tax rates do not differ between various sectors (types of property) of the economy, but differ on a geographic basis. That is, the situation is analogous to the case of a uniform property tax levied at different rates in different jurisdictions. The high interregional mobility of capital will equalize the after-tax rates of return to capital in ventures of similar risk by reducing supply in high-tax regions and increasing supply of capital in low-tax jurisdictions. In areas where the tax rate is relatively high, taxpayers will have to pay high before-tax prices to owners of capital, while the reverse is true in low-tax regions.

Also, because of the high mobility of workers, households, and shoppers within any given metropolitan region, it follows that intraurban property tax differentials will be borne by land owners in the form of capital losses. That is, the movement of capital (workers, households, and shoppers) out of the high-tax area depresses land values and rents because of the reduced demand. If labor and capital are perfectly mobile, one would expect land rents in the high-tax area to be reduced by the full amount of the tax.

In summary, the new view leads to a number of implications which extend those associated with the traditional view. First, that portion of the property tax common to all property across jurisdictions falls on the owners of capital in the form of lower rates of return than would be expected in the nontax situation. Second, in addition to their share of the average nationwide property tax burden, property owners bear a portion of the above-average tax rate differentials, particularly in urban areas. In those areas with below-average tax levels, property owners tend to benefit from the low taxes and, therefore, to be able to absorb some increase in taxes without depressing their returns to investment below national norms. Third, that portion of the property tax which is shifted to consumers is much less important than believed according to the traditional view.

Table 9 expresses the ultimate property tax burden, under different assumptions of tax shifting, as a percentage of annual income by income class. Under the traditional view (middle column), the tax is regressive for most of the bottom half of the income distribution and for the top 5%, but most significantly for the bottom 25%. The pure new view conclusion that the tax does burden capital income (last column), however, shows the tax to be regressive only for the lowest 10%; beyond that, it is essentially proportional until the upper fourth of the income distribution where the share of income going to property taxes increases to 5.6%.

It should be emphasized that the new and traditional views are complementary, not competing. If the concern is a change in the national average property tax, the new view is most appropriate and leads to the conclusion that the tax change is primarily borne by the owners of capital. If, however, the concern is the relative change in a local property tax or differentials between sectors and/or regions, the traditional view provides the appropriate framework for analysis focusing on the excise effects of local differentials.

The incidence of the property tax on Minnesota homeowners is analyzed in chapter 17. The findings of this limited analysis confirm the more general national results. Specifically, the Minnesota property tax on homeowners is regressive at the low end of the income scale and essentially proportional

TABLE 9

Alternative Estimates of the Incidence of the
Property Tax, by Income Percentiles, 1975

| Household income percentile[a] | Effective rates of tax, assuming property tax on improvements is borne in proportion to | |
|---|---|---|
| | Housing expenditures and consumptions[b] | Income from capital[b] |
| 0-5 | 11.4 | 1.8 |
| 5-10 | 5.0 | 0.9 |
| 10-15 | 3.7 | 1.0 |
| 15-20 | 3.6 | 1.1 |
| 20-25 | 3.2 | 1.3 |
| 25-30 | 2.9 | 1.4 |
| 30-35 | 2.9 | 1.3 |
| 35-40 | 2.9 | 1.4 |
| 40-45 | 2.9 | 1.5 |
| 45-50 | 3.0 | 1.7 |
| 50-55 | 2.9 | 1.7 |
| 55-60 | 3.0 | 1.9 |
| 60-65 | 3.0 | 1.9 |
| 65-70 | 3.1 | 1.9 |
| 70-75 | 3.1 | 2.0 |
| 75-80 | 3.1 | 2.2 |
| 80-85 | 3.1 | 2.2 |
| 85-90 | 3.3 | 2.5 |
| 90-95 | 3.3 | 3.3 |
| 95-99 | 3.2 | 4.3 |
| 99-100 | 2.8 | 5.6 |
| All classes[c] | 3.2 | 2.7[d] |

*Source:* Joseph A. Pechman, *Federal Tax Policy.* 4th ed. (Washington, D.C.: Brookings Institution, 1983), p. 265.

[a]Ranked from low to high incomes. Income is defined as money factor income plus transfer payments, accrued capital gains, and indirect business taxes.

[b]It is assumed that the property tax on land is borne by landlords.

[c]Includes negative incomes.

[d]The average burden of the property tax is lower because, under these assumptions, part of the tax is borne by the tax-exempt sector and is not included in the household sector.

through most other income categories. Deductibility of the tax from state and federal income taxes makes the property tax more regressive. Classification and credits offset the effect of deductibility and the circuit breaker makes the tax essentially proportional.

## ENDNOTES

1. The state does tax the flight property of air carriers engaging in air commerce.

2. This is the net levy amount actually paid by property owners in Minnesota and does not include property tax liabilities paid to the local governments by the state through the various credit programs.

3. U.S. Department of Commerce, Bureau of the Census, *Governmental Finances in 1982-83,* Washington, D.C., Government Printing Office, October 1983, Table 13. This figure represents state aid to local governments, which includes property tax credits but excludes the circuit breaker refund.

4. In order to put the role of the property tax in a perspective vis-a-vis other states, it is necessary to use data provided by the U.S. Bureau of the Census. Census data is the most comprehensive set of standardized state/local financial data available. Each state and local government has its own accounting convention so that interjurisdictional comparisons are not possible without some standardization of the data; census provides this standardization. Census revenue and expenditure numbers, therefore, may not directly correspond to numbers prepared by a given state/local government. One of the most important differences is that census uses a broad definition of general fund revenues and expenditures. Thus, census numbers indicate that property taxes are a smaller percentage of municipal own-source revenues in Minnesota than do the general fund data prepared by the state auditor's office; the numbers are not comparable.

5. U.S. Department of Commerce, Bureau of the Census, *Government Finances, 1982-83,* (Washington, D.C.: Government Printing Office, October 1984, Table 5.)

6. *Ibid.*

7. U.S. Department of Commerce, Bureau of the Census, *1982 Census of Governments, Volume 2,* (Washington, D.C.: U.S. Government Printing Office, February 1984, Table E.)

8. South Dakota, Pennsylvania, North Dakota, New York, New Hampshire, Illinois, Hawaii, and Delaware.

9. In Minnesota, 0.2% of the net tax base was locally assessed personal property. This amount included mobile homes and some personal property of public utilities.

10. Actual property tax collections usually do not grow as rapidly as implied by the growth in market values, in part because assessments do not keep pace with the growth in market values, and new exemptions and/or exclusions have the direct result of reducing the base. On the other hand, property taxes can be responsive to inflationary pressures, especially when assessments are made on a timely basis using modern techniques. See David Greytak and Bernard Jump, "The Effect of Inflation on State and Local Government Finances, 1967-74," occasional paper #25, Syracuse University, 1975.

11. This is the standard definition used in the economic literature of revenue stability. Recently, Fox and Campbell have refined this definition by distinguishing between the short- and long-run stability of tax revenue. They argue that the income elasticity of a tax is an endogenous variable that varies over the business cycle, i.e., no consistent relationship need hold between short-run and long-run elasticities over the business cycle. Given this view, a tax is regarded as being relatively stable if the short-run elasticity rises during recessions and falls during expansions so that tax revenues fluctuate less than income. See Fox and Campbell, "Stability of the State Sales Tax Income Elasticity," *National Tax Journal,* June 1984, pp. 201-12.

12. Because of the frequent changes in Minnesota's property tax laws it is difficult to isolate the change in property tax revenues due solely to economic growth. Staff calculations for the 1975-78 period, a relatively stable period for the property tax, estimated the income elasticity of property tax revenues in Minnesota was .73. In general, the various components of the real property tax base have different income (GNP) elasticities which, over the years, have been estimated to fall in the following ranges: Nonfarm residential ranges from .8 to 1.2; nonfarm nonresidential, .5 to 1.8; farm property .6 to 1.0; weighted averages for all real property .7 to 1.4. An income elasticity of 1.0 indicates a proportional revenue source where the base increases at the same rate as income, a value greater than 1.0 indicates an elastic revenue source and a value of less than 1.0 indicates an inelastic revenue source.

# 16

# Property Tax Law and Administration

## INTRODUCTION

Minnesota has the most complex property tax system in the nation. The result is taxpayer confusion, misunderstanding, and distrust. Accordingly, the purpose of this and subsequent papers is to unravel the threads that intertwine to form the confused tapestry of property taxation in Minnesota.

The next section begins with a review of the process followed to determine individual property tax liabilities. The following section discusses traditional techniques used to value property and how they are employed in Minnesota. A final section discusses differences in assessment quality across counties in Minnesota.

## DETERMINING PROPERTY TAX LIABILITIES

In Minnesota, local and county assessors, the county auditor, the township, city, or county board of commissioners, the county treasurer, and the Minnesota Department of Revenue all play vital roles in determining individual property tax liabilities. This section briefly reviews the legal responsibilities of each of these actors in the property tax system.

### ROLE OF THE COUNTY ASSESSOR

Each county is required by law (Minnesota Statutes section 273.061, subdivision 1) to have a county assessor, appointed by the county commissioners and approved by the commissioner of revenue. The county assessor estimates the market value of each property, assigns it a classification, and multiplies the estimated market value by the percentage set by law for its class. Thus, the assessed value. The market and assessed values are determined as of a specific date. For example, assessed values certified for January 2, 1984, serve as the base for taxes levied in 1984 and paid in 1985. After the values are established, the assessor sends to the owner of each property notification of its class and estimated assessed value.

Towns and cities often have the option of hiring their own town/city assessor who is then appointed by the town board or city council. At present, there are approximately 900 town and city assessors in Minnesota. The duty of the local assessor (or the county assessor in counties with county-wide assessment) is to view and appraise the value of all property in his jurisdiction. The assessor must visit each parcel listed for taxation, and estimate its market value at least every four years.[1]

The county assessor is required to

- maintain the assessment books provided by the county auditor;
- prepare and maintain all assessment cards, charts, maps, and other forms prescribed by the commissioner of revenue;
- search each year for property, real and personal, which has been omitted from the assessment roles and report all omissions to the county auditor;
- make all property classifications and assessments, based upon the information reported to him by the local assessors or his assistants;
- view and appraise all property that may be too difficult for local assessors to appraise;
- determine the eligibility for certain property tax credits from property declaration cards used to apply for homestead, native prairie, and wetlands credits; and
- act as a liaison between the commissioner of revenue and local assessors.

While the primary responsibility of the county assessor is to establish a reliable estimate of the market value for each parcel of real property in the county, this job is made more difficult by several additional administrative responsibilities imposed on the assessor. For example, in addition to estimating market value, the assessor is responsible for determining which properties are homestead properties for purposes of classification. This determination does not affect the assessor's estimation of the property's market value, yet substantial time and effort may be required. Several pieces of information not required to value the property may be required to determine homestead-class eligibility. These include: (1) where the taxpayer is registered to vote; (2) where the taxpayer has his mail delivered; and (3) where the taxpayer's children attend school; and (4) the address on the taxpayer's driver's license.

The classification process can become even more complicated in the case of a homestead property whose owner dies. To determine whether the property maintains its homestead classification, loses it entirely, or gets a fractional homestead classification, the assessor must determine: if the house is only occupied by all the heirs; if the surviving spouse retains a life interest and resides in the property; or what share of the heirs live in the property so a fractional homestead could be extended according to the extent of ownership of the heirs in occupancy.

## COUNTY VS. TOWNSHIP OR CITY ASSESSMENT

Any county in the state has the option of deciding that the assessment of taxable property in the county will be done by the county assessor (section 273.052). Any election to exercise this option must be made by the county board of commissioners by resolution. If such a resolution is adopted, the offices of all township and city assessors in that county will be terminated (section 273.055). Currently, thirteen counties have exercised this option and have full county assessment of all property.

If the county board of commissioners does not exercise its option to establish countywide assessment, individual townships and cities have the option of contracting with the county assessor to assess the property in their jurisdictions. The contract may or may not abolish the position of local assessor. The township or city entering such a contract will pay the county for these services so that, contrary to a countywide assessment system, the cost of assessment comes out of the local levy, not that of the county. At present, ten of Minnesota's eighty-seven counties have responsibility for assessing virtually the entire respective counties because of contracts with individual local governments. In these cases, assessment is essentially a countywide assessment system.

Countywide assessment has several advantages over assessments by individual local jurisdictions. The larger the assessment jurisdiction, the greater the potential benefits from economies of scale—e.g,, the more likely the jurisdiction is to benefit from computerized recordkeeping and/or computer-assisted assessment techniques. In addition, larger assessment jurisdictions will have more comparable sales data available to use in the valuation process. Also, a larger assessment jurisdiction is in a better position to afford a full-time, professional assessor. The net result of consolidating many small assessment jurisdictions with part-time assessors into a single large jurisdiction may provide more uniform treatment of property and, perhaps, more accurate assessments.

### THE APPEALS PROCESS

As a result of 1984 legislation, the appeals process is explicitly laid out. First, the aggrieved property owner must appeal the assessment to the local board of review. The local board of review is composed of the town board in each town, or the council in each city. The county assessor establishes a time for the local board of review to meet sometime between April 1 and June 30 (section 274.01). The county assessor or a delegated assistant attends the local board of review meetings and enters all changes made by the board in the assessment books.

If the property owner fails to appeal the assessment or classification to the local review board, he has no further avenues of appeal. Prior to the changes made in 1984, a property owner could bypass the local board of review and appeal his assessment directly to the state tax court.

If the property owner is not satisfied with the decision of the local board of review, that decision may be appealed to the county board of equalization. The county board of equalization is composed of the county commissioners plus the county auditor or his delegate. The county board may appoint a special board of equalization to fulfill its obligations. The board reviews the classification and assessment of individual properties and the aggregate value of each class of property. The board can make changes in either the classification or the assessed value of individual properties; however it may not reduce assessed values in the aggregate by more than 1% of the total value.

The county assessor is then required to correct all the changes made by the county board of equalization and send a copy of the corrected abstracts to the commissioner of revenue to review in his capacity as the sole member of the state board of equalization. The final list of all assessed values in the county is then sent to the county auditor's office.

While the assessors are determining the property tax base, local jurisdictions are deciding on the type and level of services to be provided. After deciding on service levels, local authorities prepare budgets reflecting the cost of those services. When the budget is prepared, local officials decide what portion of the budget will be financed by the local property tax—subject, of course, to local levy limitations, when applicable. By October 10, local authorities forward to the county auditor's office the final budget and the share to be financed by local property taxes.

The county auditor finally has both the list of properties in the county and their assessed values and the local property tax levy amounts determined by local authorities. By dividing the property tax levy by the total assessed value, the auditor determines the mill rate necessary to generate the required property tax levy. For each individual property the auditor then multiplies the assessed value by the mill rate to calculate each property owner's gross property tax liability. The auditor also subtracts any applicable credits to determine each property owner's net property tax liability. Finally, the auditor forwards the list of all properties and their net tax liability to the county treasurer, who prepares the individual property tax bills that are mailed to each property owner in January of the year the tax is payable. Property owners can contest the amount of their tax liability in district court or tax court until May 15 of the year in which the taxes are payable. The first half of the property taxes are due by May 15 and the second half are due by October 15. As the county treasurer receives the tax payments from the property owners, the money is distributed to each of the taxing jurisdictions.

# THE ASSESSMENT PROCESS

Section 272.01, subdivision 1, of the Minnesota Statutes provides that

All real and personal property in the state, and all personal property of persons residing therein, including the property of corporations, banks, banking companies, and bankers, is taxable, except Indian lands and such other property as is by law exempt . . . .

Real property includes "the land itself and all buildings, structures and improvements or other fixtures on it."[2] For the purpose of taxation, personal property includes "all goods, chattels, money and effects" plus boats; all stock of nurserymen; public stocks and securities; shares in foreign corporations; certain public utility personal property like water mains, pipes, conduits and poles; and other items. (section 272.03, subsection 2). Certain real property is exempt from property taxation by statute including cemeteries; public schools, hospitals and colleges; wetlands; native prairie; and other property in certain specified uses. Similarly, Minnesota law explicitly exempts certain personal property including all agricultural personal property (livestock, tools, implements and machinery) and business personal property.[3]

The property tax is the only major tax whose base must be estimated, rather than observed. Thus, by its very nature, the valuation of property is subjective. Assessing property requires the talents of highly trained and experienced personnel. However, since no two individuals have exactly the same experiences, individual assessors differ in the weights they assign different abstract factors—e.g., view, neighborhood quality—which may influence the value of a particular property.

Since there is no objectively discernible, true market value for an individual property, the goal of the assessor is to provide what can only be characterized as a best guess of what the property would sell for on the open market at a given time. Innumerable studies document the variation in assessed values which different assessors assign a specific property, many of which may deviate significantly from what may be a consensus estimate of true market value. Therefore, written procedures, establishing the parameters or rules governing subjective judgments that an individual assessor must make, will help reduce the variation in estimated market value between different assessors. This would result in less variation in property values, thereby minimizing some of the confusion on the part of both practitioners and the general public. However, this can be attained only if procedures are spelled out with a high degree of specificity.

The commissioner of revenue traditionally issued an *Assessor's Manual* for the guidance of assessing officials.[4] While the commissioner does provide frequent communications to county assessors addressing particular issues that are of concern at that time, no formal *Assessor's Manual* has been published since 1977. One obstacle to regularly publishing such a document is the frequent changes the legislature makes in the property tax laws. For example, even though legislative leaders agreed in advance of the 1984 mini-session not to revise the property tax, the 1984 omnibus tax bill contained thirty-six specific property tax changes. Previous legislatures have been even more aggressive in modifying provisions in the property tax laws: e.g., the 1983 legislature made 125 changes in the property tax law; in 1982, sixty-seven changes; in 1981, eighty-one changes; and in 1980, seventy-seven changes. To the extent that the legislature continues frequent alteration of the property tax laws, it will be difficult for field assessors to obtain, assimilate, and put into practice all of the changes necessary to perform their responsibilities. This type of uncertainty results in confusion and inconsistent application of the law, and, invariably, unequal assessments.

Whatever the exact provisions of assessment law, assessors generally employ three common approaches to the valuation of property endorsed by the American Institute of Real Estate Appraisers:

1) Cost approach—the current cost of reproducing a property minus depreciation from deterioration or functional and economic obsolescence;
2) Income approach—the value which the property's potential net earning power will support, based on a capitalization of net income; and
3) Market data approach—the value indicated by recent sales of comparable properties in the market place.

Typically, each of these traditional approaches to valuing property is applied to a specific, well-defined subset of property use types. However, as the 1977 *Assessor's Manual* recognizes, ". . . each approach to value, if accurately carried out should give approximately the same answer (value)." Thus, the other approaches should not be considered mutually exclusive; rather, alternative valuation techniques may be used to verify the results of the traditional approach of valuing each property type (commercial, residential, etc.)

## COST METHOD

The cost method is used frequently in the appraisal of new construction and special purchase properties. Information is obtained from developers as well as national sources and is used to estimate the cost of new construction.

In using the cost method, the assessor first determines the value of the land by examining sales of comparable land. Next, the assessor estimates the cost of replacing a building at the time of his reassessment based on the available cost data. Thus, as construction prices increase or decrease, so will the estimated cost of replacing a building. When applied to existing buildings, this replacement cost is depreciated according to the building's age and functional or economic obsolescence.

The loss from physical deterioration and functional obsolescence is the estimated cost of curing curable defects or deficiencies plus the estimated loss in utility and remaining useful life of the building, due to incurable defects. In this approach, economic obsolescence is observed and estimated according to the way it strikes the property. If a loss in rental income or occupancy is the result, the extent of the loss in value is the capitalized loss in income. Similarly, if excess space is the result of economic obsolescence, this space is discounted down to its value for some other likely use. If a loss in salability or desirability is the result of the economic influence, this loss is measured by judgment based on comparison with properties that have sold.[5]

The first appraisal of property is made when there are any improvements on the land as of January 2. At that time, it is appraised by the cost approach and placed on the records at the percentage and placed on the records at the percentage that its stage of completion bears to its estimated full value at completion.

A comparison may also be made with the builder's cost. In cases where there is a large discrepancy between the two figures, an analysis is made of the builder's cost for reconciliation of the two figures. As construction progresses, the property is revalued. The change in value reflects the stage of building completion at the time of revaluation. When the building is completed and occupancy has begun, it is again revalued—perhaps using the income approach.

It is something of a misnomer to refer to "the" cost approach. Depending on the property and the circumstances, the assessor may use the reproduction cost approach, as outlined above, or the historical cost approach. The reproduction cost approach values the current cost of reproducing exactly the existing structure, less accrued depreciation. The historical cost method produces an estimate of the improvement value by determining the original cost of construction and applying trending factors to that data. A third approach—replacement cost—may also be used. This approach seeks to estimate the cost of replacing a structure with one that would serve the function, but using current building technology and materials.

INCOME METHOD

Generally, the income method is used to value investment properties, e.g., large and heavy commercial and industrial properties and apartments of more than four units. The income method may be applied in any of several specific ways, but whatever the exact approach, determination of a capitalization rate is necessary. A fundamental relationship involved in the income method is:

$$\text{value} \times \text{interest rate} = \text{income}.$$

Thus, if one year's information is representative, and if the going average (market) rate of return on investment—i.e., the interest or yield rate—is 10%, a property costing $1,000,000 would have to produce at least $100,000 annual income to be an attractive investment [$1,000,000 x .10 = $100,000], a lesser annual income would offer a below-market return.

This same relationship can be used to determine value when the market interest rate and the (potential) income from a given property are known. Rearranging the above equation, we have:

$$\text{value} = \text{income/interest rate.}$$

Thus, if a property can yield an annual income of $1.5 million, and if the going interest rate is 12%, the value of that property is $12.5 million [$1.5/.12 = $12.5].

The application of the income approach requires information on income and operating expenses for the property being valued. In some instances, this information is readily available from schedules sent to the property owner. In other cases, general income and expense information may be obtained from standardized tables available to assessors. Both income and expenses per foot may vary substantially depending on the type of property being valued—apartment, retail store, warehouse, etc. In addition to operating expenses, a vacancy factor and a bad debt expense are allowed, which also may vary according to the type of business. A vacancy factor may range from 2% to 10% for apartments whereas a 40% vacancy factor, or higher, may be allowed for transient accommodations. Two expenses not allowed as deductions are mortgage payments and depreciation. Depreciation as such is not estimated by the appraiser because income accounts for depreciation. All the appraiser must determine with reference to depreciation is the estimated remaining productive life of the improvements so that allowance for capital recovery (depreciation) can be made in capitalization rate. The federal accelerated cost recovery system (ACRS) of 1981 has complicated the assessor's work.

An examine may help to illustrate this process. A one-hundred-unit apartment building renting each unit at $150 per month would generate $180,000 gross income per year. Assume that 54% of the gross income is allowed for expenses.[6] Assume also that this property has a 6% vacancy rate. Thus, in this example:

Actual Gross Income = $180,000 x .94 = $169,200
Estimated Expenses = $169,200 x .54 = $91,368
Estimated Net Income = $169,200 - $91,368 = $71,832

The next step in the valuation process is to capitalize the estimated net income at a rate of return prevalent in the market at the time of valuation. Just as fluctuations of construction costs may influence the valuation of property under the cost method, market trends in the rate of return on money invested, vacancy factors, rent controls, or other lease agreements and other variations in cost variables may influence the valuation of property under the income method.

The mortgage equity technique is one means of calculating the interest rates which reflects the return the mortgage holder and property owner expect to receive. For the property owner, the interest rate must be high enough to compensate for the risk involved in the investment and at least equal to the rate that could be received by placing the money in a guaranteed savings account or long-term deposit. The interest rate, in other words, must equal the investor's opportunity cost of investing the capital in another project of the same risk. Similarly, the lender will provide capital for the mortgage only if the rate received equals the rate available from other investments of the same risk. One must be able to realize a rate of return equal to or greater than the opportunity cost or the mortgage will not be made. For example, if there were a 25% equity in the building, the applicable interest rate would be determined as follows:

Mortgage: 75%   (amount of investment)
      x 12%  (opportunity rate of return equal to what could be obtained in the long-term bond market)     = .090

plus
Equity:   25%   (amount of investment)
      x 10%  (opportunity rate of return equal to what could be obtained in alternative investment, e.g., money market account)     = .025

Interest Rate     .115

There are two subjective factors which compromise the usefulness of the estimates generated using the income approach. The intent of this approach is to estimate the value of the property (land and permanent improvements), as distinct from the value of entrepreneurial and other factor services used along with the property to generate the observed level of net income. Ideally, these other influences should be filtered out through use of property income figures that reflect some norms, rather than actual outcomes for a specific property; to do otherwise is to reward inept operation with low property valuation and to penalize extraordinarily efficient operation.

The first source of error, then, is that where there is a significant variation of managerial skill among property owners. The net income that a property can potentially generate is a direct function of the entrepreneurial skill of the owner in combining factor inputs. A limited check on this source of income variation is obtained by referring to the economic rent and expenditure schedules discussed above. However, even this fails to acknowledge explicitly and allow for differences in managerial skills. An additional check would be an increased reliance on comparable sales, perhaps even if the sale does not lie within the same assessment jurisdiction.

A second inherent weakness of the income approach is "goodwill." Two motels of identical construction in similarly desirable locations may differ in their income producing capacity simply because one is named *Holiday Inn* and the other is named *Economy Motel*. It is difficult to place a specific value on the extra income potential associated with an established brand name.

## COMPARABLE SALES (MARKET DATA) METHOD

The comparable sales or market approach to valuation involves a comparison of the property being appraised with properties that have sold recently in arm's length sales—i.e., exchanges between a willing buyer and a willing seller who are unrelated. All differences, minor and major, are enumerated and evaluated according to the judgment of the appraiser. The value of the property being appraised is thereby related to the prices of comparable properties that have sold. Depreciation in this approach is not measured by the appraiser. The result of his appraisal is market value in which all depreciation has already been determined by the market itself. This method is used generally for valuing residential and small apartment/commercial properties. It is based on the principle that the value of a property tends to be set by the cost of acquisition of an equally desirable substitute property.

Minnesota law requires that a certificate of value must accompany the deed or instrument of conveyance whenever the title to real property is transferred. The certificate of value should be the amount of the full consideration paid or to be paid including any assumed lien or liens. Beginning in October 1984, the certificates also are to contain data on financing terms so that a cash equivalency price can be calculated for any sales with creative financing. If the property being transferred or any fraction thereof is exempt from taxation, the certificate should specify the reasons for the exemption. The register of deeds or registrar of titles is not required to record the certificate of value but is to forward two copies of it to the county assessor. The assessor is to record the estimated market value and the classification of the transferred property on both copies of the certificate of value and then send one copy to the state.[7]

It should be noted that a certificate of value must be filed when a contract for deed is recorded. According to the department of revenue, the compliance with this provision of the law is very lax. As a result, nearly half the sales of residential property that take place are not listed, and, therefore are not included as potential comparable sales.

To complete the process, comparable sales are examined to determine the factors and trends which influence value. Appropriate units of comparison, such as price per square foot of building, price per room, and price per apartment unit may be employed by the assessor. The assessor may be required to make adjustments to the comparable sales data based on the factors and trends which influence or affect value. These may include physical and economic conditions, location and time of sale, financing, etc. The adjustments may be expressed on a lump-sum or percentage basis and are applied to the property under review.

It is essential to have a defensible mechanism for determining which sales are arm's length transactions and can be used as comparable sales. The criteria for determining whether a sale should be classified as arm's length are often too subjective. As a result, a number of sales may not be classified as such with little, if any, justification.


## MEASURING ASSESSMENT QUALITY

Section 273.11 of the Minnesota Statutes requires that

> All property shall be valued at its market value. In estimating such value, the assessor shall . . . value each article or description of property by itself, and at such sum or price as he believes the same to be fairly worth in money.

Market value, then, is the target for the assessor and represents the usual selling price which could be obtained from an arm's-length sale. Since the actual market price is observed only when a sale takes place, the question arises: How well does the assessor estimate the market value of property in his jurisdiction? To what extent does the assessor's estimated market value—which is the product of the assessment process described above—reflect the true market value as indicated by actual sales data?

One of the primary objectives in property tax administration is the assessment of property in a uniform manner. It is important that uniformity be attained not only among local property owners but also between taxing districts since property valuations serve as a basis for:

1. tax levies by overlapping governmental units, i.e., counties, school districts, and special districts;
2. determination of net bonded indebtedness restricted by statute to a percentage of either the local assessed value or market value;
3. determination of authorized levies restricted by statutory tax rate limits; and
4. apportionment of state assistance to local governmental units, i.e., school aid formula or local government aid formula.

The consequence of nonuniform assessment is an unwarranted shift in the tax burden elsewhere to the detriment of some property owners. An equitable distribution of the tax burden is achieved only if built upon a uniform assessment.

Uniformity is obtained most easily where all properties are assessed at their full market value. Full value assessment is preferred to the alternative of fractional assessment for many reasons. Specifically, full value assessment:

- reduces the possibility of sloppy, politically oriented, or corrupt assessments, which may benefit particular property owners or classes, since comparisons between properties can be made in a more meaningful manner;
- increases uniformity, thereby improving the horizontal equity of the property tax, so that similar properties face similar tax liabilities;
- eliminates "undervaluation illusion" associated with fractional assessment that covers up the apparent inequities;
- promotes taxpayer understanding since the taxpayer is likely to be familiar with market values in his particular area; and
- assigns political responsibility for increased property tax burdens to the elected officials who set the tax rate, and allows the assessor to concentrate on estimating full market value—a difficult task even when unencumbered by political pressures associated with fractional assessments.

Because of its classification system, Minnesota relies heavily on "fractional assessments" whereby different classes of property have different ratios of assessed market value (e.g., Minnesota has three statutory ratios of assessed value to market value for nonagricultural homesteads). The result, however unintentional, is that the government creates a fiscal illusion, or plays a fiscal trick, on the taxpayer—an outcome that violates the goal of accountability in fiscal matters. This fiscal illusion occurs for two reasons:

- *Fractional assessments may lull homeowners into a false sense of well being.* For example, a person who knows his home is worth about $80,000 may feel that he has no basis for complaint if his home is assessed at $40,000—even though on average homes may be assessed at 40% of market value. This illusion could be eliminated if assessments were at 100% of value (and the mill rate proportionately decreased); and

- *Assessment errors are obscured.* Under fractional assessment any error seems smaller than it really is. If the assessment standard is 10%, for example, a $60,000 house should be valued at $6,000; while a $500 error might seem small (e.g., valuation at $6,500 instead of $6,000), it would amount to a $5,000 overstatement of home value, or more than an 8% error. Similarly, any rounding carried out by the assessor becomes more significant under fractional assessment. However, because these errors seem small, they tend to go unchallenged.

## ASSESSMENT/SALES RATIOS

In order to evaluate the degree of uniformity across properties and jurisdictions, accurate and acceptable statistical measures are needed. The technique most commonly used to measure the degree of assessment inequality is that of determining assessment/sales ratios, or the relationship of the assessor's estimated market value to the sales price of a particular property that sold. In Minnesota, if perfect assessment uniformity existed in an area, the assessor's estimated market value for a property that sold would be 100% of the actual sales price, and no ratio would deviate from that level. In practice, however, it has been observed that in most areas, the individual assessment/sales ratios range from 50% - 120% of the sales price, or actual market value.

One important way of describing a group of individual assessment/sales ratios for an area, or for a class of property, is by the use of averages. Usually three averages are considered: the mean, median, and the aggregate average ratio. These averages, or measures of central tendency, provide a simple numerical description of how closely a group of individual assessment/sales ratios approach the prescribed statutory level.

The assessment/sales ratio for an individual parcel of property sold is simply the relationship expressed as a percentage between the assessor's estimated market value and the sale price. For each parcel of real estate sold, the assessment/sales ratio is found by dividing the assessor's estimated market value by the full consideration paid. For example,

| Property | Assessor's Market Value | Sale Price | Ratio |
|---|---|---|---|
| 1 | $ 20,900 | $ 19,000 | 110.0% |
| 2 | 28,500 | 30,000 | 95.0 |
| 3 | 22,950 | 25,500 | 90.0 |
| 4 | 33,200 | 41,500 | 80.0 |
| 5 | 31,200 | 52,000 | 60.0 |
| | $136,750 | $168,000 | 435.0 |

The mean, or arithmetic average, is a measure of central tendency and provides a simple numerical description of a group of individual assessment/sales ratios. The mean is derived by first computing the assessment/sales ratio for each parcel sold, adding those ratios, and dividing this sum by the total by the number of items.

In the previous example the mean is 87%:

$$\frac{435.0}{5} = 87 \text{ Mean}$$

The mean is the most commonly used, easily understood average, but the fact that it may be substantially affected by one or a few extreme assessment/sales ratios can lead to serious consequences. Only if the sales data collected are accurate and representative should extreme individual assessment/sales ratios be allowed to affect the average.

The median, like the mean, is a measure of central tendency used to describe a group of individual assessment/sales ratios. The median is found by arranging the individual assessment/sales ratios in order of magnitude from highest to lowest, then selecting the middle ratio in the series. For example, in the previous example, the median is 90.0 and given by the third parcel.

The median, unlike the mean, is not so readily affected by an extreme individual assessment/sales ratio. The median for a group of assessment/sales ratios depends upon the position of items in the distribution rather than their magnitude, therefore undue influence is not given to unusually high or low ratios. This important feature is desirable due to the difficulty in excluding sales that might, if all the facts were known, be discarded as unusable.

The aggregate, or weighted average, is an alternative measure of central tendency. This measure is computed by dividing the total assessor's market value for the properties sold by the total sales prices of those properties. For example, from the previous example, total market value was $136,750 and total sales value was $168,000 so the weighted average ratio was 81.4:

$$\frac{136,750}{168,000} = 81.4 \text{ Aggregate average ratio}$$

In the aggregate average ratio, unlike the mean, each property sold is given a weight according to its sale price. Higher-priced properties, of course, play a more important role than lower-priced properties in the average so determined. This effect is justified if the sale of higher-priced properties bear the same relationship to all properties in the sample as those properties bear to all properties in the taxing district. Because of its statistical properties, the aggregate ratio generally is accepted as the most appropriate measure to be used in the equalization of aids.

Section 124.2131 of the Minnesota Statutes authorizes the equalization aid review committee[8] (EARC) to review the assessed values of each school district. If there is evidence that the estimated market values do not accurately reflect actual market values, the EARC must direct the department of revenue to adjust the estimated market values to offset inequities in the assessment levels across the state.[9] The law, however, does not specify the particular measure of central tendency that should be used to make the adjustment. In practice, the department of revenue computes all three measures of central tendency and uses the mean to make the actual adjustments to estimated market values.

Performance of Minnesota assessors in valuing residential properties (both homestead and nonhomestead, and including apartments with fewer than four units) is summarized in Table 1. Only residential properties are represented because they account for most real property sales and, therefore, the ratios are most reliable for this type of property. Because of the greater amount of sales for residential properties, it is often argued that assessors can be expected to perform better in valuing such properties; focusing on residential assessment performance, therefore, should place assessors in a relatively favorable light.

While the standard is 100% assessment (i.e., Minnesota law requires that the assessor's estimate of market value be equal to full market value), Minnesota counties' average residential assessment level for 1982 (taxes payable in 1983) ranged from 62% to 88%; the mean level for the eighty-seven counties was 75% (Table 1, column 1). Attainment of any specific standard is not likely, given the general rise in property value over time and the fact that assessed value figures are for a particular date (in this case January 2, 1982) while the sales data reflect prices paid in a later period. Falling as far below the assessment standard as Minnesota counties have is not unusual; still, the state reasonably could hope for somewhat better performance.

DISPERSION OF ASSESSEMENT RATIOS

The second dimension of the quality of assessment that needs monitoring is the degree to which actual assessment ratios are dispersed around the measure of central tendency. For example, for any particular taxing jurisdiction, the median assessment ratio may equal 1.0, indicating that the estimated value of the median property exactly equaled its actual selling price. However, this provides no information about the variation in the other ratios in the jurisdiction: how closely clustered around the median are the other ratios? The concern here is with the variability of assessment ratios. While any of several measures is conceptually appropriate to measure the uniformity of assessments, the coefficient of dispersion is perhaps the most commonly used measure of assessment uniformity. It measures the deviation of individual parcel ratios from the average ratio, as a percentage of that average ratio. The higher the coefficient, the less uniform are the assessments.

An example may help to clarify the nature of the coefficient of dispersion. Presented below are data (also used in illustrating the sales ratio) for five hypothetical homes that have recently sold—sales prices, estimated market values, assessment-sales price ratios (calculated), and absolute deviations of the individual parcel ratios from the median ratio:

| Property | Sales Price | Assessed Value | A/S Ratio | Absolute Deviation |
|---|---|---|---|---|
| 1 | $20,900 | $19,000 | 110.0% | 20 |
| 2 | 28,500 | 30,000 | 95.0 | 5 |
| 3 | 22,950 | 25,500 | 90.0 | 0 |
| 4 | 33,200 | 41,500 | 80.0 | 10 |
| 5 | 31,200 | 52,000 | 60.0 | 30 |

The assessment/sales ratio for each home is subtracted from the median ratio, and the difference is recorded without regard to its sign (absolute deviation from the median). These absolute deviations are summed and divided by the number of homes in the sample (65/5 = 13). Finally, this average absolute deviation is expressed as a percentage of the median ratio: (13/90) x 100 = 14.4%. Thus, the value of the coefficient of dispersion in this case is 14.4%.

The coefficients of dispersion—like the assessment sales ratios—also overstate the error in assessments because there is essentially no trending of values. For example, assessments are established as of January 2, while the actual sale could take place up to twelve months later. To the extent values increased over that period, the actual sale will be more than the assessment because the assessment is not inflated for time differences.

Just as Minnesota's assessment performance is not out of line with national experience with regard to average level of assessment, neither is it out of line in terms of uniformity. The coefficient of dispersion for 1982 ranged across counties from under 11% to over 41%, and averaged over 19% (Table 1, column 2). Nationally, the state average in 1981 was over 21%.[10] While this figure compared with the Minnesota Department of Revenue figure shows Minnesota assessment performance to be somewhat better than the national average, the national report shows Minnesota's average CD to have been above the national average, at 26.8%.[11] A difference between the state and the national exercises may help to explain their different results for Minnesota: the department of revenue study pertains to the broad category of residential property in 1982 while the census bureau study pertains only to single-family residences in 1981.[12]

## ENDNOTES

1. There is no formal requirement that the three-quarters of a jurisdiction's property not subject to onsight review in any one year have their values increased each year. There is wide disparity across assessing jurisdictions regarding the manner and extent of trending up values of properties not actually visible.

2. At an early date, railroads were subject to a tax on gross earnings in lieu of property taxes. Other kinds of transportation and communication companies are also subject to gross earnings taxes. Similarly, the mining industry is subject to a production and occupation tax, based on the quantity and value of ore produced.

3. A review of the *Commerce Clearing House State Tax Reporter* and the Minnesota Statutes dealing with property taxation turned up no explicit language exempting household personal property from taxation. Section 272.02, subsection 1(8) does provide a maximum $100 exemption for household property. The *Commerce Clearing House State Tax Reporter* states that

> "According to a December 19, 1980, communication from the Department of Revenue, Property Equalization Division, the only property accessible as personal property are the following categories:
> (1)  Mobile homes (Section 273.13, Class 2a property);
> (2)  Structures on leased public (federal and state) lands, such as cabins constructed by lessees of the public land (Section 273.13, Class 3 property);
> (3)  Structures on railroad operating rights of way (Section 273.32);
> (4)  Owner occupied residences on leased land or railroad lands;
> (5)  Real estate leased under Minnesota Statutes Section 272.01, Subdivision 2;
> (6)  Tools, implements and machinery of an electric generating, transmission or distribution system or a pipeline system transporting or distributing water, gas or petroleum products or mains and pipes used in the distribution of steam or hot or chilled water for heating or cooling buildings, which are fixtures (Section 273.13, Class 3 property); and
> (7)  Systems of electric, gas and water utilities."

And that

> "Notwithstanding this broadening of the exemption of personal property from tax, the provisions of the law defining personal property, subjecting personal property to tax, and specifically exempting only certain types of personal property from tax were not repealed but remain a part of the property tax law. Therefore, where personal property is concerned, caution must be exercised in reading and applying the provisions of the law."

Representatives from the department of revenue said that household personal property has been exempt by local option at the county level and that the 1984 legislature brought the language of the law into conformity with actual practices. No specific legislative references were available at the time this draft was printed.

4. *Commerce Clearing House State Tax Reporter,* p. 2071.

5. *Minnesota Assessors' manual,* 1977.

6. This is an estimate used for illustrative purposes only. In the absence of actual expense data, the assessor must make a determination of the average costs associated with each type of property so that a net income figure can be calculated.

7. *Minnesota Assessors' Manual,* op. cit.

8. The committee is composed of the commissioners of education, administration, agriculture and revenue.

9. Because school districts are not coterminous with local government boundaries (e.g., townships, cities, counties), different jurisdictions are responsible for assessing portions of each school district's property base. The resulting differences in assessment practices between school districts make it necessary to conduct assessments/sales ratio studies in order to describe the variations in

assessment levels to (1) ascertain prescribed statutory levies, and (2) permit compensating adjustments in state equalization aid.

10. U.S. Bureau of the Census, *Census of Governments 1982, Vol. 2, Taxable Property Values and Assessment/Sales Price Ratios* (Washington, D.C.: Government Printing Office, February 1984), Table 18.

11. *Ibid.*

12. Statistical analysis of the coefficients of dispersion in Minnesota counties was undertaken using a model similar to one employed with Virginia data. [John H. Bowman and John L. Mikesell, "Uniform Assessment of Property: Returns from Institutional Remedies," *National Tax Journal,* 31 (June 1978), pp. 153-63.] The model did not perform as well with the Minnesota data. While it accounted for more than two-thirds of the differences in Minnesota county CDs, only six of twelve independent variable were statistically significant; the most important of these was the assessment ratio. Other variables representing features of the Minnesota property tax administration structure—e.g., county-level assessment rather than city, town, or township assessment—generally were not significant. An exception was CAMA, a dummy variable for computer-assisted mass appraisal, which was marginally significant and, on average, helped to improve assessment quality. Simply using a computerized records system, however, had no significant impact on assessment quality.

# 17

# Direct Property Tax Relief

## INTRODUCTION

Direct property tax relief directly reduces the tax bills for individual parcels. Examples of direct relief include homestead exemptions, circuit breakers, deferrals, and classification. Direct property tax relief reduces the tax bills for individual property parcels but may not affect total property tax levies of governments. In contrast, indirect property tax relief provides local governments with alternative revenue sources, thereby permitting property tax levies to be lower—and/or services to be higher—than they otherwise would be. This chapter analyzes direct property tax relief programs in Minnesota.

Minnesota provides direct property tax relief through three basic approaches:

1. Classification alters the tax base by assessing different types of property at different percentages of market value;
2. Credits make the net property tax bills that certain property owners must pay less than their gross property tax bills; and
3. Tax refunds, of which the circuit breaker is by far the most important, return (refund) a portion of the local tax payments to certain taxpayers.

The classification system is the first layer in the three-tiered Minnesota direct property tax relief system; under it, the tax base is determined. The assessed value adjustments under classification are, in effect, like partial exemptions, and—as is generally the case with adjustments to the base—any revenue loss is borne locally. The state, however, bears the costs of the credits (paid to the local taxing units) and of the circuit breaker (paid to the taxpayers). These programs are discussed below in the order listed here.

## CLASSIFICATION

Within the category of real property, uniformity across the board was the almost universal legal requirement for many decades; it continues to be the standard in the majority of states, although twenty-one states plus the District of Columbia have adopted real property classification. Among

Minnesota's neighboring states, only Wisconsin does not classify real property for taxation; the other states, however, all have considerably simpler systems than Minnesota's.

Minnesota's is the oldest real property classification system in the nation, dating from 1913. It also is one of the most complex, if not the most complex. In terms of the number of classes, Minnesota has no close rival—though it is not clear exactly how many classes exist in Minnesota.

Persons familiar with the Minnesota property tax have estimated the number of classes anywhere between twenty and seventy, in part because some persons consider "classification" to include only the assessment level differences, while others also include the differentiation introduced by the various credits. But even under the traditional, narrower definition, it is not clear how many classes exist. The Minnesota Department of Revenue lists fourteen numbered classes but they appear as twenty-two entries. A second approach, listing classification percentages, reveals fifteen specific percentages plus a range of percentages (30 to 48.5) for " 'low recovery' iron ore" for taxes payable in 1984, but these fifteen percentages account for thirty-four listings.

Adding to the complexity inherent in the many classes in combination with the system of credits is the frequency of change in classification provisions. For example, from 1972 through 1984, the residential homestead classification percentages were changed five times, including a change from two to three percentage brackets beginning with taxes payable in 1981. Classification percentages were changed four times for both agricultural homesteads and agricultural nonhomesteads.

Most of the classification changes have reduced the tax base, and they generally have favored residential and agricultural properties relative to other classes. Effective rate differentials tend to create both equity and efficiency problems; and as the differentials become larger, the cause for concern tends to increase. To summarize:

*Equity.* Large effective tax rate differences between classes of property are inequitable because people who own properties of equal value do not pay equal property taxes.[1] Classification also reduces the base of the property tax so that a higher tax rate must be applied to the remaining base in order to raise a given amount of property tax revenue, causing properties not receiving preferential treatment to subsidize the properties taxed at lower percentages of market value.

*Efficiency.* When some property types or uses bear higher tax rates than others, private economic decisions (investment choices) tend to be distorted by the tax system.

## PROPERTY TAX CREDITS

Property tax credits currently account for nearly three-fourths of the state-funded direct relief—almost $622 million of $841 million for taxes payable in 1984. There are nine property tax credits. The credits and the persons eligible to receive them are:

| Credit | Eligibility |
|---|---|
| state school agricultural credit | owners of farmland, timberland, private vacation cabins |
| wetlands credit | owners of wetland |
| native prairie credit | owners of native prairie |
| reduced assessment credit | blind homeowners, permanently and totally disabled homeowners, owners of rental property providing rental housing to senior citizens and low- and moderate-income families |
| disaster credit | owners of homesteads damaged by disaster |
| agricultural preserve credit | owners of certified long-term use agricultural land in the seven-county metropolitan area |
| taconite tax relief credit and supplementary taconite tax relief credit | Iron Range homeowners, including farm homeowners |
| homestead credit | homeowners, including farm homeowners |
| power line credit | owners of homesteads and agricultural land |

Based on preliminary data for taxes payable in 1984, nearly 85% of total credits go to homeowners (homestead properties), and most of the remaining credits go to agricultural properties. Among the credit programs, the homestead credit is by far the largest ($505 million out of $622 million). The credit programs are described briefly below and are taken up in the order in which they are subtracted from the property tax bill, as listed above.

## STATE SCHOOL AGRICULTURAL CREDIT

Under the state school agriculture credit, a portion of the property tax imposed by local school districts on agricultural properties, timberlands, and certain seasonal-use cabins is paid by the state. The fraction of the tax paid via the credit varies by the type of property and, within the agricultural category, the size of the tract and its homestead or nonhomestead character. The credit percentages for taxes payable in 1984 are shown below (changes, if any, adopted in 1984 for future years are shown in parentheses):

| | |
|---|---|
| agricultural homestead: | first 320 acres, 29% (33% after 1984); next 320 acres, 13% (15% after 1984); and acreage over 640, 10%. |
| agricultural nonhomestead: | first 320 acres, 13% (15% after 1984); acreage over 320, 10%. |
| timberland: | 10% |
| cabins: | 13% (15% after 1984). |

It is said that the properties favored by the state school agriculture credit otherwise bear taxes that are high, relative to the costs that these properties impose on the local schools. Thus, the program seeks to make local school taxation better accord with the benefits received (or costs imposed) notion of tax equity. The relative relief percentages within the state school agricultural credit program are not consistent with this: agricultural homesteads receive much more favorable treatment than nonhomesteads even though the number of children per acre probably does not differ systematically between these farm types; eligible cabins and timberlands legally cannot add to local school enrollments, yet they receive relatively small tax reductions and, all other types of property that do not contribute directly to school enrollments—e.g., commercial and industrial—receive absolutely no school tax reduction.

More basic, however, is the question of whether such emphasis on the benefits principle is desired; various considerations often rule out reliance on user financing.

WETLANDS AND NATIVE PRAIRIE CREDITS

The wetlands and native prairie credits, two separate programs adopted in 1980, are so similar that they are considered together here. Ownership of either wetlands or native prairie lands that meet certain size and locational criteria gives rise to these credits. Because both these types of land are exempt from property taxation under other legal provisions, the credit offsets taxes on other, taxable land. The stated intent is to give incentive for the preservation of such lands beyond that provided by tax exemption of those lands.

Thus, one criterion for wetland and native prairie credits is ownership of other, taxable land in the same or adjacent parcels in the case of wetlands; native prairie land can be removed from the other land by as much as two cities or townships. There must be at least one acre of tax exempt wetlands to be eligible for the credit, and the minimal tract of native prairie land eligible for the credit program is ten acres.

Public subsidy for the preservation of wetlands and of native prairie lands may be warranted by public values and preferences, but the current subsidy varies directly with the market value of tillable farmland and tends to be higher in areas closer to population or where farmland is more productive, a pattern that may not reflect differences in public benefits from preservation. Moreover, the requirement that owners of wetlands and of native prairie lands also own other taxable lands (either adjacent or relatively close by) suggests—rather implausibly—that there is less public benefit from preserving wetlands or native prairie lands that are owned by persons who own no other land in the same vicinity.

REDUCED ASSESSMENT CREDIT

The reduced assessment credit, also adopted in 1980, simply provides a different approach for an earlier policy. Prior to 1981, similar property tax relief was provided solely through assessed value reductions, with costs borne locally. Now, local taxing units receive the gross property tax amounts based on the higher standard assessment percentages, while the net taxes paid by the favored properties' owners still are based on the lower percentages; the difference is the credit amount which is paid by the state.

This credit is to provide lower property taxes for selected disabled homeowners and for owners of certain apartments that are rented to the elderly and/or low- and moderate-income families; in the case of the apartments, the intent clearly is to reduce the rent paid by the tenants, and not simply the landlords' property tax bills.

*Homestead provisions.* The homestead provisions are applicable to homeowners who are legally blind and those who are permanently and totally disabled. For the blind and for permanently and totally disabled veterans, there are no income constraints on credit participation; for the permanently and totally disabled who are not veterans, however, credit eligibility is restricted to those who are unable, because of their disability, to earn enough to support themselves and who receive at least 90% of their income from certain state or federal payment programs.

*Apartment provisions.* The apartment provisions are complex because of different treatments for buildings that differ by financing, location, and/ or age; some of these differences have been introduced by recent legislation. To qualify for the reduced classification ratio, the apartment building must (1) be either a limited- or a nonprofit operation, (2) be financed by certain state or federal loan programs, and (3) provide rental housing to the elderly or to certain low- and moderate-income families.

The reduced assessment credit provisions pose several policy questions. For example, is it appropriate that the tax relief be needs-tested for one group of disabled homeowners while it is not for another subset of the disabled population? This tends to create horizontal inequities; persons with the same disabilities (though perhaps with different causes of those disabilities) and the same incomes will receive different property tax credits based on the sources, rather than the amounts, of their incomes.

More fundamentally, is this credit program needed? The department of revenue states that the targeted groups ". . . have less ability to earn income and pay the costs of [housing] . . . ." Why rely upon imperfect proxies for diminished income potential, when income itself not only can be observed, but is observed and is the basis for property tax relief under the circuit breaker program? The circuit breaker program, which includes renters as well as owners, would seem to make the reduced assessment credit redundant.

### DISASTER CREDIT

The disaster credit provides tax relief for homeowners whose homes have been damaged by a disaster—fire, flood, tornado, etc.—that results in a local declaration of emergency and/or the local area being declared a disaster area by certain federal officials. The program was adopted in 1982; 1984 legislation sets requirements as to (1) the average amount of home damage and either (2a) the number of homes damaged or (2b) the fraction of aggregate market value destroyed by the disaster.

For the credit determination, the market value of the damaged home is estimated both after disaster struck and before. Each is weighted by the appropriate fraction of the year to arrive at the adjusted estimate of market value. The excess of the local property tax based on the initial value estimate and the tax based on the weighted average of the before- and after-disaster values is the amount of the credit.

The problem addressed by this credit, unlike the credit itself, is not restricted to homestead property. Owners (and/or tenants) of damaged nonhomestead properties are left to bear property tax on the full, predisaster values of their properties for the fraction of the year after the disaster, even though their property income probably will have fallen.

### AGRICULTURAL PRESERVE CREDIT

The agricultural preserve credit is a tax reduction program intended to encourage farming within the seven-county Twin Cities metropolitan area. Participation in this program requires a total of at least forty acres in parcels of at least ten acres each, although a single parcel of at least twenty acres can participate if it is bordered by eligible land on at least two sides. Unlike most of the other credit programs, however, relief under this one is not automatic. Local government has to certify that the land in question is long-term-use agricultural land, and the owner has to establish a restrictive covenant to keep the land in agricultural use for at least eight years.

There is reason to question the effect on the decision to convert land from agricultural use of the several types of agricultural tax relief. Those requiring restrictive land use agreements, however, are the most likely to succeed in the preservation objective.

## TACONITE TAX RELIEF CREDIT

The taconite tax relief credit, adopted in 1970, is the second oldest of the credits. This credit is to benefit Iron Range homeowners, including farm homeowners, in designated "taconite tax relief areas." A "supplementary taconite tax relief credit" adopted in 1980 provides identical benefits to two specific Iron Range school districts that do not meet the exact criteria for the basic credit but that are said to warrant the same relief.

The taconite tax relief credit is funded by proceeds from the state taconite production tax. This tax is in lieu of property taxation. The rationale for the taconite tax relief credit is summarized as follows:

> Taconite production companies do not pay property tax on land which they are actively mining and on land and buildings where their production facilities are located. As a result, Iron Range communities must make up for the absence of the substantial property tax revenue they would receive from the taconite companies— if the companies were not exempt from the property tax—by imposing a property tax on homeowners which is substantially higher than the property tax of homeowners of most other communities in the state. The taconite tax relief credit is intended to reduce the yearly property tax bills of Iron Range homeowners to roughly what the bills would have been if the taconite companies did pay property taxes.[2]

The relief provided by this credit is equal to 66% of the property tax for homes located in a city or a town, and 57% of the property tax for homes not in a city or a town. In each case, there is a statutory maximum credit, with a maximum outside cities and towns set $55 below that for cities and towns. Both maximum rates rise automatically by $15 per year; they are $475 and $420 for taxes payable in 1984.

There is logic to the notion that the state should make up local revenue losses that result from state policies—in this case, the property tax exemption of taconite production and mine properties. The state-provided relief, however, is too narrow; the above rationale logically extends beyond homesteads to every other type of taxable property. Also, the taxes on homeowners and agricultural properties in the Iron Range enjoy larger reductions than those in other parts of the state, with the level of net taxes in the region being relatively low.

## HOMESTEAD CREDIT

The homestead credit, the oldest and the largest of the credits, is deducted after all other credits (although 1984 legislation places the taconite credit after the homestead credit in future years). It is equal to 54% of the (remaining) gross tax, up to a relief maximum of $650.

The homestead credit is available to all homesteads, including farm homesteads of unlimited acreage. The tax on only the first 240 acres of a farm homestead was considered in calculating homestead relief prior to 1983 legislation. But at the same time that the coverage of agricultural homestead taxes was extended, nonagricultural homestead coverage was made narrower by limiting relief to the taxes on the first $67,000 worth of market value. These changes tend to increase the net tax differentials that exist between agricultural and nonagricultural properties and between relatively high-valued homes and less-expensive homes.

The objective is to reduce by a large amount the property tax bill of every homeowner by providing a property tax credit which is subtracted from the homeowner's property tax bill. Also, the homestead credit reduces low and moderate property tax bills by a greater proportion than high property tax bills.

In addition to the obvious effects of this credit on the interclass distribution of the property tax impact, it may stimulate growth of the public sector in the various areas of the state. Due to the high relief percentage within the $650 homestead credit maximum, an additional $1 of local tax on a home not yet at the maximum will cost the homeowner only 46 cents; the state as a whole will pick up the other 54 cents. This provides a substantial incentive for local residents to tend to support local budget expansion. For homeowners already at the $650 maximum, another $1 of local tax will cost the homeowner the full $1, and approval of further local budget increases is less likely.

Applying the credit to the first "X" dollars of the property bill makes inefficient use of state aid dollars. Aid goes to relieve property tax bills in areas that have relatively low effective taxes while less relief goes to areas with higher effective tax rates. In general, millage rates are highest in cities and the percentage of homeowners affected by the $650 maximum is larger in cities than in rural areas. Some city supporters argue that the result of this state policy is to make it more difficult for cities to get tax increases approved.

## POWER LINE CREDIT

The power line credit reduces the property tax bills of owners of homestead and agricultural properties over which a high voltage power transmission line passes, provided the line was constructed after June 1974. Funding is equal to 10% of the property tax on the power line. The fraction of the credit for any given property is equal to the percentage of the total length of the line in the county that passes over that property. Prior to 1982, when the credit became effective, the utility companies made direct payments to the property owners.

The logic of this credit is not clear. A newly constructed line, as opposed to an existing line, could reduce the value of the property over which it passes; but if such construction does not occur over an existing easement, the rights to run the line presumably would have to be bought. Thus, the owners of the properties crossed by the power line should already have been compensated. Moreover, the extent to which the power line diminishes the value of the properties should be reflected in the appraised and assessed values and result in lower property tax liabilities.

## REFUND PROGRAMS

In addition to classification and property tax credits, the State of Minnesota also provides some property tax refunds.

### CIRCUIT BREAKER

The circuit breaker is the largest and oldest of the refund programs and its benefits accrue to homeowners and renters alike. Of the $178 million of benefits paid in 1984, $100 million went to renters. The renters' share is larger in part because renters tend to be more concentrated than owners in the lower income levels and because other property tax relief programs benefit homeowners.

The objective of the circuit breaker is to provide relief from property taxes in relation to income—the percentage of relief falls as income rises to an income ceiling. Minnesota, like virtually all circuit breaker states, relates property taxes to a broad income[3] measure, rather than just taxable income, to determine benefit amounts.

*How it works.* Renters with household income below $40,000 may be eligible for a circuit breaker refund; because homeowners receive a homestead credit, they may be eligible for a refund if income is $32,500 or less. (If there were no homestead credit, the $40,000 income limit also would apply to homeowners.)

Eligibility depends on the amount of property tax paid as a share of income. For any income the amount of relief increases as the amount of tax increases, although a maximum amount of relief is available at each income level.

For homeowners, the program works in stages that proceed as follows:

- First, the homeowner pays a share of the tax (e.g., the first $70 for households with incomes of $7,500).
- Next, the state pays a share up to a limit (e.g., the state pays the next $70 for the $7,500 household).

- Any remaining tax is shared by the state at a rate ranging from 95% to 50%, depending on income. There is a maximum amount available at each income level (e.g., at $7,500 income, the state pays 88% of the tax over $140 or 95% for senior and disabled households up to a maximum credit of $1,125).
- The homestead credit previously granted by the state is subtracted from the total relief allowed. The remainder is refunded to the taxpayer.
- For seniors and disabled persons, the refund works the same way except that for taxpayers under the maximum, the state pays a larger share of the tax at income levels between $5,000 and $27,500.

For renters, the refund works in the same way except that the property tax attributable to the housing unit is treated as their share of the property tax paid. No credits are subtracted in determining the circuit breaker refund to renters.

For taxes paid in 1983, circuit breaker forms had to be filed by August 31, 1984. Claims for relief filed before that date were paid in August. Circuit breaker relief for 1983 taxes is charged to the state budget for FY 1985.

*Evaluation.*   The present circuit breaker fails to serve the goals of simplicity, equity, and neutrality. The circuit breaker, operating with or without the homestead credit, can continue to provide substantial amounts of property tax relief. However, there are problems as it applies to both renters and homeowners.

Under the renter provisions of the circuit breaker, many renters receive more relief than owners with comparable income for the same personal outlays for property taxes. This happens because all property taxes assessed against a rental unit are attributed to the renter in providing circuit breaker relief. In fact, part of the tax is passed on to the renter but the rest is borne by the owner. Ideally, tax relief should be provided only for the part of the tax actually passed to renters.

There are four fundamental problems with the present circuit breaker as it applies to homeowners:

- Tax relief is positively related to property wealth—at a given income level, ownership of more property often means more tax relief. Thus, the program subsidizes people who elect to spend larger shares of their income on taxable property.
- Taxpayers have different net "tax prices," i.e., they pay different percentages of new tax assessment. This result is due to the caps on the circuit breaker at each income level and to some internal bumps in the circuit breaker design. Taxpayers experience abrupt increases in tax burden as their liabilities pass beyond the caps.
- Taxpayers have different incentives to vote for property tax increases since the taxes paid for new public services are different.

• The circuit breaker system is complex, with part of the complexity contributed by its interrelationship with the homestead credit. Without the homestead credit, the system continues to be unnecessarily complex and none of the three problems above are relieved; some problems are exacerbated.

To illustrate these issues, consider a 10% increase in mill rates; this increase will lead to a 10% rise in gross property tax bills. If the property taxes originally were 1.5% of market value, they should now be 1.65% of market value for all homes or 0.15% more across the board. Thus, the gross tax increase is:

```
$ 30 for a $ 20,000 home
$ 60 for a $ 40,000 home
$ 90 for a $ 60,000 home
$120 for a $ 80,000 home
$150 for a $100,000 home
$180 for a $120,000 home
$210 for a $140,000 home
```

We might expect the circuit breaker to soften this increase for lower-income owners of lower-valued properties so that, for example, for a low-income household the net extra tax could be distributed as:

```
$ 10 for a $ 20,000 home (.05 % of home value)
$ 30 for a $ 40,000 home (.075% of home value)
$ 60 for a $ 60,000 home (.10 % of home value)
$100 for a $ 80,000 home (.125% of home value)
$140 for a $100,000 home (.14 % of home value)
$180 for a $120,000 home (.15 % of home value)
$210 for a $140,000 home (.15 % of home value)
```

In practice, however, at a constant income level, the circuit breaker and homestead credit can produce results very different from these. Choose $25,000 income for an example. The following distribution of net marginal taxes can result:

```
$ 16 for a $ 20,000 home (.08% of home value)
$ 32 for a $ 40,000 home (.08% of home value)
$ 41 for a $ 60,000 home (.07% of home value)
$ 55 for a $ 80,000 home (.07% of home value)
$ 52 for a $100,000 home (.05% of home value)
$140 for a $120,000 home (.12% of home value)
$210 for a $140,000 home (.14% of home value)
```

This problem of varying net marginal tax rates is not relieved by eliminating the homestead credit. Figure 1 illustrates how marginal taxes are distributed after the circuit breaker adjusts to removal of the homestead credit. Taxpayers with income/home-value combinations in Regions I, II, and V of the figure will pay a fraction of tax increases with the fraction varying for different income/home-value combinations.

To interpret the figure, choose any household income level—again, $25,000 is a good illustrative value. Draw a vertical line beginning at $25,000 on the income axis. Households will pay 100% of tax increases if they own homes valued at less than $22,500 or more than about $100,000. Households in homes valued between $22,500 and $45,000 will pay 0% of any tax increases. Owners of homes worth $45,000 to about $100,000 will pay 35% of gross mill rate increases; the circuit breaker picks up the rest of the local tax increase.

The different net tax rates create nonneutral incentives to vote for or against local property tax increases. Taxpayers in Regions I, II, and V will pay 100% of gross tax increases and have relatively great pocketbook incentives to vote against additional funding for local public services. Taxpayers in Region IV will pay some of the gross tax. As you move to the left on this chart in Region IV, the taxpayers' tax price gets smaller and these households have more incentive than others to vote for higher taxes. In Region III, the state pays 100% of property tax increases and these taxpayers have every incentive to vote for new public services that will be free to them. At an effective tax rate of 2%, as depicted in the figure, Region III includes many households with mid-range incomes ($25,000 to $38,000) and slightly-below-average-value homes ($40,000 to $60,000). For

FIGURE 1
Distribution of Marginal Tax Rates Under the
Circuit Breaker with No Other Credits
(assumes effective tax rate of 2% credit before circuit breaker)

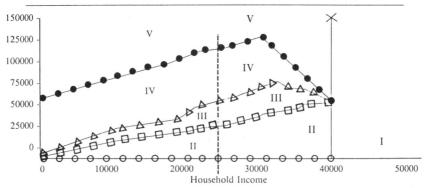

*Source:* Glenn Nelson, University of Minnesota (St. Paul) and Resources for the Future (Washington, D.C.), November 1984.

some jurisdictions, the number and share of households in this free-rider region will be quite large.

Two options have been proposed for improving the circuit breaker— eliminating the caps on credit at each income level and raising the maximum income that qualifies for relief. Neither option is a desirable choice. In the figure, eliminating the caps corresponds to eliminating Region V, and raising the income eligibility corresponds to moving Region I to the right. Neither proposal addresses the fundamental flaw of the circuit breaker, i.e., the existence of regions with net tax rates ranging from 0% to 100% of gross tax increases. The free-rider Region III remains intact as does tax-penalty Region II which levies especially heavy marginal taxes on low-valued property. Further, by removing the caps, the circuit breaker would become an unlimited subsidy for owners of high-valued property.

*An alternative to the circuit breaker.* A new program for property tax relief can be designed and implemented as a substitute for the current circuit breaker. It is an improvement over the existing circuit breaker in three respects. First, it is based on the premise that Minnesota will move to fewer classes and fewer or no credits. In contrast, the present circuit breaker is designed to mesh with the existing, multicredit system. Second, the proposal is explicit regarding the underlying values that are the foundation for property tax relief policy. And, finally, the proposal enhances the coinsurance feature of tax relief policy which requires that no taxpayer is able to vote for property tax increases knowing that the state will pick up 100% of the additional tax cost.

Under the proposed property tax credit (PTC) format, taxpayers share their tax bill with the state according to a simple fractional division—the state pays two-thirds, one-half, one-fifth, or some other fraction and the taxpayer is liable for the rest. The fraction paid by the state depends on the combination of the taxpayer's income and property wealth. Taxpayers with a larger bundle of income/wealth get a smaller fraction of relief than those with lesser bundles. Decisionmakers for the state can decide how much to spend on circuit breaker relief and set the fractions accordingly. Decisionmakers also can shape the system of fractions to provide relatively more relief to targeted groups, to achieve greater progressivity, and to create a smooth array of marginal tax rates across income and property values.

Figure 2 illustrates one example of a design for the PTC system. There are five fractional tax-sharing lines in the Figure—in practice, decisionmakers could choose as many or few of these lines as they want. Each of these lines intersects the income axis and the home value axis, and makes an arc between the two intersections; again decisionmakers can choose any pair of intersections and many shapes for the arc at each fractional level.

Each arc in Figure 2 defines the edge of the group of income/home value combinations that receive the same fraction of PTC relief. For example, in

the figure the state pays 80% of the tax bill for households with about $15,000 or less income and very little wealth, for households with home values up to $30,000 and no income, and for households on or below the arc joining these two points. The next arc defines the region of 60% PTC; these are households with income/wealth too large to qualify for 80% relief but on or beneath the next fractional boundary.

In the figure, households with up to $50,000 income and low-valued homes could get some relief; households with $120,000 homes and no income could also qualify for some relief. In general, the fraction of relief falls as wealth increases and as income increases.

Decisionmakers may want a separate relief program for renters. Alternatively, renters can be viewed as having income but no wealth; they can receive relief according to the intersections on the income axis. Thus, renters with household incomes of $15,000 or less would receive 80% relief from the property tax component in their rent and so forth.

FIGURE 2
Example of One Design for the Property Tax Credit System
Percentage of Property Tax Bill Paid by the State

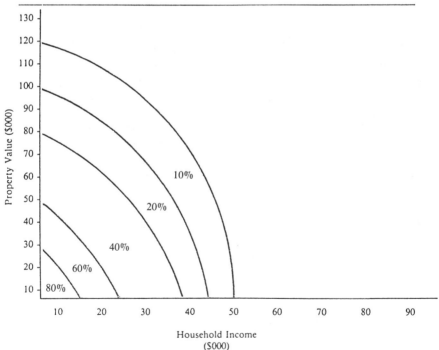

Household Income
($000)

The same PTC can be used to determine tax relief for agricultural and nonagricultural homesteads where the agricultural homestead is considered to be the residence and one acre. If the decisionmakers feel that homesteaded owners of agricultural land should be given additional relief, that fraction of relief could be determined separately through this program. For example, suppose a farm household has income of $15,000, a home on one acre valued at $30,000, and $100,000 of additional agricultural land. The farmer qualifies for a fraction of relief for taxes on the residence, based on the $15,000/$30,000 combination of income and home value. The owner also qualifies for a second fraction of relief from tax on the other acres based on the $15,000/$100,000 combination of income and agricultural land value.

The cost of this tax relief program can be set at any amount and is a policy decision. Similarly the distribution of tax relief is a policy decision. Many distributions of the relief fractions are possible for the same total cost. Thus, policymakers can choose to allocate the fractional tax relief among income/wealth classes in many different ways. Because both the total amount of relief and the distribution are policy choices, in most cases the system can be designed to be progressive: in general, net marginal tax rates could increase with income. Progressivity might not be possible if the policy choice is to have total cost quite low, coupled with a highly regressive gross tax distribution.

## TARGETED REFUND

At present, temporary relief in addition to the circuit breaker is targeted to homeowners whose property taxes have increased relatively rapidly since 1982 (payable 1983). Initially, this temporary relief was provided by 1983 legislation, but it was modified and expanded by 1984 legislation.

Specifically, there are two targeted relief measures. The first, the special property tax refund, provided relief when (1) household income was under $50,000 and (2) the tax—net of all other relief, including the circuit breaker—payable in 1984 was more than 20% above that payable in 1983 on the same property, provided the tax difference did not result from improvements to the property between the two years. In such cases, the state paid the amount of payable-1984 tax in excess of 120% of the 1983 bill. Similarly, for 1984 taxes payable in 1985, the state will pay half of the increase in excess of 112.5% of that for the previous year, to a maximum of $400 of relief. In this latter year, there is no income restriction. This relief is extended through the same procedure as the circuit breaker, via additional lines on Form M-1PR.

The second temporary relief program was adopted in 1983, the extra special property tax refund, was targeted to homestead net taxes payable in 1984 that have increased at least 10% from the previous year and result in an effective tax rate of at least 2.25%. In these circumstances, the state pays half the amount in excess of 110% of the previous year's net tax. A $200 limit on the amount of this additional tax refund was removed by 1984 legislation.

## CONGRESSIONAL MEDAL OF HONOR PAYMENTS

The final refund program was also created by 1983 law. A veteran who has received the congressional medal of honor and who meets certain Minnesota residency requirements can be refunded up to $2,000 of homestead property tax annually. Application must be made with the commissioner of revenue. Any refund under this provision is before the circuit breaker refund.

This refund clearly represents an expression of gratitude for or pride in the military service of the recipient. Whether such a feeling of gratitude should be built into the tax system is questionable; benefit is contingent upon ownership of eligible property, and is directly related to the value of that property. The total cost of the credit will depend upon the age of the recipient when the refund is first received, how long that person (or the surviving spouse) continues to live in qualifying property in Minnesota, and how high the gross taxes on that property are. Lifetime costs, however, could well run into the tens of thousands of dollars.

## EFFECTIVE TAX RATES

### FROM MARKET VALUE TO ASSESSED VALUE: CLASSIFICATION

Some notion of the effects of the Minnesota direct property tax relief programs can be seen by comparing each class's various tax base and tax amount.

Uniformity would result if three conditions were met: (1) if all properties were valued for tax purposes at the same percentage of their respective market values; (2) if a uniform tax rate were then applied to all such assessed values in calculating tax amounts; and (3) if the gross taxes thus calculated were not reduced by credits or refunds.

The tax determination process starts with the estimation of market values by assessors. Such estimates of market value for 1983 are shown in the first column of Table 1. (These values are not adjusted for differences in assessment accuracy across property classes.) The assessed values in column 2, the actual tax base, result from multiplying the legal classification percentages and the assessors' estimates of market value. The gross tax amounts in column 4 are the products of the statutory (or nominal) tax rates

TABLE 1
Relationship Between Market Value and Assessed Value
and Between Gross Tax and Tax Net of Credits
Taxes Payable in 1983
(Dollars in Millions)

| | Market Value | Assessed Value | Assessed Value/ Market Value | Gross Tax | Net Tax | Net Tax/ Gross Tax |
|---|---|---|---|---|---|---|
| Residential | $54,649.3 | $11,498.9 | 21.0% | $1150.9 | $688.0 | 59.8% |
| 3 Res. homestead | 50,028.1 | 10,223.9 | 20.4 | 1021.8 | 561.6 | 55.0 |
| 4 Res. nonhomestead | 4,442.1 | 1,243.8 | 28.0 | 126.0 | 126.0 | 100.0 |
| 9 3cc: Ag. & nonag. | 179.1 | 31.2 | 17.4 | 3.1 | .4 | 12.9 |
| Agricultural | 34,280.6 | 6,216.1 | 18.1 | 415.8 | 261.5 | 62.9 |
| 1 Ag. homestead | 23,702.2 | 4,206.2 | 17.7 | 284.3 | 150.5 | 52.9 |
| 2 Ag. nonhomestead | 10,458.2 | 1,987.1 | 19.0 | 129.3 | 109.0 | 84.3 |
| 12 Timberlands | 120.2 | 22.8 | 19.0 | 2.2 | 2.0 | 90.0 |
| Apartments | 4,721.5 | 1,588.3 | 33.6 | 164.3 | 151.5 | 92.2 |
| 5 Apartments | 3,899.5 | 1,308.9 | 33.6 | 135.0 | 135.0 | 100.0 |
| 6 Subsidized Apts. | 822.0 | 279.4 | 34.0 | 29.3 | 16.5 | 56.3 |
| Seasonal | 2,593.0 | 544.5 | 21.0 | 45.2 | 39.3 | 86.9 |
| 10 Seasonal-rec-res | 2,593.0 | 544.5 | 21.0 | 45.2 | 39.3 | 86.9 |
| Commercial | 18,698.5 | 7,730.1 | 41.3 | 763.1 | 762.7 | 99.9 |
| 7 Commercial | 9,391.5 | 3,988.1 | 42.5 | 402.9 | 402.9 | 100.0 |
| 8 Industrial | 3,767.2 | 1,608.9 | 42.7 | 163.7 | 163.7 | 100.0 |
| 11 Commercial-seasonal | 173.0 | 28.6 | 16.5 | 2.4 | 2.0 | 83.0 |
| 13 Vacant land | 1,193.8 | 477.5 | 40.0 | 47.0 | 47.0 | 100.0 |
| 14 Mineral | 67.8 | 33.9 | 50.0 | 3.8 | 3.8 | 100.0 |
| 15 Personal & PU | 3,814.5 | 1,468.0 | 38.5 | 130.7 | 130.7 | 100.0 |
| 16 Railroad | 290.8 | 125.1 | 43.0 | 12.6 | 12.6 | 100.0 |

Source: Minnesota House Research Department property tax simulation model.
*Gross tax minus credits. The circuit breaker is not subtracted out.

of the local jurisdictions and the assessed values.[4] Subtraction of credits from gross taxes results in the net tax amounts shown in column 5.

The first three columns present, for five major classes and sixteen subclasses, market and assessed value amounts, and the percentages of market value represented by assessed value. To summarize:

- For all taxable property, assessed value is only 24% of market value—i.e., market value is reduced by 76% in arriving at the actual tax base.
- The largest reduction among the five broad classes is enjoyed by agriculture (82%), followed by residential and seasonal residential (79% each); for the apartment and commercial classes, the reductions were 66% and 59%, respectively.
- While all of these reductions are quite large, their relative magnitudes are quite different. The remaining tax base (assessed value) is about twice as large a fraction of market value for the commercial class (41%) as for the agricultural, residential, and seasonal classes (18%, 21%, and 21%, respectively).
- These differences in the tax treatment produce effective tax rate differentials of better than two to one before taking into account the tax credits and refund programs.
- An important difference exists within the residential class, where homesteads are treated much more favorably than nonhomesteads (i.e., owner-occupants are favored over renters and landlords). For homesteads, the assessed value equals 20% of market value versus 28% for nonhomesteads. Because the overall assessment level is so low, this differential of only 8% becomes a 40% differential. Moreover, assessed value is a much higher fraction of market value for apartments than for other residential properties; at nearly 34%, the assessment level is almost 70% higher than that for homesteads. If one believes that tenants bear the taxes on their dwellings, so large a differential is questionable. However, the more competitive the rental market, the more likely the property tax is borne by the landlord.

## FROM GROSS TO NET TAX: CREDITS

State tax credit policies increase the interclass differentials, already large due to classification on the assessed value side. Credits create the differences between gross taxes and net taxes shown in the last three columns of Table 1. Across the five major classes, net taxes range from 60% of gross taxes for residential to 100% for commercial; the figure for agricultural property is nearly as low as that for residential (63%), while those for seasonal residential and for apartments are closer to that for commercial (87% and 92%, respectively).

Greater differentiation appears when considering sixteen classes. Net tax represents as little as 13% of gross taxes for homesteads of certain blind and disabled persons eligible for reduced assessment credit (class 3cc). For subsidized apartments participating in the same program, however, net taxes drop to 56% of gross taxes—a seemingly low figure, but more than four times as high as for the homesteads in the program. Credits reduce taxes to a lower percentage of gross taxes for agricultural homesteads than for subsidized apartments, and within the residential class, nonhomesteads receive no credits while homestead taxes are reduced to 55% of the gross amount. These figures are consistent with the strong bias in favor of homesteads previously noted.

## COMBINED CLASSIFICATION AND CREDIT EFFECTS BY TYPE OF PROPERTY

Both classification and credits affect the relationship between net taxes and market values. Substantial effective tax rate differences across classes are the result:

- the effective tax rate relative to market value is only 0.6% for agricultural homesteads compared to 4.3% for commercial property;
- residential homestead properties enjoy a relatively low 1.1% effective rate; and
- residential nonhomestead properties have a relatively high 2.8% effective tax rate.

The relatively favorable treatment of residential property, and of residential homesteads in particular, is apparent. The three-tiered application of progressively larger classification percentages, however, provides unequal preferences for homes of different values, and the limit on total homestead credit benefits likewise produces unequal percentage reductions in gross property taxes. These differences are illustrated in Table 2.

The first two columns apply the classification percentages of class 3c (residential homestead) and class 3dd (residential nonhomestead, three units or less) to arrive at assessed values. The next two columns show gross tax amounts for both the homestead and the nonhomestead homes using a nominal rate of 100 mills, an illustrative rate chosen because it is near the statewide average. The fifth column shows nonhomestead amounts as percentages of homestead amounts. This column shows that the assessment preference accorded homesteads declines as market value rises. At $40,000, the nonhomestead assessed value and tax are 60% higher than the comparable figures for homesteads, but the differential declines steadily and is only 6% for $200,000 homes.

## TABLE 2
### Comparison of Homestead and Nonhomestead Residential Taxation of Homes of Selected Market Values

| Market Value | Assessed Value | | Tax at 100 mills | | Non-HS as % of HS | HS Credit | Tax Net of Homestead Credit | | Effective Rates | | Non-HS as % of HS |
| --- | --- | --- | --- | --- | --- | --- | --- | --- | --- | --- | --- |
| | HS | Non-HS | HS | Non-HS | | | HS | Non-HS | HS | Non-HS | |
| $ 40,000 | $ 7,000 | $11,200 | $ 700 | $1,120 | 160% | $378 | $ 322 | $1,120 | .81% | 2.8% | 340% |
| 60,000 | 10,800 | 16,800 | 1,080 | 1,680 | 156 | 583 | 497 | 1,680 | .83 | 2.8 | 337 |
| 80,000 | 16,800 | 22,400 | 1,680 | 2,240 | 133 | 650 | 1,030 | 2,240 | 1.29 | 2.8 | 217 |
| 100,000 | 22,800 | 28,000 | 2,280 | 2,800 | 123 | 650 | 1,630 | 2,800 | 1.63 | 2.8 | 172 |
| 120,000 | 28,800 | 33,600 | 2,880 | 3,360 | 117 | 650 | 2,230 | 3,360 | 1.86 | 2.8 | 151 |
| 140,000 | 34,800 | 39,200 | 3,480 | 3,920 | 113 | 650 | 2,830 | 3,920 | 2.02 | 2.8 | 140 |
| 160,000 | 40,800 | 44,800 | 4,080 | 4,480 | 110 | 650 | 3,430 | 4,480 | 2.14 | 2.8 | 128 |
| 180,000 | 46,800 | 50,400 | 4,680 | 5,040 | 108 | 650 | 4,030 | 5,040 | 2.24 | 2.8 | 125 |
| 200,000 | 52,800 | 56,000 | 5,280 | 5,600 | 106 | 650 | 4,630 | 5,600 | 2.32 | 2.8 | 121 |

*Source:* Minnesota Tax Study Commission staff computations based upon current (1983, payable in 1984) property tax provisions.

TABLE 3
Percentage Distribution Tax Base and Effective Rates,
Taxes Payable 1983

| | Statewide | | Metro | | Nonmetro | |
|---|---|---|---|---|---|---|
| | % of Market Value | Effective Rate | % of Market Value | Effective Rate | % of Market Value | Effective Rate |
| Residential | 47.6% | | 68.1% | | 29.6% | |
| 3 Res. Homestead | 43.5 | 1.1 | 62.2 | 1.3 | 27.2 | .8 |
| 4 Res. Nonhomestead | 3.9 | 2.8 | 5.7 | 2.9 | 2.3 | 2.8 |
| 9 3 cc Ag. & Nonag. | .2 | .2 | .2 | .3 | .1 | .2 |
| Agricultural | 29.8% | | 11.0% | | 54.4% | |
| 1 Ag. homestead | 20.6 | .6 | 2.0 | .9 | 36.9 | .6 |
| 2 Ag. Nonhomestead | 9.1 | 1.0 | .9 | 1.7 | 16.3 | 1.0 |
| 12 Timberland | .1 | 1.7 | .0 | 1.5 | .2 | 1.7 |
| Apartments | 4.1% | | 7.1% | | 1.6% | |
| 5 Apartments | 3.4 | 3.5 | 6.2 | 3.4 | 1.0 | 3.6 |
| 6 Subsidized Apts. | .7 | 2.0 | .9 | 2.2 | .6 | 1.7 |
| Seasonal | 2.3% | | .2% | | 4.1% | |
| 20 Seasonal-rec-res | 2.3 | 1.5 | .2 | 1.8 | 4.1 | 1.5 |
| Commercial | 16.4% | | 21.8% | | 11.5% | |
| 7 Commercial | 8.2 | 4.3 | 12.5 | 4.3 | 4.4 | 4.3 |
| 8 Industrial | 3.3 | 4.3 | 5.2 | 4.4 | 1.6 | 4.3 |
| 11 Com. Seasonal | .2 | 1.2 | .0 | 1.9 | .3 | 1.2 |
| 13 Vacant Land | 1.0 | 3.9 | 1.7 | 4.0 | .5 | 3.8 |
| 14 Mineral | .1 | 5.5 | -0- | -0- | .1 | 5.5 |
| 15 Personal & PU | 3.3 | 3.4 | 2.2 | 4.0 | 4.3 | 3.1 |
| 16 Railroad | .3 | 4.7 | .2 | 4.4 | .3 | 4.3 |
| Over-all Effective Rate | | 1.7 | | 2.2 | | 1.2 |

The homestead credit (54% of tax up to a $650 maximum credit) figures in column 6 are subtracted from the gross homestead taxes in column 3 to arrive at the net homestead tax amounts in column 7; the nonhomestead net taxes in column 8 are the same as the gross taxes in column 4. These net tax amounts are divided by the appropriate market value figures to calculate effective tax rates, shown in columns 9 and 10. Column 11 expresses nonhomestead taxes as percentages of homestead taxes on homes of the same value. Compared to column 5, the column 11 figures are higher at every home value shown. Thus, the homestead credit increases the degree of homestead preference in relation to that established by classification. For a $40,000 home, the net tax (and the effective rate) is nearly two and one-half times higher than it would be the same value homestead home; at the $200,000 home level, the nonhomestead net tax is only about 20% higher vis-a-vis a homestead.

Thus, the homestead preference within the residential class is quite large at relatively low value levels and remains large even above the average home value; most of the differential is due to the homestead credit, at least at a 100-mill tax rate. But the homestead credit is of comparatively little value for very high home values. In our examples, the effective tax rate for a $200,000 homestead is nearly three times as high as that for a $40,000 home.

## ISOLATING THE GEOGRAPHICAL EFFECTS

Local taxing decisions, as well as state direct tax relief policy, lie behind the shares and effective rates. Table 3 reports tax shares and effective rates by property class statewide, and for the metro and nonmetro areas. The overall effective rates differ substantially (1.7% statewide, 2.2% in the metro area, and 1.2% in the nonmetro area), as do the effective rates for many of the sixteen classes. Application of the same state policies in different areas often result in different effective rates for the same type of property because of (1) different nominal rates, (2) the distribution of different property classes in any jurisdiction, and (3) the percentage of homestead properties that receive the maximum homestead credit.

TABLE 4
Percentage Distribution of Minnesota Net Property Taxes Under Alternative Property Tax System
Taxes Payable in 1984

| | 1 Actual '84 | 2 Current assessment no credits | 3 Uniform assessment no credits | 4 Uniform assessment all credits | 5 Two classes no credits | 6 Two classes all credits | 7 Three classes no credits | 8 Three classes all credits | 9 Five classes no credits | 10 Five classes all credits |
|---|---|---|---|---|---|---|---|---|---|---|
| RESIDENTIAL | 36.0 | 44.5 | 55.0 | 48.2 | 51.0 | 43.5 | 46.7 | 38.5 | 44.1 | 35.2 |
| 3 Residential homestead | 28.9 | 39.0 | 49.8 | 41.3 | 46.2 | 37.1 | 39.6 | 29.3 | 40.0 | 29.8 |
| 4 Residential nonhomestead | 7.1 | 5.5 | 5.1 | 6.8 | 4.7 | 6.3 | 7.0 | 9.1 | 4.0 | 5.3 |
| 9 3cc: Ag. & nonag. | 0.0 | 0.0 | 0.1 | 0.1 | 0.1 | 0.1 | 0.1 | 0.1 | 0.1 | 0.1 |
| Agricultural | 14.2 | 16.6 | 18.2 | 16.3 | 18.7 | 16.6 | 17.5 | 15.3 | 17.5 | 15.2 |
| 1 Agricultural homestead | 8.4 | 11.4 | 12.8 | 10.0 | 13.0 | 9.9 | 12.2 | 9.2 | 12.2 | 9.1 |
| 2 Agricultural nonhomestead | 5.6 | 5.0 | 5.2 | 6.1 | 5.5 | 6.4 | 5.1 | 5.9 | 5.1 | 5.9 |
| 12 Timberlands | 0.2 | 0.2 | 0.2 | 0.2 | 0.2 | 0.3 | 0.2 | 0.2 | 0.2 | 0.2 |
| Apartment | 7.8 | 6.0 | 5.1 | 6.9 | 4.9 | 6.4 | 7.0 | 9.1 | 6.1 | 7.9 |
| 5 Apartments | 6.9 | 5.3 | 4.2 | 5.7 | 4.0 | 5.3 | 5.7 | 7.5 | 5.0 | 6.5 |
| 6 Subsidized Apartments | 0.9 | 0.7 | 0.9 | 1.2 | 0.9 | 1.1 | 1.3 | 1.6 | 1.1 | 1.4 |
| Seasonal | 2.1 | 1.8 | 1.8 | 2.1 | 2.0 | 2.4 | 2.4 | 2.7 | 2.4 | 2.7 |
| 10 Seasonal-rec-res | 2.1 | 1.8 | 1.8 | 2.1 | 2.0 | 2.4 | 2.4 | 2.7 | 2.4 | 2.7 |
| Commercial/Industrial | 39.9 | 30.8 | 19.8 | 26.4 | 23.4 | 31.2 | 26.4 | 34.4 | 29.9 | 39.0 |
| 7 Commercial | 21.2 | 16.4 | 10.4 | 13.9 | 12.5 | 16.6 | 14.2 | 18.5 | 15.9 | 20.8 |
| 8 Industrial | 8.7 | 6.7 | 4.2 | 5.7 | 5.0 | 6.7 | 5.5 | 7.2 | 6.4 | 8.4 |
| 11 Commercial Seasonal | 0.1 | 0.1 | 0.1 | 0.1 | 0.1 | 0.2 | 0.2 | 0.2 | 0.2 | 0.2 |
| 13 Vacant Land | 2.4 | 1.8 | 1.2 | 1.6 | 1.4 | 1.9 | 1.6 | 2.1 | 1.9 | 2.5 |
| 14 Mineral | 0.2 | 0.1 | 0.1 | 0.1 | 0.1 | 0.1 | 0.1 | 0.1 | 0.1 | 0.1 |
| 15 Personal & PU | 6.7 | 5.2 | 3.5 | 4.7 | 4.0 | 5.3 | 4.5 | 5.9 | 5.0 | 6.5 |
| 16 Railroad | 0.6 | 0.5 | 0.3 | 0.3 | 0.3 | 0.4 | 0.3 | 0.4 | 0.4 | 0.5 |

*Source:* Calculated from the Minnesota House Research Property Tax Simulation Model for the Minnesota Tax Study Commission, 1984.

ILLUSTRATING THE EFFECTS OF CLASSIFICATION AND CREDITS

If all property were assessed at full market value, and if no tax credits were granted, but local tax differences remained, residential property would pay 55% of Minnesota's property taxes. Agriculture's share would be 18.2% with commercial/industrial at 19.8%, apartments 5.1%, and seasonal/recreational residences at 1.8% of total tax collections. These shares are reported under column 3 of Table 4; this column is labeled "Uniform assessment no credits." Column 3 of Table 5 shows the corresponding effective tax rates for the same property classes with uniform assessment and no credits.

As Table 5 shows under column 1, the actual share of total tax attributable to residential property is only about 36% and for commercial/industrial it is 39.9%. The combined effects of classification and credits reduce residential shares by about one-third (columns 3 and 1 of Table 6 also show a large fall in effective rates). Similarly the share of commercial/industrial approximately doubles, and effective tax rates bounce from about 2.8% to 4.4% of property value. After classification and credits, agriculture pays

TABLE 5
Minnesota "Effective" Property Tax Rates Under Alternative Property Tax System, 1984

| | 1 | 2 | 3 | 4 | 5 | 6 | 7 | 8 | 9 | 10 |
|---|---|---|---|---|---|---|---|---|---|---|
| | | Current | Uniform | Uniform | Two | Two | Three | Three | Five | Five |
| | Actual | assess- | assess- | assess- | classes | classes | classes | classes | classes | classes |
| | '84 | ment no | ment no | ment all | no | all | no | all | no | all |
| | | credits | credits | credits | credits | credits | credits | credits | credits | credits |
| Residential | | | | | | | | | | |
| 3 Residential homestead | 1.2% | 2.1% | 2.6% | 1.6% | 2.5% | 1.5% | 2.1% | 1.2% | 2.2% | 1.2% |
| 4 Residential nonhomestead | 3.0 | 3.0 | 2.7 | 2.7 | 2.5 | 2.5 | 3.8 | 3.8 | 2.2 | 2.2 |
| 9 3cc: Ag. & nonag. | 0.3 | 0.5 | 2.6 | 1.4 | 2.4 | 1.3 | 2.1 | 1.0 | 2.1 | 1.0 |
| Agricultural | | | | | | | | | | |
| 1 Agricultural homestead | 0.7 | 1.3 | 1.4 | 0.8 | 1.4 | 0.8 | 1.4 | 0.8 | 1.4 | 0.8 |
| 2 Agricultural nonhomestead | 1.1 | 1.3 | 1.3 | 1.2 | 1.4 | 1.2 | 1.3 | 1.2 | 1.3 | 1.2 |
| 12 Timberlands | 1.7 | 1.9 | 2.2 | 1.9 | 2.4 | 2.2 | 2.0 | 1.8 | 2.0 | 1.8 |
| Apartment | | | | | | | | | | |
| 5 Apartments | 3.7 | 3.7 | 2.9 | 2.9 | 2.7 | 2.7 | 4.0 | 4.0 | 3.4 | 3.4 |
| 6 Subsidized Apartments | 2.2 | 2.2 | 2.8 | 2.8 | 2.6 | 2.6 | 3.9 | 3.9 | 3.4 | 3.4 |
| Seasonal | | | | | | | | | | |
| 10 Seasonal-rec-res | 1.6 | 1.9 | 1.9 | 1.6 | 2.1 | 1.8 | 2.4 | 2.1 | 2.4 | 2.1 |
| Commercial/Industrial | | | | | | | | | | |
| 7 Commercial | 4.4 | 4.4 | 2.8 | 2.8 | 3.3 | 3.3 | 3.9 | 3.9 | 4.3 | 4.3 |
| 8 Industrial | 4.6 | 4.6 | 2.8 | 2.8 | 3.4 | 3.4 | 3.8 | 3.8 | 4.3 | 4.3 |
| 11 Commercial Seasonal | 1.3 | 1.5 | 1.9 | 1.6 | 2.1 | 1.7 | 2.4 | 2.1 | 2.7 | 2.3 |
| 13 Vacant Land | 4.2 | 4.2 | 2.6 | 2.6 | 3.3 | 3.3 | 3.8 | 3.8 | 4.3 | 4.3 |
| 14 Mineral | 6.2 | 6.2 | 3.4 | 3.4 | 4.0 | 4.0 | 4.4 | 4.4 | 4.9 | 4.9 |
| 15 Personal & PU | 3.7 | 3.7 | 2.4 | 2.4 | 2.7 | 2.7 | 3.2 | 3.2 | 3.5 | 3.5 |
| 16 Railroad | 4.7 | 4.7 | 2.4 | 2.4 | 3.1 | 3.1 | 3.5 | 3.5 | 4.0 | 4.0 |
| All Property | 1.8 | 2.3 | 2.3 | 1.7 | 2.3 | 1.7 | 2.3 | 1.8 | 2.3 | 1.8 |

Source: Calculated from the Minnesota House Research Property Tax Simulation Model for the Minnesota Tax Study Commission, 1984.

TABLE 6
Net Cost of Credits To State For Alternative Property Tax Policies
Minnesota Taxes Payable 1984
($000)

| Policy Alternative | Homestead | Taconite Homestead | School Agricultural Credit | Native Prairie | Wetland | All Credits | Average Statewide Mill Rate Gross Tax |
|---|---|---|---|---|---|---|---|
| 1. Status Quo (Actual '84) | $  — | $  — | $  — | $  — | $  — | $  — | 98.2 |
| 2. Classification, No Credits | -505,746 | - 19,607 | - 97,926 | -  151 | -  537 | -623,967 | 98.2 |
| 3. Uniformity, No Credits | -505,746 | - 19,607 | - 97,926 | -  151 | -  537 | -623,967 | 56.7 |
| 4. Uniformity, All Credits | 57,193 | 1,920 | 4,577 | 0 | 0 | 63,690 | 56.7 |
| 5. Two Classes, No Credits | -505,746 | - 19,607 | - 97,926 | -  151 | -  537 | -623,967 | 65.8 |
| 6. Two Classes, All Credits | 42,132 | 1,278 | 10,775 | 0 | 0 | 54,156 | 65.8 |
| 7. Three Classes, No Credits | -505,746 | - 19,607 | - 97,926 | -  151 | -  537 | -623,967 | 91.3 |
| 8. Three Classes, All Credits | 15,815 | 212 | 7,431 | 0 | 0 | 23,458 | 91.3 |
| 9. Five Classes, No Credits | -505,746 | - 19,607 | - 97,926 | -  151 | -  537 | -623,967 | 90.8 |
| 10. Five Classes, All Credits | 18,671 | 178 | 7,114 | 0 | 0 | 25,964 | 90.8 |

Source: Research Staff, Minnesota House of Representatives.

less and apartments pay more of the total tax bill. Variations within the subclasses are even greater than for the five major classes.

Comparing column 3 to column 2 (current assessment, no credits) in either table will isolate the effect of classification. Without credits, the classification system alone reduces residential collections by about one-fourth, to 44.5% of all property taxes. The share of commercial/industrial is increased through classification by about one-half to 30.8%.

Some or all of Minnesota's twenty to seventy property tax classes can be consolidated. The most complete simplification is to have one class and assess all property at the same percentage of market value. Thus, all property, regardless of its use, would pay gross taxes based on the same percentage of market value. The shares and effective rates for uniform assessment with no credits are reported in column 3 of Tables 4 and 5; column 4 reports uniform assessment with all current credits. Going to uniform assessment, with or without credits, would reduce effective rates on commercial/industrial and apartment property while increasing effective rates on agricultural and residential property.

Within both the agricultural homestead and residential homestead classes there would be a shift in relative property taxes on different properties under uniformity. If assessed at a flat rate, low-value homes would have relative increases in assessment (as compared to the current variable rate assessments) while high-value homes would have relative assessment decreases. For example, at a 20% flat rate, a $40,000 homestead is assessed at $8,000 and a $200,000 homestead is assessed at $40,000 as compared to $7,000 and $52,000, respectively, under current procedures. A similar result happens for small and large agricultural homesteads: assessed values of small homesteaded acreages would rise relative to large farms due to loss of the current preferential assessments on smaller farms.

Table 6, rows 3 and 4, indicate how much expenditures on credits would change under uniform assessment. With no credits, the state saves all of the $624 million that currently goes to credits. Or, if credits are continued, the total credit cost to the state would rise by $64 million dollars with uniform assessment. From Table 7, row 3, it is clear that the current circuit breaker would automatically offset much of the cost to taxpayers if credits are removed; circuit breaker claims could increase by $439 million, leaving a net savings to the state of $185 million after eliminating credits. If credits are retained, uniform assessment would increase eligibility claims for circuit breaker relief by $83 million; the total increased cost in credits and circuit breaker is $146 million with uniformity. These circuit breaker claims, however, can be reduced if the circuit breaker program is more carefully targeted to those specific groups requiring relief.

There are many configurations for improving classification that are less complete than uniformity and more straightforward than the current system. Tables 4 through 7 present estimates of tax effects for several of

TABLE 7
Net Cost To State Of Credits Plus Circuit Breaker Refund
Under Alternative Property Tax Policies
Minnesota Taxes Payable 1984
($000)

| Policy Alternative | Total Credits | Circuit Breaker | Net Total Relief |
|---|---|---|---|
| 1. Status Quo (Actual '84) | 0 | 0 | 0 |
| 2. Classification, No Credits | -623,967 | 246,500 | -377,467 |
| 3. Uniformity, No Credits | -623,967 | 438,700 | -185,267 |
| 4. Uniformity, All Credits | 63,690 | 82,500 | 146,190 |
| 5. Two Classes, No Credits | -623,967 | 360,000 | -263,967 |
| 6. Two Classes, All Credits | 54,186 | 33,700 | 87,866 |
| 7. Three Classes, No Credits | -623,967 | 302,853 | -321,114 |
| 8. Three Classes, All Credits | 23,458 | 34,320 | 57,778 |
| 9. Five Classes, No Credits | -623,967 | 257,600 | -366,367 |
| 10. Five Classes, All Credits | 25,964 | - 8,800 | 17,164 |

*Source:* Table and staff estimates.

these configurations, including a two-class, a three-class, and a five-class assessment system both with and without credits. The five-class system with all credits holds the distribution of tax shares and effective rates reasonably close to the current distributions, thus achieving simplicity with little adjustment in taxes. Homeowners and agricultural homesteads, however, would experience the relative internal shifts because each class would be assessed at a single internal rate.

Three-classes-with-no-credits achieves the goal of reducing relative taxes on commercial/industrial property—recall that these burdens are somewhat higher than in most other states—while shifting this burden to other classes, especially residences and agriculture. Two-classes-with-no-credits makes the same adjustment but to a greater extent. Again, in either case, there are internal adjustments for property in agriculture or residential homesteads. Some of the increased burden for homesteads is offset by allowing the credits, but they are not well-targeted to provide relief where it is most needed. High-valued homes would have lower assessments and get credit assistance if current credits are retained. The total cost of providing credits and circuit breakers through the current program would rise.

The tangled classification-credit system can be substantially remedied by going to two or three classes; at the same time, relative burdens on commercial/industrial property can be relieved. Three classes provides a moderate policy for improving classification. An associated, moderate policy is available for assisting taxpayers who are unduly burdened by the shifts among and within classes. Such a policy involves eliminating credits and the present circuit breaker and substituting the earlier-discussed income/wealth property tax relief program specifically targeted to needy taxpayers. This program can be designed to help some homeowners and farmers at a cost, perhaps, of $180 million dollars. Thus, the state could choose a system of three classes, levy the current gross amount of property tax revenues, save $624 million on ill-targeted credits, and substitute about $180 million in targeted relief for the current circuit breaker relief. The result is greater simplicity, equity, and a "surplus" of $624 million which could be used to reduce property taxes by reducing mill rates for all property owners.

## COMPARISON OF TWO RELIEF PROGRAMS—LUMP SUM GRANTS TO LOCAL GOVERNMENT VERSUS CREDITS TO TAXPAYERS

A major issue underlying a property tax relief program is a concern with political accountability. One particularly relevant concern is with the effect of intergovernmental aids (intended for mill rate reduction) on own-source local spending. The concern is that the aid system drives a wedge between those making spending and revenue raising decisions which may encourage higher local own-source spending—i.e., intergovernmental aid may be stimulative. The evidence suggests that credits are substantially more likely than grants to stimulate local spending.

Intergovernmental aids potentially can stimulate additional own-source local spending in different ways. First, a credit subtracted from the gross property tax and paid by the state reduces the effective price the property owner pays for a given level of local services. If the property owner is not at the $650 credit ceiling, each additional dollar increase in local own-source expenditures will cost only 46 cents ($1.00-.54 state-paid credit). Since the property owner pays a tax price less than the value of the increased expenditure, there will be an incentive to purchase goods/services through the public sector—e.g., tennis courts, swimming pools and perhaps even trash collection—rather than through the private sector where taxpayers pay the full cost of goods/services.

In addition, the taxpayer realizes an increase in disposable income as a result of the lower tax price paid for locally provided services. In other words, the taxpayer has more after-tax income to spend on additional public, as well as private, goods and services. Thus, a property tax credit reduces the effective cost of local services to property owners and is said to stimulate local own-source expenditures through both price and income effects.

Alternatively, a lump-sum grant from the state to local governments (e.g., LGA) does not alter relative prices, but rather only increases the amount of resources available to local jurisdictions. In fact, the government could use the additional resources for local property tax relief and actually reduce own-source revenues. Therefore, for an equal level of expenditures by the state, the potential stimulative impact of this type of intergovernmental aid is less than one with both a price and income effect.

The commission has empirically tested the hypothesis that intergovernmental aids stimulate additional local own-source expenditures using data for 174 Minnesota cities with population above 2,500.[5] The model employed used an ordinary, least-squares regression technique to explain differences in net property tax levies per capita (gross property tax levies minus all the credits). The impact of the different forms of intergovernmental aids (LGA lump-sum grants and credits) on local own-source cities in tax capacity, base composition, and "need" or preference for services.

Both property tax credits paid to cities (homestead, wetlands, and taconite credits) and local government aids, on average, tend to stimulate additional local own-source spending, i.e., own-source spending net tax levy is higher than would have been expected if there were no intergovernmental aid programs. Credits, on average, are nearly three times more stimulative than local government aid payments. Various alternative specifications of the model produced results consistent with this finding of a relatively greater stimulative effect of credits vis-a-vis lump-sum local government aids.

Several warnings are in order. First, the results reflect the situation for cities on average rather than any particular city. Second, the model explains about three-quarters of the variation in net property tax levies per capita across the 174 cities studies. Third, the empirical results can be used to estimate the impact of small incremental changes in the values of the credits and grants, but cannot be used to estimate accurately the impact of large shifts in funding for these programs.

## POLICY IMPLICATIONS

The information presented above sets the stage for a series of decisions that must be made in order to rationalize the Minnesota property tax structure. These decisions include

- the number of classes to be applied;
- the classification ratio relationships among the classes (of course, if uniformity is agreed to, the ratios are always units); and
- the design of the property tax relief system.

In its deliberations, the commission examined a wide range of alternative property tax structures, which combined various classification schemes with property tax relief devices. Based on information summarized above, the commission unanimously agreed to replace the existing property tax with a greatly simplified approach that explicitly limited the number of classes to the following three: residential homestead and agriculture (most favored classes), residential nonhomestead and apartments (next favored), and all other property.[6]

Having agreed to these three classes, the next step was to examine the policy tradeoffs among alternative three-class systems. As noted, several alternatives were examined (see the appendix to this chapter), with the final recommendation that Minnesota adopt a three-class property tax combined with a single tax relief credit (in place of the present eleven devices) that is targeted to low-income homeowners and owners of small farms (520 acres or less) and a state-to-local block grant, which amounts to approximately one-third of total property tax collections, to be distributed in a manner that equalizes fiscal disparities among local units of government.

This system is designed so that in the first year the change would be revenue neutral—i.e., in the aggregate there would be no net change in state or local revenues. In subsequent years, however, the commission's property tax would exert a downward pressure on local mill rates—an indirect but genuine form of property tax relief.

These recommendations are presented in summary form in chapter 1 and in full at the end of this chapter. The major policy implications of the commission's recommendations are to:

• simplify and make explicit the system of property tax classification;
• nearly eliminate the stimulative effect of the existing state-financed property tax relief structure, which over time encourages higher, not lower, local mill rates;
• reduce the tax burdens on high-valued residential residences and large high-valued farms and slightly increase the tax on large, low-valued farms (as the result of the combined effect of the classification-tax relief-block grant reforms);[7] and
• reduce the tax on small farms, and reduce or hold harmless the tax burden on low- and mid-income homeowners (due to the combined effect of the classification change targeted credit that is inversely related to homeowner income and real estate wealth).


## FINAL COMMENT

During the time the commission had been deliberating the property tax, the U.S. Treasury Department released details on a tax reform plan that included the elimination of the deductibility of state and local property, income, and sales taxes in computing the federal individual income tax. There is little reason to doubt that this feature of the federal tax reform will be included in the president's proposal to be sent to Congress in May 1985. (Ed. note: The president's program, released on May 28, 1985, did include this provision.)

If this provision or even a compromise (e.g., deductibility limited to the tax paid on excess of some percentage of one's AGI) is passed, it will further emphasize the importance to Minnesota of reforming its property tax laws so that the system is not designed—as it now is—to stimulate higher property taxes over time.

## RECOMMENDATIONS

### AN EQUITABLE AND EFFICIENT PROPERTY TAX STRUCTURE

The commission concludes that the present complex system of classification and multiple tax credit and refund devices, while ostensibly designed to promote equity among taxpayers, in fact results in a tax structure with many capricious and unintended results. Specifically the existing system

- builds incentives for higher local spending, and thereby higher tax burdens, for all classes of Minnesota taxpayers over the long run;
- provides tax relief in a poorly targeted manner;
- discourages efficient tax administration as well as taxpayer understanding and participation in the fiscal system, thereby placing control of the system in the hands of technicians rather than taxpayers.

Accordingly, the commission recommends elimination of the present Minnesota classified property tax and, in its place, the adoption of a system that employs three classes to be valued at full market value:

- Class I: Residential homestead and all agricultural property will be assessed at the lowest classification ratio.
- Class II: Residential nonhomestead and apartments will be assessed at the next highest classification ratio; and
- Class III: All other property will be assessed at the highest ratio.

The commission specifically notes that in its deliberations it has adopted a classification rate of 33% for Class I property, 66% for Class II property, and 100% for all other property.

Because this reform will create a fiscal windfall to the state general fund of an amount equal to approximately 30% of the statewide gross property tax collections, the commission recommends that this windfall be fully used for relief of the local property tax burden, and that this relief be provided as a combination of grants designed to equalize fiscal disparities among local jurisdictions and provide lower mill rates; and income/wealth adjusted property tax credit, (circuit breaker) targeted to homeowners, renters, and farmers with low income and low wealth.

In making this recommendation, the commission explicitly recognizes and stresses that because the present system of tax credits has been eliminated, the longer-term effect of this reform will be to reduce the incentive for increased local spending. This, in turn, will result in a fiscal system that places a downward pressure on the property tax burdens of all taxpayers, thereby effectively enhancing the Minnesota tradition of minimizing the reliance on the property tax. The commission also notes that a failure to reform the property tax system along the lines specified above will, over time, only result in increased property tax burdens on homes, farms, and commercial properties alike.

The commission further concludes that as this property tax structure is adopted, its operation will gradually permit the state to reduce reliance upon the use of the circuit breaker in favor of a property tax system that more closely approximates a tax on property value, with explicit adjustments for income to be made primarily through the vehicle of the progressive individual income tax.

## PROPERTY TAX RELIEF: THE INCOME/WEALTH ADJUSTED PROPERTY TAX CREDIT

The property tax is designed to be a tax on that part of wealth that is held in the form of real estate. Thus, the ability to pay the property tax is related to the property wealth as well as to the income of the taxpayer. Taxpayers with relatively little property and little income have less ability to pay property taxes than those who have more property, more income, or both.

The current circuit breaker program for property tax relief is very complex and designed to be integrated with the existing system of tax credits. The commission has recommended eliminating these credits; with the credits removed, the result is that as property taxes rise, some taxpayers with very low-valued homes get no relief from the state and pay all of the new tax themselves. Other taxpayers, with both incomes and homes of moderate value, get 100% relief from additional taxes, thereby creating a strong incentive for these persons to vote for all property tax increases knowing that the state will pay their share of the cost of new public services. In addition, the circuit breaker provides a greater percentage of relief (up to a maximum) for a low-income/high-property-value taxpayer than for a taxpayer with both low income and low property value. And at every included income level, there is an abrupt cap on the amount of circuit breaker relief available. As taxes rise and taxpayers reach this cap, the share of extra tax borne by the lowest-income taxpayer rise abruptly from 5% to 100% of new tax levies. For moderate-income taxpayers, the extra share jumps from 50% to 100%.

With these problems in mind, the commission recommends replacing the current circuit breaker program with an alternative system for property tax relief that is based on a combination of household income and residential value. The system would have the following characteristics:

- The amount of tax relief for any taxpayer would be a simple percentage of the total tax bill. For some taxpayers the percentage would be zero; they would get no assistance. No taxpayer would receive 100% property tax relief.
- For households with the same property wealth, the size of the fraction of state-paid relief would fall smoothly as income rises—higher-income households would get a smaller percentage of property tax relief. The percentage would become zero above some income level.
- For households with the same income, the size of the fraction of state-paid relief will fall smoothly as the home value (real estate wealth) rises—wealthier households will get a smaller percentage of relief. The size of the percentage would become zero above some property value.
- Renters and homeowners will be treated the same in determining their privileges for property tax relief. Therefore, when renters and homeowners have the same income, renters—who have no wealth in the form of an owner-occupied home—will get a larger amount of tax relief than homeowners.
- The above described program can be designed to spend no more than the current circuit breaker.
- Small farms (520 acres or less) of homesteaded agricultural land also will be eligible for property tax relief. Relief fractions for agricultural land will be determined separately from the fractions for residential property taxes. The agricultural fractions will decrease with greater value of this land. (The value of the homestead and one acre are not included for agricultural relief. These are eligible for relief under the homeowner part of the program.) The fractions also will decrease with greater household income. The relief fractions for agricultural land can be chosen in a manner to target expenditures for agricultural land relief to any designated amount.

## APPENDIX TO CHAPₗER 17

As noted in the text, the commission examined numerous alternative property tax structures. Once the decision was made to adopt three classes, the next step was to analyze the alternatives under different assumptions pertaining to the classification ratios across classes. Next studied was the effect on local mill rates of alternative amounts of a state-to-local block grant distributed in a way that equalizes fiscal disparities among competing jurisdictions (no specific formula was specified). Tables A-1 through A-3 illustrate nine sets of these alternatives that were examined. Table A-2 presents effective rates by major tax classifications, assuming the ratios of assessed value to market value are residential homestead and all agricultural, 33%; residential homestead, 66%; and all other, 100%. Table A-3 gives ratios in a 15%-20%-40% set. The commission finally voted to use the variant described in Table A-2, column 4 ($624 million grant) as its illustration for the "balanced package" described in chapter 1. This $624 million used up all but $179 million of the state general fund windfall resulting from the elimination of the nine existing property tax credits and three refund programs. Accordingly, the remaining $179 million was used on the illustration to fund the targeted property tax credit to low-income homeowners and small farms (See text discussion).

TABLE A-1

Minnesota "Effective Property Tax Rates" Based on the Three Classes Adopted by the Commission under Alternative Ratios

|  | Actual '84 | Variant 13%/26%/39% | Variant 15%/20%/40% |
|---|---|---|---|
| Residential | | | |
| 3 Residential Homestead | 1.2 | 1.8 | 2.0 |
| 4 Residential Nonhomestead | 3.0 | 3.6 | 2.7 |
| 9 3C: Ag. & Nonag. | 0.3 | 1.7 | 1.9 |
| Agricultural | | | |
| 1 Agricultural Homestead | 0.7 | 1.2 | 1.3 |
| 2 Agricultural Nonhomestead | 1.1 | 1.2 | 1.2 |
| 12 Timberlands | 1.7 | 1.3 | 1.4 |
| Apartments | | | |
| 5 Apartments | 3.7 | 3.7 | 2.8 |
| 6 Subsidized Apartments | 2.2 | 3.6 | 2.7 |
| Seasonal | | | |
| 10 Seasonal-rec./Residential | 1.6 | 3.4 | 3.2 |
| Commercial/Industrial | | | |
| 7 Commercial | 4.4 | 5.1 | 5.1 |
| 8 Industrial | 4.6 | 5.1 | 5.1 |
| 11 Commercial Seasonal | 1.3 | 3.3 | 3.1 |
| 13 Vacant Land | 4.2 | 5.4 | 5.2 |
| 14 Mineral | 6.2 | 5.5 | 5.4 |
| 15 Personal & PU | 3.7 | 4.2 | 4.1 |
| 16 Railroad | 4.7 | 5.0 | 4.9 |
| All Property | 1.8 | 2.3 | 2.3 |

*Source:* Calculated from the Minnesota House Research Property Tax Simulation Model for the Minnesota Tax Study Commission, 1984.

[1]Net of existing tax credits.

[2]Effective rates do not take into account any proposed tax relief.

TABLE A-2

| | Ratio | (Index) |
|---|---|---|
| Res. Home/Ag | 13% | (100) |
| Res. Nonhome & Apts. | 26% | (200) |
| Other | 39% | (300) |

| | Actual 84 | Variant #3 With No Mill Rate Reduction | With $803 Million for Mill Rate Reduction | With $624 Million for Mill Rate Reduction | With $300 Million for Mill Rate Reduction |
|---|---|---|---|---|---|
| **Residential** | | | | | |
| Residential Homestead | 1.2 | 1.8 | 1.3 | 1.4 | 1.6 |
| Residential Nonhomestead | 3.0 | 3.6 | 2.6 | 2.8 | 3.2 |
| 3cc: Ag and Nonag. | 0.3 | 1.7 | 1.2 | 1.3 | 1.5 |
| **Agricultural** | | | | | |
| Agricultural Homestead | 0.7 | 1.2 | 0.9 | 0.9 | 1.0 |
| Agricultural Nonhomestead | 1.1 | 1.2 | 0.9 | 0.9 | 1.0 |
| Timberlands | 1.7 | 1.3 | 0.9 | 1.0 | 1.2 |
| **Apartments** | | | | | |
| Apartments | 3.7 | 3.7 | 2.6 | 2.9 | 3.3 |
| Subsidized Apartments | 2.2 | 3.6 | 2.6 | 2.8 | 3.2 |
| **Seasonal** | | | | | |
| Seaonal - Rec/Res. | 1.6 | 3.4 | 2.4 | 2.6 | 3.0 |
| **Commercial/Industrial** | | | | | |
| Commercial | 4.4 | 5.1 | 3.6 | 4.0 | 4.5 |
| Industrial | 4.6 | 5.1 | 3.6 | 4.0 | 4.5 |
| Commercial Seasonal | 1.3 | 3.3 | 2.3 | 2.6 | 2.9 |
| Vacant Land | 4.2 | 5.4 | 3.8 | 4.2 | 4.8 |
| Mineral | 6.2 | 5.5 | 3.9 | 4.3 | 4.9 |
| Personal and PU | 3.7 | 4.2 | 3.0 | 3.3 | 3.7 |
| Railroad | 4.7 | 5.0 | 3.6 | 3.9 | 4.5 |
| **All Property** | 1.8 | 2.3 | 1.6 | 1.8 | 2.0 |

TABLE A-3

| | Ratio | (Index) |
|---|---|---|
| Res. Home/Ag | 15% | (100) |
| Res. Nonhome & Apts. | 20% | (133) |
| Other | 40% | (267) |

| | Actual 84 | Variant #3 With No Mill Rate Reduction | With $803 Million for Mill Rate Reduction | With $624 Million for Mill Rate Reduction | With $300 Million for Mill Rate Reduction |
|---|---|---|---|---|---|
| **Residential** | | | | | |
| Residential Homestead | 1.2 | 2.0 | 1.4 | 1.6 | 1.8 |
| Residential Nonhomestead | 3.0 | 2.7 | 1.9 | 2.1 | 2.4 |
| 3cc: Ag and Nonag. | 0.3 | 1.9 | 1.4 | 1.5 | 1.7 |
| **Agricultural** | | | | | |
| Agricultural Homestead | 0.7 | 1.3 | 0.9 | 1.0 | 1.6 |
| Agricultural Nonhomestead | 1.1 | 1.2 | 0.9 | 0.9 | 1.1 |
| Timberlands | 1.7 | 1.4 | 1.0 | 1.1 | 1.2 |
| **Apartments** | | | | | |
| Apartments | 3.7 | 2.8 | 2.0 | 2.2 | 2.5 |
| Subsidized Apartments | 2.2 | 2.7 | 1.9 | 2.1 | 2.4 |
| **Seasonal** | | | | | |
| Seaonal - Rec/Res. | 1.6 | 3.2 | 2.3 | 2.5 | 2.9 |
| **Commercial/Industrial** | | | | | |
| Commercial | 4.4 | 5.1 | 3.6 | 4.0 | 4.5 |
| Industrial | 4.6 | 5.1 | 3.6 | 4.0 | 4.5 |
| Commercial Seasonal | 1.3 | 3.1 | 2.2 | 2.4 | 2.8 |
| Vacant Land | 4.2 | 5.2 | 3.7 | 4.0 | 4.6 |
| Mineral | 6.2 | 5.4 | 3.8 | 4.2 | 4.8 |
| Personal and PU | 3.7 | 4.1 | 2.9 | 3.2 | 3.7 |
| Railroad | 4.7 | 4.9 | 3.5 | 3.8 | 4.4 |
| **All Property** | 1.8 | 2.3 | 1.6 | 1.8 | 2.0 |

## ENDNOTES

1. The property tax is based on the value of real property. In this context, equal treatment of equals suggests that property owners with equal-valued properties should be subject to equal property tax liabilities. This is in contrast to other taxes where equity is defined in terms of income—those with equal income pay equal taxes.

2. For a detailed discussion see Lisa A. Roden, *Minerals Taxation in Minnesota,* a technical paper presented to the Minnesota Tax Study Commission.

3. Household income extends the definition of income used for tax purposes by including otherwise exempt sources of money income, e.g., social security, pensions, and other transfer payments.

4. In moving from tax base values in column 2 to gross tax amounts in column 3, the taxing decisions of local governments come into play. These decisions are affected indirectly by state policies in many areas (e.g., local government structure and state aid) undertaken for reasons other than affecting interclass tax uniformity.

5. Michael E. Bell and John H. Bowman, "Property Tax Differences Among Cities: The Effect of Property Tax Relief Programs," in *Staff Papers,* vol. 2 of the *Final Report of the Minnesota Tax Study Commission,* ed. Robert D. Ebel and Therese J. McGuire (St. Paul: Butterworth Legal Publishers, 1985).

6. Residential homestead includes agricultural homes plus one acre. Residential nonhomestead refers to three or fewer rental units; apartments are four or more units. Agricultural includes timberland.

7. Based on staff computations for various representative residential homesteads and agricultural property by value and size. Data presented to the commission, December 8, 1984. Before the targeted credit was applied, the effective tax rate fell from 1.31% to 1.01% on large (620, 750, and 800 acres) and high-valued ($1,200/acre to $1,500/acre) farms; rose from 0.88% to 0.99% on relatively large, low-valued farms (e.g., 800 acres and $500/acre); and rose from 0.83% to 1.0% on small high- and low-valued farms (320 acres to 250 acres at $1,500/acre to $500/acre).

# 18
# Levy Limitations

## INTRODUCTION

Minnesota has a system of programs to limit the amount of property tax collected by local jurisdictions. Every local levy in Minnesota must be authorized by some state statute. In many cases, the levy is limited by the same statute that authorizes it. Cities and counties may levy for general and special purposes under four limitation programs:

Overall levy limitation
Mill rate limitation
Per capita levy limitation
Charter city limitation

As of 1984, towns are subject to relatively few levy limitations. School districts are subject to both general purpose and special purpose levy limitations. The levies of special taxing districts like hospital districts, the metropolitan council, park districts, and others, are each limited by their specific authorizing legislation. These limits are not discussed here.

This chapter is organized in two sections. The first section briefly analyzes the four levy limit programs listed above as they affect Minnesota's cities and counties.

The second section discusses the impact of the overall levy limitation on distribution of tax effort and on simplicity in the tax system. There are two basic findings of the analysis. First, the current limitations are not simple to understand or administer. Second, whether or not the overall levy limitations reduce property tax collections, they do not achieve goals in the equalization of tax effort. Improvements in distribution of tax effort must be achieved through a system of equalizing state to local government grants.

## LEVY LIMITATION PROGRAMS ON CITIES
## AND COUNTIES

Four forms of limitations on property tax levies are used in Minnesota. One, the overall levy limitation, applies to counties and larger cities. The others—the per capita limit, mill rate limit, and charter city limit—apply to various cities and each city is subject to more than one limitation. All applicable limits must be met in each city.

*Per capita limit.* Nearly all cities, no matter how small their population, are subject to the so-called *$54 per capita levy limitation.* The actual per capita limitation for payable-1985 is $252.18 and reflects cost-of-living adjustments to the $54 base established in 1971. This per capita amount limits the sum of special and general purpose levies; the total of all levies cannot exceed $252.18 multiplied by the population, as measured by recent population data.

*Mill rate limitation.* All cities are subject to the mill rate limitation. For statutory cities, the applicable mill rate is ten mills, if adjusted assessed value is $1,500,000 or more, and eleven and two-thirds mills, if less than $1,500,000. The statutory city may levy for general fund purposes up to the mill rate limit, plus a cost of living adjustment which is $198.16 per capita for payable-1985. Charter cities, including iron ore charter cities, have mill rate limitations of 13 1/3 mills plus the cost-of-living adjustment.

*Charter city limitations.* Charter cities face an additional limitation as imposed by their charter. Iron ore charter cities are limited by the cost-of-living adjustment plus the charter authorization for general fund purposes. Other charter cities are bound by the charter authorization for general fund purposes. Charter limitations apply in most smaller (third and fourth class) cities.

*Overall levy limitation.* For payable year-1985, overall levy limitations will apply in the 105 cities with 5,000 or more population and in all eighty-seven of Minnesota's counties. It is the most binding limitation measure for these cities and the counties. The amount of the overall levy limitation is the difference between the jurisdiction's adjusted levy limit base for 1985 and its grant of local government aids for 1985. Where applicable, taconite aid, natural resources aid, and reimbursement for wetlands and native prairie also are subtracted from the base. If the jurisdiction has adopted special levies that are exempt from the overall limitation,[1] the total levy certified to the jurisdiction is the sum of the exempted special levies and the levy limitation. When a jurisdiction actually levies in excess of its certified levy, the penalty can be a $1 loss in local government aid for each $3 of excess levy. This penalty is avoided if the jurisdiction agrees to go under its levy limit for the next year by the amount of the current year's excess.

MECHANICS OF THE LIMIT

The overall levy limitation was introduced as part of the package of policies referred to as the Minnesota Miracle. In order to reduce local property tax, the state legislature began making substantial grants to local governments. Then, in 1971, local levy limitations were imposed to insure that property tax burdens would fall, and that communities would not use state aid to increase the level of local spending.

In the years since 1971, there have been many complex and confusing changes in the base for calculating the levy limit in each locality. Initially, the levy limit base in each jurisdiction was set equal to the total of state aid plus the property tax levy for 1971; this base was automatically extended by 6% each year through 1981, and by 8% for 1982 and 1983. In addition to the automatic extensions, other changes include adjustments for population growth, urban development, inflation, the folding of new items into the base, and subtracting certain special aids from the base. A locality may also vote for a temporary or a permanent extension of the levy limit base. Thus, the levy limit base is not tied to the property tax base; the consequence is that levy limits are not necessarily linked to local tax capacity.

With so many changes and adjustments over time, it is unlikely that the 1984 levy limit base for each locality is comparably related to its capacity to raise property tax revenue, i.e., its property tax base. An important simplification to the program may be to establish a link between the levy limit base and the value of taxable property.

Cities and counties are eligible to levy a tax which is exempt from the limitation under twenty-two special exempt levy programs. The revenue from these levies is earmarked for the specific program. But, if the jurisdiction previously had covered this program from the limited levy, use of the exempt levy can free potential revenue allowed in the limitation.

It is hard to judge if localities are constrained to collect less property tax than they otherwise might choose. Localities have a strong incentive not to exceed their limits when each $3 of over taxation can cost $1 in local government aid. When a locality collects less than its allowable limit, the cause could be lack of demand for revenue, implying that the limit is not binding. But the cause also can be avoidance of the penalty in which case the limit is binding.

While the $3 penalty encourages a community not to levy over the limit, another penalty encouraged communities not to levy under the limit for payable years 1982 and 1983. Before payable-1982, a beginning point for determining the levy limit was the levy limit of the prior year. For 1982 and 1983, a beginning point was the lesser of the actual levy and the limitation in the prior years. Localities under the limitation in 1981 were penalized with a more narrow limitation in 1982 and 1983. Even though this procedure has been changed, some communities continue to levy to their limitation as insurance against future rule changes.

## DEALING WITH THE CONSTRAINT

Localities facing a levy limit have five options available for adjusting to the constraint:

- Collect revenue through special levies exempt from the limitation;
- Collect revenue through nonproperty tax local sources;
- Collect more property tax and pay the penalty;
- Vote to extend the levy limitation;
- Reduce the level of local public services.

The evidence below suggests that the overall limitation may be constraining in many jurisdictions and these jurisdictions may have used options (1) or (2) to adjust to the constraint. Options (3) and (4) also are used. There is no empirical evidence to establish the extent to which option (5) is used to circumvent the limit.

Table 1 presents data for jurisdictions subject to the overall levy limitation for payable years 1980 to 1984. Column (1) shows that the number of jurisdictions covered by the limit has fluctuated in recent years. In 1980 and 1981, cities of less than 2,500 were exempt from the levy limitation; in 1982 and 1983, all cities were limited; and in 1984 cities with populations below 5,000 were dropped. Columns (2) and (3) report the number over the limit and those voting to extend the levy limit. For these jurisdictions the limit

TABLE 1
Jurisdictions Subject to Overall Levy Limitation;
Data for Taxes Payable, 1980-84

|  | (1) Number of Localities | (2) Number Exceeding Levy Limit* | (3) Number Voting to Extend Limit | (4) Levy Limitation ($000) | (5) Total Under Limit ($000) | (6) Total Exempt Special Levies ($000) |
|---|---|---|---|---|---|---|
| Cities |  |  |  |  |  |  |
| 1980 | 175 | 14/9 |  | $196,334 | $27,060 | $ 94,469 |
| 1981 | 175 | 7/6 | 2 | 229,068 | 32,468 | 113,106 |
| 1982 | 885/185** | 36/23 | 4 | 268,082 | 4,898 | 93,957 |
| 1983 | 885/185** | 14/8 | 6 | 260,955 | 2,737 | 131,109 |
| 1984p | 105*** | 13/4 | 2 | 271,421 | 7,374 | 123,752 |
| Counties |  |  |  |  |  |  |
| 1980 | 87 | 7/6 |  | 308,164 | 43,721 | 230,344 |
| 1981 | 87 | 6/6 | 6 | 334,447 | 30,557 | 257,458 |
| 1982 | 87 | 8/5 | 19 | 337,638 | 11,409 | 308,956 |
| 1983 | 87 | 4/2 | 4 | 357,342 | 8,190 | 332,581 |
| 1984p | 87 | 3/3 | 3 | 396,343 | 29,734 | 369,409 |

*Source:* Staff Computations.

*The first number is all jurisdictions exceeding the levy limit, the second is the number exceeding the limit by $1,000 or more.

**All 855 cities were subject to the overall levy limitation. These data are for only the 185 cities with population of 2,500 or more.

***All cities with population of 5,000 or more.

constrained the amount of revenue the jurisdiction could collect from the property tax.

Columns (4) and (5) indicate the total of the levy limits for all jurisdictions and the amount by which the actual limited levies are under the limitation. Especially in 1982 and 1983, the unused portion of the levy privilege was very small.

Column (6) indicates the dollar value of special levies that are exempt from the levy limitation. The term *special* has two, easily confused usages in the levy limitation. Column (6) refers to the twenty-two special levies that are exempt from the overall levy limit as identified by Minnesota Statutes 275.50, subdivisions 5 and 7. The column does not report the other special levies which are subject to the overall limitation. Both levies, however, are counted as part of the total limited levy allowed to the local jurisdiction.

Comparing columns (4) and (6) and counties to cities, it is clear that exempt levies are larger in relation to the levy limitation for counties. This is due primarily to the counties' obligations for the costs of social services— Minnesota supplemental assistance, aid to families with dependent children (AFDC), medical assistance, and general assistance—which are exempt from the levy limitation. This special levy is limited to a maximum increase of 18% per year.

Data for all cities and counties subject to the overall levy limitation in payable-1984 show that sixty-two of eighty-seven counties (71%) are either within 5% or exceed their allowable limit. For cities, eighty-four (80%) are within 5% of, or over, their general purpose levy limitation.

## SPECIAL EXEMPT LEVIES

Individual cities and counties appear to use exempt special levies more intensively if they are near their levy limit. The average ratio of special levies to limited levies for 1984 is 93.2% for counties and 45.6% for cities. Only fourteen of the eighty-seven counties and thirty-two of the 105 cities are above this average. These numbers are far fewer than half the jurisdictions, implying that at least some are outliers with much greater than average ratios. If the levy limitation is extremely tight, a jurisdiction will have a strong incentive to use exempt levies, if possible, for revenues to support the specifically allowed services. The share of the allowable special levy that is unused is, on average, 7.5% for counties and 2.7% for cities. Sixty-eight of eighty-seven counties and seventy-eight of 105 cities have less than average slack.

## LOCAL NONTAX REVENUES

Another substitute for local property tax revenue is local revenue raised from nontax sources. A jurisdiction confronted with the penalty for an excess property tax levy may use nontax revenue sources even if this revenue is more costly to collect and administer. Table 2 contains aggregate data for local tax and local nontax revenues in Minnesota for various years beginning in 1972. The table also reports fees and charges and special assessments, a subcategory of nontax revenue. Columns (4) and (5) show that both total nontax receipts and the subcategory have increased as a percentage of locally generated tax since 1972, with dramatic increases from 1978 on.

The conclusion to be drawn from Table 2 is that local nontax revenue has become increasingly important, and local tax revenue decreasingly so, since the late 1970s. This alone does not prove the hypothesis that levy limitations encourage jurisdictions to exploit nontax revenue sources. For example, a greater commitment to the benefits received principle in raising local revenue could account for the same result. Indeed, the trend toward greater reliance on fees rather than taxes is nationwide with fees and charges generating about one-third of all municipal own-source revenue in 1982 as compared to less than one-fourth in the early 1970s. Although Minnesota has tended to rely more heavily than the U.S. state on nontax revenue with a total of more than one-half of own-source funds in 1982 and about one-third of funds in 1972, it may nevertheless be part of this trend.

In view of Minnesota's heavy use of nontax local revenues, it seems unlikely that these revenues could substitute for additional cuts in local government aids. In 1981, local government aid was reduced in mid-year. Many jurisdictions could not arrange for immediate offsetting increases in local levies and these localities were pressed for revenue. Local tax revenue fell in 1981 while the nominal and real values of nontax revenue rose. If

TABLE 2
Local Tax and Nontax Revenues in Minnesota

|  | (1) Total Local Tax Revenue | (2) Total Local Nontax Revenue | (3) Total Fees and Charges and Special Assessments | (4) Nontax Revenue Percent of Revenue | (5) Fees, Charges Assessment as Percent of Tax Revenue |
|---|---|---|---|---|---|
| 1972 | $ 905,467 | $ 508,905 | $327,718 | .60 | .36 |
| 1975 | 921,720 | 691,048 | 448,008 | .75 | .49 |
| 1978 | 1,261,155 | 934,914 | 627,740 | .74 | .50 |
| 1979 | 1,304,847 | 1,123,037 | 698,150 | .86 | .54 |
| 1980 | 1,382,323 | 1,337,214 | 800,877 | .97 | .58 |
| 1981 | 1,371,584 | 1,616,432 | 935,306 | 1.18 | .68 |
| 1982 | 1,407,313 | 1,750,517 | 974,663 | 1.24 | .69 |

Source: Compiled from tables in Office of the Legislative Auditor, State of Minnesota, *State and Local Government Finances in Minnesota, A Review of Trends in Revenues and Expenditures 1957-1982,* November 1983.

Minnesota broadened the local fee system in 1981, there is likely to be little slack in that system in 1984. Thus, any shift in the revenue raising responsibility to localities should be accomplished by an easing of the limitations on property tax or opening new tax sources.

## THE EFFECTS OF LIMITATIONS ON LOCAL PROPERTY TAX

Limitation of property tax revenues can have an impact on the simplicity and fairness of the tax itself. This section examines the overall limitation by these criteria.

Minnesota's system of limitations is not simple and few Minnesotans can recall the rationale for our current limitations. The original purpose of the overall levy limitation was to guarantee that the property tax reductions made possible by local government aids would occur. However, the limit for each jurisdiction is determined by procedures that change virtually every year. Jurisdictions may be unsure what the limit will be next year, what formula will be used to derive the limit, if programs will be shifted from exempt to limited levy coverage (or the reverse), and even if the jurisdiction will be subject to the program.

Accordingly, a case can be made for revising the limits or even eliminating them altogether. The options for revision include simplification and adjusting the limits in order to enhance fiscal equalization among localities.

### SIMPLIFICATION

*Adopt a long-term formula.* One clear path for simplification is to make a long-term commitment to a specific formula for determining the limit; this would avoid the annual and confusing changes in determining which programs and jurisdictions are limited and to what extent. A vehicle for simplification is to untie the levy limit base from its tangled relationship to the 1971 tax-and-aids and to establish a direct link of the levy limit base to the property tax base in each locality. This would enable any limitation measure to derive directly from the base for the tax collections that are intended to be limited. Some adjustments could be made for inflation, population change, or other items.

*Consolidate programs and increase the limit.* Simplification could involve a permanent increase in the levy limitation to fold in some exempt levies that represent ordinary or maintenance programs of the jurisdiction. However, the state may always wish to maintain some exempt levies for extra-ordinary programs like those that are imposed on the locality or that guarantee its financial interests. For example, any legally authorized program where the locality is required to provide matching funds might be kept outside the levy limit or levies protecting the principal and interest on indebtedness may need to be outside of levy limitations. The goal should be to develop a rationale for those levies which are to be exempt, and to allow exemptions only in keeping with the rationale. Other levies could then be covered by a predictable, well-defined, levy limitation.

## FISCAL DISPARITIES

Property tax capacity is not evenly distributed among jurisdictions. A property-rich jurisdiction can support any given amount of public services at a lower mill rate than a property-poor jurisdiction. Due to a lower fiscal capacity, the poorer jurisdiction must make a greater effort (in terms of millage) to support local services.

The rationale for local government aid to Minnesota's localities includes equalizing for disparities in fiscal capacity and effort. The evidence shows that LGA does tend to soften these disparities.[2]

Levy limitations do not have equalization of disparities as a direct purpose. However, the limitations are set as the difference between the levy limit base and local government aid. Thus, to the extent that aid equalizes disparities, the levy limits could reflect this equalization through a narrower range of allowable mill rates. This result, however, depends in part on the levy limit base being closely tied to the taxable property base.

The limitations may also be examined as mill rate equivalents on the equalized property value, i.e., as the mill rate which will generate the allowed and limited amount of general purpose revenue. If levy limitations and local aids actually ameliorate disparities in property tax capacity, then these mill rate equivalents will be clustered. In actuality, these equivalencies are widely dispersed and suggest that after LGA, levy limitations do not substantially perform the job of reducing disparities in fiscal effort.

For counties, mill rate equivalents range from 4.92 in Renville County to 20.51 in Lake County. This range moves more than 50% in either direction from the average value of 11.27. The evidence for cities is more dramatic. The range of mill rate equivalents is 1.10 to 55.73 while the average is 12.24.

## ELIMINATE THE LIMITS?

*Elimination of the overall levy limitations.*   From the perspective of tax effort, the mill rate equivalents show that limitation varies widely and may be capriciously felt. It is clear that the degree of limitation on the tax effort is not uniformly distributed across jurisdictions. Jurisdictions already have options for getting around these limitations. If local government aids are reduced, the original need for levy limitation is correspondingly reduced. If the homestead credit and circuit breaker programs are altered or eliminated, the state will have much less financial interest in restraining property taxation.

The negative consequences of eliminating limitations are such that, to the extent state grants and property tax relief programs persist, the state bears part of the burden of local tax decisions. Also, the state no longer has a check on the taxing behavior of local jurisdictions. To improve local accountability if levy limits are eliminated, localities could be required to make full disclosure statements before new mill rates are established. For example, property owners can be issued a statement showing their tax bill for next year at current mill rates and the corresponding bill under proposed new rates. Through this process of prior disclosure, local taxpayers potentially can influence their tax obligations and the accountability of local officials.

## RECOMMENDATION

### RESTRUCTURING THE PROPERTY TAX LEVY LIMITATION LAW

Minnesota has been a leader among the fifty states for its long-term commitment to providing state grants to local jurisdictions. These grants enable localities to provide public services at much lower property tax rates than is true for many other states. To protect the mill rate reductions, a system of overall levy limitations for larger cities and counties was adopted in 1971. In view of the state's substantial programs of property tax credits and relief, levy limits also help to guard against an unbudgeted drain on state funds. Without limitation, local property tax increases could occur and be significantly funded by state assistance to individual taxpayers.

However, the overall levy limitations need revision. They were established based on actual tax collections and state aids granted in 1971. Since then, the limits have been patched and altered, jurisdictions have been added to and dropped from the program, and some jurisdictions have voted permanent extensions of their limitations. The program needs to be thought through again, simplified, and clarified for the second half of the 1980s. Some or all of the commission's property tax recommendations will affect property tax structure at the local level, and they, in turn, may add to the need for revision of the overall levy limits.

## ENDNOTES

1. As allowed by Minnesota Statutes, section 275.50, subdivisions 5 and 7.

2. Michael E. Bell, "Minnesota's Local Government Aids Program," in *Staff Papers,* vol. 2 of the *Final Report of the Minnesota Tax Study Commission,* ed. Robert D. Ebel and Therese J. McGuire (St. Paul: Butterworth Legal Publishers, 1985).

# 19

# Property Taxation of Agriculture

As an important part of Minnesota's economy, agriculture is distinguished from most other state industries by the land- and capital-intensive processes it uses to transform raw materials into finished products. Of particular significance to this commission, however, is the role played by land. Both crop production and livestock grazing are land-based activities that are necessarily dispersed over wide geographic expanses. Farmland, of which there is a relatively fixed supply in the near- to mid-term, is priced according to the expected future returns from its use. As land appreciates, it increases the wealth of its owners, and thus (relative to most other types of realty) becomes a larger and often significant proportion of the total return from farming.

Real property wealth, however, is held in the form of unrealized capital gains. It is therefore not readily available to meet farm operating expenses, including the property tax. Instead, the tax is paid out of current income, and in many years, farming yields a relatively low income. This situation—real property wealth that is disproportionately large in relation to current income—is the cause of the hardship felt by many farmers when it comes time to pay their semiannual property tax bills. It is also the crux of most agricultural property tax issues.

This chapter examines the property taxation of agriculture from both an economic and tax standpoint. It focuses its analysis on issues related to the valuation of farmland, and to the goals and methods of providing property tax relief to farmers.

## THE STATUS OF THE FARM ECONOMY

The farm economy is about twice as important to Minnesota as it is to the United States as a whole. In 1982, the farm sector comprised 7% of total state employment (with an additional 15% of state jobs estimated to be in agricultural-related industries) and 4% of state-earned income. Comparatives figures for the U.S. were 4% and 2%, respectively.

In 1982, Minnesota 94,382 farms generated about $6.7 billion in cash receipts from the marketing of crop, dairy, livestock, and poultry products. The diversity of Minnesota's agricultural base, however, has not shielded it from the volatility in American agriculture. During the 1970s, farmers became increasingly dependent on international markets to take growing levels of production. Because of the wide swings in supply and demand in export markets, Minnesota net farm income has become very unstable. It peaked in 1973, as export demand surged to record levels, supplies fell, and farm prices rose significantly. One result of this export-driven increase in farm income was higher land values. Between 1972 and 1979, the average value per acre of Minnesota farmland rose by 319% (unadjusted for inflation). Land values continued to rise for two more years even though the farm boom generally ended in 1980 when export demand weakened, harvests were record-large, and farm prices and net income fell accordingly. Since 1981, the low prospects for a rebound in farm prices and income has prompted a sharp drop in Minnesota farmland values (down 19% between 1981 and 1983).

These powerful economic forces have buffeted the family farm, which has long been the recipient of preferential property tax treatment in Minnesota. In the past six years, the number of very large farms (1,000 acres or more) has increased by 16%, while the number of mid-size family farms (50-500 acres) has decreased by 10%. In 1982, farms of 500 acres or more accounted for 47% of the state's farmland even though they represented only 15% of total Minnesota farms. The amount of land in mid-size operations has declined from 77% in 1964 to 52% in 1982. This trend toward consolidation is also reflected in farm product sales. Farms with 1982 sales of less than $40,000 comprised 56% of farms but only 12% of total sales. Those with 1982 sales of $40,000-$100,000 comprised 25% of farms and only 26% of total sales. Farms with sales of $100,000 or more comprised 18% of farms and 62% of sales. Thus, slightly over one-sixth of Minnesota farms account for nearly two-thirds of farm sales.

Instability in the farm sector is likely to continue in the years ahead. The greater reliance on export markets has increased the industry's sensitivity to interest rates, the value of the U.S. dollar, foreign competition, and high debt levels and economic recession ahead. Predicting trends in agriculture is fraught with uncertainty, but it appears that the odds for a quick return to the prosperity of the 1970s are not good. One thing that emerges, however, is that state/local tax policy is not a major factor in determining the long-term health of the farm.

## OVERVIEW OF THE PROPERTY TAX ON AGRICULTURE

The property tax is the largest tax paid by Minnesota's agricultural sector. It is levied solely on farm real estate. Personal property, such as farm machinery and livestock, has been exempt since 1967. In 1982, farmers paid

$252 million in property taxes compared to $33 million in individual income taxes. This indicates why the property tax is at the center of agricultural tax policy issues. Before considering such issues, it is necessary to place the farm tax bill into perspective with real property taxation in Minnesota and nationally, as follows:

*Tax trends.* Between 1973 and 1984, taxes on farm property increased by 171% (unadjusted for inflation). Concurrently, the equalized market value of farm property rose by 549%, or nearly three times faster than farm property taxes. Consequently, the effective tax rate (taxes as a percent of equalized market value) decreased sharply from 1.55% in 1973 to 0.65% in 1984. Effective tax rates on farm property are considerably lower than those on other types of property.

*Geographic variation in tax burdens.* The effective tax rate on farm property varies substantially across Minnesota, ranging from 0.15% to 0.26% in Lake and Cook Counties to 0.78% and 0.90% in Washington and Ramsey Counties. Overall, seventy-six of Minnesota's eighty-seven counties have effective farm property tax rates of 0.40% to 0.69%.

*Variation in tax burdens: size and type of farm.* Small and/or lower-valued homestead farms have significantly lower tax rates than larger and higher-valued homestead farms. Moreover, homestead farms have substantially lower effective rates than nonhomestead farms. Unlike homestead farms, the effective tax rate on nonhomestead farms varies little due to farm size and not at all due to per-acre value.

*Minnesota and U.S. comparative farm tax burdens.* Prior to 1970, farm taxes per $100 of full market value in Minnesota were substantially above the national average. For example, in 1960, the effective rate in Minnesota was 1.35% compared to the national average of 0.97%. In 1970, Minnesota's effective rate was 1.69% compared to 1.08% nationally. By 1981, however, Minnesota was slightly below average (0.43% vs. 0.48% nationally). Thus, the effective tax rate on farm property decreased substantially across the nation in the 1970s, but it fell further than average in Minnesota. And compared to its neighbors, Minnesota has slightly lower effective rates than Iowa and North Dakota, and significantly lower rates than Wisconsin, South Dakota, and Nebraska.

*Property taxes as percentage of net farm income.* Throughout the late 1970s, Minnesota farm property taxes were slightly below average in relation to net farm income. For example, in 1979, they were 7% of net farm income compared to 8% nationally. These rates were considerably lower than those in surrounding states. In 1979, property taxes as a percentage of net farm income were 13.6% in Iowa, 9.6% in North Dakota, 12.4% in South Dakota, and 11.6% in Wisconsin (post-1979 data not available).

These trends indicate that major steps have been taken during the last decade to lower farm property taxes in Minnesota. As will be discussed next,

Minnesota has followed a different path from most states in providing property tax relief to farmers.

## FARM PROPERTY TAX RELIEF PROGRAMS

### TAX RELIEF GOALS

Today, virtually all states have enacted some type of property tax relief program for agricultural property. Although diverse in their structure, most states' programs are designed to address two goals: (1) to ease the cash flow problems of farmers whose real property wealth is disproportionately large in relation to current income; and/or (2) to encourage the preservation of farmland.

Acceptance of these goals by state policymakers is far from universal. First, some suggest that the cash flow pinch imposed by the property tax is not a tax problem, but rather a problem of imperfect credit markets. Therefore, the provision of broad-based permanent tax relief is an inappropriate solution; instead, a newly designed private or publicly supported lending instrument is required. Second, the need to publicly influence land use patterns varies considerably between and within states: since 1970, Minnesota's total decrease in farm acreage was 1.6% compared to 21% in Anoka County. This suggests that the provision of tax relief for preservation should be done on a limited basis, not statewide.

### TAX RELIEF METHODS

There are three primary methods used to grant tax relief to farm property:

- Use-Value Assessment allows farm property to be assessed at its value in agricultural use rather than at its market value;
- Classification explicitly assigns a lower assessment ratio to farm property than to certain other types of property (use-value assessment does this implicitly);
- Tax Credits and Refunds lower the gross property tax bills of farmers through the subtraction of a nonrefundable credit or the subsequent receipt of a property tax refund.

### MINNESOTA'S USE OF PROPERTY CLASSIFICATION AND CREDITS

Unlike most states, Minnesota has relied on its system of property classification and credits as a means of providing property tax relief to farmers. Ever since the early 1970s, the state has steadily reduced the percentage of a farm's value that is subject to tax, with farm homesteads receiving more favorable tax treatment than nonhomestead farms. Next, it has provided the state school agricultural credit, which is distributed to school districts for the reduction in farm property taxes (this credit used to be calculated by applying specific mill rates to the assessed value of given farm acreages; now it is a graduated percentage of the total property tax bill). Its structure strongly reinforces the more favorable tax treatment that is given to homestead farms by Minnesota's classification system. This is continued by the homestead credit, which pays 54% of the remaining tax bill up to a maximum $650. For purposes of receiving the credit, a farm homestead is broadly defined—owner-occupied, unlimited acreage, noncontiguous property within two townships, and farmed by owner-occupant or rented for farm use. Finally, Minnesota provides a circuit breaker refund to certain farmers depending on their household income and property tax bills.

In addition, Minnesota has implemented three less well known programs, all of which are variations of the use-value assessment method of farm property tax relief. It has two programs—green acres, enacted 1967, and metropolitan agricultural preserves, enacted 1980—that assess qualified and enrolled farmland at its value in agricultural use. And, third, since 1977, Minnesota has valued farmland at the average of its market and use-value for purposes of determining adjusted assessed values (EARC) for school aids.

Most states have relied more on use-value assessment for purposes of providing property tax relief to farmers. Their programs vary considerably in terms of scope, administration, and enforcement. However, most reject the conventionally used comparable sales (market) approach to property value. Instead, they rely on the income approach to value. This approach stresses the productivity and net earnings capacity of agricultural land. It uses soil quality, production, price and expense data to arrive at net farm income, which is then capitalized (divided by a rate of interest) to yield the use-value of farmland. Thus, use-value is a computed figure that depends on two factors: estimated net farm income and a capitalization rate.

## HOW SHOULD AGRICULTURAL LAND BE VALUED?

In reality, the question of how farmland should be valued is actually one of whether farm assessments should be lowered. In addressing this issue, it is necessary to evaluate the strengths and weaknesses of the two methods of valuation—comparable sales and income capitalization.

### COMPARABLE SALES APPROACH TO VALUE

There are several problems with the comparable sales approach to property valuation. For instance, there may be a scarcity of sales from which to establish reliable estimates of market value; crop equivalency ratings, which are a measure of soil productivity, provide for greater assessment accuracy between properties but may not be used if county-wide soil surveys are not available; if financing terms of farm sales are not adjusted, they can result in an overstatement (understatement) of value; and, it is possible to introduce a systematic bias into market valuation (e.g., if a market is dominated by one type of buyer willing to pay more or less for land).

In addition to these market problems, a common criticism is that market value taxation of agricultural land is inappropriate since it recognizes development potential and speculative value, as well as expected income from agricultural use. By recognizing these nonfarm-related anticipated increases in value, the property tax system assigns values to farmland that are generally higher than if valuations were based on income capitalization.

While the use of market value has its drawbacks, it does not necessarily imply that it should be abandoned as the standard for valuation. Its greatest handicap—the paucity of comparable sales and the subsequent inadequacy of sales data—can be substantially overcome by expanding both the geographic area and the market data used to value subject properties. Such expansion minimizes any bias in the selection and dollar adjustment of the comparable sales, and therefore allows assessors to better substantiate (and landowners to better evaluate) their analysis of the market.

No matter how improved the valuation process, however, it still does not relieve the cash flow pinch that arises from disparities in income and real property wealth. Although commonly depicted as a tax problem, this situation is more accurately a credit market problem. When viewed in this light, the solution is not broad-based permanent tax relief but rather some type of intervention in the capital or loanable funds market. A state financed tax deferral mechanism that allows farmers to defer (with interest) payment of part or all of their property tax liability is one example.

## INCOME CAPITALIZATION APPROACH TO VALUE (USE-VALUE ASSESSMENT)

Proponents of this alternative method of valuation suggest that its main advantage is that it is based on income and not wealth; therefore, it strikes at the heart of the farmer's cash flow problem—large increases in land values and taxes that outpace income.

However, in terms of its design and administration, distribution of benefits and costs, and effectiveness, the method has several drawbacks.

• It uses a volatile measure—net farm income—as the basis for determining property value. This results in land values that can fluctuate substantially over short periods of time. It also tends to politicize the determination of net farm income by creating incentives to distort and dispute state estimates.

- It usually produces values that are far below market value, even in areas where the only foreseeable use of the land is for agricultural purposes. This is because most farm income capitalization formulas are inconsistent in their treatment of prospective farm income and inflation, i.e., in estimating net farm income they do not recognize the present value of anticipated farm income, but in selecting a capitalization rate, they use market mortgage interest rates which do reflect the expected future rate of inflation.
- If net income estimates are computed over large areas and not adjusted for differences in the level and variability of farm income associated with different types of farming, the method's averaging effect will tend to overvalue marginal land and undervalue the more productive lands.
- It is an administratively complex system of property valuation in that it requires the annual or periodic collection of detailed information on local soil quality, farm income and expenses, and economic trends in the commodity markets. This type of information is best gathered and analyzed at the state level.

## DISTRIBUTION OF BENEFITS

Perhaps the most controversial aspect of use-value assessment is that it redistributes property tax burdens among property owners within a taxing jurisdiction. Because the aggregate value of agricultural land is lowered, the resulting revenue loss is made up by increasing the tax rate (assuming tax revenues are held constant). This increases the property tax liability of all nonfarm property and offsets to some degree the reduced assessment of farm property. In addition, the now lower value of rural school districts is likely to make them eligible to receive greater state school foundation aid.

Other things being equal, use-value assessment tends to confer the greatest benefits to areas where farmland values are appreciating rapidly, and where only a moderate amount of farmland is left within the taxing jurisdiction. This may or may not include the areas where farmers are most burdened by the property tax. This illustrates why use-value assessment has been called a "blunt policy instrument," i.e., it provides tax relief to all parcels of agricultural property regardless of an individual's owner's income/wealth situation.

## DISTRIBUTION OF COSTS

In most states, use-value assessment programs are locally financed through the tax shifts described above. However, if the major goal of a state's farm property assessment laws is to relieve farmers' property tax burdens (as is the case in Minnesota), then presumably such legislation yields benefits to a state as a whole and should be financed by all state taxpayers. Because state financing involves reimbursing local taxing jurisdictions for revenue lost due to lowered valuations, it provides greater benefits to agricultural landowners than locally financed programs. Despite their legislative goals, most states have balked at picking up this cost.

## EFFECTIVENESS

Despite the long-standing existence of many use-value assessment programs in other states, there is scant empirical evidence as to whether this valuation method produces a "fairer" tax distribution. What evidence exists suggests that use-value assessment is generally successful in reducing the property taxes of farmers. However, it does so by providing tax relief to all agricultural landowners regardless of their ability to pay. Moreover, unless carefully structured, it provides relief to both those who own farmland for farming purposes and those who hold farmland for purposes of value appreciation. With respect to the second goal—agricultural land preservation—it is generally agreed that use-value assessment alone is an ineffective tool for influencing land use. While it may forestall development in the short term, the opportunities for capital gains through sale or development remain unaffected; therefore, it is unlikely to have an appreciable influence on long-term land use patterns.

## PROPERTY TAX RELIEF IN THE CONTEXT OF STATE AGRICULTURAL POLICY

This study finds that it is possible to provide any amount of property tax relief to farms without embroiling the state in the policy-laden mathematics of determining agricultural use-value and the complexities of its administration. Through its present system of classification and credits, Minnesota has already done a great deal to provide property tax relief to owners of farmland. The question remains, however, does Minnesota need to do more? The projections of state farm income through 1987 are adverse. Minnesota agriculture is beset by the same problems affecting farmers nationally, i.e., high interest rates, unfavorable exchange rates, and the depressed economic condition of many importing foreign nations.

This tax policy discussion raises the greater question of how the state should meet its long-standing commitment to maintaining the family farm. A serious and extensive state commitment to this goal will require more than just the local redistribution of property tax burdens and state expenditures for property tax relief. Specifically, it may require direct state assistance to economically vulnerable farmers, or conversely, a recasting of the state's overall policy toward agriculture.

# RECOMMENDATIONS

## RETAINING THE COMPARABLE SALES APPROACH TO VALUING FARMLAND

From its study of the property taxation of agriculture, the commission concludes that the method of determining farmland value is a separate and distinct issue from that of providing property tax relief to farmers. Minnesota can provide any amount of relief to farmers without involving the state in the policy-laden mathematics of determining agricultural use-value and the complexities of its administration. Therefore, the commission recommends that the state retain the comparable sales approach to farmland valuation, and where it is not already done, such values should be adjusted to reflect soil productivity and the financing terms of farm sales.

With regard to the provision of property tax relief, the commission recommends that the farm homestead and acreage (homestead and nonhomestead) should be subject to the most preferential assessment ratio within the three-class property tax system. In addition, the farm homestead should be eligible to receive the income-wealth-adjusted property tax credit, and the first 520 acres of homesteaded agricultural land should also be eligible for such property tax relief.

## CLASSIFICATION OF TIMBERLAND AS AGRICULTURAL PROPERTY*

Under current law, the tax status of timberland is unclear and requires county officials to exercise a great deal of discretion. The relative fiscal capacities of forested counties depends in part on how timberland is designated by these officials. Some timberland parcels are taxed under the tree growth tax law, a favored tax status that is in lieu of property taxes. Because these parcels are favored, other land bears a greater property tax burden. Other timberland parcels are taxed under class 3e of the property tax; these parcels are overvalued for tax purposes, as current practice incorporates both the land and the timber growing on it as part of "land" value. The practice is contradictory to valuation procedures for other cropland, which exclude the value of the crop while taking into consideration the use for which the land can be used. The result is double taxation of timberland and some incentive for owners to cut-out-from-under the tax.

---

* The background discussion on the taxation of timber is provided by Julia Friedman in Volume II of this report.

With these issues in mind, the commission recommends that all forested land be classified under one rural/agricultural classification for nonhomestead land:

- devising statutory language to assure uniform interpretation and implementation;
- providing technical assistance from state foresters; and
- improving assessment practices and assessing all agricultural and timber parcels on bare land value.

# 20
# Gross Earnings Taxation

## INTRODUCTION

### HISTORY OF THE TAX[1]

Gross earnings (receipts) taxation in Minnesota began as early as 1857 when the legislature of the Territory of Minnesota granted a charter to Minnesota and Pacific Railroad Company. The charter provided that the company pay 3% of its gross earnings in lieu of all other taxes and property assessments. All other railroad companies came under gross earnings taxation by 1887. The tax rate rose to 4% in 1905 and to 5% eight years later.

Telephone and telegraph companies were added as gross earnings taxpayers in 1887, with a rate of 2%. After a five-year hiatus during which time they were subject to property taxation in 1897, Minnesota returned to taxing gross earnings in lieu of the property tax. The rate in that year was 3%, although it rose to 4% in 1922. Other amendments followed in 1937 to increase the rate to 7% for companies serving localities with a population exceeding 10,000, and in 1945 to provide per-phone rates for small companies.

Further additions to the set of gross earnings taxable industries included express companies and sleeping car companies in 1897 (the tax base no longer exists), boxing exhibitions in 1937 (repealed 1984), rural electric companies in 1939 and taconite railroads in 1955 (repealed after 1980). The current rate structure appears in Table 1.

TABLE 1
Gross Earnings Tax Rates

| Industry* | |
|---|---|
| Express companies | 5% |
| Rural electric cooperatives | 10 dollars per 100 members (in lieu of all personal property taxes) |
| Telegraph | 6% |
| Telephone | 4% from rural service |
| | 4% for localities with less than 10,000 population |
| | 7% from all other service |
| | 30 cents per phone if companies earnings are $1,000 or less |

*Gross earnings taxes are levied in lieu of all ad valorem property taxes.

The gross receipts tax on telephone and telegraph companies provided nearly $75.7 million in 1982, consistently about 2% of state tax collections since 1980 (see Table 2). In contrast, in the latter 1970s, when railroads were still subject to the tax, telephone and telegraph companies provided about 2.7% of state taxes.

For 1982, 95% of the gross earnings tax revenue came from taxation of telephone companies, a fraction which has steadily risen, since 1976. In fact, one firm, Northwestern Bell Telephone, has paid 75%-80% of the gross earning taxes in recent years. Finally, over the period 1980-82, about 79% of telephone company gross earnings taxes were generated at the 7% rate.

## A TAX ON TELEPHONE COMPANIES

The picture of the gross earnings tax that emerges from an examination of the data in Table 2 is of a tax on telephone companies. Although 113 telephone companies paid the tax in 1982, all but fifteen were subject only to the 4% rate. In fact, just a handful of companies (again, especially Northwestern Bell Telephone) have paid almost all of the tax. For these reasons, this discussion and evaluation of the tax will concentrate almost exclusively on the taxation of telephone companies, with emphasis on the tax situation of Northwestern Bell. Long distance (interstate) companies (e.g., American Telephone & Telegraph, Sprint, and MCI) will also be discussed.

Three administrative features are crucial to understanding how the gross earnings tax has operated. The first concerns the allocation of revenue from

TABLE 2
Gross Earnings Tax Revenue
($000)

|  | 1982 | 1981 | 1980 | 1979 | 1978 | 1977 | 1976 |
|---|---|---|---|---|---|---|---|
| Gross earnings taxes* | $75,668 | $75,206 | $69,425 | $79,551 | $73,390 | $66,584 | $59,255 |
| % of Minnesota state taxes | 2.0% | 2.2% | 2.1% | 2.5% | 2.7% | 2.7% | 2.7% |
| Telephone taxes | | | | | | | |
| at 4% | $15,546 | $14,649 | $12,824 | $12,638 | $10,720 | $ 9,584 | $ 8,162.3 |
| at 7% | 56,486 | 52,274 | 46,858 | 40,928 | 37,484 | 33,038 | 29,150 |
| Total | 72,032 | 66,498 | 59,683 | 53,566 | 48,205 | 42,622 | 37,312 |
| % of gross earnings taxes | 95.2% | 88.4% | 86.0% | 67.3% | 65.7% | 64.0% | 63.0% |
| Northwestern Bell gross earnings taxes | $59,809 | $56,098 | $50,512 | $45,236 | $41,047 | $36,329 | $31,745 |

*Source:* Data provided by Minnesota Department of Revenue.

*Excluding insurance company premiums tax

interstate service to Minnesota for tax purposes. The second concerns the implementation of the specified rate differences between small and larger localities. A third issue pertains to how telephone property would be structured if it were subject to the property tax.

*The allocation problem.*    Before divestiture (1984), the taxation of gross earnings represented an administratively simple alternative to a property tax. Companies reported revenues and paid the appropriate tax rate. The one administrative difficulty concerned the allocation of long distance revenues of AT&T to Northwestern Bell and then the further allocation to Minnesota. With the recent introduction of competition in long distance service, the same problem has been faced by MCI; However, other competitors (e.g., Sprint) have not paid gross earnings taxes.

While the Minnesota tax law mentions airline miles as the required allocation formula, AT&T has used its more complicated corporate division of revenues, a method of dividing revenues among its twenty-two associated companies. Basically, each associated company receives compensation for the value of its plant, reserves, payments to connecting companies, and taxes it incurs in providing long distance service; the remaining money is divided among the companies on the basis of the number of shares held, where a share represented $1 of net plant furnished. Since shares are allocated according to book value, thereby providing more revenue per call to the capital intensive companies, the allocation method coincidentally reinforces the property tax aspect for which gross earnings taxation substituted.

The only other long distance company that has paid gross earnings taxation to Minnesota is MCI, which allocates revenues according to the fraction of airline miles that cross over Minnesota. This method bears no relation to any economic activity such as investment or use, although it is feasible to administer.

*Tax rates.*    The gross earnings tax statute provides for three basic tax rates. The rates are "four percent . . . from service to rural subscribers," "four percent . . . from exchange business of all cities . . . having a population of 10,000 or less," and "seven percent . . . from all other business." The Minnesota Supreme Court has ruled (*Mankato Citizens Telephone Co. v. Commissioner,* 1966) that the second 4% rate class requires that both the firm's central facilities and office be in a jurisdiction of less than 10,000 to qualify for the 4% rate, regardless of the location of customers. Finally, firms with less than $1,000 of gross receipts pay 30 cents per telephone.

The revenue department implements these rate classes as follows. Service to customers in unincorporated areas is always taxed at a 4% rate regardless of the firm's office location. Service to customers in jurisdictions larger than 10,000 population is always taxed at 7% regardless of central office location. But the tax rate on service to customers in jurisdictions of less than 10,000 is taxed at the rate appropriate to the location of the firm's central office.

*State Assessment of Utility Property.*  Historically, utilities have been treated different from most other firms for state and local tax purposes, particularly concerning property taxes (Appendix 1). The different treatment primarily arose from two factors. First, utility properties present special, though certainly not insurmountable, assessment difficulties. There is little sales data showing market transactions. The income approach to valuation is contaminated by the regulation process, which is often designed to guarantee the utility a given, after-tax rate of return. And the cost-plus adjustment approach to valuation requires a measure of depreciation of utility property, which in many cases is nearly unique property.

Second, the geographic distribution of utility property is somewhat unusual. The production and distribution facilities are very unevenly distributed between local jurisdictions (in the limiting case, only a couple of electric generating plants may serve an entire state). Thus, local property taxation provides large revenue gains to a few local governments. A related, but opposite problem occurs because of the utility transmission property (e.g., electric and telephone lines, pipelines, railroad tracks). This property presumably has a single value, but with a local property tax, it would be separately assessed by each jurisdiction.

These traditional problems led many states either to levy state (rather than local) property taxes on these utilities and railroads or to substitute a different state tax (usually a gross receipts tax) for property taxes on these businesses.

Minnesota took the second route. Telephone and telegraph companies and railroads were exempt from the local property tax and subjected instead to a state tax on gross earnings. Starting in 1979, the gross earnings tax on railroads was phased out and replaced with a property tax on the operating property, with annual assessment by the state government. The value was then apportioned back to each local government, where the property is located and property taxes are levied by each of the localities. For tax purposes, the railroad operating property is treated as commercial and industrial property (see Appendix 2). Railroad property not used for operating purposes (land) continues to be subject to local taxation, as before the change. The gross earnings tax revenue from telephone companies, telegraph companies, and other sources accrues to the state's general fund, some part of which is then distributed back to local governments through the revenue sharing program.

## A BRIEF HISTORY OF THE EVOLUTION OF THE TELEPHONE INDUSTRY

### A NATIONAL MONOPOLY, 1934-59

Until relatively recently, the telephone industry seemed the classic example of a natural monopoly. Fixed costs of constructing and maintaining the nationwide network comprised the vast majority of expenditures with little additional cost for the incremental telephone call. The consequent decreasing cost structure argued for both entry restriction and rate regulation: the former, to permit attainment of minimum cost, and the latter to preclude monopolistic pricing.

The Federal Communications Act of 1934 placed communication common carriers, such as the telephone industry, under the regulatory authority of the Federal Communications Commission (FCC). The public interest, convenience, and necessity standard required the FCC to consider, in addition to economic efficiency, such other factors as the technical integrity of the system, costs, consumer choice, and universal service. For example, AT&T maintained a virtual monopoly on the manufacture and sale of the telephones themselves until the mid-1960s because of the ban on "foreign attachments." Competing equipment was forbidden on the argument that interference or even damage to the system might result from low-quality or incompatible devices. Further, above-normal returns to equipment sales allowed subsidy of residential subscribers. Similarly, competition in long distance services was forsworn, it was argued, because the technical integrity of the system required that a single firm provide all parts of the service. As a result, the monopoly on long distance allowed excess returns for cross-subsidization.

EROSION OF MONOPOLY STATUS, 1959-82

Beginning in 1959, the telephone industry entered a second phase which witnessed the gradual erosion of monopoly status, the narrowing of the scope of regulation, and the introduction of widespread competition in nearly all facets of informal transmission. The first in a series of court judgments and regulatory rulings was the 1959 "above 890" of the FCC which allocated a portion of the radio frequency spectrum to large users desiring to construct their own private microwave communications systems, and, hence, compete with AT&T's long distance monopoly. Between 1969 and 1973, the commission opened long distance private line communications to new competition, such as MCI Communications Corporation, and eliminated tariff restrictions on resale and shared use of leased lines, thereby creating a new class of value-added carriers. These companies, such as MCI and Sprint, purchase the basic long distance service from AT&T and then resell it, often with enhanced services such as conference calling and facsimile transmission. These services also limited AT&T pricing flexibility by providing a means for arbitrage among markets.

The 1969 Carterfone decision inaugurated competition in terminal equipment manufacture and sales. Later, in 1980, the FCC ruled that nondominant carriers similarly be free of rate and entry regulation.

EXHIBIT 1
Local Access and Transport Areas

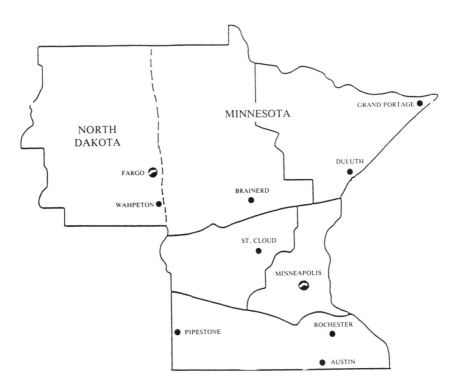

Beginning in 1984, Northwestern Bell Telephone Company now distributes information only within what are known as Local Access and Transport Areas, or LATAs. A map is shown above of Minnesota LATAs (one of which also includes half of North Dakota). A call within a user's exchange remains a local call. A call between exchanges within a LATA is a Northwestern Bell long distance call, unless it is purchased from another supplier. Northwestern Bell Telephone does not serve users across LATA Boundaries.

*Source:* Northwestern Bell, *The Changing World of Telecommunications,* 1984.

The FCC declared in 1971 that most combinations of computer and communications services were not subject to regulation. The final important FCC decision was its second computer inquiry in 1980, which attempted to divide AT&T's competitive activities, such as enhanced services and customer premises equipment, from its regulated local and long distance service.

DIVESTITURE: THE 1983 CONSENT DECREE

All of these decisions can be seen as forming a sequence of phased but relentless narrowing of the scope of the AT&T monopoly. A much more discrete event, however, was the 1982-83 settlement of the U.S. Justice Department antitrust suit against AT&T. Under those terms AT&T was to divest itself of all of its local exchange services, effectively removing the company from the local telephone service market. In its place remain eight holding companies (such as U.S. West, which services Minnesota). These companies will provide local service over AT&T's former exchanges and intraLATA or short haul interexchange (see Exhibit 1). AT&T retains ownership of Long Lines (its long distance arm), Western Electric (telephone manufacture and sales), and Bell Labs (research). The former Bell operating company may sell but not manufacture telephone equipment, and it may continue to market *Yellow Pages.*

As the industry now stands, basic local services will continue to be regulated. Most of Minnesota will be served by Northwestern Bell, although other local companies will retain a market share. Some peripheral competition for local service will be provided by mobile telephones and PBX-type equipment. AT&T will sell private long distance service according to regulated rates, but it will be subject to vigorous competition from those who resell its WATS service and also from microwave satellite transmissions. Telephone equipment manufacture, sales, and leasing will operate as a competitive industry.

This competition in equipment sales and long distance will preclude the historic subsidization of local (and residential) rates. The means by which the subsidy has been carried out was through the allocation formula described above, whereby a portion of the fixed costs of local service were allocated to long distance; some fraction of the surplus long distance revenues were also returned to the local companies. With competition there will be, of course, no surplus revenues in the long distance business. The questions remain concerning allocation of fixed costs between local and long distance, and the recovery of these costs.

In its access charge decision, the FCC ruled that local companies may continue to allocate a share of fixed costs to interstate service. This share is currently 26% nationally (26.6% in Minnesota), but it is scheduled to decline to a 25% standard by 1990. The costs are to be recovered through a system of customer fees, called "access charges." These are scheduled to begin June 1985 for residential customers and single line businesses and will not exceed $4.00 per line until 1990. Multiline business customers pay access charges of $6.00 per line as of May, 1984.

After 1990, access charges will rise until they cover the allocated portion of fixed costs (about $9 per line). Until then, the allocated portion of fixed costs not covered by access charges will be paid to the local companies by the long distance companies.


## TELEPHONE TAXATION: PROBLEMS OF DEREGULATION AND TECHNOLOGICAL CHANGE

Deregulation of the telephone industry over the last decade, recent and continuing technological changes in telecommunications, and the court-ordered divestiture of the Bell System have generated three issues of operation for the gross receipts tax as applied to telephone companies. The first issue is one of the definition of the tax base, i.e., which firms, and/or activities will be subject to the gross receipts tax. For those firms that must pay the gross receipts tax, the second and third issues are, respectively, how gross receipts should be apportioned to Minnesota for firms doing business in several states and at what rate the tax should be imposed. Depending on the resolution of these questions, a key fourth issue is whether it might be preferable to levy a tax not based on gross receipts, a property tax, on all telecommunication firms.


### DEFINITION OF THE TAX BASE

In considering the first issue of which firms are to be subject to the gross receipts tax, the starting point must be the intent of the law to tax telephone companies and the definition of those firms. For the purpose of the gross receipts tax, a telephone company is defined as "any person, firm, association or corporation, excluding municipal telephone companies, owning or operating any telephone line or telephone exchange for hire wholly or partly within this state, including radio and other advancements in the art of telephony."

It is worth noting that the above definitions became effective in 1974. Prior to that, it was only required that the organization ". . . whenever organized or incorporated, own or operate any . . . telephone line within this state . . . ." It seems that this change was made in 1973 in anticipation of the coming technological and economic changes in the industry. Yet, the new definition has not settled the question, as at least one firm (Sprint) is challenging in court its status as a telephone company.

The question of which activities are to be taxed also arises because existing local telephone companies and AT&T have reorganized to separate the regulated phone service from the other activities of those firms. Northwestern Bell left the Bell System as part of AT&T at the start of 1984, leading to the current organizational structure shown on the following chart. Northwestern Bell Telephone Company is the major firm providing traditional local phone service in Minnesota as well as Iowa, Nebraska,

North Dakota, and South Dakota. But as can be seen, Northwestern Bell Telephone is a subsidiary of the holding company called Northwestern Bell Corporation, which itself is a subsidiary of a holding company called U.S. West.

For gross receipts tax purposes, it is the revenue of Northwestern Bell Telephone Company that seems to be subject to the tax. It is also necessary that the revenue of Northwestern Bell Telephone operations in Minnesota be separated from revenue derived from operations in the other four states. In essence, the continuing state-regulated activities specified in the divestiture settlement remain part of Northwestern Bell Telephone while the other subsidiaries of Northwestern Bell Corporation compete in an unregulated market against other firms, in many cases providing new services or products.

This reorganization has implications for gross receipts tax revenues in at least three ways. All three portend a decline in gross receipts tax revenues:

- *Decline in Leasing of Equipment by Users.* First, as user telephone purchase and ownership have become more common and leasing of telephone equipment from Bell has declined, the revenue of the phone company has declined. In addition, sales of telephones are now made by subsidiaries of Northwestern Bell Corporation and AT&T as well as many other private retail firms. These activities, which are not part of the "Telephone Company," are not subject to the gross receipts tax. Moreover, in Minnesota, phone equipment owned by individuals is not subject to any personal property tax. However, the sale of telephones at retail is subject to the state sales tax.

- *Directory and Advertising.* Directories and advertising service (*Yellow Pages*) are now provided by a subsidiary of U.S. West rather than the Bell Company. As a result, the full revenues from directory provision are not subject to the gross receipts tax, although Northwestern Bell does receive a fee for selling its customer list to U.S. West Direct. These fees received are included as revenue for the gross receipts tax; and

- *Shift of Receipt Generating Activities to Nonregulated Firms.* Future organization changes are possible; they would move additional activities out of Northwestern Bell Telephone Company and into subsidiaries not subject to the gross receipts tax. For example, Northwestern Bell Telephone argues that the gross receipts tax puts Bell at a competitive disadvantage compared to other firms in the provision of centralized, multiline business phone systems. As shown in Chart 1, Centrex/Centron services are part of Northwestern Bell Telephone and subject to the gross receipts tax, while a system purchased at retail and installed by a firm for its own use generates no gross receipts tax liability (although equipment purchase is subject to retail sales tax). This personal property may be subject to ad valorem property tax of the firm. Although Northwestern

CHART 1
U.S. West (Holding Company)

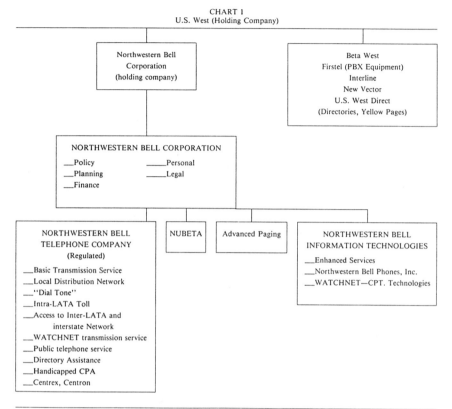

*Source:* Northwestern Bell Corporation Bulletin, July 1984.

Bell Corporation is prevented at present by the divestiture agreement from moving Centrex operations into a subsidiary, that option and actions similar to it may be possible in the future.

The implications of some communication activities being subject to the gross receipts tax and some not are four:

- a potential decrease in tax revenue of a previously taxed activity now exempt;
- a potential shift in tax revenues if one activity is now exempt;
- a potential shift in tax revenues if one activity is now exempt from gross receipts tax but subject to the local property tax (implying in many cases that these telephone or communication firms will be subject to different taxes on different aspects of their business); and
- potentially different tax treatment of different firms providing the same goods and services.

Related to the question of the definition at the tax base is the tax treatment of access charges. Recall that there will be two types of access charge payments until 1990: by residential customers and businesses to local companies and by long distance providers to the local companies. As far as gross earnings taxation is concerned, two decisions must be made. First, are the payments by long distance companies taxable receipts? Second, can long distance companies deduct the access charges from their taxable total revenues?

It would seem that if the charges are receipts to the local companies, then they are deductions for the long distance companies. Otherwise, the same service would be taxed twice.[2] The current position of the State of Minnesota is that the access charges are taxable but not deductible.

## APPORTIONMENT OF INTERSTATE REVENUES

Once it has been generally decided which firms or activities are to be subject to the tax, it is then necessary to apportion the revenue of interstate firms to determine the amount applicable to and taxable by Minnesota. With deregulation this is an especially important issue in respect to long distance carriers. As noted earlier, before divestiture AT&T revenue from interstate service was allocated to AT&T and each of the Bell System companies based on expenses and net plant investment. At this time, the revenue department and AT&T have not come to a decision as to the apportionment formula to be used now. Therefore, for our purposes, it is necessary to focus on the past discussions and decisions regarding apportioning revenues of MCI and Sprint.

*MCI Telecommunications Corporation.*    The revenue department and MCI Telecommunications Corporation agreed in 1979 to apportion revenue to Minnesota for gross receipts tax purposes "by dividing the sum of city-pair circuit airlines miles that cross Minnesota by the sum of all city-pair circuit airlines miles nationwide." A city-pair circuit airline mile is the airline distance between two cities served by MCI multiplied by the number of circuits available between those two cities.

By this method, revenue is apportioned based on the potential for city-to-city calls to "cross" Minnesota, although no measurement of actual calls made is necessary. As an example, the airline distance from Bismarck, North Dakota to Chicago is 732 miles, 309 of which cross Minnesota. The 309 miles, then, generate a proportion used to allocate total MCI revenue to Minnesota. Similarly, MCI service between locations in Minnesota and those outside of the state would generate apportionment of revenue to Minnesota. To implement this system, MCI calculates the circuit airline miles between all city-pairs served by MCI and the portion of aggregate city-pair circuit airline miles which cross Minnesota, providing its apportionment factor.

*Sprint Communications.*    In contrast to MCI, GTE Sprint Communications Corporation has contended that they are not subject to the gross receipts tax, an issue now before the tax court. But Sprint has proposed an allocation system for use if they are ruled to be subject to the tax. It is Sprint's position that because the gross receipts tax is levied in lieu of local ad valorem property taxes, revenue should be apportioned based on the fraction of the firm's taxable property value which is in Minnesota. In essence, Sprint argues for a property tax, even though it is called a gross receipts tax.

As it now stands, it appears that the three major interstate carriers, AT&T, MCI, and Sprint are each treated differently under the same tax. All precepts of good taxation would argue for similar administrative treatment of similar activities. What the appropriate single treatment is remains of issue.

To repeat, the allocation problem arises because firms that operate in Minnesota also do business outside the state. Because it is not feasible to pin-point the particular revenues which accrue from operations in Minnesota per se, total revenues for the firm are calculated and apportioned among the states in which it operates. The tax that the firm owes depends not only upon its revenues, as it would in the case of a pure gross receipts tax, but also on its apportionment formula. If a particular activity of the firm enters the apportionment formula, the firm's tax payments will vary with the level of that activity. Thus, the apportionment question contains at least three issues: consistency of treatment among telecommunications firms, administrative feasibility and cost, and opportunity for and ease of auditing.

TAX RATE

The third major issue concerns the rate at which apportioned revenue is to be taxed. As previously noted, telephone gross receipts are taxed at either 4% or 7% depending on the locations of the firm's central offices and location of customer. In practice, given the allocation systems used, it is difficult to see a reasonable way to divide the apportioned revenue of the major interstate firms into a 4% and 7% base. In fact, in 1983 MCI paid the 7% rate on all its apportioned (mileage) revenues.

Divestiture and deregulation may affect the amount of revenue from the gross receipts tax in other ways. Previously, AT&T long distance revenue was allocated to Northwestern Bell Telephone, some of which was taxed at 4% and some at 7% depending on the user's situation. After divestiture, AT&T will pay gross receipts tax on all this revenue presumably at the 7% rate, if they are treated similarly to MCI. This would increase shifts from AT&T to MCI for interstate service, revenue previously taxed at 4% could become taxed at 7%. However, if customers shift from AT&T to Sprint for long distance service, gross receipts revenues could decrease, given Sprint's claim of not being subject to the tax.

While the differential rates for the gross receipts tax on telephone companies have always posed administrative and equity problems for the tax, those problems are magnified by the growth of telephone competition and divestiture.

## EFFECTS OF DIVESTITURE ON GROSS RECEIPTS REVENUES

How will divestiture affect total gross earnings tax revenues in Minnesota? This section provides some estimates of tax revenues under several assumptions concerning allocation formulas for long distance revenues, change in tax rates, and the tax treatment of access charges. Given the rapid change in the telephone industry, these estimates must be taken with some caution.

The first issue concerns the allocation formulas allowed for apportioning, for tax purposes, long distance revenues among communities eligible for 4% tax rates and those required to pay rates of 7%. As discussed above, before divestiture AT&T and Northwestern Bell allocated revenues among communities within Minnesota based upon net plant investment. Most of the plant investment upon which the predivestiture allocation was based, however, has now been transferred to Northwestern Bell. The postdivestiture distribution by plant investment is likely concentrated in 7% communities.

The other major competitors in the long distance service market, MCI and Sprint, must also face this issue. Oral communication with MCI revealed that they have not considered the interstate allocation question. Consistency with their intrastate allocation would indicate a similar matrix of airline miles and rates charged based on the fraction of the route within 4% and 7% tax areas. The 4% rate can be interpreted as a special circumstance for long distance carriers as well, requiring that the main offices lie within a municipality with a population less than 10,000. Sprint has taken the position that, should they be required to pay gross earnings taxes, the allocation should be based upon property.

The entire intrastate allocation issue depends on the rate differential; therefore, elimination of the rate differential would obviate the allocation problem. Estimates for the revenue consequences of eliminating the 4% rate are presented below.

There remains the question of the tax treatment of access charges. The current position of the revenue department is that these are taxable as revenues accruing to the local companies, but not deductible from the revenue base of the long distance companies. The matter is currently under litigation, and the revenue consequences of this decision are quite significant. Access charge will account for 35%-40% of long distance revenues for the near future. The position of the revenue department would tax these revenues twice; should the position of the taxpayers be upheld, no tax receipts would accrue.

Table 4 presents nine estimates of gross earnings tax revenues for 1984. The assumptions considered are three for access charges and three for rates and allocation formulas. On the access charge question, possible decisions are that the charges be both deductible and taxable (in other words, taxed once as receipts of the local companies), taxable but not deductible (taxed twice), or neither taxable nor deductible (not taxed). The rate assumptions are to maintain current rate differentials and allow AT&T to continue with its predivestiture formula. Alternatively, all long distance revenues could pay 7% for all communities.

The calculations in Table 4 assume no rate increase for 1984; although an increase has been approved, no date is set. Advertising revenue has been deducted, based on the postdivestiture corporate organization of U.S. West. We also used an internal Northwestern Bell forecast of access charges.

The most likely outcome seems to be that access charges will be taxed once and that long distance carriers will pay 7%. Table 4 shows that in this case, revenues may decline only 2%. Other assumptions lead to revenues falling by nearly half or rising by more than a third. Eliminating the rate differential generates approximately $5 million in gross earnings tax revenue.

The major factor for revenue purposes is the access charge decision.

The above estimates probably overstate revenues. First, revenues from equipment leasing and the sale of enhanced services are included in the tax

TABLE 4
Postdivestiture 1984 Gross Receipts Revenue Forecasts (millions)
and Percentage of 1983

| Rate Assumptions | Access Charge Assumptions | | | | | |
|---|---|---|---|---|---|---|
| | Deductible and Taxable | (% 1983) | Not Deductible but Taxable | (% 1983) | Neither Deductible Nor Taxable | (% 1983) |
| Current Rates + Allocation formulas | $65.9 | 92% | $88.3 | 123% | $40.1 | 56% |
| Current rates for local + 7% for all long distance | $68.9 | 98% | $93.8 | 130% | $40.6 | 56% |
| All revenues at 7% | $73.3 | 102% | $98.2 | 136% | $47.8 | 66% |

*Source:* Staff Calculations.

base for the calculations in Table 3. These activities will almost certainly pay little gross receipts tax in the future. Northwestern Bell will move much of this business to its enhanced services division, and, thus, not pay gross earnings tax. Meanwhile competitors not subject to this tax will expand their share. Unfortunately data were not available to make more realistic assumptions about revenues from equipment and enhanced services.

Further, the structure of access charges will change as more of the share is shifted to end users. The Northwestern Bell forecast is that only 2.9% of access charges will be borne by end users in 1984. After 1990 the residential fees will begin to rise from $4 per line to the per-line share of allocated fixed costs, which are scheduled to be 25% of total fixed costs by 1990. This switch to end user payment implies that if the nondeductibility of access charges is upheld, the revenue gain will be temporary.

Finally, rapidly changing technology gives one pause to forecast confidently in this industry. Microwave transmissions, cellular phones, two-way cable, and many other developments will significantly change the structure of revenues.

## ECONOMIC ANALYSIS OF GROSS EARNINGS COMPARED TO PROPERTY TAXATION

The gross earnings tax in Minnesota originated as an alternative to the property tax. Accordingly, two issues are of particular interest to Minnesota in the context of the changing economic and institutional arrangement of the telecommunications industry. The first pertains to the consequences of taxing one industry with gross earnings taxation while the remainder of the economy pays property taxes. The second concern pertains to the problems of taxing alternative firms within the same industry and of taxing separate divisions of the same firms with different taxes.

For purposes of this study, there are two features of property taxation of interest. First, in that it is a tax upon capital, property taxes induce firms to substitute labor for capital. Second, as it is a tax upon factor use, the property tax is neutral so far as vertical integration is concerned. There are no tax consequences of acquiring an "upstream" or "downstream" producer.

Gross earnings taxation differs from property taxation in these two areas. Gross earnings taxes are neutral with regard to the factor mix employed by the taxed firm, but they do encourage vertical integration. The acquisition of a downstream producer eliminates a market transaction and therefore reduces taxes.

The gross earnings taxation of one industry, while the remainder of the economy pays property taxes, thus leads to greater capital intensity in the gross-earnings-taxed industry, accompanied by some tax-induced vertical integration. There is little more to be said so long as the separation between the gross-earnings-taxed and property-taxed industries is clear-cut. If, however, either closely competing product lines are taxed differently or the distinction between gross receipts taxable (e.g., regulated) and exempt (unregulated) is unclear, the problem is more complicated.

With some portion of the information transmission industry taxed according to gross earnings and the remainder subject to property tax, there are economic incentives to reallocate resources in such a way as to reduce tax payments. Two alternative taxes will collect smaller revenues than one universal tax. To see this, refer back to corporate organization of Northwestern Bell (Chart 1). The company is involved in serving regulated markets, subject to gross earnings taxation, and simultaneously competing in the unregulated sector. It must make at least two types of allocations that have important tax consequences. First, for a given corporate structure, it must decide how its taxable property is to be allocated between those divisions subject to gross earnings taxation and those paying property taxes. Certainly, corporate incentives include allocating more taxable property toward the regulated divisions, and the existence of general overhead allows some flexibility and room for interpretation. Auditing is required to assure that property falls within the appropriate tax base.

Further, the allocation of property within a given structure aside, the corporate structure itself is a matter of choice for the firm. Many factors such as cost and complementarity of the product lines play roles in the designs of the corporate structure. One factor, however is the tax consequence. Other things equal, from a corporate point of view, capital intensive product lines are better placed in its regulated gross-earnings-taxed divisions, while less capital intensive product lines can remain subject to property tax. That these incentives exist raises the issue of the nonneutrality or the existing tax system.

## FORM OF TELEPHONE PROPERTY TAXATION

In structuring a telephone company property tax, there are three separate issues: (1) who will assess the taxable value of the firms, (2) what basis or system will be used to determine assessed value, and (3) who will levy the tax on the determined value and receive the revenue?

### THE BASIS AND RESPONSIBILITY FOR ASSESSMENT

For the first issue, the options are either state government assessment or property assessment by each locality, which includes telephone company property. Of the forty-four contiguous states that impose a property tax on telephone utilities, thirty-four use the state assessment. And of these thirty-four, twenty-eight assess using the unit method, which attempts to value the whole property (personalty and real estate) as a unit, rather than examining the separate value of the component parts (see Appendix 1).

*State assessment of unit value.* It is obvious that the unit method is inappropriate for local assessment, requiring each local assessor to value the property located only in that jurisdiction, probably based on historic cost, adjusted for depreciation. The difficulties of this are well known, particularly because the value of some transmission property cannot really be separated from other aspects of the firm. The value of a telephone line depends, obviously, on the number of calls carried. In addition, local assessment can result in identical property being assessed at different values in different localities.

The state assessed property section of the Minnesota department of revenue currently assesses electric utilities, pipelines, gas distribution companies, and railroads. The department has indicated that they also have the authority to assess telephone company property.

*Local assessment of real property.* The presumption in favor of state assessment of telephone company property is not based on the viewpoint that local officials would be unable handle the assessment job (there is ample evidence that they can),[3] but rather on the view that the telephone company should continue to be treated as if it were a natural monopoly similar to electric and gas utilities. One important policy implication of acceptance of this traditional approach is that the tax neutrality goal is not violated if the telephone property tax base includes personalty as well as realty.

In a postdivestiture environment, however, the traditional view—that the telephone company is like a utility/monopoly—is being rapidly undercut as new technologies are developed and new firms enter the telecommunication industry. Now, microwave and satellite devices allow for the development of alternatives to the traditional telephone network. The average telephone user can choose from among several long distance carriers, and local customers have put into place private systems (some quite large) that bypass the traditional telephone network. Development in the computer and cable television fields will likely expand customers' service options in the future.

The convergence of these economic as well as technological forces (which were formally acknowledged with the 1982 consent decree) argues for a rethinking of the state/local tax treatment of the firms in the telecommunications industry. Specifically, Minnesota's policymakers must consider whether in view of the increasingly competitive nature of telecommunications, the telephone company must now be treated like any other commercial/industrial entity for tax purposes. If the answer is yes, the tax neutrality goal requires that the gross receipts tax be replaced by a locally assessed ad valorem tax on real property only.

## ASSESSMENT RATIO

The second issue concerns the assessment method and valuation ratios to use. Current tax law specifies an assessment ratio of 43% for real property (land and buildings) of public utilities, and 33.3% for machinery, tools, or implements used by public utilities and electric or gas distribution companies. Assuming that the real property of telephone companies would become subject to taxation if the shift is made, the assessment ratios could be, as currently specified or appropriate to any new property tax classification systems, recommended by this commission.

## DISPOSITION OF REVENUE

The final issue is the levying of the tax and disposition of the revenue. Although the property is to be assessed by the state, the tax could be collected by either the state or local governments. For instance, as previously noted, once valued, utility and railroad property is allocated to each locality where the property is located for taxation, the revenue going directly to each local government. Alternatively, the state could levy and collect the tax at an average state tax rate and then distribute the revenue to localities according to a formula. A third option, which is of particular interest because the gross receipts tax revenue accrues to the state's general fund, is to similarly have the telephone property tax be a direct state property tax. Any of the three structures is administratively feasible, the choice depending on other state intergovernmental aid programs and state revenue needs.

# REVENUE AND DISTRIBUTION EFFECTS OF PROPERTY TAX

### REAL PLUS PERSONAL PROPERTY TAXATION

In some ways, the administration of the gross receipts tax has made it equivalent to a property tax. As has been discussed, before divestiture the long distance revenue of AT&T was distributed among the Bell System Companies proportionally to the firm's net plant investment. Thus, interstate revenue of Northwestern Bell Telephone was both determined and taxed on the basis of Northwestern Bell's property relative to total AT&T and Bell System property. In essence then, part of Northwestern's revenue for tax purposes was proportional to property value. In addition, AT&T's revenue was allocated across states on the basis of the share of property value in the state.

Similarly it is noted that GTE Sprint Communications, Inc., has argued that if they are to be subject to the gross receipts tax, revenue should be apportioned to Minnesota on the basis of the fraction of the firm's property value in the state. In that case, the gross receipts tax is directly a property tax (with allowance for appropriate setting of tax rates to generate equal yield). To the extent that revenue for the gross receipts tax is apportioned on the basis of property values for these interstate service firms, transition to a telephone property tax would not alter the distribution of tax burden between these firms.[4]

At the request of the commission, the Minnesota Department of Revenue estimated the property tax liability for four telephone companies, given particular structure assumptions. The assumptions are as follows:

*Valuation method.* Unit value based both on historic cost less depreciation and net operating income capitalized at 11%; telephone system personal property included.

*Assessment ratio.*  43%

*Tax rate.*  97.85 mills (estimated 1984 state-average rate).

One estimate for Northwestern Bell Telephone, based on 1983 data, is the predivestiture firm and thus includes some value now attributable to AT&T. A second estimate for Northwestern Bell is for the regulated entry in 1984, i.e., the postdivestiture Bell. The property tax estimates are a 1984 estimate of Bell's gross receipts tax. The results are shown in Table 5.

TABLE 5
Telephone Company Property (Real Plus Personal)
Tax Estimates Before and After Divestiture
($000)

| | Predivestiture (1983) North-western Bell | Postdivestiture (1984) | | | |
|---|---|---|---|---|---|
| | | North-western Bell | Sleepy Eye Telephone Co. | Benton Co-op. | Lismore Co-op. |
| Unit value[a] | $4,259,684 | $3,726,000 | $4,542 | $3,079 | $295 |
| Minnesota taxable value | 1,813,711 | 1,588,140 | 4,528 | 2,849 | 290 |
| Minnesota assessed value | 779,896 | 670,000 | 1,947 | 1,225 | 125 |
| Property tax[b] | 76,313 | 65,560 | 191 | 120 | 12 |
| Gross earnings[c] tax | 61,534 | 39,500 | 52 | 34 | 5 |
| % Gross earnings taxed at 7% | 79% | 79% | 0% | 0% | 0% |
| Property taxes % of gross receipts tax | 124% | 166% | 367% | 353% | 240% |

[a]Estimate by Minnesota Department of Revenue
[b]97.85 mills
[c]Northwestern Bell and 1982 AT&T tax

If Northwestern Bell Telephone had been subject to a tax on real plus personal property in 1983, it is estimated that its liability would have been 24% greater than actual gross receipts tax for that year, given the assumption of the sample property tax structure. Similarly, Bell's 1983 estimated property tax is about 19% greater than the sum of Northwestern Bell's and AT&T's actual 1983 gross receipts taxes. In contrast, it appears that the three smaller companies would have faced property tax liabilities three and one-half or two and one-half times their own gross receipts taxes. In part, this difference between Bell and the smaller firms is the result of 79% of Bell's gross receipts tax being taxed at 7%, while none of the three smaller firms pays any gross receipts tax at 7%.

In addition to the change in the relative tax burden of the smaller firms, it also appears that the absolute tax burden of the smaller firms would be increased. The breakup of AT&T should have little immediate effect on the receipts or revenues of these smaller firms. Thus, both the actual 1983 gross receipt taxes and the estimated 1983 property taxes are probably relatively accurate estimates of the respective 1984 taxes. Although the ninety-eight firms taxed only at the 4% rate paid only about $5.1 million in gross receipts tax in 1982 (7% of total), their collective property taxes could have approached $12-$18 million, based on the sample of three smaller firms. In essence, these estimates suggest that the smaller firms generate much less revenue per dollar of investment (measured by historic cost less depreciation) than Bell, and thus do better with a gross receipts than property tax.

The revenue department also prepared an estimate of Bell's 1984 property tax (realty plus personalty after divestiture). The estimates shows about a 13% decline in the unit value of Northwestern Bell Telephone as a result of divestiture. Such a decrease could result from several factors. Before divestiture, consumers could lease telephone equipment from Bell. After divestiture, that property was transferred to AT&T, from whom some consumers continue to lease, while others have purchased the phones from AT&T. In either case the property of Bell decreases, in the first instance to be replaced by property newly acquired by AT&T. In addition, certain other services (and property) offered by Bell before divestiture may now be provided by one of the unregulated entities of Northwestern Bell Corporation or U.S. West.

Bell's estimated 1983 property taxes are only 7% greater than Bell's 1983 gross receipts tax but are fully 66% greater than Bell's estimated 1984 gross receipts tax, after divestiture (Table 5). It should be noted, however, that the gross receipts tax estimate assumes no access charge revenue for Bell, and thus underestimates the likely long-run revenues (and thus the property tax: gross receipts ratio) of Bell. In other words, after divestiture and without access charges, Bell looks much more like the smaller phone companies in terms of comparative property tax/gross receipts tax effects. Without access charges, Bell simply is expected to generate less revenue per investment dollar, at least initially, than the old Bell System did.

Thus, it appears that substitution of a statewide telephone company tax on real plus personal property for the gross receipts tax would likely increase the relative tax burden on local phone companies, including Northwestern Bell Telephone Company. However, this conclusion is sensitive to the access charge question, which would increase the revenue and gross receipts tax of the local companies. And further, it would decrease the long distance firms' taxes only if the receipts are not apportioned by property value in any way, or to the extent the firm pays any gross receipts tax.

REAL PROPERTY TAXATION

The discussion and numbers in the preceding section are based on the assumption that the property tax base would include personal as well as real property. Thus, the tax would be applied to such items as switching equipment, computers, tools, showroom equipment, motor vehicles, and cables in addition to buildings and structures.

If one views providers of telephone services as still operating essentially as a monopoly, then this divergence from the structure of the Minnesota property tax as it is applied to other commercial/industrial activity (i.e., on real estate only) is probably warranted. Indeed, there is even a theoretical case for the gross receipts tax.

However, in a postdivestiture world, the arguments behind the inclusion of personalty in the property tax base need to be reconsidered. This is true because "the telephone company" as a result of technological changes now finds itself participating in a broad telecommunications market no longer easily characterized as having monopoly barriers to entry.

The increasingly competitive nature of the industry appears to be particularly clear on the long distance market, which now has at least ten firms competing for customer service in Minnesota.

Although things are proceeding at a somewhat slower pace with respect to providers of local telephone service, there is increasing evidence that the "copper wire logic"—i.e., the only feasible way to provide local telephone services between two points was to string a wire or lay a cable—is rapidly becoming obsolete. Now one can not only communicate locally through wires and cables, but also through such bypass technologies as microwave, FM radio, cable TV, and satellite.

These new technologies and innovations are further evidenced by the emergence of "smart buildings" (e.g., the Minnesota world trade center now under construction) and mircosystem networks (e.g., Northern States Power, and certain Minnesota state agencies) that permit people to establish their own telephone companies, bypassing the local regulated telephone company except to connect with local numbers.

Although these technologies and innovations have not yet greatly cut into the traditional local telephone market (Northwestern Bell still handles 85%-90% of local business services), they promise to account for an increasing share of the voice communication market in the years ahead.

These developments raise important questions for Minnesota tax policy: should the ninety-four regulated local telephone companies continue to be treated as if they have their traditional monopoly power? If so, how long can this treatment be justified? If not, what is the justification for treating telephone activities—long distance as well as local—different from other commercial/industrial activities for the purpose of taxation?

If the decision is that the era of the telephone monopoly has ended (or is coming to an end), and the evidence suggests that it is, the neutrality criterion requires that the telephone companies be treated similarly to other commercial and industrial businesses. Not only should the gross receipts tax be replaced with an ad valorem tax, but also, the property tax should be levied on real estate only.

Substitution of an ad valorem real property tax on telephone businesses would entail substantial revenue loss for the Minnesota treasury, at least in the early years. Indeed, estimates derived from public documents for the commission by Gerald Garski of the Minnesota Department of Revenue indicate that if the gross earnings tax were replaced by an ad valorem tax on the real property of telephone companies, FY 1985 revenues would fall to somewhere between $6 million (if cables were considered personalty) and $10 million (cables treated as realty). Of course, the loss would be complete to the state if it were determined that assessment and collection should be turned over to local governments.

The gross earnings—ad valorem real property tax choice provides a dramatic illustration of both the importance of relationship between the state's changing economic structure and its tax policy, and the magnitude of the tradeoffs that may occur with respect to achievement of the goals of a good tax policy.

Finally, it is important to note that substitution of a property tax would not resolve all the tax difficulties of deregulation. If a statewide property tax were levied on telephone companies, the question of what constitutes a telephone company would still be at issue. However, the incentive to avoid the state property tax for a collection of local property taxes seems less than the incentive to avoid the gross receipts tax for the local property tax. In addition, a state telephone company property tax would have to continually deal with what type of property (e.g., personalty as well as real?) is taxable and how the value is to be determined. One can imagine the state's decision to tax an interstate carrier's satellite as property (real or personal?) assessable to the state. These administrative issues exist already in the thirty-four states levying a state property tax on telecommunication firms. The advantage of an ad valorem real property tax, then, is not that it will prevent technological changes from altering the tax, but rather that these firms are treated much more like other types of businesses.

## RECOMMENDATIONS

### REPLACEMENT OF THE GROSS RECEIPTS TAX ON TELEPHONE AND TELEGRAPH COMPANIES WITH LOCAL AD VALOREM TAXATION

The commission finds that the telecommunications industry is experiencing and will continue to experience fundamental and rapid changes in its economic and institutional arrangements. In particular, three factors are converging so as to change the structure of the sector. First, the industry is no longer highly regulated and monopolistic, a reality that has been validated and then reinforced by the 1983 divestiture of AT&T. Second, new technologies (satellite, microwave, and, in the future, cable and computers) have allowed the development of alternatives to the traditional telephone network. And, third, there has been a change in federal regulatory policies designed to increase competition in the industry and eventually lead to complete deregulation of long distance rates and equal access to local telephone networks of competing long distance carriers.

Accordingly, the commission concludes that the traditional method of applying gross receipts (earnings) taxes in lieu of property taxes to telephone and telegraph companies is breaking down. The result is that the dual system of taxing according to gross receipts (on regulated activities) and property tax (on the deregulated divisions) is and will continue to create unusually difficult problems of tax administration (the line between property used for regulated and deregulated activities is blurred) and violations of the commission's goal of tax uniformity or neutrality requiring taxpayers in similar circumstances to be treated similarly). Therefore, the commission recommends the short-term maintenance of the gross receipts tax (one or (two years) in order for the state to plan for the replacement of this tax with a property tax that for tax base purposes treats telecommunication businesses like other commercial/industrial activities. Thus, under existing Minnesota statutes, the tax would be levied on real property only. The responsibility for assessment and collection shall be at the local rather than state level.

In making this recommendation, the commission recognizes that this replacement will result in a revenue loss to the state general fund much larger than the additional property tax funds that will accrue to local governments. However, given the nature of the rapid changes of the telecommunications industry, this change is justified on neutrality (uniformity) grounds.

## NEED TO EXAMINE THE METHOD OF VALUING RAILROAD OPERATING PROPERTY

Under the present system of valuing railroad operating property, the state assesses property by the unit value (companywide) method and then apportions the tax collected back to local jurisdictions on the basis of several property-related criteria. There are administrative and efficiency benefits to this method, particularly when the value of the components (parcels) of a particular type of business property (e.g., utility) is difficult to separate from its role in the integrated whole. However, one cost of the unit value approach is that by not valuing according to the "highest and best use" criterion applied to other business property, total statewide assessments are often well below that which would occur if railroad operating property were treated like other businesses, regulated and nonregulated alike. In Minnesota, the use of the unit value approach resulted in a statewide tax base that is 49% of what it would be under ad valorem taxation (1984).

Although the commission recommends that the present unit value method be retained for valuing railroad operating property, it is concerned that this approach may result in undue preferential treatment of railroad operating property relative to other commercial and industrial property. Accordingly, the commission further recommends that the state examine whether greater use of an ad valorem approach or features associated with that approach can be utilized in the taxing railroad operating property.

## APPENDIX 1
## ELECTRIC AND GAS (REGULATED) UTILITY TAXATION: THE UNIT VALUE METHOD

Properties of electric and gas utilities and pipelines in Minnesota are taxed on the same basis as all other property, an ad valorem property tax method. The collected taxes are paid to the counties, municipalities, school districts, and special districts in which utility properties are located for the support of those local units of government.

Utility property includes real estate and personal property. Real property consists of land, structures (property valued at 43%), and attached machinery (property valued at 33.3%). Personal property consists of transmission lines, distribution systems, meters, services, etc. (property valued at 43%).

Since 1975, as a result of a Minnesota Supreme Court ruling in *Independent School District No. 99 vs. State of Minnesota,* investor owned utilities have been valued under the unit value concept. The previous system, known as the Hatfield formula, used only cost to determine utility property. Generally, property values are determined by using a combination of cost, income, and market value. The court held that by using only one indicator of value, the state failed to arrive at an appropriate market value for the property. It therefore instructed the department of revenue to devise a system that considered more than just cost in the valuation process. The system arrived at was the unit value method.

Under the unit value method, utility-type property (that crosses various jurisdictions) is valued in its entirety without regard to the individual components. All parts contribute equally to the total operation, regardless of their location. This state-administered approach has two important merits. First, it reflects the current economic and market conditions and can be easily adjusted when changes in those conditions occur. Second, the valuation is predictable because it is based on known factors used in the unit value formula, i.e., the rate of depreciation used in determining the value based on cost and the rate for capitalizing net operating income used in determining the value based on income.

All electric and gas utilities, except for municipal-owned utilities, are taxed on the ad valorem property tax system. Investor-owned utilities, as previously mentioned, are valued under the unit value method, while the rural cooperative utilities are valued under the Hatfield formula because they do not have an income stream that can be capitalized and translated into a market value.

## APPENDIX 2
## TAXATION OF RAILROAD PROPERTY IN MINNESOTA

This appendix discusses the taxation of railroad companies from 1979 until the present. The structure of the present tax is described, followed by a discussion of the recent Soo Line case and its impacts. Finally, alternative approaches to railroad taxation are discussed.

### FROM GROSS EARNINGS TO AD VALOREM TAXATION

In 1979 the gross earnings tax on railroads in lieu of a property tax was repealed and replaced by a property tax on railroad operating property. This action was in response to the 1976 federal "4 R's" act (Railroad Revitalization and Regulatory Reform Act), which required that state tax treatment of railroad property not discriminate relative to other commercial-industrial property, lest it unreasonably burden interstate commerce. The department of revenue felt that the gross earnings tax would not pass this test. The action by the legislature was empowered by a 1974 amendment to the state constitution allowing the legislature to alter its method of taxing railroads.

UNIT VALUATION

The legislature required that railroad property be valued using the unit basis of establishing value. Rather than valuing railroad real property separately, this approach calculates the total value of railroad property, then subtracts nontaxable property to arrive at total taxable property.

The unit basis uses three factors to calculate railroad property values: the cost approach, the income approach and the stock and debt approach. The cost factor equals the cost of all road and equipment, general expenditures, property leased to and from others, and the cost of construction work in progress. Beginning in 1984, a deduction for depreciation and obsolescence was allowed. The income fraction is calculated by averaging the net operating income of a railway for the most recent five years and applying a capitalization rate (14.6% in 1984). The stock and debt factor uses the total of liabilities and stock equity to calculate asset value using the identity: Assets = Liabilities + Equity.

If all three of these calculations can be made, the unit value is computed by weighting the income factor at 60%, the cost factor at 15%, and the stock and debt factor at 25%. If all three calculations cannot be made for a company, those that can be are weighted more heavily.

Once the unit value of a railroad's property is established, the value attributable to Minnesota is calculated. This is done by allocating total value in proportion to the ratio of the Minnesota total to the system's total of these four factors: miles of railroad tracks, ton-miles of revenue freight, gross revenue from transportation operations, and original cost of road property. The average of these four factors is calculated, giving an allocation percentage for Minnesota which is then applied to total unit value to give Minnesota unit value.

APPORTIONMENT TO LOCAL GOVERNMENT

From this value, deductions are allowed for pollution control equipment, railroad nonoperating property, and personal property. Railroad nonoperating property is property not used by the railroad in performance of rail transportation services. This property is subject to local valuation and assessment. A formula is used to calculate the personal property exclusion. The amount remaining after making these subtractions from Minnesota unit value is the statewide market value of railroad property for tax purposes. This property value is apportioned to the taxing districts in which a railroad operates in proportion to a three-factor formula based on the share of total railroad operating land value in each jurisdiction, average cost per mile of certain track cost accounts, and the share of structures of over $10,000 in original cost.

After the property values have been apportioned to the taxing districts, they are equalized. This ensures that railroad property is not assessed at 100% of its value while other commercial and industrial property is assessed at less than 100% of value. The estimated current year assessment sales ratio for commercial-industrial property in each county is calculated and multiplied by the estimated market value of operating railroad property apportioned to the jurisdiction. Thus, in a jurisdiction with a commercial-industrial sales/assessment ratio of 83%, the market value of all railroad property apportioned to taxing districts in the county will be reduced by 17%. The assessed value calculated for this property is 43% of the equalized market value, which is then taxed at the millage rates applicable in each taxing district. No credits or refunds are available for railroad property, so gross tax equals net tax.

SOO LINE CASE

In November of 1983, the state tax court decided the case of the *Soo Line Railroad vs. Commissioner of Revenue*. The court made three important rulings affecting the taxation of railroad property. First, it was ruled that the cost factor as originally designed was not a valid method of calculating unit value because depreciation and obsolescence had not been allowed. Second, railroad signals and certain other equipment were ruled to be personal property, not real property, and thus were not taxable under the Minnesota property tax. Third, it was required that the market value of railroad properties be equalized relative to commercial-industrial values in each county.

The cost factor of the unit value calculation had been based on the original cost of railroad property. The department of revenue formerly did not allow a depreciation deduction from original cost. Deductions for depreciation and obsolescence were permitted only when replacement cost was used in the calculation of unit value. The ruling disallowed this approach, arguing that any cost figures must allow a depreciation deduction. The present method now bases calculations on restated cost, which uses a depreciation accounting basis rather than a retirement-replacement-betterment accounting basis.

The second ruling determined that railroad signals and similar equipment are personal property not subject to the property tax. This was based on Minnesota Statutes section 272.03, subdivision 1 (c), which states that ". . . real property shall not include tools, implements, machinery, and equipment attached to or installed in real property for use in the business or production activity conducted thereon. . . ." Rails, ties, and track equipment were classified as real property subject to taxation.

The third major ruling required that railroad property values be equalized. Formerly this calculation was not done. The court ruled that this resulted in over-taxation of railroad property relative to commercial and industrial property. This change accounted for roughly half of the tax reduction for railroad companies.

Another part of this ruling advised the revenue department to use 14.5% as the capitalization rate in the income factor instead of the 11% previously used.

The effect of the Soo Line case was to reduce property tax revenues from the Soo Line by about 40%. For property taxes levied in 1984, payable in 1985, the revenue department estimates local revenues to be roughly $8 million. It was expected that other railroad companies would apply for refunds on the same grounds, causing similar tax reductions. This reduction in property tax revenues is a particularly serious problem for areas with a disproportionately large share of railroad property. For instance, Fridley had about $9 million in railroad property value, and Dilworth, a city of 2,600, had roughly $1 million in rail property. Northeastern Minnesota is more dependent on railroad property tax revenues than most other regions, with 2.6% of its total assessed value in railroad property compared to 0.5% statewide. For assessment years 1981 and 1982, the state is providing a partial reimbursement to certain severely affected localities.

TAX POLICY OPTIONS

The unit value approach to valuing railroad property is fundamentally different from that used to value most other property. Unit value can be described as an appraisal of an integrated property as a whole without reference to the value of its component parts. One aspect of this approach is that property is taxed only to the extent that the company is productive, i.e., has a positive unit value. This can be important for an industry like railroads that may be required to maintain certain unprofitable lines. Note, however, that a portion of the total unit value may still be allocated to such property, yielding taxes for the jurisdiction in which the unproductive property is located.

The alternative to the unit value approach to taxation of railroad property is the traditional approach to real property appraisal, which attempts to value property at its "highest and best use." This concept requires that each parcel of property be appraised as though it were being put to its most profitable use, given probable legal, physical, and financial constraints. For railroads this determination can be difficult. The value of railroad property in most cases could potentially be equal to the value of adjacent land, absent certain legal restrictions. However, this potential is not reached because of two particular circumstances of railroads. First, the value of an entire rail line is dependent on the fact that the line is continuous. Second, since railroad abandonments are restricted, property will not always be used at its highest and best use. It is not that this approach to appraisal is not helpful, simply that the reduction in property values is very difficult to measure because of these restrictions.

Gordon Moe, Minneapolis city assessor, has advanced a proposal that attempts to apply a highest and best use concept to the taxation of railroad operating property. Railroad lands would be valued at either the value per acre of adjacent land or the average value per acre of property in each taxing jurisdiction. Buildings would be valued by assessors at their fair market value. There is an important legal question about the validity of this approach. In 1981, the Texas Supreme Court ruled that valuing railroad operating property by comparing market values of adjacent land did not clearly meet the standard that assessments not be arbitrary and grossly excessive. Instead it approved of the unit value approach in this case. Whether or not this case is relevant to Minnesota is unclear.

Such a proposal, even if it raised the same taxes from railroad companies, would be likely to result in a different distribution of tax revenues among local taxing districts than it does at present. The current formula for distributing property values among taxing jurisdictions is a complicated one using three factors: the value of railroad operating land, the share of track mileage, and the distribution of railroad operating structures. Distributing taxes in proportion to local property values would generally shift revenues towards taxing jurisdictions with higher property values and higher mill rates.

Another possible change is to continue to make a statewide calculation of the taxable property base, but to include some measure of local land values in the calculation. This would have the advantage of keeping the revenue department principally responsible for administration of this tax while basing the calculation more on property market values, consistent with the taxation of other property. There are similar alternatives, compromises between a strict highest and best use approach and the current unit value method.

Neither the highest and best use nor the unit value approach are without flaws. They both can be evaluated according to the tax structure goals the commission has established:

*Certainty/Predictability.* Under the unit value approach, taxes will fluctuate with income, costs, and asset value. Under the highest and best use approach, taxes vary with other land values. Railroad companies are better able to estimate taxes under the former approach.

*Simplicity.* The unit value approach is a much more complicated calculation, but once in place it is understandable to both the companies and the revenue department. A highest and best use approach is readily understandable, although it does require assessors to value parcels of property which at present they do not. In short, administration is feasible under either approach.

*Neutrality.* The unit value approach bases a company's taxes on the taxable Minnesota portion of three values: net asset value, the asset value implied by five-year net income, and the sum of liabilities and equity values. It is quite possible that two companies could have similar Minnesota taxable unit values, but different values of property holdings. The unit value approach would yield similar taxes for these two companies (subject to variations in local mill rates) while a highest and best use approach would result in different tax bills.

If railroad companies were free to abandon lines and sell property, a property tax using the highest and best use approach would be more efficient and satisfy the commission's neutrality goal. However, because railroad properties are not able freely to abandon unproductive (nonincome-producing) properties, taxing companies at a property value higher than the value of the property to them, while restricting abandonment, creates an inefficiency. Because federal and Minnesota laws require governmental approval before allowing abandonment, this is a key consideration. The unit value approach may create incentives to adjust a company's income stream, total asset value or stated system costs. It is unclear how much these potential incentives would affect a railroad company's behavior.

*Competitiveness.* No information is currently available comparing Minnesota's level of taxes on railroad companies to other states. At present, every state with railroads now uses the unit value method, which makes compliance with Minnesota's method of taxation much easier under a unit value approach than under any other.

## ENDNOTES

1. This chapter is based on the paper by Ronald Fisher and Lawrence Martin, "Taxes and Telecommunications in an Era of Change," in *Staff Papers,* vol. 2 of the *Final Report of the Minnesota Tax Study Commission,* ed. Robert D. Ebel and Therese J. McGuire (St. Paul: Butterworth Legal Publishers, 1985).

2. Under a pure (unregulated) system, gross receipts taxation would provide an incentive to integrate vertically. In this case, however, the local companies (those which were part of the Bell system) are proscribed from selling long distance service; therefore, no merger to avoid the tax is possible.

3. For a discussion of local versus central assessments of special purpose property, see Robert D. Ebel and Joan E. Towles, *Payments In Lieu of Taxes on Federal Real Property* (Washington, D.C.: U.S. Advisory Commission on Intergovernmental Relations, 1981), vol. 1, pp. 68-70.

4. Fisher and Martin, "Taxes and Telecommunications in an Era of Change."

# 21
# Local Nonproperty Taxes

The state has primary responsibility for creating and maintaining a suitable system for financing both state and local governments. Thus, the state must plan for the overall revenue structure. This chapter helps to inform the state in overall planning by identifying nonproperty tax sources of revenue available for local finance and evaluating these sources in terms of statewide tax policy goals—simplicity, neutrality, accountability, revenue potential, and equity. The specific revenue sources to be discussed are nontax revenues from user fees and charges, local sales tax, and local income tax.

Many motivations contribute to the desire for local revenue from nonproperty tax sources. These include:

- *Property tax relief.* The property tax is capriciously related to the income-flows and real estate wealth holdings of homeowners. Also, those jurisdictions with little property value per capita bear greater burdens in raising property tax revenue.
- *Tax base equalization.* Although there are tax base disparities among jurisdictions for all local revenue sources, the disparities for local sales and income taxes may not be distributed identically with property tax disparities. Allowing two or more revenue sources may result in some equalization of tax base among localities.
- *Revenue flexibility.* Nonproperty tax revenues enable local governments to be less dependent on state aids, and they allow the localities to raise revenue from communities and others who pay no property taxes.

As has been noted above (chapters 3 and 6), Minnesota has a centralized system of raising revenue, but a decentralized spending system. In 1982, localities collected 26% of total state and local taxes, but accounted for about 70% of total expenditures. A large share of state revenue was returned to local governments to finance specific programs and to provide property tax relief.

The sources of state and local revenues in Minnesota in 1982 were presented in chapter 4. Of all local revenues in Minnesota, 41% comes from intergovernmental grants. The localities also collect property tax revenue but receive little or no revenue from income, corporation, sales, excise, inheritance, or other taxes. Localities supplement their incomes from grants and property taxes with nontax revenues like fees, service charges, and special assessments.

Localities in Minnesota use nonproperty taxes less often than other localities in the U.S. Local general sales and/or income taxes are levied by one or more local governments in thirty-three states. And both general sales and income taxes are common in large cities. Of the seventy-two cities over 200,000 population, only eighteen—including Minneapolis and St. Paul— have neither a sales tax nor an income tax. Minnesota has no local income taxes and only Duluth and Rochester have local general sales taxes. While Minnesota is low in use of nonproperty tax, this is compensated by relatively large shares of state aid and nontax revenue.

The remainder of this chapter will describe and analyze the local options for increased revenues from three revenue sources—local nontax revenues, local sales taxes, and local income taxes. A final section compares the local sales and income taxes to the property tax in terms of the efficiency, simplicity, and equity goals of state tax policy.

## NONTAX LOCAL REVENUES

Minnesota's localities make substantial use of nontax sources of revenue. The category of nontax general revenues normally includes special assessments; licenses and permits; charges for services; sewer, water, and garbage operating revenues; interest; and other miscellaneous general revenue. According to the U.S. census bureau, Minnesota local government nontax general revenue was 55.3% of local revenue in 1981, compared to 36.5% nationally. For all local jurisdictions in Minnesota, per capita nontax revenue averaged $443, nearly one-third more than per capita property tax revenue of $341. Nationally, nontax was smaller, $263, and less than property tax, $348.

For Minnesota cities (in 1981), the ratio of nontax to local tax revenue was 74.1% compared to 38.0% in all U.S. cities. The average per capita amount of nontax revenue was $330 ($161 nationally) compared to $95 ($138) of property tax. In counties, townships, special districts, and school districts, Minnesota had slightly larger proportions of nontax to tax revenues than the national average.

About three-fourths of nontax general revenue is generated as payments for locally provided public services. Payments are suitable for financing many local public functions—urban renewal, water, garbage disposal, hospitals, and many other services—and Minnesota's localities already know the effectiveness of these charges. Minnesota's relative dependence on nontax revenue may be due to the long history of local levy limitations on property taxes, or to a direct "pay for what you use" philosophy, or both.

An efficient local payments system assesses a price for the cost of a service against the immediate user of the service, whether the user is a household or a business. These charges promote efficiency only when each user pays the full cost of the public service being provided. In many cases, where users do pay fully for the services, it could be provided privately. Thus, for example, some cities have private garbage service and some have public service on a fee-for-service basis.

Charges will not be efficient if the service has additional benefits received by secondary users who do not pay for these benefits or if use of the service imposes costs on others or indirectly involves demand for additional public services. Public education is an example of a public service with second party benefits; if public education were provided only on a user fee basis, revenue would not support the appropriate level of education. Conversely, use of some public services, like city streets, imposes additional costs on second parties (for example, the time costs of traffic jams and health costs of exposure to automobile exhaust) and creates demand for additional public services (traffic control and health services). User charges will not pay the full costs of those public services that are accompanied by congestion and other detrimental, indirect effects. Either these extra costs must be subsidized by other revenues or the user fees must be high enough to discourage demand for the service.

Local jurisdictions may be able to develop some additional nontax sources of local revenue. However, the chapter on levy limitations argued that local charges are unlikely to substitute for significant cutbacks in local government aid. In the same vein, nontax revenues may not be able to accommodate a substantially greater share of the local revenue requirement. On a per capita basis, Minnesota's average local nontax bill already is greater than the national local property tax bill. User charges, considered alone, may not be able to bear a growing share of local revenue needs, given recent increases in dependence on these revenues. Between 1978 and 1982, the categories of fees, charges, and special assessments increased from 50% to 69% of total local revenue in Minnesota.

## LOCAL SALES TAX

Counties are permitted to levy a general sales tax in nineteen states; the tax rate ranges from 0.25% to 3.00%. Cities levy sales taxes in twenty-one states, including Minnesota (in the cities of Duluth and Rochester), and current rates range from 0.25% to 5.0%. Table 1 presents the data for local use of the general sales tax in other states. In some states all similar local jurisdictions have a sales tax; in other states only a few jurisdictions tax sales. In addition, Alaska borroughs and most Louisiana school districts levy sales taxes. In three states local sales taxes were authorized but not

## TABLE 1
### Local Sales Taxes By State

| Counties | Rates | Rate Limits | Voter Approval | No. of Units |
|---|---|---|---|---|
| States where all counties tax: | | | | |
| Utah[1] | .75-.875 | .875 | No | 29 |
| Washington | .5-1.0 | 1.0 | No | 39 |
| Virginia | 1.0 | 1.0 | No | 95 |
| Illinois | 1.0 | 1.25 | No | 102 |
| California | 1.25 | 1.25 | No | 58 |
| Louisiana[2] | 1.0-2.0 | 3.0 | Yes | 63 |
| Tennessee[3] | 1.0-2.25 | 2.25 | Yes | 94 |
| States where at least 50% of the counties tax: | | | | |
| North Carolina | 1.0 | 1.5 | No | 99 |
| New York[4] | 1.0-3.03 | 3.0 | No | 51 |
| Georgia | 1.0 | 1.0 | Yes | 128 |
| Ohio | .5-1.0 | 1.0 | No | 59 |
| Wyoming | 1.0 | 1.0 | Yes | 15 |
| Missouri[5] | .375-.5 | 1.0 | Yes | 70 |
| States where less than 50% of the counties tax: | | | | |
| Kansas | .5-1.0 | 1.0 | Yes | 51 |
| Colorado[6] | .25-2.0 | 4.0 | Yes | 27 |
| New Mexico | .25 | .25 | Yes | 10 |
| Alabama | .5-3.0 | None | No | 41 |
| Arkansas | 1.0 | 2.0 | Yes | 11 |
| Nevada[7] | .25 | .25 | Yes | 1 |
| Cities | | | | |
| States where at least 98% of cities tax: | | | | |
| California | 1.0 | .85-1.0 | No | 434 |
| New Mexico[8] | .25-.75 | .75 | No | 98 |
| Texas | 1.0 | 1.0 | Yes | 1,117 |
| Virginia | 1.0 | 1.0 | No | 41 |
| Washington[9] | .5-1.0 | 1.0 | No | 273 |
| Illinois | .5-1.0 | 1.0 | No | 1,253 |
| Utah[10] | .75-.875 | .875 | No | 219 |
| Other states where at least half the cities levy tax: | | | | |
| Arizona | 1.0-2.0 | None | No | 70 |
| Oklahoma | 1.0-4.0 | None | Yes | 427 |
| Alabama | .5-3.0 | None | No | 310 |
| Alaska | 1.0-5.0 | 6.0 | No | 92 |
| Colorado | 1.0-4.0 | * | Yes | 170 |
| Louisiana | .3-3.5 | ** | Yes | 161 |

*Continued on next page*

Table 1—*Continued*

| Counties | Rates | Rate Limits | Voter Approval | No. of Units |
|---|---|---|---|---|
| States where less than half the cities tax: | | | | |
| Missouri | .5-1.0 | 1.0 | Yes | 360 |
| South Dakota | 1.0-2.0 | 2.0 | Yes | 74 |
| Kansas | .5-1.0 | 1.0 | Yes | 83 |
| New York | 1.0-3.0 | *** | No | 29 |
| Tennessee | .25-2.25 | 2.25 | Yes | 16 |
| Nebraska | 1.0-1.5 | 1.5 | Yes | 12 |
| Minnesota[11] | 1.0 | 1.0 | Yes | 2 |
| Arkansas | 1.0 | 2.0 | Yes | 32 |

1   Limits will increase to 1.0% in 1987.
2   The combined local rate (parish, municipality, and school district) may not exceed 3.0%.
3   Maximum local rate with county precedence.
4   The combined city and county rate may not exceed 3.0%. Cities may preempt 1.5%, but cities and counties generally negotiate the division of taxing authority.
5   St. Louis County rate is 3.0%.
6   Combined local rates may not exceed 4.0%; combined local state rate may not exceed 7%. A temporary state-local limit of 7.5% expires July, 1984, when the state sales tax is reduced from 3.5% to 3.0%.
7   The state made the 3.75% county sales tax mandatory in 1981, effectively raising the state rate and returning the 3.75% to the county of origin. In 1981 counties were authorized to levy an additional 0.25% for transit.
8   Increases to 1.0% in July, 1984.
9   If the county in which a city is located levies a tax, the city rate is lowered to 0.425%. An additional 0.5% may be levied with voter approval.
10  Rate limits will increase to 1.0% in 1987; resort communities with qualifying transient populations may levy an additional 1.0%.
11  Rochester's 1.0% tax is authorized by special legislation and is dedicated for a flood control and recreation improvement project.
 *  4% maximum rates, not precluding county tax of 1%; total state, county, and city rates may not exceed 7.0%.
 ** Total parish, municipal and school district rates may not exceed 3.0% unless otherwise authorized.
*** Total city and county rate may not exceed 3.0%; city may preempt 1.5%. The combined limit for New York City and Yonkers is 4.5%. In counties covered by the Metropolitan Communities Transportation District, the combined limit is 3.5%.

*Source:* Compiled by J. Fonkert. Some data taken from ACIR, *Significant Features of Fiscal Federalism,* 1982-83, table 55, pp. 83-85.

levied as of 1983—Wisconsin and Florida, with taxes authorized in counties, and North Dakota, with city taxes. In Minnesota the tax is prohibited unless it is specifically authorized by the state. This authorization has been granted to two cities. Duluth may levy and administer a 1% sales tax. Rochester has temporary authority for a 1% local sales tax, the proceeds of which must be allocated to flood control. The Rochester tax—like recently instituted sales taxes in other states—is administered by the state.

City sales taxes are most widespread in Illinois, California, and Texas. In these states, cities with populations from 50,000 to 200,000 typically raise 25% to 50% of local tax revenue from the general sales tax.

County sales taxes are universal in California, Illinois, and Washington and, in each case, the county tax is collected only outside city limits. These counties typically raise 7% to 15% of their tax revenues through the general sales tax.

## IMPLEMENTATION

Of those states that levy local sales taxes, only Alaska has no statewide sales tax. In most states, the state administers the sales tax for administrative ease. Coordination of the local and state tax often is achieved through "piggybacking," or adding the state and local tax rates together. The state collects the revenue and returns the local share to the jurisdiction of origin. State administration is feasible in part because, since the 1950s, most state laws authorizing local sales taxes have shared the following common features: the local tax bases coincide closely with state tax bases, the range of local tax rates is limited, and the county rather than the city is the preferred taxing unit.

If Minnesota chooses to institute a local sales tax, the tax may be mandatory—i.e., a single tax rate authorized and required of all counties (or for all cities and nonurban areas of counties)—or the tax can be optional. Under the optional approach, the tax could apply to all jurisdictions or some. The rate of tax could be set by the state or the rate can vary, at local option, across an allowable range.

## MANDATORY TAX

Minnesota could choose to require local governments to use a general sales tax. If this authorization narrowly adopts the three features identified above as common in other states, it would:

1. select a uniform rate, or at most, a narrow range of tax rates, for all local taxing jurisdictions—perhaps 1%;
2. authorize only counties (or cities and nonurban areas of counties) to tax sales; internal distribution of revenues to other jurisdictions would be each county's responsibility; and
3. define the local sales tax base to conform to the state sales tax base.

Such a local tax should be approximately neutral within the state, i.e., it should have little or no impact on the pretax prices of products or on the location and level of economic activity. There may be some loss of competitiveness for sales in counties bordering on other states.

This tax functions as if the state were to raise the general sales tax by 1%
and redistribute the revenues to the county of origin. Those counties with
more taxable goods and services per capita would receive more revenue per
capita.

OPTIONAL TAX

A local sales tax that is optional across jurisdictions has both efficiency
benefits and losses. It is beneficial for various jurisdictions to provide
different levels of public service and charge correspondingly variable tax
prices for those services. Taxpayers, then, can live in the jurisdiction that
produces the bundle of public services they most want to buy at the lowest
price.

An additional benefit of the optional sales tax is that it imports tax to
high-sales jurisdictions. Shoppers who do not live in the jurisdiction (and do
not pay property tax there), nonetheless will pay sales tax. This tax payment
is efficient because shoppers inevitably use local public services as part of
the shopping activity.

In terms of efficiency losses, taxpayers may be able to travel to a low-tax
jurisdiction to shop for taxable goods, then return to the high-tax
jurisdiction to consume public services. These shoppers will not pay their
share for locally-provided public services. This is the "border" problem that
produces two undesirable outcomes. First, it decreases the ability of an
optional local sales tax to raise revenue. Second, it works to discourage sales
in the high-tax jurisdiction and to encourage sales in bordering low-tax
jurisdictions.

Recent research indicates that the overall effect of the border problem is
slight at low-tax rates, although the short-run impact on particular retailers
may be significant. The stores most likely to be affected are those carrying
"big ticket" durable goods—e.g., vehicles, appliances, and furniture—and,
to a lesser extent, food stores. In the long-run, the tax disparities will affect
relative land values and, to some extent, neutralize the short-run impacts.

A sales tax levied only in cities or urban counties may result in the border
problem; many cities and urban counties share borders with nonurban,
presumably tax-free areas. The tax could encourage sales and shopping in
the nonurban fringe. If a border result occurs, less revenue is collected as
some sales move to the nonurban fringe. If cities/urban counties share
borders, as in the seven-county Twin Cities metropolitan area, border
problems occur only at the perimeter of the metro area. The problem is not
likely to be severe because there are few convenient shopping locations on
the fringe of the metro area.

In chapter 10 it was shown that the statewide sales tax is shown to be
somewhat regressive on income. Thus, the local sales tax also is likely to be
generally regressive across Minnesota income classes.

# LOCAL INCOME TAXES

Local income taxes are levied in eleven states and are especially widespread in Maryland (where all counties must levy a surcharge to the state income tax) and Pennsylvania (where 86% of both municipalities and school districts levy an income tax). Minnesota does not have local income taxation.

Table 2 lists the eleven states and the jurisdictions that use the local income tax. In most cases, voter approval is not required for the local income tax and, again in most cases, the tax is either a flat rate tax or a surtax—a fixed percentage of the state income tax obligation. For Indiana, Pennsylvania, and Michigan, both state and local income taxes are flat rate taxes. The Iowa surtax is allowed to school districts and must be used in conjunction with an increase in property taxes.

### IMPLEMENTATION

State administration of the local tax is possible if, as in Minnesota, there also is a state income tax. When the local tax is based on the same definition of taxable income and piggybacked on the state tax, state collection and administration should be cost effective. A taxpayer can file one form to declare liability for both taxes; the state can collect and return revenues to the taxing locality. This approach eliminates duplicated efforts in compliance as well as duplicated costs of enforcement. When structured in this way, the local income tax is progressive or regressive to the same degree as the state tax.

### DEFINITION OF TAXABLE INCOME

Table 2 shows that some localities tax according to state taxable income and others base the tax—especially for nonresidents—on wages. A tax only on wages draws an arbitrary distinction between wages and other sources of income and favors taxpayers with income from capital gains and returns to property. The generation of incomes from capital gains and property depends upon public services. A more equitable approach would be to broaden the definition of taxable income, e.g., to conform to the federal code or, in the case of Minnesota, the state definition.

### SELECTION OF TAX RATE

States can choose between having a local rate structure, with either flat or variable rates, and adoption of the state's structure of rates. Ideally, the choice of rate structure should be guided by a benefits principle. That is, if demand for local services rises proportionally with income, a flat rate is

TABLE 2
Local Income Taxes, as of October 1983

| | # of Units | Type of Tax | Tax Base | Rates | Rate Limits | Voter Approval | Treatment of Nonresidents |
|---|---|---|---|---|---|---|---|
| **Counties:** | | | | | | | |
| Indiana | 38 (42%) | flat rate | state taxable income | 0.5-1.0 | 1.0 | N | Nonresident rate = 0.25% |
| Kentucky | 9 (8%) | flat rate | wages | 0.1-2.7 | none[1] | N | Larger cities tax nonresidents at lower rates; Jefferson County gives credit for Louisville tax |
| Maryland | 24 (100%) | 20-50% surcharge on state income tax | | | 20-50% | N[2] | By residence only |
| **Cities:** | | | | | | | |
| Alabama | 8 (2%) | flat rate | wages | 1.0-2.0 | none | N | Both residents and nonresidents taxed at place of earning |
| Delaware | 1 | flat rate | wages | 1.25 | 1.25 | N | Both residents and nonresidents taxed at place of earning |
| Kentucky | 60 (14%) | flat rate | wages | .25-2.7 | none | N | |
| Michigan | 16 (3%) | 1.0-3.0% surcharge on state tax | | | 1.0-3.0 | N | Nonresidents taxed at half the resident rate |
| Missouri | 2 | flat rate | wages | 1.0 | 1.0 | Y | Nonresidents taxed on portion of income earned within city |
| New York | 1 | graduated[3] | state taxable income | .4-2.0[4] | none[4] | N | Flat 0.45% rate on nonresident wages |
| Ohio | 459 (48%) | flat rate | state taxable income | .25-2.5 | none | N[5] | Nonresidents taxed on wages earned in the cities |
| Pennsylvania | 2,220 (86%) | flat rate | wages | .25-4.96 | 1.0[6] | N | Tax is generally imposed on nonresidents but jurisdiction of residents has priority |
| **School Districts:** | | | | | | | |
| Iowa | 44 (10%) | Surtax on state tax allowed when costs exceed state aid and property tax limit; state comptroller sets limits; rates range from 3.5-16.0% | | | | Y | By residence only |
| Ohio | 4 (1%) | flat rate | state taxable income | 0.5-1.0 | .25-1.0 | Y | |
| Pennsylvania | 444 (86%) | flat rate | wages | 0.5-1.0 | 1.0 | N | Jurisdiction of residence has priority |

*Source:* ACIR, *Significant Features of Fiscal Federalism,* 1982-83, table 57, pp. 88-89.

[1] Counties may levy up to 0.5 % for school purposes.
[2] County tax is mandatory within rate limits.
[3] New York City uses nine brackets; top bracket begins at $30,000 adjusted gross income.
[4] Surtaxes must be approved by state legislature. For $15,000-20,000 adjusted gross income bracket there are surtaxes of 5.0% and 2.5% in 1983 and 1984, respectively. For higher brackets there is a 1983 surtax of 10.0% and a 1984 surtax of 5.0%.
[5] Tax rates greater than 1.0% require voter approval.
[6] Seventeen cities, including Philadelphia (4.96%), Pittsburgh (2.625%), and Scranton (2.5%) have taxes above the general 1.0% limit. Home rule cities may add an additional 1.0%.

appropriate; if demand rises faster than income, a progressive rate structure is preferred. For simplicity and cost effectiveness, a percentage charge on tax obligation to the state is desirable, so long as the state's rate structure is compatible with the benefits principle. If the locality administers its own tax, the rate structure should be simple and easy to administer.

### TREATMENT OF NONRESIDENTS

The ability to tax incomes of nonresidents is a feature unique to the local income tax. This feature promotes efficiency and may help relieve disparities in the distribution of tax base.

To illustrate, suppose town A has a user fee system to pay for local public services and town B has an income tax. Some services will accrue to people as residents in the two towns, others accrue both to commuters and to those residents who earn income in each town. For clarity, suppose the per capita cost of residential services is greater than the cost of those that are work related.

Town B must tax both residents and workers in order for the income tax to be neutral. Consider Allen, Barbara, and Chris; Allen lives and works in B, Barbara lives in B and works in A, Chris works in B and lives in A. To have tax neutrality, each person should pay some income tax to Town B, with Allen paying relatively the most (for two sets of services), followed by Barbara (for residential), and with Chris paying the least (for work-related services). If B taxes only residents to cover both categories of public services, the tax is not neutral. Chris never pays for work-related services and Barbara pays for them twice. Clearly there is an incentive for people to work in B, but live in A.

Most states using local income taxes have recognized the resident-taxation problem. As Table 2 shows, the majority tax both residents and nonresidents, with nonresidents paying a lower tax rate. Thus there should be few income tax-based incentives for population or employment to move around within the state.

High-income workers often commute to low-income communities to work; this especially is true in large urban areas. A local option income tax in the employing jurisdiction could tax residents, whose lower incomes are taxed at lower marginal rates as well as nonresidents, whose higher incomes are taxed at higher marginal rates. Thus, for some jurisdictions, the local tax is a way to import tax base with proportionately greater yield than the residential tax base offers.

## COMPARING THE LOCAL TAX OPTIONS

The policy question rises as to which local tax or combination of taxes—sales, income, and property—best serves the goals of state tax policy. The local taxes may be mandatory or optional, with different implications for accountability and revenue. Each tax has inefficient nonneutral features that can be partly but not fully alleviated. Among localities, there is a wide range in fiscal capacity for each tax. Finally, because of tax base disparities, options taxes can be used in some jurisdictions to provide property tax relief. In terms of distribution of tax base, neutrality, and progressivity, the local income tax is somewhat superior to the local general sales tax.

## REVENUE PRODUCTION UNDER A MANDATORY TAX

The state can allow and require that the local tax option be applied uniformly on all taxpayers. For example, every taxpayer, regardless of place of residence, would pay a 1% local sales tax or a 10% surcharge on Minnesota net income tax[1] or 10% more-or-less property tax. In Minnesota, 1982, local property tax receipts in 1982 were approximately $1,372 million and net income tax receipts totaled $1,699 million. For 1983, the 6% sales tax yielded $961 million (stated in 1982 dollars). Thus, if residents in each county paid a uniform local tax as indicated, a rough estimate of the yield is:[2]

1.) $961,331 ÷ 6 = $160,222—local sales tax revenue
2.) $1,699,195 x 10% = $169,920—local income tax revenue
3.) $1,372,187 x 10% = $137,219—change in local property tax revenue

These yields are close enough in value to consider the three programs as near substitutes in generating revenue, at least for these marginal changes in tax rates. The state could authorize and collect sales or income taxes, then rebate the revenue to the counties to spend and/or to distribute to other jurisdictions.[3]

## ACCOUNTABILITY

Accountability of local tax authorities is greater when the local tax is not mandatory for all taxpayers. If, for example, the state uniformly implements a 1% local sales tax, potentially all jurisdictions receive revenue. Some jurisdictions will not want or need additional revenue to finance local expenditures. Local authorities could use the revenue to cut property taxes or they could find ways to spend this money. Nothing in the uniform procedure automatically holds the local decisionmakers accountable for the choice between tax relief and expenditures.

Tax authorities are held fully accountable if every taxing jurisdiction votes to approve the local tax levy. The state still can establish the allowable tax rate and tax base and can collect and return revenue to the jurisdiction. Yet, by requiring local approval before the tax is imposed, there is no issue about whether the revenue is for property tax relief or for expenditures.

EFFICIENCY OF THE LOCAL TAX OPTIONS

There are efficiency gains and losses to be realized from each of the three taxes. The property tax is levied against a nearly immobile base—only some taxable property can actually move from one jurisdiction to another and, even for mobile properties, the time frame is quite long. Thus the property tax does not directly affect the relocation of most taxable property. However, nonresidents have an incentive to commute into the property tax jurisdiction and use services free-of-charge. Because of the free-rider possibilities, residents have some incentive to move from jurisdictions that rely heavily on property taxes.

The sales tax and income tax bases are more mobile, and, in some cases, the tax can drive the tax base away. For the local option income tax, neutrality is significantly enhanced when both residents and commuters are taxed so that there is no particular advantage to living in a tax-free jurisdiction while working in a tax-paying locality. Over the long run, however, the tax on commuters adds a small marginal incentive for employment to move to a nontaxing jurisdiction.

With the local sales tax, the potential nonneutral effects occur at the borders, although the "border" can be the entire jurisdiction if the jurisdiction is geographically small. In a metropolitan area, a single taxing jurisdiction likely would lose many sales, as shoppers "free-ride" on public services in a tax-free area. If all adjoining metropolitan jurisdictions implement the tax, the migration of tax base would be much less significant.

FISCAL DISPARITIES

There are disparities in tax capacity regardless of which tax is used. High per capita sales jurisdictions get more sales tax revenue per capita; the same is true for per capita property value and property tax revenue, and to some extent for per capita income and income tax revenue. With a dual tax (by residence and workplace) some disparities are relieved in respect to the income tax.

By adding the options of sales and income taxes to the local tax base, local fiscal disparities could be somewhat reduced. Consider the 172 larger cities in Minnesota. All but eight of those below the property tax median are above the median for sales tax base per capita, or income tax base per capita, or both. By selecting the correct local option, all but eight cities with below-average property tax base can improve their fiscal capacity relative to other cities.

If local option taxes are implemented and do reduce local fiscal disparities, grants of local government aid are likely to be affected. As other commission analysis shows, local government aids are partly determined by the goal of equalizing local fiscal disparities.[4] Thus, an increase in local tax base may be partly offset by relative loss in state grants.

# RECOMMENDATION

## MAINTAIN STATUS QUO RELATING TO GENERAL LOCAL NONPROPERTY TAXATION

Minnesota has an established tradition of state support to local jurisdictions in order to alleviate disparities among localities in the ability to provide public services. As a result, Minnesota's property tax rates are low compared to other states, and state grants per capita are correspondingly high. State aid per capita exceeds the amount of net property tax per capita.

Another component of the Minnesota tradition—a component intended to preserve the equalizing feature of state grants—is to prohibit the local use of nonproperty taxes, including the local general sales tax and the local income tax. Localities are permitted to charge on a fee-for-service basis for some public services (for example, sewage management, public parking, and higher education programs) and localities do rely heavily on fees and user charges.

In keeping with current policy, and in order to protect the equalizing benefits of state grants, the commission recommends continuing the prohibition against new local general sales and local income taxes. The commission recognizes that in the case of an unusual and specific local need, a locality can request a special law from the legislature allowing a local nonproperty tax for a limited time period. This is a continuation of current policy that, for example, has allowed Rochester a temporary 1% local general sales tax.

# ENDNOTES

1. Levied as 10% by place of residence or, possibly, as 6²/₃% by place of residence and 3¹/₃% by place of employment.
2. City-by-city yields for 175 Minnesota cities are provided by Jay Fonkert in "Revenue Diversification," a technical paper presented to the commission.
3. There are other options for distribution, e.g., the state can rebate city receipts to the cities and noncounty receipts to the counties of origin.
4. Michael E. Bell, "Minnesota's Local Government Aids Program," in *Staff Papers*, vol. 1 of the *Final Report of the Minnesota Tax Study Commission*, ed. Robert D. Ebel and Therese J. McGuire (St. Paul: Butterworth Legal Publishers, 1985).

# Index to Figures and Tables

# Subject Index